MW01029148

NEPALI
Practical Dictionary

NEPALI
Practical Dictionary

NEPALI-ENGLISH
ENGLISH-NEPALI

Prakash A. Raj

Hippocrene Books, Inc.
New York

For information address:
HIPPOCRENE BOOKS, INC.
171 Madison Ave.
New York, NY 10016
www.hippocrenebooks.com

Library of Congress Cataloging-in-Publication Data

Nepali-English English-Nepali practical dictionary / Prakash A.
Raj.
    pages cm.
 ISBN-13: 978-0-7818-1271-9 (pbk.)
 ISBN-10: 0-7818-1271-2 (pbk.)
1. Nepali language--Dictionaries--English 2. English
language--Dictionaries--Nepali. I. Prakash A. Raj
 PK2597.N3883 2013
 491.4'95321--dc23
                            2013027144

Printed in the United States of America.

INTRODUCTION

Nepali is an Indo-European language that is spoken in Nepal and parts of northeastern India. It is a link language between the different ethnic groups that inhabit Nepal. It is estimated that 15 million out of Nepal's total population of 30 million speak Nepali as their mother tongue and another 10 million are able to communicate in it. Nepali is written in Devanagari script, similar to the Hindi, Sanskrit, and Marathi languages. Many speakers of Nepali have migrated from the hills to the Terai in the past four decades. The major language spoken in Sikkim state in India east of the Nepalese border is Nepali and it is the major language spoken in Darjeeling and Kalimpong in West Bengal state. It is also spoken in southeastern Bhutan, although the Bhutanese government has expelled many ethnic Nepalis who lived there in the 1990s, and who now still live in refugee camps in Nepal or have immigrated to the U.S. or countries in Europe.

Nepali is closely related to the Hindi spoken in India and is distantly related to English, French, Spanish, and other European languages, as well as to Persian (Farsi). Much of the vocabulary is derived from Sanskrit, with many loan words from Arabic and Persian. Some knowledge of Sanskrit helps to understand Nepali as it is written in newspapers and books, though colloquial Nepali contains far fewer Sanskrit words. Speakers of Hindi or Urdu often find it very easy to learn Nepali because of similarity in both the vocabulary and grammar.

Nepal is a multiethnic and multilingual country. Many Tibeto-Burmese languages are commonly found, such as Newari (in the Kathmandu valley), Gurung (in the hills around Pokhara), Magar (in the western hills) and Sherpa (the dialect of those who live around Mount Everest). Many non-native Nepali speakers have adopted Nepali as their primary language of communication, since it is still the official language of many institutions in the country (such as schools and government offices), though a proposed transition of Nepal to a federal system may change this, and give these minority languages greater prominence in everyday life in Nepal.

Pronunciation Guide

Vowels

अ　**o** as in "m<u>o</u>ther" (मा ma)

आ　**ā** like "a" in "f<u>a</u>ther" (मा ma)

इ　**i** as in "m<u>i</u>rror" (मि mi)

ई　**ī** like "ee" in "sl<u>ee</u>p" (मी mi)

उ　**u** as in "p<u>u</u>t" or "p<u>u</u>ll" (मु mu)

ऊ　**ū** like "oo" in "f<u>oo</u>l" (मू mu)

ए　**e** like "a" in "m<u>a</u>ke" (मे ma)

ऐ　**ai** like "e" in "wh<u>e</u>n" (मे mai)

ओ　**o** as in "m<u>o</u>st" or "h<u>o</u>st" (मो mo)

औ　**au** like "ou" in c<u>ou</u>gh (मौ mau)

Consonants

क　**ka** like "ca" in "<u>ca</u>ll"

ख　**kh** like "co" in "<u>co</u>ld" (aspirated)

ग　**g** as in "si<u>ng</u>"

घ　**gh** as in "<u>gh</u>ost" (aspirated)

ङ　**ng** as in "swi<u>ng</u>"

च **c** like "ch" in "child"

छ **ch** like "ch" in "church" (aspirated)

ज **j** like "ge" in "bridge"

झ **jh** no exact English equivalent. Similar to an aspirated **j** in "jhodpur"

ञ' no English equivalent, but close to the English "n"

ट **t** as in "top"

ठ **th** like "t" in "toast" (aspirated)

ड **d** as in "door"

ढ **dh** like "d" in "dam"

ण **n** as in "nine"

त **t** as in "mantra"

थ **th** as in "through"

द **d** like "th" in "the"

ध similar to aspirated "d" sound

न **n** as in "name"

प **p** as in "cup"

फ **ph** as in "philosophy"

ब **b** as in "but"

भ **bh** does not have an equivalent in English similar to aspirated "b". Many from the Indian sub-continent will pronounce "v" as "bh" which is incorrect.

म **m** as in "me"

य **y** as in "you"

र **r** as a rolled "r" similar to "rest"

ल **l** as in "loss"

व **v** as in "<u>v</u>erb"

श **s** like "sh" in "<u>sh</u>irt"

ष **s** like "sh" in "ca<u>sh</u>"

स **s** as in "<u>s</u>ee"

ह **h** as in "<u>h</u>ome"

क्ष (ksh), त्र (tra), and ज्ञ (gya) have no equivalent sounds in English.

There is little difference in pronunciation of **s** and **sh** in Nepali. While the written Devanagari alphabet still differentiates between the two, the Romanization system used in this book does not maintain this legacy distinction from the Sanskrit language. Words containing "f" and "z" are pronounced as "ph" and "j", respectively, and can be considered equivalent in Nepali. Unlike in Hindi, which contains a large number of words containing "z" (borrowed from Urdu, Persian, and Arabic), the Nepali language does not preserve this phonetic distinction in loan words from those sources.

It's also important to note that some letters in the Devanagari alphabet, such as "bh," "jh," and "dh," don't have equivalent sounds in English. The best way to pronounce "bh" is to join the lips and blow air out lightly. The official name of India, for example, is *Bharat* and the "bh" is pronounced as an aspirated "b," *not* the same "b" sound as in the English "boy."

Nepali Grammar

NOUNS

Nouns in Nepali don't have articles, as they do in English. For example:

a man	**mānche** मान्छे
the man	**mānche** मान्छे

Singular and Plural Nouns

Plurals are formed by simply adding "–haru" to the noun or pronoun. For example:

bird	**charā** चरा
birds	**chrāaharu** चराहरु
sister	**bahini** बहिनी
sisters	**bahiniharu** बहिनीहरु

PRONOUNS

Nepali has four different kinds of "*you*" or second person pronouns. The most formal of these is *tapāi*. It's best to stay on the safe side and use *tapāi*, when in doubt: using other informal types of "*you*" might offend some people as being inappropriate. *Timi* may be used for close friends or to address junior family members.

	Singular	Plural
1st per.	I म **ma**	we हामी **hāmi**
2nd per.	you तिमी **timi**	you तिमीहरु **timiharu**
2nd per. *(formal)*	you तपाई **tapāi**	you तपाईहरु **tapāiharu**

WORD ORDER

The structure of a sentence in Nepali is simple. The verb comes at
the end of the sentence and is usually preceded by the pronoun and
noun (object and/or subject). For example:

Ma tarkāri phal khānchu.
(Ma = I, tarkāri = vegetable, phal = fruit, khānchu = eat)
I eat vegetables and fruits.

VERBS

Infinitives *(regular and irregular)*

khānu खानु	to eat
uthnu उठ्नु	to get up
basnu बस्नु	to sit down
bolnu बोल्नु	to speak
khelnu खेल्नु	to play
hunu हुनु	to be
garnu गर्नु	to do

The present-tense endings for these regular verbs are:

Singular
1st per.   -chu छु
2nd per.   *inf.* + huncha हुन्छ *(hon.)*
3rd per.   *(m.)* -cha छ
             (f.) -chin छिन्

These endings are added to the verb stem. Note that "inf. +
huncha" is used to create an honorific form. To be on the safe side,
it is better to use it on all occasions unless you're talking to a child.

Conjugation of "bolnu" (*to speak/talk*)
(the verb root of "bolnu" is "bol"):

I speak Nepali.
Ma Nepali bolchu.
म नेपाली बोल्छु

You speak Nepali. *(hon.)*
Tapāi Nepali bolnuhuncha.
तपाई नेपाली बोल्नुहुन्छ

He/She speaks Nepali.
U Nepali bolcha/bolchin.
उ नेपाली बोल्छ

He/She speaks Nepali. *(hon.)*
Uni nepali bolchan/bolchin.
उहाँ नेपाली वोल्नु \ हुन्छ

We speak Nepali.
Hāmi Nepali bolchaun.
हामी नेपाली वोल्छौँ

They speak Nepali.
Uhānharu Nepali bolnuhuncha.
उहाँहरु नेपाली बोल्नु हुन्छ

"*You talk*" is *tapāi bolnuhuncha* and "*He talks*" should be *wahāan bolnuhuncha*. (The infinitive is followed by -huncha to create the honorific form.)

Infinitives *(irregular)*

There is no hard and fast rule for distinguishing regular and irrregular verbs.

    jānu जानु   to go
    hunu हुनु   to be

Present tense conjugation of "jānu" (*to go*)

I go	**Ma jānchu** म जान्छु
You go	**Tapāi jānuhuncha** तपाई जानुहुन्छ
He/She goes	**U jāncha/janchi** उ जान्छ \ जान्छी
He goes *(hon.)*	**Uhān jānuhuncha** वहाँ जानु हुन्छ
We go	**Hāmi jānchaun** हामी जान्छौं
They go	**Uhanharu januhuncha** उहाँहरुजानु हुन्छ

The Verb "to be"

There are two forms of the verb "*to be*" in Nepali (similar to the Spanish distinction between *ser* and *estar*). The first form indicates a fact such as being some place. The second form indicates the action of doing something or being there.

Conjugation of "hunu" (*to be*)

I am	**Ma hun** म हुँ
	Ma chu म छु
You are	**Timi hau** तिमी हौ
	Timi chau तिमी छौ
	Timiharu chau तिमीहरु छौ *(pl.)*
You are *(hon.)*	**Tapāi hunuhuncha** तपाई हुनुहुन्छ
He/She is *(hon.)*	**Uhān hunuhuncha** उहाँ हुनुहुन्छ
He/She is *(hon.)*	**U cha / Uni chan** उ छ उनी छन्
We are	**Hāmi (haru) haun** हामीहरु हौं
	Hami (haru) chaun हामीहरु छौं

You are *(pl.)* **Timiharu hau** तिमीहरुहौ

You are *(hon. pl.)* **Tapāiharu hunuhuncha** तपाईहरु हुनुहुन्छ

They are *(hon.)* **Uhān hunuhuncha** उहाँ हुनुहुन्छ

Ma Nepali hun. म नेपाली हुँ
I am a Nepali.

Ma yahan chu. म यहाँ छु
I am here.

Ma amerika mā chu. म अमेरिकामा छु
I'm in America.

Ma khandai chu. म खाँदै छु
I am eating.

Yo ke ho? यो के हो
What is this?

Yo mero ghar ho. यो मेरो घर हो
This is my house.

Yo mero ghadi ho. यो मेरो घडी हो
This is my watch.

Usko ghar rāmro cha. उसको घर राम्रो छ
His house is beautiful.

Mero ghar yahān cha. मेरो घर यहां छ
My house is here.

Ghadi yahān cha. घडी यहां छ
The watch is here.

Imperatives

To give commands, use the imperative form. The imperative is
formed when the verb root is followed by the following pronoun
endings:

I	**ma**	म
you	**timi** तिमी *or* **tapāi** तपाई	
we	**hāmi** हामी	

The verb root "bas" from "basnu" (*to sit*) is followed by "a" or
"nos" to make "*sit down*" in the following example. However,
there are many exceptions to this rule. The verb root "khāa" from
"khāanu" (*to eat*) is followed by "u" to make "khāu" and "nos"
to make "khāanos" (*hon.*).

Sit down!	**Basa!**	बस	
Sit down! *(hon.)*	**Basnos!**	बस्नुस	बस्नोस्
Eat!	**Khau!**	खाउ	खाउँ
Eat! *(hon.)*	**Khāanos!**	जाउ	खानोस्
Tell!	**Bhana!**	भन	
Tell! *(hon.)*	**Bhannos!**	भन्नोस्	

The prefix **na** (न) is added before the imperative to indicate
negation:

Don't sit.	**Nabasa.**	नवस
Don't sit. *(hon.)*	**Nabasnos.**	नवस्नोस्
Don't tell.	**Nabhana.**	नभन
Don't tell. *(hon.)*	**Nabhannos.**	नभन्नोस्

Verb tenses

Present:
I eat.
Ma khānchu. म खान्छु

Present Progressive:
I am eating.
Makhādaichu. म खाँदैछु

Simple Future:
I will eat.
Ma khānechu. म खानेछु

Immediate Future:
I will eat later.
Ma ekkai chin pachi khanchhu. म एक छिन पछि खानेछु

Future:
I will eat later.
Ma ekai chin pachhi khānechu. म एकछिन पछि खान्छु

Recent Past:
I ate.
Maile khāyen. मैले खाए

Remote Past:
I had eaten.
Maile khāeko thiyen. मैले खाएको थिएँ *(nasal, similar to French)*

Progressive Past:
I used to eat.
Maile khāne garthen. मैले खाने गर्थेँ म खाने गर्थेँ *(nasal)*

Negative Verb Forms

For a negative statement, the verb is normally followed by "na," the word meaning "*no*." The negative in the case of honorifics is slightly more modified than just adding "na."

Present tense negatives are as follows:

Ma Nepāli bolchu. म नेपाली वोल्छु
I speak Nepali.
Ma Nepāli boldina. म नेपाली बोल्दिन
I don't speak Nepali.

U Nepali bolchan/bolchhi. उ नेपाली वोल्छ\वोल्छी
He/She speaks Nepali.
U Nepali boldaina/boldina. उ नेपाली बोल्दैन
He/She does not speak Nepali.

Uni Nepali bolchhin. उनी नेपाली वोल्छिन्
She speaks Nepali.
Uni Nepali boldinan. उनी नेपाली वोल्दिनन्
She does not speak Nepali.

Tapāi Nepali bolnuhuncha. तपाई नेपाली वोल्नु हुन्छ
You speak Nepali. *(hon.)*
Tapāi Nepali bolnuhudaina. तपाई नेपाली बोल्नु हुन्न
You don't speak Nepali. *(hon.)*

Hāmi Nepali bolchaun. हामी नेपाली बोल्छौं
We speak Nepali.
Hāmi Nepali boldainaun. हामी नेपाली बोल्दैनौं
We don't speak Nepali.

Uhan Nepali bolnuhuncha. उहाँ नेपाली वोल्नुहुन्छ
He/She speaks Nepali. *(hon.)*
Uhān Nepali Bolnuhunna. उहाँ नेपाली वोल्नु हुन्न
He/She does not speak Nepali. *(hon.)*

Uahānharu Nepali bolnuhuncha. उहाँहरु नेपाली वोल्नुहुन्छ
They speak Nepali. *(hon.)*
Uhānharu Nepali bolnuhunna. उहाँहरु नेपाली वोल्नु हुन्न
They do not speak Nepali. *(hon.)*

Ma khādaina (khaanna). म खाँदिन (खान्न)
I do not eat. *(negative present tense)*
Ma khādai chaina. म खाँदै छैन
I am not eating. *(negative present progressive tense)*
Ma khānechaina. म खाँदै छैन
I will not eat. *(negative simple future tense)*
Ma ekkaichhin pachi khaanchu. म एकै छिन पछि खानेछु
I'll eat after a while.
Maile khāina. मैले खाइन
I did not eat. *(negative remote past tense)*
Maile khānthene. म खान्थें
I used to not eat. *(progressive past tense)*

Ma sanga chaina ... म सँग छैन
I don't have ...
Malai cahinna... मलाई चाहिन्न
I don't need ...

Saying "yes" and "no"

Ho and **hoina** represent "*yes*" and "*no*" respectively.

Is this a dog?
Ke yo kukkur ho? के यो कुकुर हो?

   Yes, it's a dog.
   Ho, yo kukkur ho. हो, यो कुकुर हो।

   No, it's not a dog.
   Hoina, yo kukkur hoina. होइन, यो कुकुर होइन

The verb "to have"

The verb "*to have*" is generally marked by "sanga" which is used if you have something with you.

I have	**Ma sanga** म सँग
You have	**Tapāin sanga** तपाई सँग
She/He has	**U/Uni sanga** उ/उनी सँग
He has *(hon.)*	**Uahān sanga** ऊहा संग
We have	**Hāmi sanga** हामी संग
They have *(hon.)*	**Uniharu sanga** उनीहरु संग
They have *(hon.)*	**Uahānharu sanga** उहांहरु संग / उहाँहरु सँग

Ma sanga pāisā chha. म संग पैसा छ
I have money.

However, "sanga" is not always used to denote "*have*," especially if you possess something:

Mero ghar chha. मेरो घर छ
I have a house.

Tapāinko ghar chha. तपाईको घर छ
You have a house. *(hon.)*

Usko/Unko ghar chha. उसको/उनको घर छ
He/She has a house.

Uahānko ghar chha. उहाँको घर छ
He has a house. *(hon.)*

Hāmro ghar chha. हाम्रो घर छ
We have a house.

Uahānharuko ghar chha. उहाँहरुको घर छ
They have a house.

Yo mero ghar ho. यो मेरो घर हो
This is my house.
Mero ghar chha. मेरो घर छ
I have a house. (*Literally*, My house is.)

Tyo tapāinko kalam ho. त्यो तपाईको कलम हो
That is your pen.
Tapāin sanga kalām cha. तपाईसँग कलम छ
You have a pen.

ADJECTIVES

Adjectives in Nepali come before the noun, for example:

kālo black   **kālo kukur** black dog
neelo blue   **neelo lugā** blue dress

Some common adjectives are:

small	**sāno** सानो
big	**thulo** ठूलो
many	**dherai** धेरै
white	**seto** सेतो
little, few	**alikati** अलिकति, **kam** कम
thin	**dublo** दुब्लो

Masculine, feminine, and plural forms of adjectives:

small boy	**sāno keto** सानो केटो
small boys	**sāno ketaharu** सानो केटाहरु
small girl	**sāni keti** सानी केटी
small girls	**sāna ketiharu** साना केटीहरु

Demonstrative adjectives also come in front of the noun.

this book	**yo kitāb** यो किताब
that book	**tyo kitāb** त्यो किताब
these books	**yi kitābharu** यी किताबहरु
those books	**ti kitābharu** ती किताबहरु

Comparatives

The word *bhandā* is used to make a comparison:

Malāi yo bhandā sasto chāhiyo.
मलाई यो भन्दा सस्तो चाहियो
I need something cheaper than this.

Tapāin ko ghādi bhandā mero sāno cha.
तपाईंको घडी भन्दा मेरो सानो छ
My watch is smaller than yours.

The term *sab bhandā* is used to denote a superlative:

Sita ko kitāb sab bhandā rāmro* cha.
सीताको किताब सबभन्दा राम्रो छ।
Sita has the best book.

*The word "rāmro" is used to mean *"beautiful," "nice,"* or *"being of good quality."*

Possessives

In most cases, **-ko** is added to make a noun or pronoun possessive.
In some cases, **-ro** is added to make a noun or pronoun possessive.
For example:

| my | **mero** मेरो |
| our | **hāmro** हाम्रो |

his   **usko** उसको

The possessives are:

Singular

1st Per.	my	**mero** मेरो
2nd Per.	your	**tapāinko** तपाईको
3rd Per.	his/her	**usko/unko** उसको / उनको
3rd Per. *(hon.)*	his/her	**uhānko** उहाँको

Plural

1st Per.	our	**hamro** हाम्रो
2nd Per.	your	**timiharuko** तिमीहरुको
2nd Per. *(hon.)*	your	**tapaiharuko** तपाईहरुको
3rd Per.	their	**uniharuko** उनीहरुको
3rd Per. *(hon.)*	their	**uhanharuko** उहाँहरुको

my house	**mero ghar** मेरो घर
your house	**tapāiko ghar** तपाईको घर
his/her house *(hon.)*	**uhānko ghar** उहाँको घर
their house	**uniharuko ghar** उनीहरुको घर
their house *(hon.)*	**uahānharuko ghar** उहाँहरुको घर

Abbreviations

abbrev.	abbreviation
adj.	adjective
adv.	adverb
anat.	anatomical
art.	article
aux.	auxiliary
f.	feminine
fin.	financial
gram.	grammatical
hon.	honorific
interj.	interjection
leg.	legal
m.	masculine
med.	medical
mil.	military
n.	noun
num.	number
opp.	opposite
per.	person
phr.	phrase
pl.	plural
pref.	prefix
prep.	preposition
sing.	singular
v.	verb
v.i.	intransitive verb
v.t.	transitive verb
zoo.	zoological

NEPALI-ENGLISH
DICTIONARY

अ

अकस्मात akasmāt *adj.* sudden
अकेला akelā *adj.* alone
अखंड akhanda *adj.* unbroken
अखवार akhabār *n.* newspaper
अब सम्म ab samma *adv.* up to
 now
अभाग्य abhāgya *n.* unfortunate
अभागी abhāgi *adj* unfortunate
अभाव abhāv *n.* scarcity
अभिवादन abhibādan *n.* salute
अभिनन्दन abhinandan *n.*
 congratulations
अभिमान abhimān *n.* pride
अभिलेख abhilekh *n.* record
अभिनय abhinaya *n.* acting
अभिनेता abhinetā *n.* actor
अभिरुचि abhiruci *n.* interest
अभियोग abhiyog *n.* accusation
अभिभावक abhibhāwak *n.*
 guardian
अभिव्यक्ति abhibyakti *n.* expression
अभ्यास abhyās *n.* exercise
अभ्यस्त बन्नु abhyast bannu *v.i.*
 accustom
अचल acal *adj.* stationary
अचम्म acamma *n.* surprise
अचर acar *n.* constant
अचार acār *n.* pickle
अचल सम्पति acal sampatti *n.*
 real estate
अचम्म acamba *adj.* surprising
अजीर्ण ajirna *adj.* indigestion
अजिङ्गर ajingar *n.* python
अति ati *adj.* excess
अदालत adālat *n.* court

अड्डा addā *n.* office
अधम adham *adj.* inferior
अधबैंसे adhbaise *adj.* middle-aged
अधिक adhik *adj./adv.* more
अधिकार adhikār *n.* authority
अधिकार मा लिनु adhikār mā linu
 v.t. occupy
अधिकार मा राख्नु adhikār mā
 rakhnu *v.t.* retain
अधिकारी adhikāri *n.* officer
अधिवक्ता adhivaktā *n.* advocate
आधिकारिक adhikārik *adj.* official
अचानक achānak *adv.* suddenly
अछूत achut *adj.* untouchable
अडकल adkal *n.* guess
अधिकतम adhiktam *adj.* maximum
अधिकृत adhikrit *adj.* officer
अधिन adhin *adj.* dependent
आधिनायकवाद adhināyakvād *n.*
 authoritarianism
अधिमूल्य adhimuly *n.* surcharge
अधिस्थापन adhisthāpan *v.* to
 install
अधिसुचना adhisucanā *n.*
 notification
अधिसूची adhisuci *n.* schedule
अधिवेशन adhibesan *n.* session
अध्यक्ष adhyaksha *n.* chairman
अध्ययन adhyayan *n.* study
अध्यापक adhyāpak *n.* teacher
अध्यात्म adhyātma *n.* spiritual
अध्याय adhyāy *n.* chapter
अधिवर्ष adhivars *n.* leap year
अधुरो adhuro *n.* incomplete
अदृश्य adrsya *adj.* invisible

अन्तर antar *n.* difference
अफ्रीकी afriki *n./adj.* African
अफसोस afsos *n.* regret
अगम्य agamy *adj.* inaccessible
अघाउनु aghāunu *v.* to be filled up with food
अगस्त agast *n.* August
अघि aghi *adv.* before, front of
अग्लो aglo *adj.* high
अग्र भाग agra bhag *n.* visor
अग्रदर्शी agradarsi *adj.* prospective
अग्राधिकार agrādhikār *n.* priority
अग्रदीप agradip *n.* headlight
अगुआ aguā *n.* pioneer
अहिले ahile *adv.* now
अझ ajha *adv.* yet, still
अकादमी akādami *n.* academy
अक्सर aksar *adv.* usually
अक्टूबर aktubar *n.* October
अकुशल akusal *adj.* unskilled
अलग alag *adj.* separate
अलग गर्नु alag garnu *v.t.* isolate, separate
अलग हुनु alag hunu *v.i.* differ, separate
अलार्म घडी alāram ghari *n.* alarm
अलावा alāvā *adv.* moreover
अलिकति alikati *adj.* a little
आलिंगन alingan *n.* embrace
अलमारी almāri *n.* wardrobe
आलोचना गर्नु alocanā garnu *v.t.* criticize
अलोकप्रिय alokpriya *adj.* unpopular
अल्प alp *adj.* meager
आल्प्स alps *n.* Alps
अल्पमत alpmat *n.* minority
अल्पसंख्यक alpsankhyak *n.* minority
अम्ल amal *n.* acid

अमर amar *adj.* immortal
अंगरक्षक angaraksak *n.* guard
अँध्यारो andhero *n.* darkness
अन्धकारमय बनाउनु amdhkārmay banāunu *v.t.* darken
अमेरीकी ameriki *n./adj.* American
अंचल anchal *n.* zone
अंग्रेज angrez *n.* Englishman
अंग्रेजी angrezi *n./adj.* English
अँगुली anguli *n.* finger
अमिलो amilo *adj.* sour
अमोनिया amoniyā *n.* ammonia
अनादर anādar *n.* disobey
अन्न anna *n.* grain
अन्नपूर्ण annapurna *n.* a peak in the Himalayas
अनाज anāj *n.* grain
अनपढ anapadh *adj.* illiterate
अनार anār *n.* pomegranate
अनाथ anāth *n.* orphan
अनावश्यक anāvasyak *adj.* unnecessary
अनावश्यकता anāvasyaktā *adv.* needlessly
अनभिप्रेत anbhipret *adj.* unintentional
अनि ani *adv.* then
अनुकरण anukaran *n.* imitation
अनुत्पादन anutpādak *adj.* unproductive
अनुदार anudar *adj.* ungenerous
अनुगमन anugaman *n.* monitoring
अन्डा andā *n.* egg
अंदाज andāz *n.* estimate
अंधोपन andhāpan *n.* blindness
अंधविश्वास andhavisvās *adj.* superstition
अंधो andho *adj.* blind
अनाधिकार प्रवेश गर्नु andhikār praves garnu *v.i.* trespass
अंग anga *n.* any

अंगूर angur *n.* grape

अनिवार्य anibarya *adj.* compulsory

अनिर्णीत anirnit *adj.* undecided

अनिश्चय aniscay *n.* suspense

अनिश्चित aniscit *adj.* uncertain, doubtful

अनिश्चितता aniscita *adj.* uncertainty

अनिष्ट anist *adj.* undesired

अंजान anjān *adj.* unknown

अंजीर anjir *n.* fig

अंकगणित ankganit *n.* arithmetic

अंकित गर्नु ankit garnu *v.t.* imprint

अंकुर ankur *n.* sprout

अनमोल anmol *adj.* valuable

अनेक anek *adj.* several

अनुच्छेद anucched *n.* paragraph

अनौपचारिक anaupacharik *adj.* unofficial

अनकनाउनु ankanāunu *v.* hesitate

अंत anta *n.* finish

अंत मा anta mā *adv.* finally

अंतर antar *n.* difference

अंतरिम antarim *n.* interim

अन्तरिक्ष antariks *n.* space

अन्तरमुखी antarmukhi *adj.* self-centered

अन्तर्राष्ट्रीय antarrāstriya *adj.* international

अंतर्वार्ता antarbārtā *n.* interview

अंत्येष्ठि antesthi *n.* funeral

अंत: प्रेरणा antarprernā *n.* impulse

अनिश्चित aniscit *adj.* uncertain

अन्तिम antim *adj.* last

अन्त्येष्ठि antesthi *n.* cremation, burial

अनुभव anubhav *n.* experience

अनुभवी व्यक्ति anubhavi vyakti *n.* experienced person

अनुभूति anubhuti *n.* sensation

अनुचित anucit *adj.* improper

अनुदान anudān *n.* grant

अनुकरण anukaran *n.* imitation

अनुक्रमिका anukramik *n.* index

अनुकूल गर्नु anukul garnu *v.t.* adopt

अनुमान anumān *n.* guess

अनुमानित anumānit *adj.* estimated

अनुमान गर्नु anumān garnu *v.t.* estimate, guess

अनुमति anumati *n.* permission

अनुमति दिनु anumati dinu *v.t.* allow

अनुमति पत्र anumati patr *n.* permit

अनुवाद गर्नु anubad garnu *v.t.* translate

अनुपस्थित anuupasthit *adj.* absent

अनुपस्थिति anupasthiti *n.* absence

अनुहार anunhār *n.* face

अनुपात anupat *n.* proportion

अनुपंयुक्त anuparyukta *adj.* unfit

अनुराग anurāg *n.* affection

अनुरोध anurodh *v.i./n.* request

अनुसन्धान anusandhān *n.* research

अनुशासन anusāsan *n.* discipline

अनुत्तरदायी anuttardāyi *adj.* unaccountable

अनुवाद anuvād *n.* translation

अनुवादक anuvādak *n.* translator

अन्यलोकवासी anyalikavāsi *adj.* alien

अन्यथा anyathā *adv.* otherwise

अन्यथा गर्नु anyathā garnu *v.i.* undo

अपारदर्शी apārdarsi *adj.* opaque

अपर्याप्त aparyāpt *adj.* insufficient

अपहरण apaharan *n.* kidnapping

अपरहरणकारी apaharankāri *n.* kidnapper

अपमान apmān *n.* insult

अपमान गर्नु apmān garnu *v.t.* insult

अपमानिक apmānik *adj.* rude

अपमानजनक apmānjanak *adj.* offensive

अपराध aprādh *n.* offense, crime

अपराधी aprādhi *n.* criminal

अपराधिकरण aprādhikaran *n.* criminalization

अपरिवर्तनीय aparivartaniya *adj.* unchangeable

अप्राप्ति aprāpti *n.* loss

अप्रसन्न गर्नु aprasann garnu *v.t.* displease

अप्रत्यक्ष apratpaks *adj.* indirect

अपूरणीय apuraniya *adj.* irreparable

अपूर्ण विराम apurn virām *n.* colon *(gram.)*

अपूर्ण apurna *adj.* incomplete

अपूर्व apurva *adj.* extraordinary

अप्सरा apsarā *n.* fairy

अपवाद apvād *n.* exception

अफिसर aphisar *n.* officer

अफिम aphim *n.* opium

अफिस aphisar *n.* office

अफसोस aphsos *n.* regret

अफगानिस्तान afghanistan *n.* Afghanistan

अरबी arabi *n.* Arabic language

अरब arab *n./adj.* Arab

अराजकता arājaktā *n.* anarchy

अडचन arcan *adj.* handicapped

अर्ध-विराम ardh-virām *n.* semicolon

अर्पण arpan *n.* gift

अर्थ arth *n.* significance

अर्थात् arthāt *adj.* namely

अर्थ मन्त्री arthamantri *n.* finance minister

अर्थव्यवस्था arthavyavasthā *n.* economy

अर्थशास्त्र arthasāstra *n.* economics

अर्थशास्त्री arthsāstri *n.* economist

अस्वस्थ aswastha *adj.* sick

अशुद्धि asuddhi *adj.* incorrect

असहयोग asahayog *n.* non-cooperation

असफल asaphal *adj.* unsuccessful

अस्तित्व astistwa *n.* existence

अथक athak *n.* tireless

अठार athāra *num.* eighteen

अठारौं āthāraum *adj.* eighteenth

अति ati *adj.* extra

अतिरंजना गर्नु atiranjanā garnu *v.t.* exaggerate

अति गोप्य ati gopya *adj.* top secret

अतिरिक्त atirikt *n.* extra

अतिरिक्त पुर्जा atirikt purja *n.* spare parts

अतीत atit *adj.* past

अतिथि atithi *n.* guest

अतिथिगृह atithigriha *n.* guest house

अत्याचार atyācar *n.* oppression

अत्याचारी atyācāri *adj.* oppressive

अत्यावश्यकता aāvasyaktā *n.* urgency

अत्तो atto *n.* false accusation

अद्भुत adbhut *adj.* surprising

अनिकाल anikāl *n.* famine

अलिखित alikhit *adv.* unwritten

अवधि avadhi *n.* term, period

अवैध avaidh *adj.* illegal

अवेर aver *adj.* late

अवश्य avasya *n.* certainly

अवश्यमेव avasyamev *adv.* necessarily

अवतार avatār *n.* incarnation

अवकाश avkās *n.* retirement

अवलोकन गर्नु avlokan garnu *v.t.* scan

अवश्यंभावी avsyambhāvi *adj.* unavoidable

अवशेष avses *n.* residue

अवतरण avtaran *n.* landing

अवयव avyav *n.* organ

अयोग्य ayogya *adj.* ineffective, unfit

अवसर avsar *n.* opportunity

अवस्था avasthā *n.* stage, phase

अवहेलना avahelnā *n.* contempt

अवज्ञा गर्नु avagyā garnu *v.t.* defy

अव्यवसायी avyavasāyi *n.* amateur

अविराम avirām *adj.* continuous

अविलंब avilamb *adv.* shortly

अविश्वास avisvās *n./v.t.* distrust, mistrust

अशक्त asakt *adj.* unable

अश्लील aslil *adj.* obscene

अशुद्ध asuddha *adj.* impure

आशावादी āsāvādi *n.* optimist

आशान्वित asānvit *adj.* optimistic

अशिष्ट asisth *adj.* impolite

असन्तोषजनक asantosjanak *adj.* unsatisfactory

असंवैधानिक asamaidhanik *adj.* unconstitutional

असामान्य asāmānya *adj.* extraordinary

असंभव asambhav *adj.* impossible

असंभाव्य asambhāvya *adj.* unfeasible

असफल asaphal *adj.* unsuccessful

असफलता asphaltā *n.* failure

असमर्थ asamarthā *n.* inability

असभ्य asabhya *adj.* uncivilized

असमर्थता asamarthatā *n.* unable

असामयिक asāmayik *adj.* untimely

असमान asamān *adj.* unequal

असर asar *n.* effect

असरदार asardār *adj.* effective

असली asli *adj.* real

असहनीय asahaniya *adj.* unbearable

असहमत हुनु asahamat hunu *v.i.* disagree

असहमति asahamti *n.* disagreement

असाधारण asādhāran *adj.* uncommon

असुरक्षा asuraksā *n.* insecure

असुरक्षित asuraksit *adj.* unsafe

अस्थायी asthāyi *adj.* temporary

अस्तित्व astitva *n.* existence

असिना asinā *n.* hail

अस्ति asti *adj.* day before yesterday

अस्थिर asthir *adj.* unstable

अस्पताल aspatāl *n.* hospital

अस्पताल गाडी aspatāl gāri *n.* ambulance

अस्पष्ट aspast *adj.* vague, illegible

अस्पष्टता aspastata *n.* ambiguity

अस्मिता asmitā *n.* pride

अस्वस्थ asvasth *adj.* unwell

अस्वाभाविक asvābhabik *adj.* unnatural

अस्विकार asvikaran *n.* rejection

अस्वीकार गर्नु aswikār garnu *v.i.* reject

अस्वीकृत aswikrit *adj.* rejected

असी assi *num.* eighty

असोज asoj *n.* sixth Nepalese month

अतिसार atisar *n.* diarrhea

अत्यन्त atyanta *adj.* very much
अहंकार ahankār *n.* conceit
अहाता ahātā *n.* compound
अहानिकर ahānikar *adj.* harmless
अहितकर ahitkar *adj.* malignant
अहिंसा ahimsā *n.* non-violence
अहिले ahile *adv.* now
अक्ष aks *n.* axis
अक्षम aksam *adj.* incompetent
अक्षर aksar *n.* syllable
अक्षरेपि aksarepi *n. used in legal documents, means "in letters instead of numerals." 500 would be "five hundred" in letters.*
अक्षांश aksāns *n.* latitude
अज्ञान agyān *n.* ignorance
अयोग्य ayogya *adj.* unfit
अपरेशन āprasan *n.* operation

आ

आइन्दा āindā *adv.* from now on

आलम्पिक ālampik *adj.* Olympic

आकाशवाणी ākasvāni *n.* radio

आकस्मिक ākasmik *adj.* accidental

आकस्मिकता ākasmikatā *n.* contingency

आकाश ākāsh *n.* sky

आक्रामक ākrāmak *adj.* aggressive

आक्रोश ākros *n.* scolding

आँकडा ānkadā *n.* date

आँखा ankha *n.* eye

आँखा को ānkha ko *adj.* visual

आँखा झिम्काउनु ānkha jhimkāunu *v.i.* blink

आँखा फादेर हर्नु āmkha fādera hernu *v.i.* stare

आँखी भुइँ ānkhi bhuin *n.* eyebrows

आँखीझ्याल ankhikhyāl *n.* lattice window

आग्लो āglo *n.* wooden door bolt

आँप āamp *n.* mango

आँधी āndhi *n.* storm

आँट āant *n.* boldness

आँसू ānsu *n.* tear (from eye)

आँगन āngan *n.* courtyard

आंशिक ānsik *adj.* partial

आइतवार āitabār *n.* Sunday

आउनु āunu *v.i.* to come

आउँ āun *n.* dysentery

आईमाई aimai *n.* woman

आकाश ākās *n.* sky

आकार ākār *n.* figure

आकर्षक ākarsak *n.* attraction

आकर्षण ākarsan *adj.* attractive

आक्रमण ākraman *n.* attack

आकर्षित गर्नु ākarsit garnu *v.t.* attract

आकांक्षा ākānksa *n.* aspiration

आक्सीजन āksijan *n.* oxygen

आकस्मिक ākasmik *adj.* sudden

आख्यान ākhyān *n.* legend

आक्षेप āksep *n.* accusation

आगन्तुक āgantuk *n.* visitor

आगमन āgman *n.* arrival

आगलागी āglāgi *n.* fire

आगामी āgāmi *adj.* forthcoming

आगो āgo *n.* fire

आग्रह āgraha *n.* request

आग्रह गर्नु āgrah garnu *v.i.* request

आघात āghāt *n.* blow

आचरण ācaran *n.* conduct

आचार ācar *n.* rule

आचार संहिता ācār samhita *n.* code of conduction

आचार्य ācārya *n.* professor; degree in Sanskrit; surname for Nepali Brahmins

आछन्न ācchann *adj.* overcast

आज āj *adv.* today

आजकल ājkal *adv.* nowadays

आज सम्म āj samma *adj.* up-to-date

आजन्म ājanma *adv.* existing from birth

आजीवन ājivan *adv.* lifelong

जिविका ājivikā *n.* livelihood

आँटा ātā *n.* flour

आठ āth *num.* eight

आठौं āthaun *adj.* eighteen

आडम्वर ādamhar *n.* false pride

आरु āru *n.* peach

आतंक ātanka *n.* terror

आतंकवाद ātankabad *n.* terrorism

आतंकवादी ātankabadi *n.* terrorist

आत्मा ātma *n.* spirit

आत्मकथा ātmakathā *n.* autobiography

आत्मगत ātmagat *adj.* subjective

आत्मरक्षा atmaraksa *n.* self-defense

आत्महत्या ātamhatyā *n.* suicide

आत्महत्या गर्नु ātamhatyā garnu *v.t.* to commit suicide

आत्म-समर्पण गर्नु ātm-samarpan garnu *v.t.* surrender

आत्म निर्णय atma nirnaya *adj.* self-reliant

आर्थिक ārtik *adj.* financial

आर्थिक सहायता ārthik sahāyatā *n.* subsidy, assistance

आदर ādar *n.* respect

आदरणीय ādaraniya *adv.* respectfully

आदर गर्नु ādar garnu *v.t.* respect, venerate

आदर्श ādars *n./adj.* ideal

आदान-प्रदान ādān-pradān *n.* reciprocity

आदिकवि ādikavi *n.* early poet in Nepal

आदेश ādes *n.* command

आदेश दिनु ādes dinu *v.t.* command

आध्योपान्त ādyopānta *prep. phr.* from beginning to end

आधा ādhā *adj.* half

आधान adhan *n.* pledge

आधार adhāsr *n.* basis

आधारहीन ādhārhin *adj.* false

आधार कर्म ādhār karm *n.* groundwork

आधारभूत ādhārbhut *adj.* fundamental

आधार-सामाग्री ādhār-sāmagri *n. pl.* data

आधारित ādhārit *adj.* based

आधिकारिक ādhikarik *adj.* official

आधुनिक ādhunik *adj.* modern

आधुनिक काल ādhunik kāl *n.* modern age

आनंद ānand *n.* joy, happiness

आन्द्रा āndrā *n.* intestine

आनंदोत्सव ānandostav *n.* carnival

आन्दोलन āndolan *adj.* agitation

आन्तरिक āntarik *adj.* internal

आफू āphu *n.* self

आफ्नो āphno *adj.* own

आपत्ति āpatti *n.* objection

आपसी āpsi *adj.* mutual

आँप ānp *n.* mango

आपतकाल āpātkal *n.* emergency

आप्रवास āprabās *n.* migration

आप्रवासी āprabasi *n.* immigrant

आफन्त āphanta *n.* relatives

आभार ābhār *n.* gratitude

आभारी ābhāri *adj.* grateful

आम हडताल āmhartāl *n.* general strike

आरक्षण āraksyan *n.* reservation

आस्तिक āstik *n.* believer

आशंका āsankā *n.* doubt, apprehension

औपचारिक aupcārik *adj.* formal

आलटाल āltāl *n.* procrastination

आपूर्ति āpurti *n.* supply

आम ām *adj.* typical, regular

आमन्त्रण āmantran *n.* invitation

आम रास्ता ām rāstā *n.* thoroughfare

आम्दानी āmdāni *n.* income
आमा āmā *n.* mother
आमा बाबु āmā bābu *n.* parents
आमाज्यु āmājyu *n.* sister-in-law
आम्लेट āmlet *n.* omelet(te)
आय āya *n.* income
आयकर āyakar *n.* income tax
आयात āyāt *n.* import
आयाम āyām *n.* dimension
आयात गर्नु āyāt garnu *v.t.* import
आयु āyu *n.* age
आयोग āyog *n.* commission
आयोजक āyojāk *n.* organizer
आयोजना गर्नु āyojana garnu *v.t.* convene
आयातकार āyātkār *adj.* oblong
आयतकर ayatkar *n.* income tax
आलोक ālok *n.* light
आलोचक ālocak *n.* critic
आलोचना ālocanā *n.* review
आलोचनात्मक ālocanatmak *adj.* critical
आलोपालो ālopālo *n.* turn
आज्ञा āgyā *n.* permission
आलु alu *n.* potato
आलुवखडा ālubakhadā *n.* plum
आज्ञा भंग गर्ने agyā bhang garnu *v.t.* disobey
आज्ञा को पालना गर्नु agyā ko palna garnu *v.t.* obey
आज्ञाकारी āgyākāri *adj.* obedient
आज्ञापालन āgyapālan *n.* obedience
आविष्कार गर्नु aviskār garnu *v.t.* invent
आवश्यक āvasyak *adj.* necessary
आवश्यकता āvasyakitā *n.* necessity

आवाज āvāz *n.* voice, sound
आवारा āvārā *n.* tramp
आवास āvās *n.* lodging
आविष्कार āviskār *n.* invention
आवेदन गर्नु āvedan garnu *v.t.* apply
आवेदन पत्र āvedan patr *n.* application
आरक्षण ārakshan *n.* reservation
आरम्भ ārambha *n.* beginning
आराम ārām *n.* comfort
आरोप ārop *n.* allegation
आर्जन ārjan *n.* earning
आशा āsā *n.* expectation, hope
आशाजनक āsājanak *adj.* hopeful
आशा गर्नु āsā garnu *v.t.* hope
आशीर्वाद asirvād *n.* blessing
आशीर्वाद दिनु asirvād dinu *v.t.* bless
आश्चर्य ascarya *n./v.t.* surprise
आश्चर्यचकित हुनु ascaryacākit hunu *v.i.* wonder
आश्चर्यजनक āscaryajanak *adj.* wonderful
आश्वासन āsvāsan *n.* assurance
आश्वासन दिनु āsvāsan dinu *v.t.* reassure

इ

इंकार inkār *n.* refusal
इंकार गर्नु inkār garnu *v.t.* refuse
इन्कलाव inkalab *n.* revolution
इंजन injan *n.* locomotive
इंजीनियर injiniyar *n.* engineer
ईंटा int *n.* brick
इंतजाम intajām *n.* arrangement
इंद्रिय indriya *n.* sense
इकाई ikāi *n.* unit
इखालु ikhālu *adj.* jealous
इच्छा icchā *n.* wish
इच्छाधीन icchādhin *adj.* optional
इच्छापत्र icchāpatra *n.* will (leg.)
इजलास ijālas *n.* judicial sitting
इजाजत ijājat *n.* permission
इतरलिंगी intarlingi *adj.* heterosexual
इति itihās *adj.* final
इतिहास itihās *n.* history
इत्यादि ityadi *adv.* so on
इन्धन indhan *n.* fuel
इनाम inām *v.t.* award
इनाम inām *n.* reward
इनाम दिनु inām dinu *v.t.* reward
इनार inār *n.* well
इन्जिनियर inginiyar *n.* engineer
इलाज ilāj *n.* medical treatment
इन्साफ insāph *n.* justice
इन्द्रजात्रा indrajātrā *n.* festival of Indra observed in Kathmandu
इन्द्रधनुष Indradhanus *n.* rainbow (Sanskrit origin)
इन्द्रेनी Indreni *n.* rainbow (Nepali origin)
इतर itar *adj.* another

इस्तरी गर्नु istari garnu *v.t.* iron
इस्पात ispāt *n.f.* steel
इस्लाम islām *n.* Islam
इस्लामी islāmi *adj.* Islamic
इलाका ilākā *n.* area
इशारा isārā *n.* signal
ईर्ष्या irsyā *n.* envy
इष्टमित्र istamitra *n.* friends
ईर्ष्यालु irsyālu *adj.* jealous
ईमानदार imāndār *adj.* honest
ईमानदारी imāndāri *n.* honesty
ईसाई isāi *n./adj.* Christian
ईसाई धर्म isāi dharma *n.* Christianity
ईसापूर्व isāipurva B.C.
ईसवी सन् isāvi san A.D.
ईश्वर iswar *n.* god

उ

उकालो ukālo *n.* upward slope

उकुस मुकुस ukusmukus *adj.* uncomfortable

उक्साउनु uksāunu *v.t.* urge

उखान ukhān *n.* proverb

उक्त ukta *adj.* supposed to be

उखु ukhu *n.* sugarcane

उग्र ugra *adj.* terrible

उग्रवाद ugravād *n.* extremism

उग्रवादी ugravādi *adj.* extremist

उच्च uccatā *adj.* high

उचाई ucai *n.* height

उचित ucit *adj.* fair

उच्चता uccatā *n.* height

उच्चस्तरीय uccastariya *adj.* high level

उच्चारण uccāran *n.* pronunciation

उजुर ujur *n.* complaint

उर्जा urjā *n.* energy

उर्जा संरक्षण samraksan *n.* energy conservation

उज्यालो ujyālo *adj.* bright

उज्वल ujwal *adj.* illuminated

उठाउनु uthāunu *v.i.* raise

उठाउनु uthāunu *v.t.* lift

उडान udān *adj.* (act of) flying

उडुस udus *n.* bedbug

उध्यान udhyan *n.* garden

उत्तर uttar *n.* north

उत्तरी uttari *adj.* northern

उत्तरदायित्व uttardāyitwa *n.* responsibility

उत्तरदायी uttardāyi *adj.* responsible

उत्तिर्ण uttirna *n.* promotion

उत्तेजना uttejanā *n.* excitement

उत्थान utthān *n.* progress

उत्पादन utpādan *n.* production

उत्पिडन utpidan *n.* oppression

उत्सव utsav *n.* celebration

उत्साह utsāha *n.* enthusiasm

उत्साहप्रद utsāhaprad *adj.* encouraging

उता uta *adv.* on the other side

उत्थान utthān *n.* progress

उत्पादन utpādan *n.* production

उत्पिडन utpidan *n.* oppression

उत्सव utsav *n.* celebration

उत्साह utsāha *n.* enthusiasm

उत्साहप्रद utsāhaprad *adj.* encouraging

उनी uni *pron.* he, she

उन्नत unnat *adj.* prosperous

उन्नति unnati *n.* prosperity

उदाउनु udāunu *v.* rise

उन्मूलन unmulan *n.* eradication

उदास udās *adj.* depressed, sad

उदास हुनु udās hunu *v.t.* depress

उदार udār *adj.* liberal

उदाहरण adāharan *n.* example

उद्धार uddhār *n.* deliverance

उध्योग udhyog *n.* industry

उध्योगी udhyogi *adj.* industrious

उध्योगपति udhyogpati *n.* industrialist

उद्धरण uddharan *n.* annotation

उपकार upkār *n.* welfare

उपदेश upades *n.* preaching

उपन्यास upanyās *n.* novel

उपन्यासकार upanyāskār *n.* novelist

उपनिवेश upanibes *n.* colony

उपयुक्त upyukta *adj.* appropriate, fit

उपभोक्ता upabhoktā *n.* consumer

उपयोग upayog *n.* application, use, usefulness

उपयोगिता upayogita *n.* utility

उपयोग गर्नु upayog garnu *v.* use

उपमहाद्वीप upamāhadwip *n.* subcontinent

उपयोगी upayogi *adj.* useful

उपकुलपति upakulpati *adj.* vice chancellor

उपलब्धि upalabdhi *n.* achievement

उपस्थिति upasthiti *n.* presence

उपस्थित रहनु upsthit rahanu *v.t.* attend

उपाय upāya *n.* means

उपहार upahār *n.* present, gift

उपहास upahās *n.* ridicule

उपेक्षा गर्नु upeksā garnu *v.t.* disregard

उम्मेदवार ummedbār *n.* candidate

उफ्रनु uphranu *v.i.* jump

उड्नु udnu *v.i.* fly

उर्वरक urvarak *n.* fertilizer

उत्कृष्ट utkrista *adj.* excellent

उत्कीर्ण utkrina *n.* carving

उत्खनन utkhanan *n.* excavation

उत्तेजित गर्नु uttejit garnu *v.t.* alarm

उत्तेजना uttejanā *n.* excitement

उलंघन ullanghan *n.* infringement

उलंघन गर्नु ullanghan garnu *v.t.* infringe

उल्लेख ullekh *n.* citation

उल्लेख गर्नु ullekh garnu *v.t.* specify

उल्लेखनीय ullekhaniya *adj.* remarkable

उल्टो ulto *adj.* opposite

उष्णा ushna *adj.* hot

उहाँ uhan *pron.* he

ऊँट unt *n.* camel

ऊँचाई uncāi *n.* height

ऊन un *n.* wool

ऊनी uni *adj.* woolen

ए

एडस् eds *n.* AIDS

ए.सी. e.si *n.* air-conditioning

एक ek *num.* one

एकदम ekdam *adv.* suddenly

एक पटक ekpatak *adv.* once

एकै बेलामा हुनु ekai belāmā hunu *v.i.* coincide

एक हुनु ek hunu *v.t.* unite

एकड ekar *n.* acre

एकत्र गर्नु ektra garnu *v.i.* concentrate

एकदम ekdam *adv.* all of a sudden

एकलिंगी eklingi *adj.* unisex

एक्लो eklo *adj.* alone

एकमत ekmat *adj.* unanimous

एक्स रे eks-kiran *n.* X-ray

एकसुरो eksuro *adj.* monotonous

एकता ektā *n.* unity

एकत्र हुनु ekatra hunu *v.t.* assemble

एक हुनु ek hunu *n.* alliance

एकाएक ekāek *adj.* sudden

एकादशी ekādasi *n.* eleventh day

एकाधिक ekādhik *adj.* plural

एकाधिकार ekādhikār *n.* monopoly

एकाधिनायक ekādhināyak *n.* dictator

एक्कासी ekkāsi *adv.* all of a sudden

एकीकरण ekikaran *n.* unification

एकीकृत ekikrit *adj.* unified

एकांत ekānt *n.* seclusion

एघार eghāra *num.* eleven

एघारौं eghāraun *adj.* eleventh

एजेंट ejent *n.* agent

एथियोपिया ethiopia *n.* Ethiopia

एरियल eriyal *n.* aerial

एशिया esiyā *n.* Asia

एलर्जी संबन्धी elarj sambhandhi *adj.* allergic

एलर्जी हुनु elari hunu *v.i.* to be allergic

एलर्जी elarji *n.* allergy

एप्रन epran *n.* apron

ऐंठन ainthan *n.f.* cramp

ऐच्छिक aicchik *adj.* voluntary

ऐडमिरल aidmiral *n.* admiral

ऐतिहासिक aitihāsik *adj.* historical

ऐन ain *n.* law

ऐना ainā *n.* mirror

ऐन्टेना aintenā *n.* antenna

ऐले aile *adv.* now

ऐलुमिनियम ailuminiyam *n.* aluminum

ऐश ais *n.* luxury

ऐश्वर्य aisearya *n.* glory

ऐस्परिन aisprin *n.* aspirin

ओ

ओइलाउनु oilāunu *v.* fade away
ओखती okhati *n.* medicine
ओखर okhar *n.* walnut
ओछ्यान ouchyān *n.* bed
ओछ्याउनु ochyāunu *v.* lay
ओठ oth *n.* lip
ओडार odār *n.* cave
ओरालो oprālo *n.* descent
ओहदा ohadā *n.* post

औ

औकात aukāt *n.* means
औचित्य aucitya *n.* justification
औजार aujār *n.* tool, implement
औद्योगिक audhyogik *adj.*
  industrial
औपचारिक aupacārik *adj.* formal
औपचारिकता aupacarikta *n.*
  formality
औधी audhi *adv.* very much
औलो aulo *n.* malaria
औंला aunla *n.* finger
औषधी ausadhi *n.* medicine
औषधीय ausadhiy *adj.*
  pharmaceutical
औसत ausat *n./adj.* average
औलो aulo *n.* malaria
औपचारिक aupacariktā *n.*
  formality
औंठी aunthi *n.* finger ring
औंला aunlā *n.* finger
औषधालय ausadhālaya *n.*
  pharmacy
औषधोपचार ausadhopacar *n.*
  medical treatment

क

कंपनी kampani *n.* company
कंबल kambal *n.* blanket
कंकाल kankāl *n.* skeleton
कंगारु kangāru *n.* kangaroo
कंगाल kangāl *n./adj.* very poor
कवि kabi *n.* poet
कविता kabitā *n.* poetry
कब्जा kabja *n.* possession
कचरा kacrā *n.* refuse
कचहरी kacahari *n.* court
कचौडी kacauri *n.* bread and vegetable breakfast
कचौरा kacaura *n.* cup
कच्चा kaccā *adj.* raw
कक्षा kaksā *n.* class
कछुवा kacuwā *n.* tortoise
कदम kadam *n.* step
कदर kadar *n.* appreciation
कट्टर kattar *adj.* orthodox
कटु katu *adj.* bitter
कठ kantha *n.* neck
कठपुतली kathputli *n.* pawn
कठबैद्य kathvaidya *n.* quack (fake doctor)
कठिन kathin *adj.* difficult
कठिनाई kathināi *n.* difficulty
कठोर kathor *adj.* strict, rigid
कठोरता kathoratā *n.* strictness
कडा गर्नु karā garnu *v.t.* toughen
कडा बनाउनु karā banaunu *v.t.* stiffen, harden
कडा हुनु karā hunu *v.t.* stiffen
कडापन karāpan *n.* hardness
कडी kadi *n.* link
कराही karāhi *n.* cauldron

करोड karod *num.* ten million
करोडपति karodpati *n.* multi-millionaire
कण्ठी kanthi *n.* necklace
कण्टक kantak *n.* nuisance
कन्ठ गर्ने kantha garne *v.* memorize
कण kan *n.* particle
कर्तव्य kartabya *n.* duty
कता katā *adv.* where
कति kati *adv.* how much
कतै katai *adv.* somewhere
कथनीय kathaniya *adj.* deserving to be said
कथन kathan *n.* statement
कथा kathā *n.* story
कथाकार kathakār *n.* story writer
कथानक kathānak *n.* plot
कथावाचक kathāvācack *n.* narrator
कदम kadam *n.* step
कदर kadam *adv.* never
कन्जुस kanjus *adj.* greedy
कन्डम kandam *n.* contraceptive
कन्तुर kantur *n.* small box
कन्या kanyā *n.* young girl
कन्यादान kanyādān *n.* ritual in Hindu marriage
कपडा kapadā *n.* textile, clothing
कपट kapat *n.* trick
कसान kaptān *n.* captain
कप्यूटर kampyutar *n.* computer
कपास kapās *n.* cotton
कपास kapāl *n.* hair
कफ kap *n.* phlegm

कफी kafi *n.* coffee

कब kab *n.* cub

कबाब kabab *n.* roasted meat

कब्जा kabja *n.* seizure, possession

कबाड kabār *n.* junk

कबुल kabul *n.* agreement

कबुलियतनामा kabuliyatnamā *n.* written agreement

कबज kabz *n.* constipation

कर्म karma *n.* work; destiny

कर्मचारी karmachāri *n.* government official

कम kam *adj.* less

कमलपित्त kamalpitta *n.* jaundice

कमसल kamsal *adj.* inferior (quality)

कमी kami *n.* shortage

कर्मी karmi *n.* carpenter

कम गर्नु kam garnu *v.t.* diminish

कम से कम kam se kam *adj.* at least

कम हुनु kam hunu *v.i.* reduce, fade

कमजोर kanjor *adj.* weak

कमजोर गर्नु kamzor garnu *v.t.* weaken

कमजोरी kamzori *n.* weakness

कमल kamal *n.* lotus

कमलो kamalo *adj.* soft

कम्मर kammar *n.* waist

कमाई kamāi *n.* earning

कमाउनु kamaunu *v.i.* earn

कमारो kamāro *n.* slave

कमी kami *n.* shortage

कम्ती kamti *adj.* less

कमीज kamij *n.* shirt

कमिलो kamilo *n.* ant

कमैया kamaiyā *n.* tenant farmer

कम्पन kampan *n.* vibration

कम्पायमान हुनु kampāymān hunu *v.i.* vibrate

कर kar *n.* tax

करकार्यालय karkaryalaya *n.* tax office

करदाता kardālā *n.* taxpayer

करणी karani *n.* sex

करदाता kardātā *n.* taxpayer

कर आधार kar ādhār *n.* tax base

कर संकलन kar sankālan *n.* tax collection

कर योग्य karyogya *adj.* taxable

कर कार्यालय kar kāryālaya *n.* tax office

करघा karghā *n.* loom

कराह karāh *n.* moan, groan

कराउनु karāhaunu *v.i.* groan, cry

करुणा karaunā *n.* compassion

करुणामय karaunāmaya *adj.* compassionate

कर्जा karja *n.* debt

कर्मवाच्य karamvācy *adj.* passive

कर्मचारी karamcāri *n.* employee

कर्मी karmi *n.* carpenter

कमिला kamilā *n.* ant

कर्ण karna *n.* ear

कलम kalam *n.* pen

कलश kalas *n.* urn

कलंक kalank *n.* spot

कलह kalaha *n.* dispute

कला kalā *n.* art

कमिशन kamisan *n.* commission

कलाकार kalākār *n.* artist

कलात्मक kalātmak *adj.* artistic

कलेज kalej *n.* college

कलेजो kaleko *n.* liver

कल्पना kalpnā *n.* fiction

कल्पना गर्नु kalpnā garnu *v.t.* imagine

कल्पित kalpit *adj.* imaginary

कल्याण kalyān *n.* welfare

कल्याणकारी kalyān kāri *adj.* auspicious

कवि kavi *n.* poet

कवियत्री kaviyatri *n.* poetess

कविता kavitā *n.* poem

कविराज kaviraj *n.* ayurvedic physician

कविसम्मेलन kavi sammelan *n.* meeting of poets

कसरत kasrat *n.* exercise

कसरी kasari *adv.* how

कस्नु kasnu *v.t.* screw, tighten

कसम खानु kasam khānu *v.t.* swear

कष्ट kasta *n.* trouble

कष्टकर kastakar *adj.* causing pain

कसाई kasāi *n.* butcher

कसरी kasari *adv.* how

कसुर kasur *n.* guilt

कसौंडी kansaudi *n.* brass cooking pot

कस्तूरी kasturi *n.* mountain deer

कस्तो kasto *adv.* how

कस्नु kasnu *v.t.* tighten

कहाँ kahān *conj./inter.* where

कहानी kahāni *n.* story

कहावत kahāvat *n.* proverb

कहिले kahile *adv.* when

कहिले काहिँ kahile kahile *adv.* sometimes

कहिले पनि होइन kahile pani hoina *adv.* never

काँक्रो kānkro *n.* cucumber

काँचो kānco *adj.* raw

कस्तो kasto *adj.* of what kind

कस्नु kasnu *v.t.* lighten

कक्षा kaksā *n.* classroom

काँध kāndh *n.* shoulder

काँप्नु kānpnu *v.i.* tremble

काउली kāuti *n.* cauliflower

काकताली kāktali *adj.* accidental

काका kākā *n.* uncle

काकी kāki *n.* aunt

काख kākh *n.* lap

काग kāg *n.* crow

कागतिहार kāgtihar *n.* first day of Tihar (festival held in November)

काउंटर kānpanu *v.i.* tremble

काजु kāju *n.* cashew

कागती kāgati *n.* lemon

कागज kāgaj *n.* paper

काज kāj *n.* temporary work

कान्छा kanchā *n./adj.* youngest

काटनु katnu *v.t.* amputate

काटने kātne *n.* something to cut with

काटने kātne *v.t.* delete

कार्टून kārtun *n.* cartoon

काठ kāth *n.* wood

काँतर kānthar *n.* coward

काथलिक kāthlik *adj.* Catholic

काथलिक धर्म kāthlik dharam *n.* Catholicism

कात्रो kātro *n.* shroud

कान kān *n.* ear

कानपासा kānpāsā *n.* earring

काँगियो kāngiyo *n.* comb

कान दुख्नु kān dukhnu *n.* earache

कानेखूसी गर्नु kānekhusi garnu *v.i.* whisper

कानून kānun *n.* legislation, law

कानूनी कारवाही kānuni kārbāhi *n.* legal punishment

कानूनी kanuni *adj.* legal

कानो kāno *adj.* blind in one eye

कान्ति kānti *n.* beauty

कान्छी kānchi *adj.* youngest female

कान्छीआमा kanchi āma *n.* stepmother

कान्छो kancho *n.* youngest

कान्छोवाबु kanchobābu *n.* uncle

कापी kāpi *n.* notebook
काफल kāphal *n.* a kind of fruit
काफी kāfi *adj./adv.* enough
काफी-गृह kāfi grhā *n.* coffee
काबू kābu *n.* control
काम kām *n.* work
कामचलाउ kāmcalāu *adj.* caretaker
कामकाज kāmkāj *n.* business
कामदेव kāmdev *n.* god of love
काम गर्नु kām garnu *v.i.* function
कामचोर kāmcor *n.* lazy person
काम को दिन kām ko din *n.* weekday
कामयाब हुनु kāmyāb hunu *v.i.* succeed
कामसूत्र kamsutra *n.* Kāma Sutra
कामना kamanā *n.* desire
कामी kāmi *n.* smith, blacksmith
काल kāl *n.* time; death
काल्पनिक kālpanik *adj.* imaginary
कायर kāyar *n.* coward
कायम kāyam *adj.* fixed
कायल kāyal *adj.* convinced
कारण kāran *n.* cause
कारखाना kārkhānā *n.* workshop
कारवाही kārvahi *n.* action
कारण kāran *n.* cause, reason
कारागार kārāgar *n.* jail
कारतूस kārtus *n.* cartridge
काल kāl *n.* time
कालीगर kaligar *n.* artisan
कारोबार kārobār *n.* transaction
कारिन्दा kārindā *n.* clerk
कार्यालय kāryālay *n.* bureau
कार्य kārya *n.* act, deed
कार्यकर्ता kāryakartā *n.* worker
कार्यकलाप kāryakalāp *n.* activity
कार्य गर्नु kārya garnu *v.i.* work
कार्यकारिणी karyakārini *adj.* executive

कार्यक्रम kāryakram *n.* program
कार्यपत्र karyapātra *n.* working paper
कार्यसमिति kāryasamiti *n.* executive committee
कार्यपालिका karyapālika *n.* executive
कार्यसम्पादन kāryasampādan *n.* achievement
कार्यविवरण karyavivaran *n.* job description
कार्यभार kāryabhār *n.* responsibility of work
कार्यसूची kāryasuci *n.* agenda
कार्यवाहक karyavāhak *adj.* officiating
कार्यान्वयन kāryanvan *n.* implementation
कार्यान्वयन kāryanvanayan *v.i.* implement
क्रांति krānti *n.* revolution
काग kāg *n.* crow
कालर kālar *n.* collar
काल्पनिक kālpanik *adj.* artificial
कालो kālo *adj.* black
कालोबजार kālo bajār *n.* black market
कालेज kālej *n.* college
काल्पनिक kālpanik *adj.* imaginary
काव्य kāvya *n.* poetry
काष्ठ kāstha *n.* wood
काष्ठकला kāsthakalā *n.* woodwork
काष्ठमण्डप kāsthamandap *n.* Kathmandu
किताबखाना kitabkhāna *n.* record keeping office of government
कि ki *conj.* either, or
किंवदंती kinvadanti *n.* rumor
किताब kitāb *n.* book
काष्ठकला kāsthakalā *n.* woodwork

किताब को पसल kitāb ko pasal *n.* bookstore

किन kina *conj.* why

किनभने kinabhane *conj.* because

किनमेल kinmel *n.* shopping

किनारा kinārā *n.* edge, margin

किफायत kiphāyat *n.* saving

किरण kiran *n.* ray (sunlight)

किरा kira *n.* insect

किरात kirāt *n.* inhabitants of eastern hills of Nepal mainly called Rai, Limbu and Sunuwar

किराना kirāna *n.* grocery

किरिया kiriya *n.* funeral rites

किर्ते kirte *n.* forgery

किला killā *n.* nail

किल्ला killā *n.* fort

किलोग्राम kilogrām *n.* kilo (gram)

किलोमीटर kilomitar *n.* kilometer

किसमिस kismis *n.* raisin

किशोर kisor *n.* teenager

किश्ती kisti *n.* tray

किसान kisān *n.* farmer; peasant

किसिम kisim *n.* kind

किस्मत kismat *n.* fortune

किस्सा kissā *n.* anecdote

कीट kit *n.* insect

कीटाणु kitānu *n.* germ

कीर्ती kirti *n.* fame

कीर्तन kirtan *n.* hymn

कीरा kirā *n.* worm

कीला kila *n.* nail

कुइरे kuire *adj.* white (man)

कुटपीट kutpit *n.* beating

कुट्नु kutnu *v.t.* beat

कुटिल kutil *adj.* crooked

कुटी kuti *n.* cottage

कुटिर उद्योग kutir udyog *n.* cottage industry

कुटुम्ब kutumba *n.* family

कुंडली kundali *n.* coil

कुतुहल kutuhal *adj.* curiosity

कुत kut *n.* rent paid by tenant

कुकर kukar *n.* cooker

कुकुर kukur *n.* dog

कुखुरो kukhuro *n.* cock

कुप्रो kupro *n.* hunchback

कुमारी kumāri *n.* miss (girl)

कुमार kumār *n.* small boy

कुमारित्व kumaritwa *n.* virginity

कुमाले kumāle *n.* potter

कुल्चिनु kulchinu *v.* trample

कुरबानी kurbāni *n.* sacrifice

कुर्सी kursi *n.* seat, chair

कुराकानी kurākani *n.* conversation

कुरा kurā *n.* fact

कुराउटे kurāute *adj.* talkative

कुल kul *adj./adv.* total

कुलच्छिन kulaksin *adj.* jinx

कुलीन kulin *n.* good family

कुल्ली kulli *n.* porter

कुल्ला गर्नु kulla garnu *v.i.* gargle

कुवा kuwā *n.* well

कुशल kusal *adj.* clever

कुशलता kusaltā *adj.* skillful

कुश्ती kusti *n.* wrestling

कुश्ती लड्नु kusti larnu *v.t.* wrestle

कुसुम kusum *n.* flower

कुसुन्डो kusunda *n.* an ethnic group in Nepal (mainly residing in forested areas)

कुहिरो kuhiro *n.* mist, haze

कूटनीति kutniti *n.* diplomacy

कूटनीतिज्ञ kutnitigya *n.* diplomat

कृतज्ञ kritagya *adj.* grateful

कृतघ्न kritaghna *adj.* ungrateful

कृपा kripā *n.* grace

कृपालु kripālu *adj.* gracious

कृपया kripyā *interj.* please

कृषक krisak *n.* farmer

कृषि krisi *n.* agriculture

कृषिऋण krisirin *n.* agricultural loan

कृषि उत्पादन krisi utpādan *n.* agricultural production

कृष्ण krisna *adj./n.* Krishna (an incarnation of Vishnu); black

केंद्र kendra *n.* center

केंद्रीय kendriya *adj.* central

के ke *pron.* what

केटा ketā *n.* young boy

केटी keti *n.* young girl

केटाकेटी ketāketi *n.* small children

केक kek *n.* cake

केरा kerā *n.* banana

केतली ketali *n.* kettle

केन्द्र kendra *n.* center

केन्द्रीकरण kendrikaran *n.* centralization

केन्द्रीय kendriya *adj.* central

केन्द्रीय सरकार kendriya sarkār *n.* central government

केन्द्रीय बैंक kendriya bank *n.* central bank

केन्द्रीय संगठन kendriya sangathan *n.* central organization

केरकार kerkār *n.* cross examination

केवल keval *adv.* just, only (ma keval mānis hun, I'm only a man)

केही kehi *pron.* something (malāi kehi cāhiyo, I need something)

कैंची kainchi *n.* scissors

कैंटीन kaintin *n.* cafeteria

कैद kaid *n.* captivity

कैदी kaidi *n.* prisoner

कैन्सर kainsar *n.* cancer

कैपसूल kaipsul *n.* capsule

कैफीन kaifin *n.* caffeine

कैमरा kaimarā *n.* camera

कैल्सियम kailsitam *n.* calcium

कष्ट kasta *n.* hardship

को ko *pron.* who

कोइला koilā *n.* coal

कोइली koili *n.* cuckoo

कोही kohi *pron.* someone

कोही पनि koi pani *pron.* anyone

कोही पनि होइन kohi pani hoina *pron.* none

कोही होइन koi hoina *pron.* nobody

कोख kokh *n.* womb

कोट kot *n.* coat

कोटा kotā *n.* quota

कोटेशन kotesan *n.* quotation

कोठा kotha *n.* room

कोदो kodo *n.* millet

कोण kon *n.* angle

कोपिला kopilā *n.* bud

कोमल komal *adj.* sensitive, delicate

कोमलता komaltā *n.* delicacy

कोइला koilā *n.* coal

कोलेस्टेरोल kolesterol *n.* cholesterol

कोर्रा korrā *n.* whip

कोषाध्यक्ष kosādhtaksha *n.* treasurer

कोश kos *n.* treasury

कोशिकीय kosikiy *adj.* cellular

कोशिश kosis *n.* try

कोशिश गर्नु kosis garnu *v.t.* try

कोसेली koseli *n.* gift, present

कौसी kausi *n.* balcony

कौंसल kaumsal *n.* consul

क्रमानुसार राख्नु kramānusār rākhnu *v.t.* grade

क्रमिक krāmik *adj.* gradual

क्रमश kramasha *adv.* step by step

क्रान्ति krānti *n.* revolution
क्रान्तिकारी krāntikāri *adj.* revolutionary
क्रिकेट kriket *n.* cricket
क्रिया kriyā *n.* verb
क्रियाकलाप kriyākalap *n.* activity
क्रियाविधि kriyāvidhi *n.* procedure
क्रियाविशेषण kriyāvisesan *n.* adverb
क्रियाशील kriyāsil *adj.* lively
क्रिसमस krismas *n.* Christmas
क्रीडा krida *n.* game
क्रेन kren *n.* crane
क्रुर krur *adj.* cruel
क्रुद्ध kruddha *adj.* angry
क्रोध krodh *n.* anger
क्रोधी krodhi *adj.* angry
क्लब kalab *n.* club (social)
क्लीनर klinar *n.* janitor, maid
क्लर्क klark *n.* clerk
क्वार्ट kvyārt *n.* quart
क्षति ksati *n.* loss
क्षमा ksamā *n.* forgiveness
क्षमा-याचना ksakmā-yācnā *n.* apology
क्षणीक ksanik *adj.* momentary
क्षत्री ksetri *n.* Hindu warrior caste
क्षयरोग ksaya rog *n.* tuberculosis
क्षेत्र ksetra *n.* zone
क्षेत्रफल ksetraphal *n.* area
क्षेत्रीय ksetriya *adj.* regional

ख

खम्बा khambhā *n.* pillar, post, pole

खच्चर khaccar *n.* mule

खजाना khajana *n.* treasure

खर्क kharka *n.* Alpine grassland

खजानची khanjānci *n.* cashier

खजूर khajur *n.* date

खटखटाउनु khatkhatāunu *v.i.* knock

खण्ड khand *n.* fraction

खण्डकाव्य khanda kāvya *n.* short epic

खण्डन khandan *n.* rebuttal

खण्डहर khandahar *n.* ruins

खड्ग khadga *n.* sword

खडा kharā *adj.* vertical

खडा हुनु kharā hunu *v.t.* stand

खडेरी khaderi *n.* drought

खतम khatam *n./adj.* finish

खतरनाक khatarnāk *adj.* dangerous

खतरा khatarā *n.* menace

खनिज पदार्थ khanij padārtha *n.* mineral

खन्नु khannu *v.* dig

खनजोत khanjot *n.* cultivate

खपत khapat *n.* consumption

खप्पिस khappis *n.* experienced

खबर khabar *n.* news

खबरपत्रिका khabar patrikā *n.* newspaper

खबरदार khabardār *interj.* beware

खम्बा khambā *n.* pillar

खरबूजा kharbuzā *n.* melon

खराब गर्नु kharāb garnu *v.t.* corrupt

खराब हुनु kharāb hunu *v.i.* decay

खलक khalak *n.* dynasty

खलनायक khalnāyak *n.* villain

खलबली khalbali *n.* turmoil

खरानी kharāni *n.* ashes

खराब kharab *adj.* faulty

खरायो khārayo *n.* rabbit

खरीद kharid *n.* purchase

खरीदनु kharidnu *v.t.* buy

खरीदार kharidār *n.* buyer

खरीदारी kharidāri *n.* shopping

खर्च kharca *n.* expense

खर्च गर्न सक्नु kharca garna saknu *v.t.* afford

खर्च गर्नु kharca garnu *v.t.* depend

खस khas *n.* largest ethnic group in Nepal

खसी khasi *n.* castrated goat

खस्रो khasro *adj.* rough

खस्नु khasnu *v.* fall

खाँचो khancho *n.* necessity

खाजा khajā *n.* midday meal (lunch)

खाम khām *n.* envelope

खाट khāt *n.* cot

खाडल khādal *n.* ditch

खाडी khāri *n.* gulf, bay

खाता khātā *n.* account

खातिर khātir *n.* sake

खाद khād *n.* manure

खानी khāni *pron.* mine

खाना khānā *n.* food

खानेलायक khāne lāyak *adj.* edible

खाद्य khādya *adj.* food

खाद्यान्न khādyānna *n.* foodstuff

खानु khānu *v.* eat

खाली khāli *adj.* vacant, empty

खाली गर्नु khāli garnu *v.t.* empty

खारिज khārij *adj.* dismissed

खास khās *adj.* special

खास तौर ले khās taur le *adv.* especially

खास्टो khāsto *n.* shawl

खिन्न khinn *adj.* depressed

खिर knir *n.* rice pudding

खिया khiyā *n.* rust

खिलाफ khilāf *conj.* against

खिलौना khilaunā *n.* toy

खींचनु khincnu *v.t.* tow

खुकुरी khukuri *n.* sword

खुट्टा khutto *n.* foot

खुद khud *pron.* ourselves, myself

खुद्रा khudrā *n.* retail

खुदाई khudāi *n.* excavation

खुरपा khurpā *n.* hoe

खुरपानी khurpani *n.* apricot

खुला khulā *adj./v.t.* open

खुल्नु khulnu *n.* opening

खुर्सानी khursāni *adj.* chilly

खुशी khusi *n.* happiness

खुशीले khusi le *adj.* willing

खूंखार khunkhār *adj.* fierce

खेत khet *n.* field

खेतीयोग्य kheti yogya *adj.* arable

खेती kheti *n.* cultivation

खेतालो khetālo *n.* farm labor

खेतीबारी khetibāri *n.* agriculture

खेद khed *n.* regret

खेर kher *n.* waste

खेल khel *n.* game

खैनी khaini *n.* tobacco product

खेल्नु khelnu *v.t.* play

खेलकूद khelkud *n.* sport

खेलनु khelnu *v.t.* play

खेल-प्रतियोगिता khel-pratiyogitā *n.* tournament

खेलाडी khelādi *n.* sportsman

खेलौना khelaunā *n.* toy

खेल्नु khelnu *v.* to play a game

खोक्रो khokro *adj.* hollow

खोक्नु khoknu *v.* to cough

खोज khoj *n.* discovery, find

खोजी khoji *n.* inquiry

खोज गर्नु khoj garnu *v.t.* search

खोज्नु khojnu *v.t.* seek

खोप khopari *n.* vaccination

खोपनु khopnu *v.* vaccinate

खोपडी khop *n.* skull

खोला khola *n.* small river

खोल्नु kholnu *v.t.* unwrap

खोसिनु khosinu *v.i.* to be dismissed

खोस्नु khosnu *v.t.* snatch away

ख्याति khyati *n.* fame

ख्याक khyāk *n.* ghost

ख्याल khyāl *n.* joke

ग

गंजो ganjā *adj.* bald

गँगटो gangato *n.* crab

गँजडी ganjadi *n.* hashish addict

गँडयौलो gandyaulo *n.* earthworm

गाँठो gānthon *n.* knot

गाँठो बाँध्नु gāntho bāndhnu *v.t.* knot

गंगा gangā *n.* Ganges River

गंध gandh *n.* odor

गँवार ganwār *adj./n.* uncultured

गंभीर gambhir *adj.* serious

गाऊँ gāun *n.* village

गच्छे gacche *n.* ability

गज gaj *n.* yard

गजल gajal *n.* lyrical poetry

गजव gajab *adj.* very strange

गठन gathan *n.* forming

गठबन्धन gathabandhan *n.* coalition

गठबन्धन सरकार gathabandhan sarkār *n.* coalition government

गडबड garbar *n.* unrest

गडबड गर्नु garbar garnu *v.t.* tamper

गडगडाहट gargrāhat *n.* rumble

गडबड गर्नु garbar garnu *v.t.* upset

गढा gaddhā *n.* dent, pit

गढ garh *n.* fortress

गण gan *n.* group, troop

गणक ganak *n.* calculator

गणना gananā *n.* counting

गणना गर्नु gannā garnu *v.t.* count

गणतंत्र gantantra *n.* republic

गणतंत्री gantantri *n./adj.* republican, non-royalist

गणपूरक ganapurak *n.* quorum

गणराज्य ganarājya *n.* republic

गणित ganit *n.* arithmetic

गणेश ganesh *n.* Ganesh (Hindu god)

गत gat *n.* past

गति gati *n.* motion, pace

गतिलो gatilo *n.* descent

गति सीमा gati simā *n.* speed

गतिविधि gatibidhi *n.* activity

गतिरोध gātirodh *n.* impasse

गतिशील gatisil *adj.* dynamic

गते gate *n.* any day in Nepali calendar

गद्दी gaddi *n.* throne

गधा gadhā *n.* donkey

गन्ध gandha *n.* smell

गन्धहीन gandhhin *adj.* odorless

गन्धक gandhak *n.* sulfur

गन्तव्य gantabya *n.* destination

गनाई ganai *n.* counting

गफ gaph *n.* gossip

गफी gaphi *adj.* gossipy

गफ गर्नु gaph garnu *v.i.* gossip

गरज garaj *n.* thunder, roar

गर्जनु garajnu *v.i.* roar

गरम garam *adj.* warm

गर्मि garmi *n.* warmth

गरीब garib *adj.* poor

गरीबी garibi *n.* poverty

गरुड garur *n.* eagle

गर्दन gardan *n.* neck

गर्भ garbha *n.* womb

गर्भपात garabhpāt *n.* abortion

गर्भवती garabhvati *adj.* pregnant

गर्भाशय garbhāsy *n.* uterus, womb

गर्भाधान garbhādan *n.* conception

गलत galat *adj.* mistaken, wrong

गल्ती galti *n.* fault, error

गलनु galnu *v.i.* thaw

गला घोट्नु galā ghotnu *v.t.* choke, strangle

गलाउनु galāunu *v.t.* thaw

गल्ली galli *n.* lane

गलैंचा galaica *n.* carpet

गवैया gavaiyā *n.* singer

गवाह gavāh *n.* witness

गवाही gavāhi *n.* evidence

गवाही दिनु gavāhi dinu *v.t.* testify, witness

गर्व garv *n.* pride

गश्ती gasti *n.* patrol

गहन gahan *adj.* profound

गहुँ gahun *n.* wheat

गहना gahanā *n.* ornament

गहिरो gahiro *adj.* deep

गहिराई gaharāi *n.* depth

गयल हुनु gayal hunu *v.* be absent

गयल gayal *n.* absent

गाँठो बाँध्नु gantho bāndhanu *v.t.* knot

गाउँ gāun *n.* village

गाउँले gaunle *n.* villager

गाडी gāri *n.* vehicle

गाँजा gānja *n.* marijuana

गाजर gājar *n.* carrot

गाड्नु gārnu *v.t.* bury

गाढा बनाउनु gārhā banāunu *v.i.* thicken

गाइड gāid *n.* guide

गाडा gādā *n.* cart

गाडी gādi *n.* vehicle

गाढा gārhā *n.* thick, close

गाढा बन्नु gārhā bannu *v.i.* thicken

गाना gānā *n.* song

गाई gāi *n.* cow, buffalo; गाई वस्तु gāi bastu *n.* cows, buffaloes

गाई जात्रा gaijātrā *n.* festival in Kathmandu valley in August in memory of dead

गायक gāyak *n.* singer

गायकदल gāyakdal *n.* chorus

गायक-मण्डल gāyak-mandal *n.* choir

गायन gāyan *n.* singer

ग्राहक gāhak *n.* customer

गायब gāyab *n.* disappearance

गायब हुनु gāyab hunu *v.i.* disappear

गायिका gāyikā *n.* singer

गाला gālā *n.* cheek

गाली-गर्नु gāli garnu *v.t.* swear

गिजा gijā *n.* gum *(anat.)*

गिलास gilās *n.* glass *(cup)*

गिटार gitār *n.* guitar

गिदी gidi *n.* brain

गिद्ध giddha *n.* vulture

गिनती गर्नु ginti garnu *v.t.* reckon

गिरजाघर girjāghar *n.* church

गिर्नु girnu *v.t.* fall

गिराउनु girāunu *v.t.* drop

गिरावट girāvat *v.t.* fall

गिरफ्तार giraftār *n.* arrest

गिरफ्तार गर्नु giraftār garnu *v.t.* arrest

गिरफ्तारी giraftāri *n.* seizure

गीत gitār *n.* song

गीति-नाटय giti-nātya *n.* opera

गीता gitā *n.* Gita *(holy scripture of Hindus)*

गीलो gilā *adj.* wet

गुट gut *n.* gang

गुटबन्दी gutbandhi *n.* clique

गुठी guthi *n.* trust

गुठीयार guthiyār *n.* trustees

गुह्य guhya *n.* secret

गुँड gundā *n.* nest

गुँद gund *n.* gum *(glue)*

गुजरात gujrat *n.* Gujarat *(Indian state)*

गुजराती gujrati *adj.* inhabitant of Gujarat

गुच्छा guccā *n.* marble

गुच्छा gucchā *n.* cluster

गुण gun *n.* virtue

गुणी guni *n.* recognizing merit

गुण गान gungān *n.* praise of merit

गुणा gunā *n.* multiplication

गुणात्मक gunātmak *n.* qualification

गुणा गर्नु gunā garnu *v.t.* multiply

गुनगुनाउनु gungunāunu *v.* hum

गुन्द्रुक gundruk *n.* dried vegetable

गुन्डा gundā *n.* tramp

गुन्डागिरी gunda giri *n.* hooliganism

गुनासो gunāso *n.* grievance

गुप्त gupt *adj.* secret, occult

गुप्तीकुरा guptikuro *n.* hidden fact

गुप्त पुलिस gupti pulis *n.* secret police

गुप्तरोग gupta rog *n.* venereal disease, STD

गुप्तचर guptcar *n.* detective, scout

गुप्तवेश guptabhes *n.* disguise

गुफा gufā *n.* cave

गुब्बारा gubbārā *n.* balloon

गुभाजु gubhāju *n.* Newar Buddhist priest

गुमाउनु gumāunuu *v.* lose

गुमनाम gumnām *adj.* anonymous

गुम्बद gumbad *n.* dome

गुम्बा gumbā *n.* monastery

गुराँस gurāns *n.* rhododendron

गुरु guruvār *n.* teacher

गुरुआमा guruāmā *n.* female teacher

गुरुवार guruvār *n.* Thursday

गुरुपूजा gurupuja *n.* Teacher's Day (holiday)

गुरुत्व gurutwa *n.* gravity

गुलाब gulāb *n.* rose

गुलाब को बिरुवा gulāb ko biruwā *n.* rosebush

गुलाबजामुन gulābjāmun *n.* gulabjamun *(a Nepali dessert)*

गुलाबी gulābi *adj.* pink

गुलियो guliyo *adj.* sweet

गहूँ gahun *n.* wheat

गृह grih *n.* home

गृहमंत्री griha mantri *n.* Minister of Interior

गृह मंत्रालय grih mantrālaya *n.* home ministry

गृह कार्य griha kārya *n.* homework

गृह सचिव griha saciv *n.* home secretary

गृहयुद्ध griha yuddha *n.* civil war

गृहिणी grihini *n.* housewife

ग्रेनाइट grenāit *n.* granite

गैरज gairaj *n.* garage

गैर-कानूनी gair-kānuni *adj.* illegal

गैलन gailan *n.* gallon

गैलरी gailari *n.* gallery

गैस gais *n.* gas

गोरु goru *n.* dull

गोरु तिहार gorutihar *n.* third day of Tihar festival celebrated in November

गोठालो gothālo *n.* shepherd; cowboy

गोता gotā *n.* dive

गोता लगाउनु gotā lagāunu *v.t.* dive

गोदाम godām *n.* warehouse

गोबर gobar *n.* cowdung

गोभी gobhi *n.* cauliflower

गोरा gorā *adj.* white

गोरेटो goreto *n.* trail

गोल gol *adj.* round

गोलावारुद golābārud *n.* arms, ammunition

गोलभेडा golbheda *n.* tomato

गोला golā *n.* sphere

गोली goli *n.* pill; bullet

गोली हान्नु goli hannu *v.t.* shoot

गोल्फ golf *n.* golf

गोप्य gopya *adj.* confidential

गोप्यता gopyatā *n.* secrecy

गोपनीय gopaniya *adj.* secret

गोवध gobadh *n.* cow slaughter

गोष्ठी gosthi *n.* seminar

गोस्वारा हुलाक goswāra hulāk *n.* general post office

गोस्वारा goswāra *n.* government office

गौरव gaurav *n.* glory

ग्रह grah *n.* planet

ग्राह grāha *n.* crocodile

ग्रहण grahan *n.* eclipse

ग्राहक grāhak *n.* customer

गन्थ grantha *n.* book

ग्रामीण grāmin *adj.* rural

ग्रीष्म grisma *n.* summer

ग्रीष्मावकास grismāvakās *n.* summer vacation

ग्लोब glob *n.* globe

घ

घंटा ghantā *n.* hour

घंटी ghanti *n.* bell

घटक ghatak *n.* ingredient

घटना ghatanā *n.* occurrence

घटनाक्रम ghatnākram *n.* sequence of events

घटनास्थल ghatnāsthal *n.* site

घट्नु ghatnu *v.i.* decrease

घटस्थापना ghatasthāpanā *n.* first day of Dashain festival *(celebrated in October)*

घटाई ghatāi *n.* shortening

घटाउनु ghatāunu *v.t.* decrease

घटाव ghatāv *n.* reduction

घटिया ghatiyā *adj.* inferior

घटुवा ghatuwā *adj.* diminishing

घडा gharā *n.* pitcher

घडियाल ghariyal *n.* crocodile

घडी ghari *n.* clock, wristwatch, watch

घडी घडी ghari ghari *adv.* time to time

घडेरी ghaderi *n.* real estate

घण्टाघर ghantāghar *n.* clock tower

घण्टी ghanti *n.* bell

घटित हुनु ghatit hunu *v.i.* occur

घनघोर ghanghor *adj.* dangerous

घनचक्कर ghanacakkar *adj.* great mistake

घनिष्ठ ghanisth *adj.* intimate

घनिष्ठता ghanisthatā *n.* intimacy

घन ghan *n.* cube

घरपट्टि gharpatti *n.* landlord

घनफुट ghanafut *n.* cubic foot

घनत्व ghanitwa *n.* density

घनिष्ठ ghanistha *adj.* very close

घमण्ड ghamanda *n.* pride

घमण्डी ghamandi *adj.* proud

घर ghar *n.* home

घर घराना ghar gharānā *n.* home and other property

घरधनी ghardhani *n.* landlord

घरभाडा gharbhādā *n.* house rent

घरानिया gharāniyā *adj.* well-bred

घरेलु gharelu *adj.* domestic

घस्रने जन्तु ghasrane jantu *n.* reptile

घाघर ghāghar *n.* skirt

घाम ghām *n.* sunlight

घाँटी ghāti *n.* throat

घाँस ghās *n.* grass

घाइते ghāite *adj.* injured

घातक ghatāk *n.* killer

घायल गर्नु ghāyal garnu *v.t.* injure

घाउ ghāu *n.* wound, cut

घाट ghat *n.* bathing place along river banks

घाटा ghāta *n.* loss

घिन ghin *n.* hate

घुमाव ghumāv *n.* turn

घुँडा ghundā *n.* knee

घुँडा टेक्नु ghundā teknu *v.i.* kneel

घुमफिर ghumphir *n.* wandering

घुम्नु ghumnu *v.* walk

घुमाउरो ghumāuro *adj.* bent

घुम्टो ghuhmto *n.* veil

घुसार्नु ghusārnu *v.t.* insert

घुस्नु ghusnu *v.i.* penetrate

घुसखोरी ghuskhori *n.* bribery
घुस ghus *n.* bribe
घुसखोर ghuskhor *n.* bribe taker
घृणा योग्य ghirnā yogya *adj.* disgusting
घृणा ghrinā *n.* scorn
घेरा gherā *n.* enclosure
घोटाला ghotalā *n.* disorder
घोडा ghorā *n.* horse
घोडी ghori *n.* mare
घोकनु ghoknu *v.* learn by rote
घोर ghor *adj.* terrible
घोषणा ghosanā *n.* declaration
घोडचढी ghod chadi *n.* horse rider
घोडदौड ghoddaud *n.* horse race
घोडेटो ghoreto *n.* horse track
घोषणा गर्नु ghosanā garnu *v.t.* announce, declare

च

चक्का cakka n. wheel
चकचके cacake adj. mischievous
चक्का जाम cakkā jām n.
  vehicular strike
चंदा candā n. subscription
चंदन को काठ candan ko kāth n.
  sandalwood
चकित cakit adj. surprised
चक्कु cakku n. knife
चक्कर ले आक्रांत cakkar le ākrant
  adj. dizzy
चक्र cakr n. wheel
चक्रपथ cakrapath n. highway
  around a city
चक्रवृद्धिब्याज cakrabriddhi byaj n.
  compound interest
चटाई catāi n. mat
चटनी catni n. sauce
चटामरी catāmari n. rice flour bread
चट्टान cattān n. rock
चट्याङ catyāng n. lightning
चढाई carhāi n. invasion; climb
चढनु carhnu v.i. ride, mount
चढाउनु carhāunu v.t. offer
चतुर catur adj. ingenious, clever
चतुराई caturāi n. cleverness
चना canā n. gram
चन्दन candan n. sandlewood
  paste
चन्द्र candra n. moon
चन्द्रग्रहण candragrahan n. lunar
  eclipse
चप्पल cappal n. sandal
चपाउनु capāunu v.t. chew
चपाटि capati n. wheat bread

चर्म carma n. leather
चर्मरोग carmarog n. skin disease
चमक camak n. glare
चम्काउनु camkaunu v.t./v.i. shine
चमत्कार camatkār n. miracle
चमत्कारी camatkāri adj.
  miraculous
चमकीलो camkilo adj. brilliant
चमेरो camero n. bat (animal)
चमेना camenā n. light breakfast
चमेली cameli n. jasmine
चम्चा camchā n. spoon
चरन caran n. feet; cow pasture
चरम caram adj. extreme
चरेस cares n. marijuana
चरित्र caritra n. character
चरित्रहत्या caritrahatyā n.
  character assassination
चरित्रहीन caritrahin adj. without
  moral character
चर्नु carnu v. graze
चर्च carc n. church
चर्चा carca n. talk, discussion
चयन cayan n. selection
चरा cara n. bird
चंचल cancal adj. restless
चहलपहल cahalpahal n. activity
चल संपति cal sampatti n.
  movable property such as car,
  money
चलनु calnu v.t./v.i. move
चलन calan n. custom
चश्मा casmā n. eyeglasses
चश्मा बनाउने casmā banaune n.
  optician

चाँदी candi *n.* silver
चाँदी को भाँडा cāndi ko bhānd *n.* silverware
चाक cāk *n.* chalk
चाकर cakar *n.* servant
चाकलेट cāklet *n.* chocolate
चाकलेट रंग को cāklet rang ko *adj.* maroon
चाख्नु caknu *v.* taste food
चानचुन cancun *adj.* very little
चलानी calāni *n.* dispatch
चलाख calākh *adj.* clever
चलाखी calākhi *n.* cleverness
चल्ला callā *n.* chicks
चलता पुर्जा caltā purjā *adj.* active; clever
चाबी cābi *n.* key
चायदान cāydān *n.* teakettle
चियादानी cāydāni *n.* teapot
चार cār *num.* four
चाटनु cātnu *v.* lick
चाल चलन cāl calan *n.* conduct
चालीस cālis *num.* forty
चालीसौं calisaun *adj.* fortieth
चालू cālu *adj.* current, active
चामल cāmal *n.* rice
चाहनु cāhanu *v.t.* desire
चाहिंदो cāhindo *adj.* necessary
चाहिन्न cahinna *n.* lack of need for something
चासो chāso *n.* concern
चिउँडो chiundo *n.* chin
चिउरा ciurā *n.* flat rice
चिकित्सा cikitsā *n.* therapy
चिकित्सालय cikitsālay *n.* clinic
चिकित्सक cikitsak *n.* therapy; doctor, physician
चिडियाखाना ciriyākhana *n.* zoo
चिडचिडा circirā *adj.* fractious
चिडचिडी circiri *adj.* hasty

चिढाउनु cidhāunu *v.t.* tease
चित्र citra *n.* painting, photo
चित्रकार citrakār *n.* painter
चित्र जस्तो citra jasto *adj.* picturesque
चित्रण गर्नु citran garnu *v.t.* depict
चित्रित citrit *adj.* portrayed
चित्रकार citrakār *n.* painter
चित्रकारी citrakari *n.* painting
चित्रपट citrapat *n.* tapestry
चिलाउनु cilāunu *v.* itch
चिसो ciso *adj.* cold
चिन्ता गर्नु cintā garnu *v.t.* worry
चिंता cintā *n.* concern, worry
चिता citā *n.* funeral pyre
चिन्ह cinh *n.* mark, trace
चिनजान cinjaan *n.* recognition
चिन्नु cinnu *v.* recognize
चिट्ठी citthi *n.* letter
चिप्लो ciplo *adj.* slippery
चिच्याउनु cicyāunu *v.t.* scream
चिहान chihān *n.* tomb
चिया ciya *n.* tea
चिप्लेटी cipleti *n.* game
चीज cij *n.* thing
चीज cij *n.* cheese
चीन China *n.* china
चीनी cini *n./adj.* sugar
चील cil *n.* eagle
चुंबक cumbak *n.* magnet
चुंबकीय cumbakiya *adj.* magnetic
चुक्नु cuknu *v.* miss
चुकुल cukul *n.* tower bolt *(for doors)*
चुप cup *adj.* silent
चुप गर्नु cup garnu *v.t.* silence
चुन cun *n.* lime
चुनिनु cuninu *v.* to be elected
चुनाव cunāv *n.* election
चुनौती cunauti *n.* challenge

चुनौती दिनु cunauti dinu *v.t.* challenge

चुम्बकीय cumbakiy *adj.* magnetic

चुम्बन cumban *n.* kiss

चुरा curā *n.* bangle

चुरोट curot *n.* cigarette

चुरौटे curaute *n.* Muslim minority group in Nepal's hill country

चुम्बन गर्नु cumban garnu *v.* kiss

चुस्की cuski *n.* sip

चूक cuk *n.* default

चुक्नु cuknu *v.i.* fail

चुटाई cutāi *n.* beating

चुटनु cutnu *v.* beat

चुल्हो culho *n.* stove

चुल्है निम्ता culhai nimtā *n.* family invitation

चूर्ण curn *n.* powder

चुस्नु cusnu *v.t.* suck

चेक cek *n.* check

चेवा cewā *n.* peek, check

चेष्टा cestā *n.* move, gesture; try

चेला celā *n.* disciple, pupil

चेन cen *n.* chain

चेप्टो cepto *adj.* wide

चेपाङ cepāng *n.* ethnic group living in western hills

चेरी ceri *n.* cherry

चेष्ठा cesthā *n.* attempt

चेतनशील cetansil *adj.* conscious

चेतना cetana *n.* consciousness

चेतावनी दिनु cetāvani dinu *v.t.* warn

चोखो cokho *adj.* unpolluted

चोट cot *n.* hurt, wound

चोट लगाउनु cot lagāunu *v.i.* hurt

चोट खानु cot khanu *v.t.* hurt

चोट्टा cotta *n.* swindler, thief

चोरवजार corbajar *n.* smuggling market

चोर cor *n.* thief

चोरी cori *n.* theft

चोरी गर्नु cori garnu *v.t.* steal

चोलो colo *n.* blouse

चौक cauk *n.* square

चौकी caukāi *n.* checkpost

चौकीदार caukidār *n.* watchman

चौतारा cautāra *n.* platform for resting

चौतर्फी cautarphi *adj.* all round

चौकिनु caukinu *adj.* wary

चौडा caurā *adj.* wide

चौडा गर्नु caurā garnu *v.t.* widen

चौडाई caurāi *n.* width

चौतारी cautāri *n.* platform

चौथाई cauthāi *n.* One-fourth

चौथो cautho *adj.* fourth

चौध caudah *num.* fourteen

चौधौं caudahaun *adj.* fourteenth

चौपट caupat *n.* damage

चौर chaur *n.* meadow

चौंरीगाइ chaurigāi *n.* yak

च्याउ cyāu *n.* mushroom

च्यामे cyāme *n.* sweeper, cleaner

च्यात्नु cyātnu *v.* tear, rip

छ

छ cha *v.* is
छकाउनु chakāunu *v.* deceive
छड char *n.* rod
छडी chari *n.* wand
छरितो charito *adj.* efficient
छर छिमेकी charchimeki *n.* neighbors
छर्नु charnu *v.* scatter
छल chal *n.* deception
छलफल chalphal *n.* discussion
छलाँग chalāng *n./v.i.* gallop
छपाई chapāi *n.* printing
छपाउनु chapāunu *v.* print
छप्पर chappar *n.* shed
छत chat *n.* roof
छट्टु chattu *n./adj.* cunning
छत्रछायाँ chatrāchāyā *n.* shelter
छर्नु charnu *v.* scatter
छहरा chaharā *n.* waterfall
छहारी chahāri *n.* shade
छाड्नु chādnu *n.* leave
छाडा chādā *adj.* out of control
छाउनी chāuni *n.* cantonment
छाता chātā *n.* umbrella
छाती chāti *n.* chest (anat.)
छान्नु chānnu *v.t.* select
छात्र chātra *n.* pupil
छात्रा chātrā *n.* female pupil
छात्रवास chātravās *n.* boarding
छात्रवृत्ति chātravrtti *n.* scholarship
छात्रजीवन chātrajivan *n.* student life
छानवीन chānbin *n.* selection
छानबीन गर्नु chān-bin garnu *v.t.* investigate

छाना chānā *n.* roof
छनोट chanot *n.* selection
छाप chāp *n.* stamp
छापाखाना chāpākhānā *n.* printing press
छान्नु chānnu *v.t.* choose
छानिनु chāninu *v.* be selected
छाप chāp *n.* stamp
छाप्रो chāpro *n.* cottage
छापा chāpā *n.* raid
छापामार chāpāmār *n./adj.* guerilla
छाप्नु chāpnu *v.t.* print
छायाँ chāyā *n.* shadow, shade
छायाँ दार chāyā dār *adj.* shady
छाल chāl *n.* wave
छाला chālā *n.* leather
छिटपुट chitput *adj.* random
छिटो chito *adj.* quick
छिमेक chimek *n.* neighborhood
छिमेकी chimeki *n.* neighbor
छुच्चो chucco *adj.* miser
छुटकारा chutkārā *n.* relief
छुट्टी chutti *n.* holiday, vacation
छुतहा chuthā *adj.* infectious
छूट chut *n.* omission
छूट दिनु chut dinu *v.t.* exempt
छुट्टिनु chuttinu *v.* separate
छुनु chunu *v.t.* touch
छुरा churā *n.* blade
छेत्री chetri *n.* caste name in Nepal
छोरा chora *n.* son
छोरी chori *n.* daughter
छोडी दिनु chodi dinu *v.t.* quit
छुटकारा chukara *n.* release

छुट्टीनु chuttinu *v.* be separated
छेउ cheu *n.* side
छोटो choto *adj.* small
छोटो चित्तको chotocittako *adj.*
  mean-spirited
छोट्याउनु chottyāunu *v.* shorten
छ्यासमिस chyāsmis *n.* mixture
छुल्याहा chulyāhā *n.* backbiter,
  informer
छोड्नु chodnu *v.t.* leave, launch

ज

जंगल jangal *n.* wood
जंगली jangali *adj.* wild
जंगली जनावर jangali janāvār *n.*
  wildlife
जंजीर janjeer *n.* chain
जग jag *n.* jug
जगत jagat *n.* world
जगमग jagmag *n.* glitter
जगाउनु jagāunu *v.* awaken
जग्गा jaggā *n.* land
जङ्गली jāngali *adj.* uncivilized
जनरल janaral *n.* general
जब jaba *adv./conj.* when
जननी janani *n.* mother
जनाना janānā *adj.* feminine
जमानत jamānat *n.* bail
जमीन jamin *n.* ground, land
जाँच jānch *n.* thigh
जज jaj *n.* judge
जटिल बनाउनु jatil banāunu *v.t.*
  complicate
जड jar *n.* root
जन jana *n.* people
जनगणना janaganana *n.* census
जन आन्दोलन janaandolan *n.*
  popular movement
जनता janatā *n.* people
जनमत संग्रह janamat sangraha
  n. referendum
जनगणतन्त्र janaganātantra *n.*
  people's republic (political term)
जनमुखी janamukhi *adj.* people-
  oriented (political term)
जनधनत्व janaghanatwa *n.*
  density of population
जनशक्ति jansakti *n.* manpower

जनजाति janjāti *n.* tribe
जनप्रतिनिधि janapratinidhi *n.*
  people's representative
जनरल janaral *n.* general
जनसंख्या janasankhyā *n.*
  population
जनसहभागिता janasahabhāgita
  n. people's participation
जनस्वास्थ janaswāsthya *n.*
  public health
जनसाधारण janasādhāran *n.*
  general public
जनवरी janvari *n.* January
जनवादी janavādi *n.* communist
जनयुद्ध janayuddha *n.* people's
  war
जन्म janma *n.* birth
जन्मनु janmanu *v.i.* be born
जन्म-भूमि janm-bhumi *n.*
  homeland, native land
जन्मकैद janmakaid *n.* life
  sentence
जन्म तिथी janma tithi *n.* date of
  birth
जन्मदिन janmadin *n.* birthday
जन्म जयन्ती janma jayanti *n.*
  birth anniversary
जन्मजात janmajāt *adj.* born
जन्मसिद्ध janmasiddha *adj.* by
  birth
जब jaba *adv.* as, when
जब कि jab ki *adv.* as
जब सम्म jab samma *prep./conj*
  until, while, unless
जबर्जस्ती jabarjasti *n.* by force
जम्नु jamnu *v.i.* freeze

जम्मा jammā *adj.* total

जम्मा गर्नु jammā garnu *v.t.* gather

जमाउनु jamāunu *v.t.* fix, freeze

जमानत jamānat *n.* bail

जमाना jamāna *n.* time

जमीन jamin *n.* land

जमीनदार jamindār *n.* landowner

जम्मा हुनु jammā hunu *v.i.* gather

जन्मस्थान janmasthān *n.* birthplace

जर्मन jarman *n./adj.* German

जर्मनी jarmani *n.* Germany

जरुरत jarurat *n.* necessity

जरुरी jaroori *adj.* necessary

जरिवाना jariwānā *n.* fine

जरो jaro *n.* fever

जर्सी jarsi *n.* jersey

जल jal *n.* water

जलचर jalcar *adj.* aquatic

जलन jalan *n.* jealousy

जल्नु jalnu *v.* burn

जलमग्न jalmagna *adj.* waterlogged

जलपान jalpān *n.* refreshment

जलपानगृह jalpāngrha *n.* café

जलमार्ग jalamārga *n.* water route

जलयात्रा गर्नु jalyātrā garnu *v.t.* sail

जलवायु jalvāyu *n.* climate

जलविज्ञान jalavigyān *n.* hydrology

जलसमाधि jalasamādhi *n.* water burial

जलस्रोत jalasrot *n.* water source

जलाधार क्षेत्र jalādhār ksetra *n.* watershed area

जल्लाद jallād *n.* hangman

जस्तो jasto *adj.* such

जस्तै jastai *adv.* for example

जस्ता jastā *n.* zinc

जय jaya *n.* victory

जयन्ती jayanti *n.* anniversary

जवान javān *adj.* youthful

जवानी javāni *n.* youth

जवाब javāb *n.* response, reply

जवाब दिनु javāb dinu *v.t.* reply

जवाहरात javāhrāt *n.* jewelry

जहाँ jahān *conj.* where

जहाज jahāz *n.* ship, vessel

जहान jahān *n.* family; wife

जहिले jahile *adv.* when

जाग्नु jāgnu *v.* waking up

जाँगर jangar *n.* activity

जाँच jānc *n.* scrutiny

जाँचबुझ jancbujh *n.* investigation

जाँच गर्नु jānc garnu *v.t.* examine

जाँच्नु jāncnu *v.t.* view

जाँच-पडताल jānc-partāl *n.* investigation

जाँच-पडताल गर्नु jānc-partāl garnu *v.t.* inspect

जाँड jānd *n.* beer

जाउलो jāulo *n.* cooked rice

जाकेट jāket *n.* jacket

जाग्नु jāgnu *v.i.* awake

जागरण jāgaran *n.* wake, waking up

जागीर jāgir *n.* government service

जागरुक jāgaruk *adj.* aware, alert

जाडो jāro *n.* winter

जात jāt *adj./n.* caste

जातभात jātbhāt *n.* related to caste

जातिभेद jātibhed *n.* caste discrimination

जातीय jātiy *adj.* racial

जात्रा jātrā *n.* festival

जादू jādu *n.* magic, charm

जादू गर्नु jādu garnu *v.t.* charm

जादूगर jādugar *n.* magician

जानी जानीकन jani jāni kana *adv.* knowingly

जानकार jānkār *adj.* conscious

जानकारी jānkāri *n.* information

ज्यान बचाउनु jān bacāunu *v.t.* save

जानीबूझी jānbujhi *adj.* deliberate

जनावर janavar *n.* animal

जानु jānu *v.i.* go

जान्नु jānnu *v.t.* know

जापान jāpān *n.* Japan

जापानी jāpāni *n./adj.* Japanese

जायदाद jāydād *n.* estate

जार jār *n.* wife's lover

जाल jāl *n.* net

जालसाजी jālsāji *n.* forgery

जालसाजी गर्नु jālsāji garnu *v.t.* falsify, forge

जालझेल jāljhel *n.* fraud

जासूस jāsus *n.* spy

जासूसी jāsusi *n.* espionage

जिउ jiunu *n.* body

जिउनार jiunār *n.* eating

जिजु आमा jijuāmā *n.* grandmother

जिजु बुवा jijubuwā *n.* grandfather

जिद्दी jiddi *adj.* obstinate

जिन jin *n.* gin

जिन्दगी jindagi *n.* life

जिन्दावाद jindābād *adj.* long live (slogan)

जिप zip *n.* zipper

जिप्सी jipsi *n.* gypsy

जिन्सी jinsi *n.* non-monetary goods

जिब्रो jibro *n.* tongue

जिम्दार gimdār *n.* landowner

जिम्मा jimmā *n.* responsibility

जिम्मा दिनु jimmā dinu *v.* to give responsibility

जिम्मेवार jimmebār *adj.* responsible

जिम्मेवारी jimmevāri *n.* liability

जिल्ला jillā *n.* county, district

जिरेल jirel *n.* an ethnic group living in eastern hills of Nepal

जिल्ला अदालत jillā adālat *n.* district court

जिल्ला न्यायाधीश jillā nyāyādhis *n.* district court judge

जिल्ला प्रशासन jillā prasāsan *n.* district administration

जिल्ला स्तरीय jillā stariya *adj.* district level

जिज्ञासा jigyāsa *n.* inquisitiveness

जिज्ञासु jigyāsu *adj.* inquisitive

जीत jit *n.* victory

जीतनु jitnu *v.t.* win

जीउनु jiunu *v.i.* live

जीर्ण jirna *adj.* old

जीवाणु jivānu *n.* germ

जीवाणुहीन बनाउनु jivānuhin banāunu *v.t.* sterilize

जीवविज्ञान jivavigyān *n.* biology

जीवन jivan *n.* life

जीवन्त jivanta *adj.* living

जीवन काल jivan kāl *n.* lifetime

जीवन पद्धति jivan paddhati *n.* lifestyle

जीवन-स्तर jivan-star *n.* standard

जीवन यापन jivan yāpan *n.* livelihood

जीवनी jivani *n.* biography

जीविका jivikā *n.* livelihood

जीवित jivit *adj.* alive

जीवित रहनु jivit rahanu *v.i.* survive

जिज्ञाशा jigyāsā *n.* inquisitiveness

जिज्ञासु jigyāsu *adj.* inquisitive

जुआ juā *n.* gambling

जुवाडे juādi *adj.* gambler

जुङ्गा jungā *n.* moustache

जुङ्गे junge *adj.* moustached

जुका jukā *n.* leech

जुक्ति jukti *n.* means

जुटाउनु jutāunu *v.t.* furnish

जुट jut *n.* jute

जुम्लाहा jumlāhā *n.* twin

जुम्सो jumso *adj.* lazy

जुलाई julāi *n.* July

जुवाइँ juvain *n.* son-in-law

जुलाहा julāhā *n.* weaver

जुता jutā *n.* shoe

जुता को पालिस juttā ko pālis *n.* shoe polish

जुठो jutho *v.* pollute food

जुन jun *n.* moonlight

जुनार junār *n.* orange

जून jun *n.* June

जुम्रो jumro *n.* lice

जूरी juri *n.* jury

जुलुम julum *n.* tyranny

जुलुस julus *n.* procession

जेट jet *n.* jet

जेठ jeth *n.* month in Nepali calendar

जेठो jetho *n.* firstborn male

जेठी jethi *n.* firstborn female

जेठाजु jethaju *n.* brother-in-law

जेठाबा jethābā *n.* uncle

जेठान jethān *n.* brother-in-law

जेठानी jethani *n.* sister-in-law

जेठीसासु jethisāsu *n.* sister-in-law

जेथा jethā *n.* property

जेब jeb *n.* pocket

जेबकट jebkat *n.* pickpocket

जेबखर्च jebkharcha *n.* pocket money

जेब्रा jebrā *n.* zebra

जेल jel *n.* jail

जेल प्रशासन jel prasāsan *n.* jail administration

जेलखाना jelkhānā *n.* prison

जेली jeli *n.* jelly

जैन jain *n.* Jain *(follower of Jainism)*

जेहनदार jehandar *adj.* intelligent

जैतुन jaitun *n.* olive

जैम jaim *n.* jam

जैविक jaivik *adj.* biological

जैसी jaisi *n.* a kind of Brahmin *(supposed to be lower rank)*

जो jo *pron.* which

जोई joi *n.* wife

जोईपोई joipoi *n.* husband/wife

जोकर jokar *n.* joker

जोखनु jokhnu *v.* weigh

जोखिम jokhim *n.* venture, risk

जोगिनु joginu *v.* be saved

जोगी jogi *n.* holy man

जोगिनी jogini *n.* female ascetic

जोत्नु jotnu *v.* cultivate

जोड jor *n.* joint; total

जोडी jori *n.* pair, couple

जोड्नु jornu *v.t.* unite, join, assemble

जोताहा jotāhā *n.* tenant; plowman

जोवन jovan *n.* youth

जो कोही jo koi *pron.* whoever

जोत jot *n.* cultivation

जो सुकै jo sukai *pron.* whosoever

जोश josh *n.* passion, excitement

ज्यान jyān *n.* life

ज्यानमारा jyanmāra *n.* murderer

ज्यापु jyāpu *n.* a Newar peasant caste

ज्यामी jyāmi *n.* laborer

ज्याला jyāla *n.* remuneration

ज्यावल jyāwal *n.* working tools

ज्योति jyoti *n.* light

ज्योतिषी jyotishi *n.* astrologer

ज्योतिष jyotish *n.* astrology

ज्वर jwar *n.* fever

ज्वलन्त jwalanta *adj.* brilliant, burning

ज्वाला jwāla *n.* flame

जौ jau *n.* barley

ज्यादा jyādā *adj.* more

ज्यादा मन पराउनु jyada man parāunu *v.t.* prefer

ज्यादति jyādati *n.* injustice

ज्वार-भाटा jvār-bhātā *n.* tide

ज्वलनशील jvalansil *adj.* inflammable

ज्वाला jvālā *n.* flame

ज्वालामुखी पहाड jvālāmukhi pahār *n.* volcano

झ

झगडा jhagrā n. quarrel
झगडालु jhagrālu adj. quarrelsome
झगडिया jhagadiya n. litigant
झटका jhatkā n. tug, jerk
झटकेलो छोरो jhatkelo choro n.
  stepson
झण्डा jhandā n. flag
झण्डै jhandai adv. almost
झरना jharnā n. waterfall
झर्कनु jharkanu v.i. talk irritably
झरी jhari n. long spell of rain
झर्रो jharro adj. pure
झन्झट jhanghat n. trouble
झलक jhalak n./v.t. glimpse
झ्याल jhyāl n. window
झाडी jhadi n. dense forest
झाड़ू jhāru n. mop
झारा jhāra n. work without
  payment
झाँक्री jhankri n. witch doctor,
  shaman
झाँगड jhāngad n. ethnic group of
  Nepal
झिंगो jhingā n. fly
झ्याउरे गीत jhyāure geet n.
  Nepali folk song
झारफुक jharphuk n. exorcism
झिक्नु jhiknu v. withdraw
झिंजो jhinjo n. trouble
झिंगटी jhingati n. shingle
झील jhil n. lake
झिसमिसे jhismise n. dawn
झुक्नु jhuknu v.t. submit
झुक्नु jhuknu v.i. crouch, incline
झुकाउनु jhukāunu v.t. bend
झुकाव jhukāv n. trend

झुण्ड jhund n. swarm
झुन्डनु jhundanu v.i. hang
झुटो jhuto n. lie
झुप्रो jhupro n. cottage
झुल jhul n. mosquito net
झुल्नु jhulnu v.t. swing
झुलाउनु jhulāunu v. give false
  hopes
झोंका jhonkā n. gust
झोक jhok n. anger
झोपडी jhopari n. lodge
झोलुङ्गे पुल jholunge pul n.
  suspension bridge
झोला jholā n. knapsack, bag

ट

टकसार taksār *n.* mint

टंकी tanki *n.* tank, reservoir

टट्टू tattu *n.* pony

टन tanki *n.* ton

टल्कनु talkanu *v.* shine

टन्टा tantā *n.* annoyance

टन्टलापुर घाम tantalāpur ghām *adj.* very hot due to sunshine

टमाटर tamātar *n.* tomato

टमाटर को रस tamātar ko ras *n.* tomato juice

टहलुवा tahaluwā *n.* janitor; sentry

टाई tāi *n.* tie

टाउको tāuko *n.* head

टाँसिनु tāsinu *v.* cling

टाँक tānk *n.* button

टाँका tānkā *n.* stitch

टाँग tāng *n.* leg

टाँग्नु tāngnu *v.t./v.i.* hang

टाई tāi *n.* necktie

टाइप गर्नु tāip garnu *v.t.* type

टाइपिस्ट tāipist *n.* typist

टार्च tārc *n.* torch

टान्सिल tānsil *n.* tonsil

टाल्नु tālnu *v.* avert, postpone

टाढा tādhā *adj.* far

टापु tāpu *n.* island

टायल tāyal *n.* tile

टिकट tikat *n.* ticket, stamp

टिकनु tikanu *v.* remain

टिन tin *n.* tin

टिप्पणी tippani *n.* comment, remark

टिप्पणी गर्नु tippani garnu *v.t.* comment

टीका tikā *n.* mark on forehead

टीम tim *n.* team

टिवि चेनल tivi cainal *v.* channel

टुक्रा tukrā *n.* piece

टुप्पा tuppā *n.* top

टूथपेस्ट tuthpest *n.* toothpaste

ट्यूब tuyub *n.* tube

टुलिप tulip *n.* tulip

टुपी tupi *n.* small hair on head kept by Brahmins

टुक्रा tukrā *n.* piece

टुट्टा tuttā *n.* loss

टुहुरो tuhuro *n.* orphan

टेढो terho *adj.* crooked

टेबिल tebil *n.* table

टेनिस tenis *n.* tennis

टेपरेकार्डर teprekārdar *n.* tape

टेलिफोन teliphon *n.* telephone

टेलिफोन गर्नु telifon garnu *v.t.* dial

टेलिभिजन telivijan *n.* television

टैंक taink *n.* tank

टैक्सी taiksi *n.* taxi

टोक्नु toknu *v.* bite

टोकरी tokari *n.* basket

टोपी topi *n.* hat, cap

टोली toli *n.* batch

ट्रक trak *n.* truck

ट्राक्टर traktar *n.* tractor

ट्रान्जिर स्ट tranjistar *n.* transistor

ट्राम trām *n.* tram, streetcar

ट्राइसिकल trāisikal *n.* tricycle

ठ

ठट्टा thattā *n.* joke

ठकुरी thakuri *n.* ethnic group of Nepal to which the former royal family belonged

ठेकदार thekdar *n.* contractor

ठग thag *n.* thug

ठग्नु thagnu *v.* cheat

ठगिनु thaginu *v.* be cheated

ठंडा thandā *adj.* chilly

ठंडा गर्नु thandā garnu *v.t.* chill, cool

ठाँउ thāun *n.* place

ठालु thālu *n.* village elder

ठिक thik *adj.* right, correct, appropriate, well, sound

ठिक गर्नु thik garnu *v.t.* fix

ठिक छ thik cha *interj.* OK!

ठिटो thito *n.* boy

ठिटी thiti *n.* girl

ठुलो thulo *adj.* elder; big

ठुलो उद्योग thulo udhyog *n.* big industry

ठूलो घाउ thulo ghau *n.* wound

ठेल्नु thelnu *v.t.* propel

ठेउला theulā *n.* measles

ठेला thelā *n.* cart

ठेक्का thekkā *n.* contract

ठेकेदार thekedār *n.* contractor

ठोकर खानु thokar khānu *v.i.* stumble

ठेगाना thegānā *n.* address

ठोस thos *n./adj.* solid

ड

डण्डा dandā *n.* stick, pole, shaft

डटनु datnu *v.* remain steadfast

डढनु dahnu *v.* burn

डकर्मी dakarmi *n.* mason

डर dar *n.* fright, fear, terror

डराउनु daraunu *v.t.* fear

डराउने गराउनु darāune garaunu *v.t.* frighten

डराएको daraeko *adj.* afraid

डलिया daliyā *n.* basket

डाक dāk *n.* mail, post

डाकघर dākghar *n.* post office

डाका हाल्नु dākā halnu *v.t.* to rob

डाकु dāku *n.* robber

डाक्टर dāktar *n.* doctor

डाक्नु dāknu *v.* call

डायरी dāyari *n.* diary

डायल dāyal *n.* dial

डाहा dāha *n.* jealousy

डालर dālar *n.* dollar

डिब्बा dibbā *n.* bin; tin

डिग्री digri *n.* degree

डिजल dizal *n.* diesel

डिट्ठा ditthā *n.* clerk

डिप्लोमा diploma *n.* diploma

डिसमिस dismis *n.* dismiss

डीन din *n.* dean

डुङ्गा dungā *n.* boat

डुवाउनु dubāunu *v.t.* drown; dip

डुब्नु dubnu *v.t.* drown

डुल्नु dulnu *v.* wander

डेगची degaci *n.* saucepan

डेढ dedh *adj.* one and a half

डेरा derā *n.* temporary dwelling

डेरी deri *n.* dairy

डैश dais *n.* dash

डोम dom *n.* a low-caste people from Terai

डोर dor *n.* temporary government camp for such purpose as surveying

डोरी dori *n.* rope

डोल dol *n.* pail

डोलनु dolnu *v.i.* swing, oscillate

ढ

ढंग dhang *n.* manner
ढाक्नु dhāknu *v.* cover
ढाँट्नु dhāntnu *v.* lie
ढक्कन dhakkan *n.* lid, cover, cap
ढल्नु dhalnu *v.* fall down
ढल dhal *n.* sewage
ढल्कनु dhalkanu *v.* lean
ढाल dhāl *n.* shield; incline
ढाँचा dhānca *n.* structure
ढीलो dhilo *adj.* late
ढिपी dhipi *n.* obstinacy
ढिलाई dhilāi *n.* slowness
ढुकुटी dhukuti *n.* treasure
ढुङ्गा dhuhngā *n.* stone
ढोका dhokā *n.* gate, door
ढोग्नु dhoknu *v.* salute
ढोल dhol *n.* drum

त

तँ tan *pron.* you

तंबू tambu *n.* tent

तकलिफ taklif *n.* trouble

तकसाल taksāl *n.* mint

तकिया takiyā *n.* pillow

तकिया को खोल takiyā ko khol *n.* pillowcase

तक्मा takmā *n.* medal

तगडा tagada *adj.* strong

तटस्थ tatstha *adj.* neutral

तटस्थता tatasthatā *n.* neutrality

तटीय tatiya *n.* waterfront

तत्व tattva *n.* element

तत्काल tatkāl *adv.* at that time

तथ्य tathyā *n.* fact

तथा tathā *conj.* and

तना tanā *n.* stem, trunk

तनाव tanāv *n.* tension

तन्नेरी tanneri *n.* youth

तलब talab *n.* wage

तपस्वी tapasvi *n.* monk

तपसिल tapsil *n.* detail

तपाई tapāi *pron.* you

तपाईको tapaiko *pron.* your

तपाई आफै tapāi aphai *pron.* yourself

तब taba *adv.* then

तबला tabalā *n.* drum

तमाम tamām *adj.* entire

तमाशा tamāsā *n.* show

तमाखु tamākhu *n.* tobacco

तमीज tamij *n.* good manners

तर्क tark *n.* reason

तरकारी tarkari *n.* vegetable

तरवार tarvār *n.* sword

तरवुजा tarbujā *n.* watermelon

तल आउनु tala āunu *v.i.* descend

तल tala *prep./adj.* below

तलब talab *n.* salary

पारपाचुके talāk *n.* divorce

तलाक दिनु talāk dinu *v.* divorce

तलाश talas *n.* search

तष्कर taskar *n.* smuggler

तष्करी taskari *n.* smuggling

तस्वीर tasvir *n.* photo

तस्वीर tasvir *n.* painting

तह tah *n.* fold

तहखाना tahkhānā *n.* cellar

तथ्य tathya *n.* fact

तर tara *conj.* but

तराई tarāi *n.* area south of Nepal along the Indian border

तरह तरह tarah tarah *adj.* various

तरीका tarika *n.* manner

तर्कशास्त्र tarksāstra *n.* logic

तर्कहीन tarkhin *adj.* mindless

तर्कसंगत tarksangat *adj.* logical

तराजू tarāju *n.* balance

तरुण tarun *n.* young man

तरुणी taruni *n.* young woman

ताँगा tānga *n.* horse-drawn vehicle

तावा tavā *n.* pan

तावेदार tāvedar *n.* servant

तामा tāmā *n.* copper

ताक tāq *n.* niche

ताज tāj *n.* crown

ताजा tāja *adj.* fresh

ताजा गर्नु tājā garnu *v.t.* freshen

तातो tato *adj./n.* hot

तातोपानी tāto pāni *n.* hot water

तान्तु tātnu *v.* be angry
तात्कालिक tātkālik *adj.* contemporary
तात्पर्य tātparya *n.* meaning
तानसेन tānsen *n.* city in Palpā
तान्नु tānnu *v.t.* extend
तानाशाह tānāsāh *n.* dictator
तापन tāpan *n.* heating
तापमापी tāpmāpi *n.* thermometer
तामा tāmā *n.* computer; bamboo shoot
तार tār *n.* cable
तारा tārā *n.* star
तारनु tārnu *v.* save from rebirth (Hinduism)
तालचा tālcha *n.* lock
ताल tāl *n.* lake
ताला लगाउनु tālā lagāunu *v.t.* lock
तास tās *n.* brocade
तलाउ tālāu *v.t.* pond
तारिफ tarif *n.* praise
तारीख tārikh *n.* date
तालिका tālika *n.* inventory
तालिम tālim *n.* training
ताली बजाउनु tāli bajāunu *v.t.* clap
तिजौरी tijauri *n.* safe
तितर-बितर हुनु tatar bitar hunu *v.t.* scatter
तिरस्कार tiraskār *n.* scolding, censure
तिहार tihār *n.* festival celebrated in Nepal in November including the festival of lights
तीखो tikho *adj.* sharp
तीतो tito *adj.* hot (spicy)
तीन tin *num.* three
तिर्खा tirkha *n.* thirst
तीनपुस्ते tinpuste *n.* three generations of a family

तिमी timi *pron.* you
तिम्रो timro *pron.* your
तिर्थ मंदिर tirth mandir *n.* shrine
तिर्थ यात्रा tirthyātrā *n.* pilgrimage
तिक्ष्ण tikshna *adj.* sharp
तीज teej *n.* Hindu festival for women celebrated in September
तिर्थ tirtha *n.* place of pilgrimage
तिर्थयात्री tirthyātri *n.* pilgrim
तीस tis *num.* thirty
तिव्र tivra *adj.* intense, strong
तुर्की turki *adj.* Turkish
तुच्छ tucch *adj.* trivial
तुच्छ वस्तु tucch vastu *n.* trifle
तुलना tulnā *n.* comparison
तुलनात्मक tulanātmak *adj.* comparative
तुलना गर्नु tulnā garnu *v.t.* compare
तुरुन्त turunta *adv.* immediately
तुहुनु tuhunu *v.* abort
तुषार tusār *n.* frost
तूफान tufān *n.* storm
तूफानी tufāni *adj.* stormy
तेजाब tejāb *n.* acid
तेह्र terah *num.* thirteen
तेह्रौं terahaun *adj.* thirteenth
तेस्रो tesro *adj.* third
तेल tel *n.* oil
तयार taiyār *adj.* ready, set
तयार गर्नु taiyār garnu *v.t.* prepare
तैयारी taiyāri *n.* preparation
तोप top *n.* cannon
तौल taulanu *n.* weight
तोला tola *n.* weight for gold *(normally used in Nepal and N. India)*
तौलिया tauliya *n.* towel
तौलनु taulanu *v.t.* weigh
तोरण toran *n.* gate
तोरी tori *n.* mustard

त्यहाँ tyahān *adv.* there

त्यो tyo *pron.* he, it

त्रास trās *n.* fear

त्रिकोण trikon *n.* triangle

त्रिभुवन Tribhuwan *n.* grandfather
of last Nepali king

त्रिवर्षीय tribarsiya *adj.* thrice-
yearly, tri-annually

त्याग दिनु tyāg dinu *v.t.* renounce
(to give up worldly possessions)

त्याग tyāg *v.t.* relinquish

थ

थकाइ thakā *n.* tiredness

थकाली thakāli *n.* ethnic group
of Nepal living in west Nepal
known as innkeepers

थप्पड thappar *n.* slap

थाकेको thakeko *adj.* tired

थान thān *n.* stall

थाक खोला thak kholā *n.* region in
west Nepal

थाक्नु thāknu *v.* to be tired

थामी राख्नु thāmirākhnu *v.t.* sustain

थाप्लो thāplo *n.* head

थालनी thālani *n.* beginning

थाहा jānkari *n.* knowledge

थाली thāli *n.* dish, plate

थारु thāru *n.* ethnic group of
Nepal living in the Terai

थिएटर thietar *n.* theater

थुक्नु thuknu *v.t./v.i.* spit

थुक्पा thuhkpa *n.* Tibetan dish
containing soup and dumplings

थुनाई thunāi *n.* arrest

थुनिनु thuninu *v.* be arrested

थैलो thailo *n.* bag

थैली thaili *n.* pouch

थोक thok *n.* wholesale good

थोत्रो thotro *adj.* old

थोरै thorai *adj.* less

द

दंगा dangā *n.* riot
दंड दिनु dand dinu *v.t.* punish
दंडनीय dandaniya *adj.* punishable
दण्डित dandit *adj.* punished
दंड को आदेश dand ko ādes *n.* sentence
दंपती dampati *n.* couple
दंभी dambhi *n.* snob
दंभ-भरेको dambh-bhareko *adj.* snobbish
दखल dakhal *n.* interference
दगा dagā *n.* betrayal
दण्ड danda *n.* penalty
दन्तचिकित्सक dantcikitsak *n.* dentist
दबाउनु dabāunu *v.t.* depress, curb, squash
दबाएको dabayeko *adj.* depressed
दबाव dabāv *n.* stress, pressure
दफा daphā *n.* article (of a law)
दफन daphan *n.* burial
दफन गर्नु daphan garnu *v.* bury
दफ्तर daphtar *n.* office
दमन daman *n.* oppression
दमन-गर्नु daman garnu *v.t.* oppress
दम dam *n.* asthma
दम को रोगी dam ko rogi *adj.* asthmatic
दमकल damkal *n.* fire brigade
दया dayā *n.* pity, mercy
दया गर्नु dayā garnu *v.i.* pity
दयालु dayālu *adj.* merciful
दर dar *n.* rate
दस्तुर dasture *n.* custom

दरकार darkār *n.* necessity
दरवार darbār *n.* palace
दरवारी darbāri *adj.* relating to palace
दराज daraj *n.* closet
दरिद्र daridra *adj.* poor
दरिद्रता daridratā *n.* poverty
दरखास्त darkhāst *n.* rate
दर्जन darjan *n.* dozen
दर्जा darja *n.* rank
दर्जी darji *n.* tailor
दर्द dard *n./v.i.* ache
दर्दनाक dardnāk *adj.* painful
दर्पण darpan *n.* mirror
दर्शक darsak *n.* spectator
दर्शन darsan *n.* appearance
दर्शन शास्त्र darsan sāstra *n.* philosophy
दर्शनीय darsaniya *adj.* worth seeing, worth a visit
दल dal *n.* flock; party
दलाल dalāl *n.* broker
दलीय daliya *adj.* relating to a party
दलित dalit *adj.* a Hindu caste
दलदल daldal *n.* swamp
दशमिक dasmik *adj.* decimal
दस das *num.* ten
दस लाख das lākh *n.* million
दसौं dāsaun *adj.* tenth
दसैं dasain *n.* festival celebrated in Nepal in October
दस्तखत dastkhat *n.* signature
दस्तावेज dastāvej *n.* deed
दह daha *n.* pond

दाहिने dahine *adj.* right

दही dahi *n.* yogurt

दक्षिण daksin *n.* south

दक्षिण-पश्चिम daksin-pascim *n.* southwest

दक्षिण-पश्चिमी daksin-pascimi *adj.* southwestern

दक्षिण-पूर्व daksin-purv *n.* southeast

दक्षिण-पूर्वी daksin-purvi *adj.* southeastern

दक्षिणी daksini *adj.* southern

दक्षिणा dakshinā *n.* donation, fee

दखल dakhal *n.* possession

दाँत dānt *n.* tooth

दाँत को dānt ko *adj.* dental

दाँत को दुखाई dānt ko dukhai *n.* toothache

दाउ पेच dāu pech *n.* hazard

दाख dākh *n.* grape

दाखिल dākhil *v.* admit

दाग लगाउनु dag lagāunu *v.t.* stain

दाजु dāju *n.* elder brother

दारी dāri *n.* beard

दादा दाई dādā *n.* elder brother

दाइजो daijo *n.* dowry

दाउरा dāura *n.* firewood

दान dān *n.* clarity

दानवकस dān bakas *n.* deed

दान मा दिनु dān mā dinu *v.t.* donate

दवाव dabab *n.* pressure

दाम dām *n.* cost, price

दाय dāy *n.* inheritance

दालचीनी dālcini *n.* cinnamon

दावत dāvat *n.* banquet

दावा dāvā *n.* claim

दावा गर्नु dāvā garnu *v.t.* claim

दायाँ dayān *adj.* right

दायित्व dāyitwa *n.* responsibility

दारिम dārim *n.* pomegranate

दारी dāri *n.* beard

दाल dāl *n.* lentil

दाल भात dāl bhāt *n.* main food in Nepal consisting of rice and lentil soup

दास dās *n.* slave

दासता dāsatā *n.* slavery

दासप्रथा dāsprathā *n.* slavery

दार्शनिक dārsanik *n.* philosopher

दाह संस्कार dāh sanskār *n.* Hindu cremation rite

दिउँसो diuso *n.* afternoon

दिगो digo *adj.* sustainable

दिदि didi *n.* elder sister

दिमाग dimāg *n.* brain

दिन din *n.* day

दिन को खाना din ko khānā *n.* lunch

दिनु dinu *v.t.* give

दिलचस्प dilcasp *adj.* interesting

दिलचस्पी dilcaspi *n.* interest

दिलचस्पी लिनु dilcaspi linu *v.t.* interest

दिवंगत divangat *adj.* deceased

दिवस divas *n.* day

दिवाला divālā *n.* bankrupt

दिव्य divya *n.* divine

दीप deep *n.* lamp

दीपक deepak *adj.* illuminating

दीर्घ dirgha *adj.* long

दिशा disā *n.* direction

दिसा disā *n.* human excrement

दिशाकोण disākon *n.* bearing

दिसेम्बर disembar *n.* December

दीक्षा dikshā *n.* instruction

दिक्षान्त diksānta *n.* convocation

दुई dui *num.* two

दुई पटक dui patak *adv.* twice

दुईतल्ले duitāle *adj.* two-story building

दुपट्टा dupattā *n.* scarf

दुकान dukān *n.* store

दुकानदार dukāndār *n.* shopkeeper

दुख dukh *n.* affliction

दुख दिनु dukh dinu *v.t.* afflict

दुखदायी dukhdāyi *adj.* troublesome

दुखपूर्ण dukhapurna *adj.* painful

दुख्नु dukhnu *v.t.* sting

दुखी dukhi *adj.* unhappy

दुगुना dugunā *adj.* double

दुग्ध dugdha *n.* milk

दुराशय durāsaya *n.* bad intention

दुर्गन्ध durgandha *n.* bad smell

दुष्कर duskar *adj.* tough

दुश्मनी dusmani *n.* enemity

दुश्मन dusman *adj./n.* enemy

दुष्कर्म duskarm *n.* misdeed

दुबलो-पातलो dublo-patlo *adj.* skinny

दोभासे dubhāsiyā *n.* interpreter

दुरुपयोग durupyog *n.* abuse

दुरुपयोग गर्नु durupyog garnu *v.t.* abuse

दुरुस्त गर्नु durust garnu *v.t.* refit

दुरा durā *n.* ethnic group of Nepal living in western hills

दुराग्रही durāgrahi *adj.* obstinate

दुर्गम क्षेत्र durgam ksetra *n.* remote area

दुर्गा durgā *n.* Hindu goddess

दुर्गुण durgun *n.* vice

दुर्भाग्य durbhāgya *n.* misfortune

दुर्घटना durghatnā *n.* accident

दुर्लभ durlabh *adj.* scarce

दुश्मन dusman *n.* enemy

दूतावास dutāvās *n.* consulate

दूध dudh *n.* milk

दूर dur *adv.* far

दूरदर्शी durdarsi *adj.* farsighted

दूरदर्शिता durdarsitā *adj.* foresighted

दूरबीन durbin *n.* telescope

दूर संचार dursancār *n.* telecommunication

दूरी duri *n.* distance

दुरुस्त durusta *adj.* exactly the same

दूबो dubo *n.* green grass

दुलहा dulahā *n.* groom

दुलही dulahi *n.* bride

दूषित गर्नु dusit garnu *v.t.* contaminate

दृष्टि dristi *n.* sight

दृष्टि dristi *adj.* optical

दृश्य drsya *n.* scene, view

दृष्टान्त dristānta *n.* example

दृढ drh *adj.* tenacious, firm

दृढता dridhatā *n.* firmness

देख्नु dekhnu *v.t.* see

देखभाल dekhbhāl *n.* upkeep

देखि dekhi *prep.* from

देउराली deurāli *n.* near the top of hill;

देउसी deusi *n.* ritual during Tihar festival when groups of people visit homes to ask for alms

देय dey *adj.* due

देन den *n.* contribution

देवदार devdār *n.* cedar

देवनागरी devanāgari *n.* Devanagari writing script *(used by Nepali, Hindi, and Marathi)*

देवता devatā *n.* god, divine being

देवल deval *n.* temple

देवर devar *n.* brother-in-law

देवरानी deorāni *n.* sister-in-law

देउडा deudā *n.* folk song in far west hills of Nepal used in New Year

देवी devi *n.* goddess

देब्रे debre *n.* left

देश des *n.* country

देशनिकाला desnikālā *n.* exile

देशद्रोह desdroh *n.* treason

देशभक्त desbhakt *n.* patriot

देशभक्तिपूर्ण dedsbhaktipurn *adj.* patriotic

देशीय desiy *n.* native

देह deha *n.* body

देहाती dehāti *adj.* rustic

देहाती dehāti *n.* peasant

देहान्त dehanta *n.* death

दैनिक dainik *adj.* daily

दैनिकपत्रिका dainik patrika *n.* daily newspaper

दैनिक भत्ता dainik bhattā *n.* daily allowance

दैनिकी dainiki *n.* dairy

दैविक daibik *adj.* divine

देशांतर daisantar *n.* longitude

दोपहर dopahar *n.* midday

दोष dos *n.* blame

दोभासे dobhase *n.* interpretor

दोषारोपन dosāropan *n.* blame

दोषी dosi *adj.* guilty

दोसल्ला dosallā *n.* shawl

दोषदर्शी dosdarsi *adj.* cynical

दोषी ठहराउनु dosi tharāunu *v.t.* accuse

दोहराउनु doharāunu *v.t.* revise

दोहरी dohari *n.* duet song

दोस्त dost *n.* friend

दोस्ती dosti *n.* friendship

दोस्रो dosro *adj.* second

दौड daur *n.* run

दौडनु dauranu *v.t.* run

दौरा सुरुवाल daurā suruwal *n.* Nepali traditional dress

दौरान daurān *adv.* during

दौलत daulat *n.* wealth

द्रोह droha *n.* hospitality

द्रोही drohi *n./adj.* hostile

द्वन्द dwanda *n.* conflict

द्वार dwār *n.* gate

द्विपक्षीय dwipaksiya *adj.* bilateral

द्विप dwip *n.* island

द्वीभाषी dvibhāsi *adj.* bilingual

द्वेष dwes *n.* malice

ध

धकेलनु dhakelnu *v.t.* push

धक्का dhakkā *n.* shock, jog

धडकन dharkan *n.* beating of heart

धैर्य dhairya *n.* patience

धन dhan *n.* wealth

धन संपति dhan sampatti *n.* wealth

धनी dhani *n.* wealthy

धनीमानी dhani māni *adj.* wealthy and reputable

धन राशि dhan rāsi *n.* plus

धनुवात dhanurbāt *n.* tetanus

धन्यवाद dhanyavād *n.* thanks

धन्यवाद दिनु dhanyavād dinu *v.t.* give thanks

धपाउनु dhapāunu *v.* send someone away

धब्बा dhabbā *n.* stain

धन्दा dhandā *n.* business

धमनी dhamani *n.* artery

धमकी dhamki *n.* threat

धम्की दिनु dhamki dinu *v.t.* threaten

धमाका dhamākā *n.* blast, crash

धमिरा dhamirā *n.* termite

धरती dharti *n.* earth

धरोट dharot *n.* deposit

धर्म dharma *n.* religion

धर्मनिरपेक्ष dharma nirapeksa *n.* secular

धर्मशाला dharmasālā *n.* inn

धर्मनिष्ठ dharmnisth *adj.* pious

धर्मपिता dharmapitā *n.* godfather

धर्मपुत्र dharmaputra *n.* godson

धर्मपुत्री dharmaputri *n.* goddaughter

धर्ममाता dharmamātā *n.* godmother

धर्मयुद्ध dharmayuddha *n.* religious war

धर्मात्मा dharmatmā *adj.* religious

धर्माधिकार dharmādhikar *n.* religious advisor to king

धर्मान्तरण dharmantaran *n.* religious conversion

धाउ dhāu *n.* ore

धागो dhāgo *n.* string

धातु dhātu *n.* metal

धातुकर्मी dhātukarmi *n.* blacksmith

धान dhān *n.* paddy, rice

धानुक dhānuk *n.* ethnic group living in southeastern part of Nepal

धारणा dhārnā *n.* concept

धावक dhāvak *n.* runner

धावन मार्ग dhāvan mārg *n.* runway

धारा dhārā *n.* stream, current

धाराप्रवाह dhārāpravāh *adj.* fluent

धार्मिक dhārmik *adj.* religious

धितो dhito *n.* collateral

धिमाल dhimāl *n.* ethnic group living in east Nepal

धीर dhir *adj./n.* bold, steadfast / boldness, steadfastness

धुआँ dhuān *n.* smoke

धूर्त dhurta *n./adj.* cunning

धुनु dhunu *v.t.* wash

धुरन्धर dhurandhar *n./adj.* might, great(ness)

ध्रुव dhruv *n.* pole

धुलाई को मशीन dhulāi ko masin
  n. washing machine

धुनु dhunu *v.* wash

धुप dhup *n.* sunshine

धुप को चश्मा dhup ko casmā *n.*
  sunglasses

धुपताग्रता dhuptāgratā *n.* suntan

धूलो dhulo *n.* dirt

धोका dhokā *n.* deceit

धोकेवाज dhokābaj *adj.* deceitful

धोका दिनु dhokā dinu *v.t.*
  deceive, trick

धोती dhoti *n.* dress

धोवी dhobi *n.* washerman

ध्यान dhyān *n.* attention

ध्यान दिनु dhyān dinu *v.t.* pay
  attention

ध्यान भंग गर्नु dhyān bhang
  garnu *v.t.* distract

ध्वनि dhvani *n.* sound

ध्वनिविज्ञान dhvanivigyān *n.*
  phonetics

ध्वज dhvaj *n.* flag

ध्वस्त dhwasta *adj.* destroyed

न

नकल गर्नु nakal garnu *v.t.* imitate

नकली nakali *adj.* artificial, counterfeit

नकर्मी nakarmi *n.* ironsmith

डकैति nakabajani *n.* burglary

नक्शा naksa *n.* map

नक्सालवादी naksālvadi *n.* Naxalite *(term used for Maoist insurgent in India)*

नकाब nakab *n.* mask

नकारात्मक nakārātmak *adj.* negative

नङ्ग nang *n.* nail

नङ्गा nangā *adj.* nude

नगद nagad *n.* cash

नगर nagar *n.* town

नगरा nagarā *n.* big drum

शहरिकरण nagarikaran *n.* urbanization

निगिच nagich *adv.* near

नगरीय nagriya *adj.* urban

नगरपालिका nagarpālikā *n.* municipality

नग्न nagna *n.* nude

नजरवन्द najarband *n.* house arrest

नग्नता nagntā *n.* nudity

नत्र natra *adv.* otherwise

नतीजा natija *n.* result

नदी nadi *n.* river

नष्ट गर्नु nast garnu *v.t.* ruin

नपुंसक napunsak *adj.* neuter, impotent

नब्बे nabbe *num.* ninety

नमकीन namkin *adj.* salty

नमस्ते namaste *n.* greeting

नमस्कार namaskār *n.* greeting, hello

नमस्कार गर्नु namaskār garnu *v.t.* greet

नमूना namunā *n.* pattern, sample

नमूना लिनु namunā linu *v.t.* sample

नम्र namra *adj.* polite

नम्रता namratā *n.* politeness

नमी nami *n.* humidity

नयाँ nayā *adj.* new

नयाँ गर्नु nayā garnu *v.t.* renovate

नयाँ वर्ष nayā barsa *n.* New Year

नर nar *n.* male

नरभक्षी narbhaksi *adj.* maneater

नरक narak *n.* hell

नरिवल nariwal *n.* coconut

नर्स nars *n.* nurse

नर्सरी narsari *n.* nursery

नली nali *n.* tube

नलकूप nalakup *n.* tube well

नरम naram *adj.* soft

नराम्रो narāmro *adj.* ugly

नवंबर navanbar *n.* November

नवजात navjāt *n./adj.* newborn

नववर्ष navvars *n.* new year

नववधु navabadhu *n.* newlywed wife

नवीकरण navikaran *n.* renovation

नवीन navin *adj.* new

नवीनता navintā *n.* novelty

नशा nasā *n.* intoxication

नहर nahar *n.* canal

नक्षत्र nakshatra *n.* star

नष्ट गर्नु nast garnu *v.t.* destroy

नसीहत nasihat *n.* reprimand

नुहाउनु nuhāunu *v.t./v.i.* bathe

नाउ nāu *n.* boat

नाऊ nāu *n.* barber

नाउ को पसल nāu ko pasal *n.* barbershop

नाक nāk *n.* nose

नाका nākā *n.* barrier

नाङ्गो nāngo *adj.* naked

नागरिक nāgrik *n.* citizen

नागरिक कानून nāgarik kanoon *n.* civil law

नागरिक समाज nāgarik samāj *n.* civil society

नागरिकता nāgriktā *n.* citizenship

नागरिकता प्रमाणपत्र nāgariktā pramān patra *n.* citizenship certificate

नाच nāc *n.* dance

नाचनु nācnu *v.i.* dance

नाटक nātak *n.* drama, play

नाता nātā *n.* relationship

नातावाद nātāvād *n.* favoring of relatives

नाटक nātak *n.* drama

नातेदार natedār *n.* relative

नाटकीय nātakiyā *n.* dramatic

नाठो nātho *n.* illegal lover

नाती nāti *n.* grandson

नातिनी nātini *n.* granddaughter

नादान nādān *adj.* foolish

नान nān *n.* naan, thick bread

नाप nāp *n.* measure

नापी nāpi *n.* survey

नाप्नु nāpnu *v.* measure

नाफा nāphā *n.* profit

नावालक nabālak *adj.* minor

नाभि nābhi *n.* navel

नाम nām *n.* reputation, name

नामपत्र nāmpatra *n.* label

नामसारी nāmsāri *n.* changing ownership

नाम दिनु nām dinu *v.t.* christen

नामर्दी nāmardi *n.* impotence

नामर्द nāmarda *adj.* impotent

नामंजुर nāmanjur *adj.* reject

नायक nāyak *n.* leader

नायव nāyab *n.* assistant

नारा nārā *n.* slogan

नारायणी nārāyani *n.* a river in west central Nepal

नारी nāri *n.* female

नाली nāli *n.* sink; drain

नालिस nālis *n.* lawsuit

नाश nās *adj.* destruction

नासनु nāsnu *v.* destroy

नासपाती nāspāti *n.* pear

नाश्ता nāstā *n.* breakfast

नास्तिक nāstik *n.* atheist

नास्तिकवाद nāstikvād *n.* atheism

नाइट्रजन nāitrajan *n.* nitrogen

निकट nikat *adj.* near

निंदा गर्नु nindā garnu *v.t.* damn

निबंध nibandh *n.* essay

निमंत्रण nimantran *n.* invitation

निमंत्रण दिनु nimantran dinu *v.t.* invite

निकट nikat *adj./adv.* nearby

निकटदर्शी nikatdarsi *adj.* nearsighted

निकटवर्ती nikatvarti *adj.* adjacent

निकालनु nikalnu *v.t.* expel

निकाला nikālā *n.* expulsion

निकास nikās *n.* outlet

निकाय nikāya *n.* organization

निकुन्ज nikunja *n.* park

निगम nigam *n.* corporation

निचोड nicor *n.* extract

निज nij *adj.* self

निजी niji *adj.* personal

निजामती nijāmati *adj.* civil

निजामती सेना nijāmati sewā *n.* civil service

निडर nidar *adj.* fearless

नित्य nitya *adj.* eternal

नित्यकर्म nityakarma *n.* routine

निदान nidān *n.* diagnosis

निर्देशिका nirdesikā *n.* directory

निधि nidhi *v.t.* fund

निधो nidho *n.* decision

निमन्त्रण nimantran *n.* invitation

निम्न nimna *adj.* following

निम्न माध्यमिक nimna madhyamik *n.* lower secondary school *(includes grades 6 thru 8)*

निम्न लिखित nimna likhit *adj.* following

निरपेक्ष nirapeksha *adj.* impartial, indifferent

निरर्थक nirarthak *adj.* meaningless

निष्क्रिय niskriya *adj.* inactive

निरीह niriha *adj.* depressed

निशुल्क nishulka *adj.* free of charge

नियति niyati *n.* destiny

नियन्त्रक niyantrak *n.* controller

नियन्त्रण niyantran *n.* control

नियम niyam *n.* rule

नियमित niyamit *n.* regular

नियात्रा niyātra *n.* travelogue

नियुक्त गर्नु niyukt garnu *v.t.* employ, appoint

नियुक्ति niyukti *n.* appointment

नियोजक niyojak *n.* employer

निरक्षर nirakshar *adj.* illiterate

नियोजन niyojan *n.* appointment

निरस्त्र nirastra *adj.* unarmed

निराकार nirākār *adj.* abstract

साकाहारी nirāmis *adj.* meatless, vegetarian

निराहार nirāhār *adj.* fasting

निराला nirālā *adj.* extraordinary

निराश nirās *adj.* without hope

निराश गर्नु nirās garnu *v.t.* frustrate

निराशा nirāsā *n.* frustration

निराशाजनक nirāsājanak *adj.* hopeless

निराशपूर्ण nirāsāpurn *adj.* bleak

निराशावादी nirāsāvādi *adj.* pessimistic

निरीक्षक niriksak *n.* inspector

निरीक्षण niriksan *n.* inspection

निरोधक nirodhak *n./adj.* contraceptive

निर्जीव nirjiv *adj.* lifeless

निर्णय nirnaya *n.* decision

निर्णय गर्नु nirnaya garnu *v.t.* award

निर्णायक nirnāyāk *adj.* decisive

निद्रा nidrā *n.* sleep

निद्रा लाग्नु nidrā lāgnu *v.t.* sleep

निर्दल nirdal *adj.* partyless (where political parties are not allowed)

निर्दयी niardayi *adj.* merciless

निर्देश nirsesh *n.* direction

निर्देशक nirdesak *n.* director

निर्देशन nirdesan *n.* direction

निर्दोष nirdos *adj.* innocent

निर्धारित nirdhārit *adj.* determined

निर्धारित गर्नु nirdhārit garnu *v.t.* determine

निर्धो nirdho *adj.* weak

निर्भर nirbhar *adj.* dependent

निर्भर हुनु nirbhar hunu *v.* be dependent

निर्भिक nirbhik *adj.* fearless

निमित nimitta *n.* cause

निर्माण nirmān *n.* make, manufacturer

निर्माण गर्नु nirmān garnu *v.t.* manufacture, erect

निम्न nimna *adj.* low; following

निर्यात niryāt *n.* export

निर्यात गर्नु niryāt garnu *v.t.* explore

निलम्बन nilamban *n.* suspension

निर्वाचन nirvācan *n.* election

निर्वाचन आयोग nirvācan āyog *n.* election commission

निर्वाचन क्षेत्र nirbācan ksetra *n.* constituency

निर्वाचित nirvacit *adj.* elected

नूतन nutan *adj.* new

निर्वासित गर्नु nirvāsit garnu *v.t.* deport

निर्वासन nirvasan *n.* ostracism, exile

निवारक nivārak *adj.* preventive

निवारण nivāran *n.* prevention

निवारणीय nivārniya *adj.* preventable

निवास nivās *n.* dwelling

निवासस्थान nivas-sthan *n.* home

निवासी nivāsi *n.* resident

निवेदक nivedak *n.* petitioner

निवेदन nivedan *n.* request

निवेदन गर्नु nivedan garnu *v.t.* request

निशाना nisānā *n.* aim

निश्चल niscal *adj.* still

निश्चय niscay *n.* assurance

निश्चायक niscāyak *adj.* definitive

निश्चित niscit *adj.* certain

निश्चित गर्नु niscit garnu *v.t.* ascertain

निशा nisā *n.* night

निषेध nisedh *n.* prohibition

निषेधित nisedhit *adj.* prohibited

निष्ठा nista *n.* faith

निष्ठुर nisthur *adj.* cruel

निष्पक्ष nispaksa *adj.* impartial

निष्कर्ष niskarsa *n.* conclusion

निस्सन्तान nissantān *adj.* childless

निसाफ nisāph *n.* justice

निस्कनु niskanu *v.* go out

नीति niti *n.* policy

नीलम nilam *n.* sapphire

नीलो nilo *adj.* blue

नीलपुष्प nilpusp *n.* violet

नुन nun *n.* salt

नूतन nutan *adj.* new

नेता netā *n.* leader

नेपाल nepāl *n.* Nepal

नेपाली nepali *adj.* Nepalese

नेवारी newāri *n.* Nepali language

नैतिक naitik *adj.* moral

नोकर nokar *n.* servant

नोकरी nokari *n.* service

नोक्सान noksān *n.* harm

नौलो naulo *adj.* new

नौसेना nausena *n.* navy

न्याय nyāya *n.* justice

न्यायपालिका nyāyapālika *n.* judiciary

न्यायप्रणाली nyāyapranāli *n.* judicial system

न्यायसेवा nyāyasewā *n.* judicial service

न्यायधीश nyāyadhis *n.* judge

न्यायालय nyāyālaya *n.* court

न्यायिक nyāyik *adj.* judicial

न्यून nyun *adj.* less

न्वारन nwāran *n.* naming ceremony

नुहाउनु nuhāunu *v.t./v.i.* take a bath

नृत्य nritya *n.* dance

प

पंक्ति pankti *n.* row

पंक्तिबद्ध गर्नु panktibaddh garnu *v.t.* line

पंखा pankhā *n.* feather, plume; wing; fan

पंचम pancam *adj.* fifth

पंचर pancar *n.* puncture

पंचर गर्नु pancar garnu *v.t.* puncture

पछुताउनु pachutāunu *v.t.* repent

पंजा panjā *n.* Claw; glove

पंद्र pandra *num.* fifteen

पन्ध्रौँ pandrahaun *adj.* fifteenth

पंडा pandā *n.* priest in a place of a pilgrimage

पंडित pandit *n.* scholar

पकड pakar *n.* grip

पक्का pakkā *adj.* definite

पक्का गर्नु pakka garnu *v.t.* confirm

पचाउनु pacāsaun *v.t.* digest

पचास pacās *num.* fifty

पचासौँ pacāsaun *adj.,* fiftieth

पटरी patari *n.* rail

पट्टी patti *n.* tablet; bandage

पढाउनु padhāunu *v.t.* teach

पतलून patlun *n.* pants

पत्ता pattā *n.* address

पत्ता लगाउनु pattā lagāunu *v.t.* detect

पति pati *n.* husband

पत्थर patthar *n.* stone

पत्नी patni *n.* wife

पतन pattan *n.* port

पथ path *n.* trail, path

पथिक pathik *n.* passerby

पद pad *n.* post

पदक padak *n.* medal

पदवी padavi *n.* rank, title

पदयात्री padayatri *n.* pedestrian, trekker

पदच्युत गर्नु padcyut garnu *v.t.* dismiss

पदयात्रा गर्नु padyātrā garnu *v.t.* hike, trek

पदाधिकारी padādhikāri *n.* officer

पनडुब्बी pandubbi *n.* submarine

पनीर panir *n.* cheese

पन्ना pannā *n.* page

पम्प pamp *n.* pump

पम्प गर्नु pamp garnu *v.t.* pump

पर para *adv.* far

परखाल parkhāl *n.* wall

परजीवी parjivi *n.* parasite

परजीवी parjivi *adj.* parasitic

परदा pardā *n.* screen

परदेस जानु pardes jānu *v.i.* emigrate

परम param *adj.* extreme

परमाणु parmānu *n.* atom

पराल parāl *n.* straw

परसी parsi *adv.* day after tomorrow

परस्पर paraspar *adj.* mutual

पराक्रम parākram *n.* valor

परेवा parewā *n.* pigeon

परम्परा paramparā *n.* tradition

परवर्ती parvari *adj.* latter

पहलवान pahalwān *n.* wrestler

पहिचान pehicān *n.* recognition, identity

पहिलो pahilo *adj./adv.* first

पत्र-व्यवहार patr-vyavahār *v.i.* correspond

पर्यटक paryatak *n.* tourist

पर्यटन paryatan *n.* tourism

पर्याप्त paryāpt *adj.* adequate

पर्यवेक्षक paryaveiksak *n.* supervisor

पर्यवेक्षण paryaveksan *n.* observation

पर्यवेक्षण गर्नु paryaveksan garnu *v.t.* supervise

पर्याय paryāy *n.* synonym

पर्वतमाला parvatmālā *n.* range

पर्स pars *n.* purse

पराकाष्ठा parākāstā *n.* climax

परामर्श parāmarsa *n.* climax

परामर्शदाता parāmarsdātā *n.* consultant

परिक्रमा parikramā *n.* process of revolving

परिक्रमा गर्नु parikramā garnu *v.t.* revolve

परिकल्पना parikalpnā *n./v.t.* design

परिचय paricay *n.* acquaintance; introduction

परिचय दिनु paricay dinu *v.t.* introduce

परिचर paricar *n.* caretaker

परिचारिका paricāriikā *n.* stewardess

परिचित paricit *adj.* familiar

परिचित हुनु paricit hunu *v.t.* acquaint

परिच्छेद paricched *n.* chapter

परित्याग गर्नु parityāg garnu *v.t.* abandon

परिपक्वता paripakvattā *n.* maturity

परिभाषा paribhāsā *n.* definition

परियोजना pariyojnā *n.* project

परिवर्तन parivartan *n.* change, alteration

परिवर्तन गर्नु parivartan garnu *v.t.* modify

परिवर्तनीय parivartaniya *adj.* changeable

परिवहन parivahan *n.* transport

परिवार parivār *n.* family

परिशिष्ट parisist *n.* supplement, appendix

परिश्रम parishram *n.* labor

परिषद parisad *n.* council

परिस्थिति paristhiti *n.* circumstances

परी pari *n.* fairy

परीक्षा pariksā *n.* examination

परीक्षण pariksan *n.* trial

पल pal *n.* moment

पलक palak *n.* eyelid

पलायन palāyan *n.* escape

पलायन गर्नु palāpan garnu *v.t.* escape

पवित्र pavitra *adj.* holy

पश्चिम pascim *n.* west

पश्चिमी pascimi *adj.* western

पशु pasu *n.* beast

पशुचिकित्सक pasucikitsak *n.* veterinarian

पसल pasal *n.* shop

पसीना निकाल्नु pasinā nikalnu *v.i.* perspire

पसीना pasinā *n.* sweat

पसीना बहाउनु pasinā bahaunu *v.t.* sweat

पहिचान pahicān *n.* identification

पहिरिनु pahirinu *v.t./v.i.* wear

पहिलो pahilo *n.* first

पहेलो pahelo *adj.* yellow

पहलू pahalu *n.* aspect

पहिले pahile *adv.* before

पहेली paheli *n.* puzzle

पहुँच pahunc *n.* reach

पहाड pahār *n.* mountain

पहाडी pahāri *n.* hill; folk

पहेली paheli *n.* riddle

पक्ष paksa *n.* fortnight; party in a lawsuit

पक्षी paksi *n.* bird

पत्रकार patrakār *n.* journalist

पत्र-लेखक patra-lekhak *n.* correspondent

पत्र-व्यवहार patra-vyavahār *n.* correspondence

पत्रिका patrikā *n.* magazine

पाँच pānc *num.* five

पाचौँ pancaun *adj.* fifth

पाखण्ड pākhanda *n.* hypocricy

पाक्षिक pāksik *adj.* fortnightly (once in a fortnight)

पाखण्डी pākhandi *n.* hypocrite

पागल pāgal *adj.* crazy, insane, mad

पाचक pāchak *n.* digestive

पाजामा pājāmā *n. pl.* pajamas

पाको pāko *adj.* mature

पाठ pāth *n.* lesson

पाठक pāthak *n.* reader

पाठशाला pāthsālā *n.* school

पाठ्यक्रम pāthyakram *n.* course

पाठ्यपुस्तक pāthyapustak *n.* textbook

पात pāt *n.* leaf

पातकी pātaki *n.* sinner

पादरी pādari *n.* Christian priest

पाउनु pāunu *n.* find

पानी pāni *n.* water

पाप pāp *n.* sin

पाप गर्नु pāp garnu *v.i.* sin

पापी pāpi *n.* sinner

पापिनी pāpini *n.* sinner woman

पायलट pāylat *n.* pilot

पार pār *adv.* across, over

पारस pāras *adj./n.* valuable

पारगमन pārgaman *n.* transit

पारसल pārsal *n.* parcel

पार्टी pārti *n.* party

पारम्परिक pāramparik *adj.* traditional

पारिश्रमिक pārisramik *n.* remuneration

पाउन्ड pāund *n.* pound

पाल pāl *n.* tent

पाली pali *n.* turn

पाहुना pahuna *n.* guest

पाल्तु pāltu *adj.* domestic (animal)

पाल्तु बनाउनु pāltu banaunu *v.t.* tame

पाल्नु pālnu *v.t.* keep as a pet

पाल-नाव pāl-nāv *n.* sailboat

पालिश pālis *n.* polish

पालुङ्गो pālungo *n.* spinach

पट्टा pattā *n.* lease

पाउरोटी pāuroti *n.* loaf

पासपोर्ट pāsport *n.* passport

पास pās *adj.* close

पासा pāsā *n.* die, dice

पास हुनु pās hunu *v.t.* to pass an examination

पाउहना pāuhnā *n.* guest

पात्र pātra *n.* vase

पात्रो pātro *n.* calendar

पिँजरा pinjarā *n.* cage

पित्त pitta *n.* gall

पिता pitā *n.* father

पिता-जी pitā-ji *n.* father

पितामह pitāmaha *n.* paternal grandfather

पितृ pitri *n.* paternal ancestor

पिशाच pisāc *n.* ghost, demon

पियानो piyāno *n.* piano
पिरैमिड piraimid *n.* pyramid
पिस्तौल pistaul *n.* pistol
पीछा गर्नु pichā garnu *v.t.* chase
पीठ pith *n.* back
पीडा pidā *n.* torment
पीडाहीन pirāhin *adj.* painless
पीडित pirit *adj.* oppressed
पीप pip *n.* pus
पीर pir *n.* anxiety
पिस्नु pisnu *v.t.* pound, grind
पुरस्कार दिनु puraskār dinu *v.t.*
  recompense
पुरानो ढंग को purāno dhang ko
  adj. antique
पुनसंरचना punarsanrachanā *n.*
  restructuring
पुलिंग purlling *adj.* masculine
पुस्तक pustak *n.* book
पुस्ता pustā *n.* generation *(familial)*
पूँजी puji *n.* stock, capital
पूजा pujā *n.* worship
पूजा गर्नु pujā garnu *v.t.* worship
पुजारी pujāri *n.* temple priest
पुछ्नु pucnu *v.* wipe
पुतली putali *n.* butterfly; doll
पुत्र putra *n.* son
पूरा purā *adj.* whole
पूरा गर्नु purā garnu *v.t.*
  supplement, complete, satisfy
पुरी puri *n.* bread
पुरा purā *n.* total
पुराण purān *n.* Hindu mythology
पुरानो purāno *adj.* old
पुरुष purus *n.* man
पुरुषत्व purusatwa *n.* manhood
पूर्ण purn *adj.* full, complete
पूर्ण-विराम purn-virām *n.* period
  (gram.)
पूर्णिमा purnimā *n.* full moon
पूर्व purv *adj.* east

पूर्व दिन purv din *n.* eve
पूर्वज purvaj *n.* ancestor
पूर्वाग्रह purvāgrah *n.* prejudice
पूर्वानुमान purvānumān *n.*
  forecast
पूर्ववर्ती purvavarti *adj.* previous
पूर्वी purvi *adj.* eastern
पृथक्करण prithakkaran *n.*
  insulation
पृथक गर्नु prithak garnu *v.t.*
  insulate
पेँसिल pensil *n.* pencil
पेट pent *n./v.t.* paint
पेट दुखेको pet dukheko *n.*
  stomachache
पेट बोक्नु pet boknu *adj.* pregnant
पेटी peti *n.* belt
पेट्रोल petrol *n.* gasoline
पेट्रोलियम petroliyam *n.*
  petroleum
पेनी peni *n.* penny
पेपरमिंट pepermint *n.* peppermint
पेय pey *n.* beverage
पेल्नु pelnu *v.* push
पेवा peva *n.* personal property
पेशा pesā *n.* occupation, profession
पेशी pesi *n.* presentation
पेस्ट्री pestri *n.* pastry
पेस्ता pesta *n.* pistachio nut
पैडल paidal *n.* pedal
पैक गर्नु paik garnu *v.t.* pack
पैकेज paikej *n.* package
पैत्रिक paitrik *adj.* ancestral
पैदल जानु paidal janu *v.t.* walk
पैदल पार गर्नु paidal pār garnu
  v.i. wade
पैदल घुम्नु paidal ghumnu *v.i.*
  hike
पैदल यात्री paidal yatri *n.* hiker
पैमफलिट paimflit *n.* pamphlet
पैसा paisā *n.* cash

पैसा दिनु paisā dinu *v.t.* pay
पोइ poi *n.* husband
पोइला poila *n.* elopement
पोते pote *n.* glass bead
पोथी pothi *adj.* female
पोर्सिलेन porsilen *n.* porcelain
पोल pol *n.* backbiting
पोलैंड poland *n.* Poland
पोल्ट्री poltari *n.* poultry
पोस्ट-कार्ड post-kārd *n.* postcard
पोशाक posāk *n.* costume
पोषण posan *n.* nutrition
पोषण गर्नु posan garnu *v.t.* foster
पोहर pohar *n.* last year
पौडी खेल्नु paudi khelnu *v.t.* swim
पौरख paurakh *n.* bravery
पौत्र pautra *n.* grandson
पौराणिक paurānik *n.* myth
पौवा pauva *n.* inn
प्लग plag *n.* plug
प्लैटिनम plaitinam *n.* platinum
प्यादा pyādā *n.* pawn
प्याज pyaj *n.* onion
प्यार pyār *n.* love
प्यारो pyāro *n./adj.* beloved
प्यार गर्नु pyār garnu *v.t.* express, reveal
प्याला pyāla *n.* cup
प्यास pyās *n.* thirst
प्रकट हुनु prakat hunu *v.t.* appear
प्रकार prakār *n.* sort, type
प्रकाण्ड prakānda *n./adj.* great
प्रकाश prakās *n.* light
प्रकाशक prakāsak *n.* publisher
प्रकाशन prakāsan *n.* publication
प्रकाशित गर्नु prakāsit garnu *v.t.* publish
प्रकृति prakrti *n.* nature *(flora & fauna)*
प्रकृतिक दृश्य prakrtik drisya *n.* scenery

प्रकोप prakop *n.* disaster
प्रक्रिया prakriyā *n.* process
प्रख्यात prakhyat *adj.* famous
प्रगति pragati *n.* progress
प्रगति गर्नु pragati garnu *v.t.* progress
प्रगतिशील pragatisil *adj.* progressive
प्रगाढ pragādh *adj.* deep
प्रचार pracār *n.* circulation
प्रचारक pracārak *n./adj.* missionary
प्रचारित गर्नु pracārit garnu *v.t.* circulate
प्रचण्ड pracand *adj.* violent
प्रचण्ड धारा pracand dhārā *n.* torrent
प्रचुर pracur *adj.* abundant
प्रचुरता pracuratā *n.* plenty
प्रजा prajā *n.* subject
प्रजातन्त्र prajatantra *n.* democracy
प्रणाम pranām *n.* salutation
प्रति prati *pref.* anti-
प्रतिकार गर्नु pratikār garnu *v.t.* remedy
प्रतिकूल pratikul *n.* adverse
प्रतिक्रिया ल्याउनु pratikriyā garnu *v.i.* react
प्रतिनिधि pratinidhi *n.* representative
प्रतिष्ठा pratisthia *n.* dignity, prestige
प्रतिष्ठित pratisthit *adj.* dignified
प्रतिध्वनि pratidhvani *n.* echo
प्रतिबंध pratibandh *n.* curb
प्रतिबंधित pratibandhit *adj.* restricted
प्रतिभाशाली pratibhāsāli *n.* genius
प्रतिभा pratibhā *n.* brilliance
प्रतिमा pratimā *n.* icon
प्रतिज्ञा pratigyā *n.* promise
प्रतिज्ञा गर्नु pratigyā garnu *v.* promise

प्रतियोगिता pratiyogita *n.*
competition

प्रतियोगी pratiyogi *n./adj.*
competitor

प्रतिलिपि pratilipi *n.* copy

प्रतिलिपि गर्नु pratilipi garnu *v.t.*
copy

प्रतिद्वन्द्दी pratidvanddvi *n./adj.*
rival

प्रतिद्वन्द्दिता pratidvanddvitā *n.*
rivalry

प्रतिरोधी pratirodhi *adj.* resistant

प्रतिस्थापित गर्नु pratisthāpit
garnu *v.t.* substitute

प्रतिक pratik *n.* token

प्रतीकार्थ pratikārth *adj.* symbolic

प्रतिक्षा pratiksa *n.* waiting

प्रतिक्षालय pratiksālāy *n.* lounge,
waiting room

प्रतिक्रिया pratikriyā *n.* reaction

प्रतिगामी pratigāmi *adj.*
regressive

प्रतिवेदन pratedan *n.* report

प्रतिस्पर्धा pratispard *n.*
competition

प्रथम pratham *adj.* first

प्रतित हुनु pratit hunu *v.i.* seem

प्रतिशत pratisat *adv.* percent

प्रतिशोध pratisodh *n.* revenge

प्रताप pratāp *n.* majesty

प्रत्यक्ष pratyaksa *adj.* direct

प्रत्येक pratyek *pron.* everyone

प्रथा prathā *n.* custom

प्रथम pratham *adj.* first

प्राथमिक prāthmik *adj.* primary

प्राथमिकता prāthmiktā *n.* priority

प्रदान गर्नु pradān garnu *v.t.* grant

प्रदूषण pradusan *n.* pollution

प्रदूषित pradusit *adj.* polluted

प्रदूषित गर्नु pradusit garnu *v.t./v.i.*
pollute

प्रदर्शनी pradarsani *n.* exhibition

प्रदर्शन pradarsan *n.*
demonstration, display

प्रदर्शन pradarsan *v.t.* demonstrate

प्रदर्शनकारी pradarsankāri *n.*
demonstration

प्रदर्शित गर्नु pradarsit garnu *v.t.*
display, exhibit

प्रदेश prades *n.* province, state

प्रादेशिक pradesik *adj.* regional

प्रधान pradhān *n.* chief

प्रधान अपक ध्या pradhān
adhyāpak *n.* headmaster

प्रधानमत्री pradhān mantri *n.*
prime minister

प्रमाण pramān *n.* proof

प्रमाणपत्र pramānpatra *n.*
laboratory

प्रस्ताव prastāb *n.* proposal

प्रबन्ध prabandha *n.* management

प्रभाव prabhāv *n.* influence

प्रत्येक pratek *pron.* everyone

प्रज्ञा pragyā *n.* intelligence

प्रयत्न prayatna *n.* attempt

प्रवचन pravasan *n.* talk

प्रमुख pramukh *adj.* principal,
main

प्रविधि pravidhi *n.* technology

प्रहरी prahari *n.* police

प्रशिक्षित गर्नु prasiksit garnu *v.t.*
train

प्रशासन prāsasan *n.* administration

प्रयोगर prayogar *n.* application

प्राकृतिक prākrtik *adj.* natural

प्राधिकरण prādhikaran *n.*
authority

प्रासि prāpti *n.* gain, acquisition

प्रास गर्नु prāpt garnu *v.t.* gain

प्राविधिक prābidhik *n.* technical

प्रारंभिक prārambhik *n./adj.* initial

प्रेमी premi *n.* lover

प्रेमिका premikā *n.* lover, girlfriend

प्रेरित गर्नु prerit garnu *v.t.* motivate

प्रेम prem *n.* love

प्रेम-लीला prem-lilā *n.* romance

प्रेयसी preyesi *n.* beloved

प्रेरणा preranā *n.* inspiration, motive

प्रेरणा दिनु prernā dinu *v.t.* inspire

रेमिटेन्स presit rupayā *n.* remittance

प्रेषित गर्नु presit garnu *v.t.* remit

प्रेस pres *n.* press

प्रोत्साहन protsāhan *n.* encouragement

प्रसारण केंद्र prasāran kendra *n.* station

प्रौढ praudh *n.* mature adult

प्लास्टिक plāstik *n./adj.* plastic

प्लेटफार्म pletfārm *n.* platform

प्वाला pwāl *n.* hole

फ

फंदा phandā *n.* trap
फँसाउनु phansāunu *v.t.* trap
फकाउनु phakāunu *v.i.* seduce
फकिर phakir *n.* Muslim holy man
फरक pharak *n.* difference
फजुल phajul *adj.* useless
फडफडाउनु phajul *v.t.* flap
फडफडाहट farfarāhat *n.* flap
फटकार phatkār *n.* reprimand
फटकारनु phatkārnu *v.t.* reprimand
फटाहा phatāhā *n.* liar
फटाही phatāhi *n.* lie
फराकिलो pharākilo *adj.* wide
फल phal *n.* fruit
फलदायी phaldayi *adj.* productive
फलाहार phalāhār *n.* diet
  consisting of only fruits
फलनु फूलनु phalnu-phulnu *v.i.*
  thrive
फलानो phalāno *pron.* somebody
फलाम phalām *n.* iron (metal)
फर्किनु pharkinu *v.t.* return
फरिया phāriya *n.* sari
फलित-ज्योतिष phalit-jyotis *n.*
  astrology
फलामको सामान phalāmko sāmān
  n. ironic stuff
फलोद्यान phalodyān *n.* orchard
फाइदा phaidā *n.* benefit
फाइल fāil *n.* file
फाइल मा राख्नु fāil mā rākhnuu
  v.t. file
फाँसी phānsi *n.* death by hanging
फाँट phānt *n.* field, department
फालतु phāltu *adj.* useless

फेरी देखिनु pheri dekhinu *v.i.*
  reappear
फेरी बनाउनु pheri banāunu *v.i.*
  reform
फिर्ता phirtā *n.* return
फिरौती phirauti *n.* ransom
फिका पर्नु phikā parnu *v.t.* fade
फुटकर phuhtkar *n.* retail
फागुन phāgun *n.* eleventh Nepali
  month (February-March)
फुच्ची phucci *n.* small girl
फुटबल phutbāl *n.* football
  (soccer)
फुर्ती phurti *n.* activity
फूफाजु phuphāju *n.* uncle
फूफु phuphu *n.* aunt
फुर्सद phursat *n.* spare time
फूल phul *n.* flower
फूलपाती phulpati *n.* seventh day
  in Dashain festival
फूल्नु phulnu *v.i.* bloom
फेरि pheri *adv.* again
फोक्सो phokso *n.* lungs
फोहर phohar *adj.* dirty
फोस्रो phosro *adj.* useless
फैलनु phailānu *v.t.* expand, spread
फैलाव phailāv *n.* spread
फैशन phaisan *n.* fashion
फौज phauj *n.* army

ब

बंडल bandal *n.* bundle

बकपत्र bakpatra *n.* statement made in court

बकुला bakullā *n.* crane (bird)

बक्यौता bakyautā *n.* unpaid dues

बख्खु bakkhu *n.* Tibetan jacket

बखत bakhat *n.* time

बगर bagar *n.* riverside

बताउनु batāunu *v.* tell, explain

वँदेल bandedl *n.* wild boar

बंगला bangalā *n.* cottage

बंगलादेशी banglādeshi *n.* resident of Bangladesh

बन्द band *adj.* closed

बंद गर्नु band garnu *v.t.* enclose

बंदागोभी bandgobhi *n.* cabbage

बंद हुनु band hunu *v.i.* cease

बन्दी bandi *n.* prisoner

बन्दी बनाउनु bandi banāunu *v.t.* detain

बंदूक banduk *n.* gun

बाँदर bāndar *n.* monkey

बंदरगाह bandargāh *n.* harbor

बंदोबस्त गर्नु bandobast garnu *v.t.* arrange

बंधक bandhak *n.* hostage

बंधन bandhan *n.* tie

बक्सा baksā *n.* trunk

बगली bagli *n.* pocket

वगलीमारा baglimāra *n.* pickpocket

बचत bacat *n.* savings

बचत खाता bacat khāta *n.* savings account

बचाउनु bacāunu *v.t.* rescue, save

बचाव bacāv *n.* rescue, save

बच्चा baccā *n.* child

बजनु bajnu *v.* sound

बजट bajat *n.* budget

बजै bajai *n.* grandmother

बज्र bajrā *n.* thunderbolt

बजाउनु bajāunu *v.t.* play

बटन batan *n.* button

बटुआ batuā *n.* wallet

बडा badā *adj.* big

बढाउनु barhnu *v.i.* swell

बढिया barhiyā *adj.* fine, great

वढी barhi *adj.* more

बडा barā *adj.* major

बतास batās *n.* air

बत्ती batti *n.* light

बथान bathān *n.* herd

बनस्पति banaspati *n.* vegetation

बयल bayal *n.* ox

बयंलगाडा bayalgāda *n.* bullock cart

बत्तीस battis *num.* thirty-two

बदनामी badnāmi *n.* disgrace

बदमास badmas *n.* scoundrel

बदमासी badmāsi *n.* misconduct

बदला badalā *n.* revenge

बदला लिनु badlā linu *v.* to take revenge

बदलिदिनु badali dinu *v.t.* alter

बदलनु badalnu *v.t.* change, vary

बम bam *n.* bomb

बदला badlā *n.* revenge

बधाई badhāi *n.* congratulation

बमोजिम bamojim *prep.* according

बन ban *n.* forest

बन्चरो bancaro n. axe
बन्डा bandā n. division
बनाउनु banāunu v.t. make
बनावट banāwat n. structure
वंशज banshaj n. descendent
बन्धु bandhu n. relative
बन्दी bandi n. captive
बनावट banāvat n. make-up
बनावटी banāvati adj. artificial
बन्दगोभी bandagobhi n. cabbage
बन्द गर्ने band garnu v.t. close
बन्देज bandej n. restriction
बन्दुक banduk n. gun
बन्दोवस्त bandabasta n.
  arrangement
वन्दोवस्त गर्नु bandobast garnu
  v. arrange
बन्धक bandhak n. hostage
बफादार baphādar adj. loyal
बमोजिम bamojim adv. according
बराबर barābar adj. equal
बरफ baraph n. ice
बरफी barphi n. sweet dish
बरखी barkhi n. death anniversary
  ritual
बरु baru adj. rather
वराजु barāju n. great-grandfather
वरन्डा barandā n. veranda
वरखा barkhā n. rainy season
बरखास्त barkhāst n. dismissal
बरखास्त गर्नु barkhast garnu v.
  dismiss
वरखी barkhi n. annual mourning
वर्तमान bartamān adj. present
बयान bayān n. description,
  testimony
बल bal n. strength
बरखास्त गर्नु barkhasta garnu v.
  dismiss
बलात्कार balātkār n. rape

बलात्कार गर्नु balātkār garnu v.t.
  rape
बलि bali n. sacrifice
बली bali adj. strong
बल्कि balki adv. rather
बल्ब balb n. bulb
बस bas n. noun
बसन्त basant n. spring (season)
बसाइँ basāin n. migration
बस्नु basnu v. sit
बस्ती basti n. settlement
बस्तु bastu n. domestic animal
बहकाउनु bahkāunu v.t. seduce
बहिनी bahini n. sister
बहनु bahanu v.t. flow
बहर bahr n. calf
बहस bahas n. argument
बहस गर्नु bahas garnu v.t. argue
बहादुर bahādur adj. brave
बहादुरी bahāduri n. bravery
बहाउनु bahāunu v.t. drain
बहाव bahāv n. flow
वहाना bahānā n. excuse
बहिरो bahiro adj. deaf
वहिष्कार bahiskār n. boycott
बहिष्कृत bahiskrtā n. outcast
बहुदल bahudal n. multiparty
बहु विवाह bahu vivāh n.
  polygamy, polyandry
बहुमत bahumat n. majority
वहुमूल्य bahumulya adj. costly
वहु संरक्षक bahusamkhyak n.
  majority
बहुल bahul adj. multiple
बहुलता bahultā n. diversity
बहुला bahulā adj. insane
बाहिर bāhira adj. outside
बहुतायत bahutāyat n. abundance
बहुवचन bahuvacan adj. plural
बा bā n. father

बाबु bābu *n.* father

बाबु आमा babu āma *n.* parents

बाग bāg *n.* garden

बागवानी bāgbāni *n.* horticulture

बालक bālak *n.* child

बाल विवाह bāl vivāh *n.* child marriage

वातावरण batābaran *n.* environment

बाकी bāki *adj.* remaining

वाँचनु bāncnu *v.t.* survive

बाचक bācak *n.* narrator

बाँडनु bandnu *v.t.* distribute, divide

बाँडा bāndā *n.* goldsmith

वाँझो bānjho *n.* barren

बाँदर bāndar *n.* monkey

बाँध bāndh *n.* dam

बाँस bāns *n.* bamboo

बाँसुरी bānsuri *n.* reed

बाख्रा bākhrā *n.* goat

बाच्छो bāccho *n.* calf *(zoo.)*

बाट bāta *prep.* from

बाठो bātho *adj.* clever

बाजा bājā *n.* musical instrument

बाज bāj *n.* eagle

बाक्लो bāklo *adj.* thick

बाघ bāgh *n.* tiger

बाजी bāji *n.* bet

बांङ्गो bāngo *adj.* bent

बायाँ bāyan *adj.* left

बाण bān *n.* arrow

बालश्रम bāl sram *adj.* child labor

विगारनु bigarnu *v.t.* damage

बाहुल्य bāhulya *n.* majority, plenty

बाह्य bāhya *adj.* external

वीउ biu *n.* seed

विउँतनु biuntanu *v.* be awake

वित्ता birtā *n.* rent free land that existed before 1950 in Nepal

विक्री bikri *n.* sale

बिताउनु bitāunu *v.* spend (time)

बिगार bigar *n.* loss

बिगार्नु bigārnu *v.* spoil

विग्रनु bigranu *v.* be spoiled

विघ्न bighna *n.* hindrance

विछौना bichaunā *n.* bed

विजुली bijuli *n.* electricity

बिजुली को धक्का bijuli ko dhakkā *v.t.* shock

वीज गणीत bijganit *n.* algebra

विदा bidā *n.* leave

विटुलो bitulo *adj.* impure

विदाई bidāi *n.* farewell

वियुत bidyut *n.* electricity

बिना binā *adv.* without

विन्ती binti *n.* request

बिफर biphar *n.* smallpox

बिरयानी biryāni *n.* fried or roasted meat and rice

बीमा bimā *n.* insurance

बीमा को नीति bimā ko niti *n.* policy

बिराउनु birāunu *v.* be guilty

बिरामी birāmi *n.* sick person

विरालो birālo *n.* cat

बिरुवा biruwā *n.* plant

विलकुल bilkul *adv.* entirely

विर्सनु birsanu *v.* forget

बिसन्चो bisanco *n.* unwell

वीस bis *num.* twenty

विसेक bisek *n.* recovery from illness

विस्कुट biskut *n.* biscuit

विस्मात bismāt *n.* sorrow

विहान bihāna *n.* morning

विहावारी bihābāri *n.* marriage

बिहे bihe *n.* marriage

बुईंगल buingal *n.* attic

बुझ्नु bujhnu *v.* understand

वुद्धि buddhi *n.* wisdom
बुझाई bujhāi *n.* understanding
बुझाउनु bujhāunu *v.t.* be understood
वुटी buti *n.* herb
वुढो budho *adj.* old man
बुढामामा budhāmāmā *n.* uncle
वुढिया budhiya *adj.* old woman
बुढेसकाल budheskāl *n.* old age
बुद्ध buddha *n.* Buddha
बुध्दु buddhu *adj.* stupid
बुवा buva *n.* father
बुहारी buhari *n.* daughter-in-law
वोक्सी boksi *n.* witch
वोक्सो bokso *n.* wizard
बेइज्जती beijat *n.* disgrace
बेइमान beimān *adj.* dishonest
वेइमानी beimāni *n.* dishonesty
बेकार bekār *adj.* vain
बेकुफ bekuf *adj.* stupid
बेकम्मा bekammā *adj.* useless
बेतलवी betalabi *n.* someone working without getting paid
वेपत्ता bepattā *adj.* lost
वेफायदा bephāyadā *n.* loss
वेच्नु becnu *v.* sell
बेरोजगार berojgār *adj.* unemployed
वेरोजगारी berojgāri *n.* unemployment
बेला belā *n.* time
बेलायत belāyat *n.* Britain
बेलुका belukā *n.* evening
बेलुन belun *n.* balloon
बेस bes *adj.* better
बेहोस behos *adj.* unconscious
वेसार besār *n.* turmeric
बैगनी baigani *n./adj.* violet
वैंक bank *n.* bank
वैठक baithāk *n.* meeting
वैठक baithāk *n.* living room

बैना bainā *n.* advance
बैल bail *n.* ox
वोका bokā *n.* goat
बोक्सी boksi *n.* witch
बोसो boso *n.* fat
वोरा borā *n.* bag
बोझ bojh *n.* load
वोट bot *n.* plant
वोल्नु bolnu *v.* speak
वौलाहा baulāhā *adj.* insane
वोली boli *n.* speech
वौद्ध bauddha *n.* Buddhist
वौद्धिक bauddhik *adj.* intellectual
व्यापार byāpar *n.* commerce
व्यापारी byāpari *n.* businessman
व्याज byāj *n.* interest
ब्राह्मण brahman *n.* Brahman
ब्रह्मा brahmā *n.* Brahmā
ब्रह्मचारी brahmacari *n./adj.* celibate
ब्रह्माण्ड brahmandā *n.* universe

भ

भईं bhain *n.* ground
भईंकटहर bhainkatahar *n.* pineapple
भकभकाउनु bhakbhakāunu *v.i.* stammer
भंग bhang *v.* violate
भँगेरो bhangero *n.* sparrow
भंटा bhanta *n.* eggplant
भंडार bhandār *n.* storeroom
भंडार मा हुनु bhandār mā hunu *n.* stock
भंभर bhanvar *n.* whirlpool
भइपरी आउने bhai pari āune *adj.* casual
भक्त bhakt *n.* devotee
भक्ति bhakti *n.* devotion
भगवान् bhagvān *n.* god
भगवती bhagwati *n.* goddess
भजन bhajan *n.* hymn
भमरा bhamarā *n.* kind of insect
भलादमी bhalādmi *n.* gentleman
भलाई bhalāi *n.* wellness
भला bhalā *n.* welfare
भत्कनु bhatkanu *v.i.* collapse
भटमास bhatmās *n.* soybean
भट्टी bhatti *n.* furnace
भड्काउनु bhādkaunu *v.* encourage
भविष्य bhavisya *n.* future
भविष्यवाणी bhavisyavāni *n.* prophecy
भवदीय bhavadiya *adj.* yours
भतिजा bhatija *n.* nephew
भतीजी bhatiji *n.* niece
भत्ता bhattā *n.* additional allowance
भरेको bharāko *adj.* crowded
भर्खर bharkhar *adv.* just now

भद्दा bhaddā *adj.* clumsy
भदौ bhadau *n.* fifth month in Nepali calendar
भद्र bhadra *adj.* gentle
भद्रगोल bhadragol *n.* disorder
भन्सार bhasār *n.* customs
भन्सार अधिकृत bhasār adhikrit *n.* customs officer
भन्सार अड्डा bhasār addā *n.* customs office
भन्सार महसुल bhasār mahsul *n.* customs duty
भन्नु bhannu *v.* tell
भनसुन bhansun *n.* flattery
भरपाई bharpāi *n.* receipt
भराई bharāi *n.* filling
भर्नु bharnu *v.t.* fill
भरपूर bharpur *adj.* entirely
भर्ना bharnā *n.* admission
भंयकर bhayankar *adj.* terrible
भय bhaya *n.* fright, fear
भयानक bhayānak *adj.* terrific
भर पर्नु bhar parnu *n.* depend
भर पर्दो bhar pardo *adj.* dependable
भरती गर्नु bharti garnu *v.t.* recruit
भरोसा bharosā *n.* reliance
भरपाई bharpai *n.* receipt
भस्म bhasma *n.* ash
भस्मकलश bhasmklas *n.* urn
भवन bhawan *n.* building; palace
भव्य bhabya *adj.* huge
भाई bhāi *n.* brother
भाइटीका bhaitikā *n.* Hindu festival celebrated in November
भाउ bhāu *n.* cost
भाउजु bhāuju *n.* sister-in-law

भाका bhākā n. term
भाग bhāg n. segment, portion
भाँग bhang n. marijuana
भाँडो bhāndo n. utensils
भरिया bhariya n. porter
भरी bhari adj. full
भरेङ्ग bhareng n. stairway
भवितव्य bhavitavya n. unexpected
  happening
भाग्नु bhāgnu v.i. run
भाग लगाउनु bhag lagāunu v.i.
  divide
भागवण्डा bhāgbandā n. partition
भाग्नु bhāgnu v.i. flee
भाग्य bhāgya n. lot, luck
भांजा bhānja n. nephew
भांजी bhānji n. niece
भान्छा bhānchā n. kitchen
भाडो bhāro n. freight
भाँडनु bhāndnu v.t. spoil
भात bhāt n. rice
भान्सा bhānsa n. kitchen
भान्सा गर्नु bhānsa garnu v.t. eat
भार bhār n. gravity, load
भारत bhārat n. India
भारतीय bhāratiya n./adj. Indian
भारदार bhārdār n. noble
भार उठाउनु bhar uthaunu n.
  weight
भारोपेली bhāropeli adj. Indo-
  European
भारी bhāri adj. weight
भाला bhālā n. spear
भालु bhālu n. bear
भाले bhāle n. male
भावना. bhāvnā n. feeling
भावनात्मक bhāvnātmak adj.
  emotional
भाषा bhāsā n. language
भाषाशास्त्र bhāsāstra n. linguistics
भाषाशास्त्री bhāsāsāstri n. linguist

भाषीक bhāsikā n. dialect
भावना bhāvanā n. sentiment,
  feeling
भावुक bhāvuk adj. passionate
भावी bhavi n. future
भाषण bhāsan n. speech
भाषण दिनु bhashan dinu v.t.
  address
भाषिक bhasik adj. linguistic
भाष्कर bhāskar n. sun
भिज्नु bhijnu v. soak
भिडंत bhirant v.t. encounter
भिन्न bhinna adj. distinct
भिन्न-भिन्न bhinn-bhinn adj.
  diverse
भिक्षा माग्नु bhiksā mamgnu v.i.
  beg
भिक्षुक bhikshuk n. monk
भिक्षु bhiksu n. monk
भिक्षुणी bhiksuni n. nun
भीड bheed n. crowd
भिड्नु bhidnu v. fight
भित्तो bhitto n. wall
भिनाजु bhināju n. elder sister's
  husband
भित्र bhitrā adj. indoor
भित्री bhitri adj. internal
भित्रिनी bhitrini n. concubine
भित्रीमधेश bhitri madhes n. inner
  Terai in southern Nepal
भुट्न bhutun v. roast
भुटेको bhuteko adj. roasted
भीड bhirant n. crowd
भिरालो bhirālo adj. sloppy
भिडन्त bhidanta n. fight
भिन्न bhinna adj. different
भिन्नता bhinnatā n. difference
भीषण bhisan adj. terrible
भुक्नु bhuknu v.i. bark
भुखमरी bhukmari n. starvation
भुवन bhuwan n. earth

भुकतान bhugtān *n.* payment

भूकंप bhukampa *n.* earthquake

भूगोल bhugol *n.* geography

भूगर्वशास्त्र bhugarbha sāstra *n.* geology

भूत bhut *n.* ghost

भूतपूर्व bhuttpurba *adj.* past, former

भू-संरक्षण bhusamraksan *n.* soil conservation

भू परिवेक्षित bhuparivesthit *adj.* landlocked

भूमि bhumi *n.* land

भूमिगत bhumigat *adj.* underground

भूमिका bhumikā *n.* role; introduction

भूमिसुधार bhumi sudhār *n.* land reform

भूमिहीन bhumihin *adj.* landless

भूल bhul *n.* lapse, mistake

भुल्नु bhulnu *v.* forget

भूल-भूलैया bhul-bhulaiyā *n.* maze

भूविज्ञान bhuvigyān *n.* geology

भेंट bhent *n.* visit, meeting

भेट्नु bhetnu *v.* meet

भेटघाट bhetghāt *n.* meeting

भेटी bheti *n.* offering

भेडा bherā *n.* sheep

भू-परिवेष्ठित bhu paribesthit *adj.* landlocked

भेद गर्नु bhed garnu *v.t.* distinguish

भेदभाव bhedbhav *n.* discrimination

भेला bhelā *n.* gathering

भेष bhes *n.* appearance

भैंसी bhainsi *n.* buffalo

भोज bhoj *n.* feast

भोजपुरी bhojpuri *n.* a language spoken in the southern Terai

भोक bhok *n.* hunger

भोकमरी bhokmari *n.* starvation

भोकहडताल bhokhadtāl *n.* hunger strike

भोगवन्धक bhogbhandhak *n.* mortgage

भोगचलन bhogcalan *n.* possession

भोजन bhojan *n.* meal

भोजनालय bhojanalaya *n.* restaurant

भोजनकक्ष bhojan kaks *n.* dining hall

भोजन गर्नु bhojan garnu *v.i.* dine

भोला-भोला bholā-bholā *adj.* naïve

भोलि bholi *adv.* tomorrow

भोर bhor *n.* dawn

भोट bhot *n.* Tibet

भोटे bhote *n.* Tibetan

भौतिक bhautik *adj.* physical

भौतिक सम्पति bhautik sampatti *n.* physical property

भौतिक शास्त्र bhautik shastra *n.* physics

भौगर्भिक bhaugarbhik *adj.* geological

भ्याउनु bhyaunu *v.t.* manage

भ्यागुतो bhyāguto *n.* frog

भ्रम bhram *n.* error

भ्रमण bhraman *n.* travel

भ्रमण आदेश bhraman ādes *n.* travel order/authorization

भर्मण भत्ता bhrman bhattā *n.* travel allowance

भ्रमण गर्नु bhraman garnu *v.i.* ramble

भ्रष्ट bhrast *adj.* corrupt

भ्रष्टाचार bhrastācār *n.* corruption

भ्रष्टचारी bhrastācari *adj.* corrupt

भ्रान्ति bhrānti *n.* illusion

भ्रमाक bhrāmak *adj.* misleading

म

म ma *pron.* I

मकै makai *n.* maize

मखमल makhmal *n.* velvet

मगज magaj *n.* brain

मंगलवार mangalvār *n.* Tuesday

मंसीर mangsir *n.* eighth month in Nepali calendar

मंच manc *n.* platform

मंजन manjan *n.* toothpaste

मंजूर गर्नु manjur garnu *v.t.* approve

मंजूरी manjuri *n.* acceptance

मंडप mandap *n.* temporary building built for a festival or wedding

मण्डली mandal *n.* circle

मन्त्र mantra *n.* sacred text

मंत्रालय mantrālay *n.* ministry

मंत्री mantri *n.* minister; secretary

मंद mand *adj.* sluggish

मंदिर mandir *n.* temple

मई mai *n.* May

मक्खन makkhan *n.* butter

मगर magar *n.* ethic group in Nepal living in western hills

मचान macān *n.* scaffold

मजबूत majbut *adj.* strong

मजबूत गर्नु majbut garnu *v.t.* strengthen, reinforce

मजदुर majdur *n.* worker, labor

मजा maja *n.* pleasure

मजाक majak *n.* joke

मंजूरी manjuri *n.* approval

मटर matar *n.* pea

मट्टीतेल matitel *n.* kerosene

मञ्च manch *n.* seat

मत mat *n.* option

मगणना त matgananā *n.* vote counting

मत संग्रह matasangraha *n.* referendum

मतलवी matlabi *adj.* selfish

मणि mani *n.* jewel

मण्डप mandap *n.* pavilion

मटर matar *n.* pea

मठ math *n.* monastery

मतदान matdān *n.* poll

मतदाता matdātā *n.* voter

मति mati *n.* mind

मतियार matiyār *adj.* accessory

मदद madad *n.* help

मदद गर्नु madadgarnu *v.t.* help

मदरसा madarasā *n.* Muslim school

मदारी madāri *n.* snake charmer

मदिरा madirā *n.* liqueur

मदिरालय madirālaya *n.* bar

मधु madhu *n.* honey

मधुर madhur *adj.* sweet

मधुमख्खी madhumakkhi *n.* bee

मधुमास madhumās *n.* honeymoon

मधुमेह madhumeh *n.* diabetes

मधुमेही madhuhmehi *adj.* diabetic

मधेश madhesh *n.* southeastern Nepal where Madhesh people live

मधेशी madhesi *adj.* inhabitant of Madhesh in Nepal

मध्य madhya *n.* middle

मध्यपश्चिम madhyapaschim *n.* Midwest

मध्यम madhyam *adj.* middle

मध्यस्थ madyastha *n.* middleman

मध्ययुग madhyayug *adj.* middle

मध्यकालीन madhyakālin *adj.* medieval

मध्यपूर्व madhyapurba *n.* Middle East

मध्याह्नपूर्व madhyāhnpurv *adj.* a.m.

मध्यादिन madhyadin *n.* midday

मध्यांतर madhyāntar *n.* interval

मध्यावदी madhyābadi *n.* mid-term *(as in examination)*

मध्यमांचल madhyamāncal *n.* central region

मध्यरात्रि madhyarāti *n.* midnight

मन man *n.* mind

मनकामना manakāmanā *n.* desire

मनगढन्त mangadhanta *adj.* fictitious, fabricated, not true

मनपराउनु manparāunu *v.i.* like

मनन manan *n.* analysis

मनमोहक manmohak *adj.* pleasant

मनसाय manasāya *n.* intention

मनाही manāhi *n.* prohibition

मंत्री mantri *n.* minister

मनाउनु manāunu *v.t.* persuade

मन-बहलाव man-behlāv *n.* recreation

मन्दबुद्धि mandbuddhi *adj.* dull

मनचिकित्सक mansicikitsak *n.* psychiatrist

मन पर्नु man parnu *v.t.* like

मन-माना man-mānā *adj.* arbitrary

मनुष्य manusya *n.* man

मनोनयन mano-nayan *n.* nomination

मनोभाव manobhāv *adj.* passionate

मनोमालिन्य manolālinya *n.* animosity

मनोहर manohar *adj.* handsome, graceful, fancy, fair

मनोविज्ञान manovigyān *n.* psychology

मनोरंजक manoranjak *adj.* entertaining

मनोरंजन manoranjan *n.* entertainment

मनोरंजन गर्नु manoranjan garnu *v.t.* entertain

मनोरंजन manoranjan *n.* sport

मनोरम manoram *adj.* elegant

मनोविश्लेषण manovislesan *n.* psychoanalysis

मनोवृत्ति manovrtti *n.* attitude

मन्तव्य mantavya *n.* comment

मनोवैज्ञानिक manovaigyānik *adj.* psychological

मनोवैज्ञानी manovaigyāni *n.* psychologist

मंजन manjan *n.* toothpaste

मंजुरीनामा manjurināma *n.* agreement

मफल maphat *adj.* without cost, free

ममता mamata *n.* affection

मयूर mayur *n.* peacock

मरोड्नु marornu *v.t.* twist

मर्द mard *n.* male

मरण maran *adj.* dying

मरेको mareko *adj.* dead

मरदाना mardānā *n.* masculine

मरम्मत marammat *n.* repair

मरम्मत गर्नु marammat garnu *v.t.* repair, restore

मरनु marnu *v.i.* die

मरुभूमि marubhumi *n.* desert

मसल masal *n.* mussel

मसान masān *n.* cremation ground for the dead

मसाला masālā *n.* spice

मसालेदार masāledār *adj.* spicy

मसूर masur *n.* lentil

मर्म marma *adj.* vital

मर्मस्पर्शी maramsparsi *adj.* touching

मर्यादा maryādā *n.* correct behavior

मल mal *n.* manure

मलमल malmal *n.* muslin

मलमास malmās *n.* leap month *(there's one every three years in Nepali calendar)*

मलाई malāi *n.* cream

मलाई malāi *v.* give to me

मलाई झिक्नु malāi jhiknu *v.t.* skim

मलामी malāmi *n.* mourner at a funeral

मलेरिया maleria *n.* malaria

मलनु malnu *v.t.* rub

मलिलो malilo *adj.* fertile

मल्लाह mallāh *n.* sailor

मस्त mast *adj.* satisfied

मसजिद masjid *n.* mosque

मसान masān *n.* cremation grounds

मसला masalā *n.* spice

मसान्त masānta *n.* last day of any Nepali month

मसी masi *n.* ink

मसौदा masaudā *n.* draft

महंगो mahango *adj.* expensive

महंगी mahangi *n.* rise in prices

मह maha *n.* honey

महन्त mahanta *n.* monk living in a monastery

महत्व mahatva *n.* importance

महत्वहीन mahatvahin *n.* unimportance

महत्वपूर्ण mahatvapurn *adj.* important, vital, substantial

महत्वाकांक्षा mahatvākānksā *n.* ambition

महत्वाकांक्षी mahatvākānksi *adj.* ambitious

महसूस mahasus *n.* feeling

महर्षि maharsi *n.* great sage, wise man

महल mahal *n.* place

महसूल mahasul *n.* revenue

महसूस गर्नु mahasus garnu *v.t.* perceive

महा mahā *adj.* big

महाकवि mahākabi *n.* great poet

महाकाली mahākāli *n.* Hindu goddess

महाकाव्य mahākāvya *n.* epic

महाजन mahājan *n.* banker

महात्मा mahātmā *n.* great soul

महादेव mahādev *n.* Siva *(Hindu god, also spelled Shiva)*

महान् mahān *adj.* great

महादेश mahādesh *n.* continent

महानता mahānta *n.* greatness

महान्यायधिवक्ता mahānyādhivakta *n.* attorney general

महानुभाव mahānubhāv *n.* noble person

महाभारत mahābhārat *n.* Hindu epic

महामारी mahāmāri *n.* epidemic

महातरंग mahātrang *n.* swell

महामहिम mahāmahim *adj.* excellency

महाद्वीप mahāvdip *n.* continent

महाप्रबन्धक mahāprabandak *n.* general manager

महाराजधिराज mahārājādhirājā *n.* king

महारानी mahārāni *n.* queen

महायान mahāyān *n.* Mahayana Buddhism

महायुद्ध mahāyuyddha *n.* great war

महालेखापरीक्षक mahālekhapariksak *n.* auditor general

महावाणिज्यदूत mahāvānijyadut *n.* consulate general of government in a foreign country

महासभा mahāsabha *n.* congress

महासचिव mahāsaciv *n.* secretary general

महासागर mahāsāgar *n.* ocean

महासेनानी mahāsenāni *n.* colonel

महाशय mahasaya Mr.

महाशाखा mahāsākhā *n.* main branch of an organization

महिमा mahimā *n.* glory

महिला mahilā *n.* woman

महिला संगठन mahilā sangathan *n.* women's organization

महिनावारी mahinābari *n.* (menstrual) period

महिना mahinā *n.* month

मशीन masin *n.* machine

मस्जिद masjid *n.* mosque

महोत्सव mahotsav *n.* great festival

मास mās *n.* a kind of lentil

मांसपेशी mānspesi *n.* muscle

मांस māms *n.* flesh; meat

माँग māmg *n.* demand

मासु māsu *n.* flesh; meat

मांसाहारी mamsāhari *adj.* non-vegetarian

माँग्नु māgnu *v.t.* demand, request, require

माघ māgh *n.* tenth month in Hindu calendar

माइक māik *n.* microphone

माइत māita *n.* home of wife's parents

माइल māil *n.* mile

माईज्यु māijyu *n.* aunt *(maternal)*

माओवादी maobādi *n./adj.* Maoist

माकुरा mākura *n.* spider

माकुराको जालो makura ko jālo *n.* spider web

माखो mākho *n.* fly

माग्ने māgne *n.* beggar

माग्नु māgnu *v.* demand

माडल mādal *n.* model

माणिक mānik *n.* ruby

मात्रा mātrā *n.* dose

माता-पिता mātā-pitā *n.* parents

माता-जी mātā-ji *n.* mother

मातामह mātāmaha *n.* mother's father

मात्रा mātrā *n.* quantity

मातृभाषा mātri bhāsa *n.* mother tongue

माथा māthā *n.* forehead

माथि māthi *prep.* above

मादक mādak *adj.* alcoholic

मादल mādal *n.* a kind of drum often used in religious performances

मादा mādā *n.* female

माध्यम mādhyam *n.* material

माध्यमिक विद्यालय mādhyamik vidyālaya *n.* high school

मान mān *n.* honor *(award)*

मानक mānak *n./adj.* standard

मान्नु mānnu *v.t.* acknowledge

मानचित्र māncitra *n.* chart

मानव अधिकार mānav adhikār *n.* human rights

मानवीय mānaviya *adj.* human
माननीय mānaniya *adj.* honorable
मानसिक mānsik *adj.* mental
मानसिक सन्तुलन mānsik santulan *n.* sanity
मानक mānak *n.* standard
मानहानि mānhāni *n.* libel
मान्नु mānnu *v.t.* regard
मानिस mānis *n.* man
माना चामल mānā cāmal *n.* maintenance, alimony
मानव mānav *n.* man
मानव जाति manāv jāti *n.* mankind
मानवशास्त्र mānav sāstra *n.* anthropology
मानवीय mānviya *n.* human
मानवोचित mānvocit *adj.* humane
मानविकी mānaviki *n.* humanities
मानवता mānvatā *n.* humanity
मानव वस्ती mānav basti *n.* human settlement
मानसिक तनाव mānsik tanāv *n.* stress
मानहानी mānhāni *n.* libel
मानार्थ mānārtha *adj.* honorary
मानीटर mānitar *n.* monitor
मानिस mānis *n.* man
मान्छे mānce *n.* mankind
मान्य mānya *adj.* valid
मान्यता mānyatā *n.* recognition; identity
माप māpa *n.* gauge
मापांक māpānk *n.* module
माफ māph *n.* forgiveness
माफी māphi *n.* pardon
मामला māmlā *n.* affair
मामा māmā *n.* uncle
मामी māmi *n.* aunt
मामूली māmuli *adj.* ordinary
मार्नु mārnu *v.t.* kill

मारगरीन mārgarin *n.* margarine
मार्टर mārtar *n.* mortar
माल māl *n.* ware
मालदार māldār *n.* rich
मालपोत mālpot *n.* land revenue
मालसामान mālsāmān *n.* personal effects
माला mālā *n.* garland
मालिक mālik *n.* owner
मालिक्नी mālikni *n.* owner
माली māli *n.* gardener
माया maya *n.* love
मायालु māyālu *n.* lover
माया गर्नु māyā garnu *v.i.* love
मार mār *n.* beating
मार्नु mārnu *v.* kill
मारिनु mārinu *v.* be killed
मारकाट mārkāt *n.* killing
मारबाडी mārvari *n.* Indian traders from Mārwār in Rajasthan
मालिक mālik *n.* employer, boss, proprieter
मालिक हुनु mālik hunu *v.t.* possess
मालिश mālis *n.* massage
मास्टर māstar *n.* instructor, teacher
मार्शल mārsal *n.* marshal
माफी māfi *n.* excuse
माफ गर्नु māf garnu *v.t.* excuse
मार्ग mārg *n.* avenue, track
मार्गदर्शन mārgadarsan *n.* showing the way
मार्च mārc *n.* march
माटो māto *n.* soil
माता mātā *n.* mother
मातृसत्तात्मक mātrisattātmak *adj.* matriarchal
मिटाउनु mitāunu *v.t.* erase
मिठाई mithāi *n.* candy, sweets

मिठास mithās *n.* sweetness
मितव्ययिता mitvyaytā *n.* thrift
मितव्ययी mitvyaya *adj.* thrifty
मित mit *n.* friend
मिति miti *n.* date (calendar)
मितेरी miteri *n.* friendship
मिथिला mithilā *n.* an area in south Nepal
मित्र mitra *n.* ally
मित्रता mitratā *n.* friendship
मिनट minat *n.* minute
मिथ्या mithyā *adj.* false
मिनाहा mināhā *n.* reduction
मिलन milan *n.* meeting, union
मिलनसार milansār *n.* social
मिलापत्र milāpatra *n.* document of compromise
मिलावट milāvat *n.* mixture
मिरगी miragi *n.* epilepsy
मिलाउनु milāunu *v.t.* mix, join
मिलीमीटर milimitar *n.* millimeter
मिस्र misran *n.* Egypt
मिश्रण misran *n.* mixture, mix
मिश्रित misrit *adj.* mixed
मिस्त्री mistri *n.* carpenter
मीठो बनाउनु mitho banāunu *v.t.* make tasty
मीठो बिस्कुट mitho biskut *n.* cookie
मिठाई mithāi *n.* sweet
मील-पत्थर mil-patthar *n.* milestone
मीनार minār *n.* tower
मीनार को शिखर minār ko sikhar *n.* spire
मुख mukh *n.* mouth
मुआवजा muāwaja *n.* compensation
मुक्का mukkā *n.* fist; punch
मुक्का हान्नु mukkā hannu *v.t.* punch

मुक्केबाजी mukkebāzi *n.* boxing
मुकुट mukut *n.* crown
मुक्त mukta *n./adj.* emancipator
मुक्त गर्नु mukt garnu *v.t.* release
मुक्ति mukti *n.* salvation
मुक्तिनाथ muktinath *n.* temple north of Himalayas
मुखिया mukhiyā *n.* clerk in governmental service
मुख्य mukhya *adj.* main, chief, major
मुख्य न्यायधीश mukhya nyāyadhis *n.* chief justice
मुख्य मन्त्री mukhya mantri *n.* chief minister
मुख्य भू-भाग mukhya bhu-bhāg *n.* mainland
मुख्य सचिव mukhya sacib *n.* chief secretary
मुख्यालय mukhyālay *n.* headquarters
मुगा mugā *n.* coral
मुजुर mujur *n.* peacock
मुतनु mutnu *v.* urinate
मुताविक mutābik *adj.* corresponding
मुठभेड muthbhed *n.* fight
मुद्दा muddā *n.* case
मुद्दती खाता muddati khatā *n.* certificate of deposit
मुद्रक mudrak *n.* printer
मुद्रणालय mudranālaya *n.* press
मुद्रा mudrā *n.* seal, stamp
मुद्रा-स्फीति mudrā-sphiti *n.* inflation
मुद्रीत mudrit *adj.* printed
मुना munā *n.* planet
मुनि muni *n.* holy man, sage
मुन्द्रि mundri *n.* earring
मुफ्त muft *adj.* free

मुट्ठा mutthā *n.* roll

मुरदा murdā *adj.* dead

मुरब्बा murabbā *n.* marmalade

मुर्गा murgā *n.* rooster

मुरली murali *n.* flute

मुलतबी multabi *n.* postponement

मुलुक muluk *n.* country

मुलुकी ऐन mulukiain *n.* civil code

मुरली बजाउने murli bajāune *n.* piper

मुस्किल muskil *adj.* difficult

मुर्ख murkha *n.* fool

मुर्खता murkhatā *n.* foolishness

मुसलमान musalmān *n.* Muslim

मुसलमानी musalmāni *adj.* Muslim

मुसो muso *n.* mouse

मुस्कराउनु muskarāunu *v.i.* smile

मुस्कराहट muskarāhat *n.* smile

मुहान muhān *n.* source

मुहावरा muhāvarā *n.* idiom

मुहार muhār *n.* face

मुहूर्त muhurta *n.* auspicious occasion

मूँग mung *n.* peanut

मूठ muth *n.* handle

मूत्रीय mutriy *adj.* urinary

मूर्ति murti *n.* statue

मूर्तिपूजक murtipujāk *n.* idolater

मूर्ति बनाउनु murti banāunu *v.i.* sculpt

मूर्तिकार murtikār *n.* sculptor

मूल mul *n.* original

मूला mulāā *n.* radish

मूली muli *n.* main person

मूल भाषा mul bhāsā *n.* native language

मूलवाटो mainroad *n.* main road

मूलवासी mulvāsi *n.* native

मूलढोका muldhokā *n.* main gate

मूलधन muldhan *n.* principal

मूलवाटो mulbāto *n.* main road

मूल समिति mul samiti *n.* main committee

मूल्य mulya *n.* value

मूल्य तालिका mulya tālika *n.* price chart

मूल्यांकन mulyānkan garnu *n.* evaluation

मूल्यांकन गर्नु mulyānkan garnu *v.t.* valuation

मूल्यवान mulyavān *n./adj.* valuable

मृत mrit *n./adj.* dead

मृतक mritak *n.* dead person

मृत्तिका mrittiikā *n./adj.* ceramic

मृग mriga *adj.* dear

मृगतृष्णा mrgatrsan *n.* mirage

मृत्यु mrityu *n.* death

मृत्युदण्ड mrityu danda *n.* capital punishment

मृत्युशैया mrityu saiyā *n.* deathbed

मृदुल mridul *adj.* mild

मेजर mejar *n.* major *(in college)*

मेघ megh *n.* cloud

मेघ गर्जन megh garjān *n.* thunderstorm

मेच mech *n.* chair

मेचे mece *n.* ethnic group of Nepal

मेधावी medhāvi *adj.* wise

मेन्यू menyu *n.* menu

मेटनु metnu *v.* erase

मेयर meyar *n.* mayor

मेरो mero *pron.* mine

मेरुदण्ड merudanda *n.* spine

मेला mel *n.* conjunction

मेल-मिलाप melā *n.* fair

मेल-मिलाप गर्नु mel-milāo garnu *v.t.* reconcile

मेवा mewā *n.* papaya

मेहनत mehanat *n.* toil
मेहनत गर्नु mehanat garnu *v.t.* toil
मेहनती mehenati *adj.* diligent
मेक्सिको mexico *n.* Mexico
मैकेनिक maikenik *n.* mechanic
मैत्री maitri *n.* friendship
मैत्रीपूर्ण maitripurna *adj.* full of friendship
मैडम maidam *n.* madam
मैथिल maithil *n.* inhabitant of Mithila
मैथिली maithili *n.* language spoken in Terai region
मैथुन maithin *n.* sexual intercourse
मैदान maidān *n.* plain
मैन main *n.* wax
मैनवत्ती mainbatti *n.* candle
मैनेजर mainejar *n.* manager
मैलो mail *adj.* filthy
मोचन mocan *n.* release
मोज moj *n.* pleasure
मोजा mojā *n.* sock
मोटो moto *adj.* thick, fat
मोटामोटी motmoti *adv.* approximately
मोटाउनु motāunu *v.* grow fat (gain weight / get rich from bribes)
मोटाई motāi *n.* thickness
मोतियाबि न्दु motiyābind *n.* cataract
मोड mode *n.* curve
मोटरकार motarkar *n.* automobile
मोटर साइकिल motar sāikil *n.* motorcycle
मोटल motel *n.* motel
मोठ moth *n.* land register
मोडेम modem *n.* modem
मोती moti *n.* pearl

मोफसल mophasal *n.* area outside capital city
मोम लगाउनु mom lagāunu *v.t.* wax
मोमो momo *n.* dumpling
मोल mol *n.* offer
मोलभाउ गर्नु mol bhāu garnu *v.* bargain
मोसम mosam *n.* orange
मोह लिनु moh linu *v.t.* fascinate
मोही mohi *n.* tenant farmer
मोहियानी हक mohiyāni hak *n.* tenancy right
मोहकता mohktā *n.* glamour
मोहनी mohani *n.* magic, spell
मोहर mohar *n.* postmark
मोहर लगाउनु mohar lagāunu *v.t.* postmark
मोक्ष moksa *n.* deliverance
मौका mauka *n.* opportunity
मौखिक maukhik *adj.* oral
मौजदात maujdat *n.* balance
मौद्रिक maudrik *adj.* monetary
मौन maun *adj.* silent
मौरी mauri *n.* bee
मौलिक maulik *adj.* original
मौसम mausam *n.* weather
मौसम पूर्वानुमान mausam purvānumān *n.* weather forecasting
मौसमी यंत्र mausami yantra *n./adj.* seasonal machinery; appliance
म्याद myād *n.* term
म्यानेजर myanejar *n.* manager
म्युजियम miujiyam *n.* museum
नगरपालिका miunisipālity *n.* municipality
मौसम विज्ञान mausam bigyān *n.* meteorology

य

यजुर्वेद yajurved *n.* one of four vedas *(along with Rigved, Samved and Atharvaved)*

यथार्थ Yathartha *adj.* virtual

यथावत स्थिति yathāvat sthiti *n.* status

यदि Yadi *conj.* if

यदा-कदा yadā-kadā *n.* occasional

यता Yatā *adv.* here

यती Yeti *n.* snowman of legends living in the Himalayas

यतिखेर Yatikhera *adv.* at present

यत्न Yatna *n.* attempt

यश Yash *n.* fame

यहाँ Yahā *adv.* here

यहूदी Yahudi *adj.* Jewish

यहूदी को मंदिर yahudi ko mandir *n.* synagogue

यथार्थ Yathartha *adj.* real

यथासंभव yathā sambhav *adv.* as far as possible

या yā *conj.* or

याक yāk *n.* yak

यातना yātna *n.* torture

यातायात yātāyāt *n./v.i.* traffic

यातना दिनु yatnā dinu *v.t.* torment

यात्रा yātrā *n.* traveler

यात्रा लेखक yātrā lekhak *n.* travel writer

याद गर्नु yād garnu *v.t.* remember

याद दिलाउनु yād dilaunu *v.t.* remind

यायावर yāyāvar *n.* wandering

घुमन्ते जाति yāyāvari *adj.* nomadic

यिनी yini *pron.* he

युक्ति yukti *n.* device

युद्ध yuddh *n.* war

यूनानी yunāni *n.* Greek

यूरोपियन yuropiyan *n./adj.* European

यस्तो yasto *adj.* such

युग yug *n.* age

युद्ध yuddha *n.* war

युद्धबन्दी yuddhabandhi *n.* prisoner of war

युद्धविराम yuddhabirām *n.* ceasefire

युवक yuvak *n.* youth

युवति yuvati *n.* young woman

युवराज yuvarāj *n.* crown prince

युवराज्ञी yuvaragyi *n.* crown princess

युरोप yurop *n.* Europe

युवा yubā *n.* youth

युवा पिंढी yuyubā pindhi *n.* young generation

युवा वर्ग yubā varga *n.* youth group

यूरोपीय yuropiya *adj.* European

यो yo *pron.* it, this

योग yog *n.* yoga

योगदान yogdān *n.* contribution

योगासन yogāsan *n.* yoga posture

योग्य yogya *adj.* qualified, deserving

योग्य बनाउनु yogya banāunu *v.t.* enable

योग्य हुनु yogya hunu *v.i.* enable

योग्यता yogyatā *n.* competence

योग्यताक्रम yogyatākram *adj.* merit-based

योजना yojnā *n.* plan

योजनाकार yojnākār *n.* planner

योजनावद्ध yojnabaddha *adj.*
planned

योजना बनाउनु yojnā banaunu
v.t. plan

योजना आयोग yojnā āyog *n.*
planning commission

योजना विद् yojnavid *n.* planning
expert

योजनास्थल yojanasthal *n.* project
site

यौन yaun *n.* sex

यौनिक yaunik *adj.* sexual

र

रंग rang *n.* color, dye

रंगको मात्रा rang ko mātrā *n.* shade

रंग-विरंगा rang-virangā *adj.* fancy

रंग लाउनु rang launu *v.t.* paint, dye

रंग भेद rangbhed *n.* apartheid

रंगरुट rangrut *n.* recruit

रंगमंच rangmanc *n.* stage

रंगीन काँच rangin kāmc *n.* stain

रंगाई rangiā *n.* coloring

रइस rais *n.* rich man

रकसैक raksaik *n.* rucksack

रकम rakam *n.* property

रकमी rakami *n.* someone who's money minded

रगत ragat *n.* blood

रक्तचाप raktacāp *n.* blood pressure

रक्त चन्दन rakta candan *n.* sandalwood

रक्षक raksak *n.* escort, protector

रक्षण raksan *n.* protection

रक्षार्थ साथ जानु raksārth sāth janu *v.t.* escort

रक्षा raksā *n.* protection

रक्षित raksit *adj.* protected

रक्षा गर्नु raksā garnu *v.t.* protect

रक्सी raksit *n.* alcoholic

राखेर बिर्सनु rakherar birsanu *v.t.* to put something down and forget about it

रखौटी rakhauti *n.* concubine

रुखो rukho *adj.* sullen

रचना racnā *n.* composition

रचना गर्नु racnā garnu *v.t.* compose

रचनात्मक racnātmak *adj.* original

रचित racit *adj.* created by

रजिस्टर rajistar *n.* register

रजिस्टरि डाक rajistari dāk *n.* registered mail

रजत rajat *n.* silver

रजत जयन्ती rajat jayanti *n.* silver jubilee

रजनी rajani *n.* night

रणनीति ranniti *n.* tactic

रण्डी randi *n.* prostitute

रण्डीवाजी randibāji *n.* prostitution

रण्डीकोठी randikothi *n.* brothel

रत्न ratn *n.* gem

रथ rathi *n.* chariot

रथी rathi *n.* lieutenant general

रद्द radd *adj.* null

रद्द गर्नु radd garnu *v.t.* cancel, nullify

रद्दी raddi *n.* garbage

रफू गर्नु rafu garnu *v.t.* darn

रबी rabi *n.* winter crop

रबर rabar *n.* rubber

रबाफ rabāph *n.* excess in living

रम ram *n.* rum

रवाना हुनु ravānā hunu *v.t./v.i.* depart

रविवार ravivār *n.* Sunday

रस ras *n.* juice

रबाना rawānā *n.* departure

रवि ravi *n.* sun

आनन्द लिनु ras linu *v.t.* enjoy

रसायन विज्ञान rasāyan vigyan *n.* chemistry

रसद rasad *n.* pantry, mess *(military)*

रसबरी rasbari *n.* Nepali sweet made from milk products

रसीद rasid *n.* receipt

रसिक rasik *n.* hedonist

रहनु rahanu *v.i.* remain

रहस्य rahasya *n.* mystery

रहर rahar *n.* interest

रहरलाग्दो raharlāgdo *adj.* pleasing

राई rāi *n.* rye

राई rāi *n.* ethnic group of Nepal living in eastern hills

राक्षस raksas *n.* monster

राख rākh *n.* ash

राख्नु rākhnu *v.t.* keep, save, put

राँगो rāngo *n.* buffalo *(male cow)*

राँडी rānd *n.* widow

राजा rājā *n.* monarch

राजकाज rājkāj *n.* state affairs

राजकुमार rājkumār *n.* prince

राजकुमारी rājkumāri *n.* princess

राजगुरु rājguru *n.* royal preceptor

राजगद्दी rājgaddi *n.* throne

राजकीय rājkiya *adj.* royal

राजकोष rājkos *n.* treasury

राजघराना rajgharānā *n.* royal family

राजतन्त्र rājtantrā *n.* monarchy

राजदरवार rājdarbār *n.* royal palace

राजदूत rājdut *n.* ambassador

राजधानी rājdhāni *n.* capital

राजनयिक rājnayik *n.* diplomat

राजनीति rāhniti *n.* politics

राजनीतिशास्त्र rājniti sāstra *n.* political science

राजनीतिज्ञ rājnitigya *n.* politician

राजनीतिकरण rājnitikaran *n.* politicization

राजनेता rājnetā *n.* statesman

राजपत्र rajpatra *n.* gazette

राजपुरोहित rajpurohit *n.* royal priest

राजद्रोह rajdroha *n.* treason

राजस्व rājaswa *n.* revenue

राजनैतिक rājnaitik *adj.* political

राजभवन rājbhavan *n.* place

राजहंस rājhans *n.* swan

राजपथ rājpath *n.* highway

राजसी rājsi *adj.* majestic

राजीनामा गर्नु rajināmā garnu *v.i.* resign

राजीनामा rajināma *n.* resignation

राज्य rājya *n.* kingdom

राज्यसिंहासन rājyasimhāsan *n.* royal throne

राज्यरोहण rājyārohan *n.* enthronement

राज्याभिषेक rājyābhisek *n.* coronation

राज्यपाल rājyapāl *n.* governor

राज्यसभा rājyasabhā *n.* upper house of Indian Parliament

राणा rānā *n.* name of oligarchy ruling Nepal for a century

राती rāti *n.* night

राती भरी rāti bhari *adv.* overnight

रात को खाना rāt ko khānā *n.* supper

रातो rāto *adj.* red

रातो पान्डा rāto pāndā *n.* red panda

रानी rāni *n.* queen

रामतोरियाँ rāmtoriyan *n.* okra, ladyfinger

रामवाण rāmbān *n.* effective medicine

राम्रो rāmro *adj.* good

राम्ररी rāmrari *adv.* effectively

राय rāy *n.* opinion

रायो rāyo *n.* mustard

राष्ट्र rāstra *n.* nation
राष्ट्रीय rāstriy *adj.* national
राष्ट्रीय जनावर rāstriy janāwar *n.* national animal
राष्ट्रीय झन्डा rāstriy jhandā *n.* national flag
राष्ट्रीय निकुञ्ज rāstriy nikunja *n.* national park
राष्ट्रीय फूल rāstriy phul *n.* national flower
राष्ट्रीयता rāstriyatā *n.* nationality
राष्ट्रपति rāstrapati *n.* president
राक्षस rāksyas *n.* demon
राष्ट्रभाषा rāstrabhāsa *n.* national language
राष्ट्रबैंक rastrabank *n.* central bank
राष्ट्रसेवक rāstrasevak *n.* government officials
राष्ट्रगान rāstragān *n.* national anthem
राष्ट्रमण्डल rāstramandal *n.* commonwealth
राष्ट्रवाद rāstravād *n.* nationalism
राष्ट्रवादी rāstravādi *adj.* nationalist
राष्ट्रसंघ rāstrasangha *n.* League of Nations
राष्ट्रीयकरण rāstriyakaran *n.* nationalization
राष्ट्रीयता rāstriyatā *n.* nationality
राहदानी rāhadāni *n.* passport
राइफल rāifal *n.* rifle
राशन rāsan *n.* nation
राशी rāsi *adj.* mass
राशी चक्र rāsi cakr *n.* zodiac
रासायनिक rāsāynik *adj.* chemical
रासायनिक पदार्थ rāsāyanik padārth *n.* chemical
रिकापी rikāpi *n.* saucer
रीम rim *n.* ream
रिक्त rikta *adj.* vacant

रिस ris *n.* anger
रिक्सा riksā *n.* rickshaw
रिसाउनु risāunu *v.i.* get angry
रिस ris *n.* anger
रितिथिति ritithiti *n.* customs
रितो ritto *adj.* empty
रिन rukho *n.* debt
रिझ righ *n.* liking
रुनु runu *v.* cry
रुख rukh *n.* tree
रुखो rukho *adj.* rough
रुघा rugh *n.* flu
रुपान्तरण rupāntaran *n.* transformation
रुमाल rumāl *n.* handkerchief
रुचि ruci *n.* liking
रेखा rekha *n.* line
रेखाचित्र rekhācitra *n.* graph
रेखांकित गर्नु rekhānkit garnu *v.t.* underline
रेडियो rediyo *n.* radio
रेडियो स्टेशन redio stesan *n.* radio station
रेस्तराँ restarām *n.* restaurant
रेलिंग reling *n.* railing
रेल पटरी rel patari *n.* railway
रेलगाडी relgāri *n.* train
रेलवे relve *n.* railroad
रेशम resam *n.* silk
रैल raili *n.* rally
रोक rok *n.* stop, restriction
रोक्नु roknu *v.t.* stop
रोकी राख्नु roki rakhnu *v.t.* withhold
रोकेट roket *n.* rocket
रोक्नु roknu *v.t.* restrain
रोकथाम rokthām *n.* prevention
रोकटोक roktok *n.* obstruction
रोग rog *n.* disease
रोगन rogan *n.* polish

रोगी rogi *n.* patient

रोगाहा rogaha *adj.* sickly

रोगमुक्ति rogmukti *n.* cure

रोचक rocak *adj.* interesting

रोज roj *n.* day

रोजगार rojgar *n.* employment, work

रोजगारी rojgāri *n.* employment

रोजाई rojāi *n.* selection

रोज्नु rojnu *v.* select

रोगाणु नष्ट गर्नु rogānu nast garnu *v.t.* disinfect

रोगाणुनाशक rogānunāsak *n.* disinfectant

रोटी roti *n.* bread

रोडा rodā *n.* concrete

रोदीघर rodighar *n.* dancehall in western hills of Nepal

रोप्नु ropnu *v.* sow

रोपनी ropani *n.* measure of land

रोपाई ropāin *n.* rice planting

रुनु runu *v.i.* cry, weep

रोब rob *n.* dignity, prestige

रोष ros *n.* rage

रौं raun *n.* hair

रौनक raunak *n.* elegance, grace

ल

लँगडो langado *adj.* lame
लंगर langar *n.* anchor
लंबाई lambāi *n.* length
लखपति lakhpati *n.* millionaire
लक्ष्य laksay *n.* goal
लक्षण laksan *n.* symptom, characteristic
लक्षित lakshit *adj.* designated
लक्ष्मी lakshmi *n.* goddess of wealth
लक्ष्य lakshya *n.* aim, target
लगभग lagbhag *adv.* nearly, about, approximate
लगत lagat *n.* list
लागी राख्नु lāgi rākhnu *v.t.* persist
लगाम lagām *n.* mouthpiece
लगाउनु lagāunu *v.t.* install; spread
लगानी lagāni *n.* investment
लगातार lagātār *adv.* continuously
लचिलो lacilo *adj.* flexible
लज्जित lajjit *adj.* ashamed
लज्जालु lajjalu *adj.* shy
लज्जा lajjā *n.* shame
लट lat *n.* strand
लडाई larāi *n./v.t.* battle
लडाकु larāku *adj.* militant
लचक lacak *n.* flexibility
लड्नु ladnu *v.t./v.i.* fight
लडाइँ ladāin *n.* battle
लड्डु laddu *n.* sweet
लघु laghu *adj.* mini
लत lat *n.* bad habit
लचिलो lacilo *adj.* flexible
लट्ठा lattā *n.* log
लजालु lajālu *adj.* shy
लम्फु lamphu *n.* fool

लज्जा lajjā *n.* shame
लस्सी lassi *n.* yogurt drink
लब्ध labdha *adj.* received
लसपस laspas *n.* illicit sexual relationship
लसुन lasun *n.* garlic
लक्षण laksan *n.* symptom
लक्ष्य laksya *n.* target
लक्षित laksit *adj.* targeted
लक्ष्मी laksmi *n.* goddess of wealth, consort of Vishnu
लगत lagat *n.* list
गभग lagbhag *adv.* almost
लहर lahar *n.* wave
लट्ठ lattha *adj.* intoxicated
लट्ठी latthi *n.* stick
लांच lānc *n.* launch
लाइवेरी laibreri *n.* library
लाइन lāin *n.* line
लाइसेंस lāisens *n.* license
लाउडस्पीकर lāudspikar *n.* loudspeaker
लाकर lākar *n.* locker
लाख lakh *num.* one hundred thousand
लागत lāgat *n.* cost
लागु पदार्थ lāgu padārtha *n.* intoxicant
लागू गर्नु lāgu garnu *v.t.* implement
लागू हुनु lāgu hunu *v.t.* apply
लाटरी lātari *n.* raffle
लम्बाई lambāi *n.* length
लाटो lāto *n.* dumb
लाटोकोसेरो lāto kosero *n.* owl
लाचार lācār *adj.* helpless

लाज lāj *n.* shame

लाजमर्दो lājmardo *adj.* shameful

लादनु lādnu *v.t.* load

लाबी lābi *n.* lobby

लामखुट्टे lāmkhutte *n.* mosquito

लाभ lābh *n.* profit, gain

लाभ पुर्‍याउने lābh puryāunun. *v.t.* benefit

लाभदायक lābhdāyak *adj.* beneficial

लाभप्रद lābhprad *adj.* profitable

लाभांस lābhāms *n.* dividend

लाभान्वित lābhānwit *adj.* benefited

लापरवाह lā-parvāh *adj.* careless

लापरवाही lā-parvāhi *n.* negligence

लामो lāmo *adj.* long

लाल lāl *adj.* red, inflamed

लालपुर्जा lālpurjā *n.* landowners certificate, deed

लालमोहर lālmohar *n.* royal decree

लालच lālach *n.* greed

लाल वाइन lāl vāin *n.* red wine

लालटेन lālten *n.* lantern

लालीगुराँस lāligurāns *n.* rhododendron

लायक lāyak *adj.* suitable

लाश lās *n.* corpse

लाश जाँच lāsjānch *n.* autopsy

लाहुरे lāhure *n.* Gurkha soldier

लै जानु lai jānu *v.t.* carry

लिनु linu *v.t.* take

लिखत likhat *n.* written

लिंग ling *n.* penis; sex

लिम्बु limbu *n.* ethnic group of Nepal living in eastern hills

लेख्नु lekhnu *v.t.* write

लिची lichi *n.* litchi, lychee

लिपि lipi *n.* script

लिफ्ट lift *n.* elevator

लुक्नु luknu *n.* robber

लुगा lugā *n.* dress

लुटेरा luterā *n.* robber

लुब्ध lubdha *adj.* greedy

लुरे lure *adj.* weak, coward

लु लाग्नु lu lagnu *v.t.* to get heatstroke

लूट lut *n.* robbery

लूटनु lutnu *v.t.* rob

लुटिनु lutinu *v.i.* be robbed

लै जानु le jā *v.t.* take

लेक lek *n.* highland

लेक लाग्नु lek lagnu *v.* get altitude sickness

लेख lekh *n.* article

लेखा lekhā *n.* audit

लेख्नु lekhnu *v.* write

लेखक lekhak *n.* writer

लेखकस्व lekhakaswa *n.* royalty

लेखन सामाग्री lekhan sāmagri *n.* stationery

लेखपढ lekhpadh *n.* reading and writing

लेखा lekhā *n.* accounting

लेखाजोखा lekhājokhā *n.* evaluation

लेखापाल lekhāpāl *n.* accountant

लेखा परीक्षक lekhā pariksak *n.* auditor

लेजर lezar *n.* laser

लेनदार lendār *n.* creditor

लेन-देन गर्नु len-den garnu *v.t.* deal

लेन्स lens *n.* lens

लेबल lebal *n.* tag

लेबल लगाउनु lebal lagāunu *v.t.* label

लैंगिकता laingik *n.* sexuality

लैङ्गिक laingiktā *n.* gender

लैटिन laintin *n.* Latin

लोक lok *n.* world

लोकतांत्रिक lokatantrik *adj.*
  democratic
लोककथा lokkathā *n.* folktale
लोक गीत lok git *n.* folk song
लोकतंत्र loktantra *n.* democracy
लोकतांत्रिक koltantrik *adj.*
  democratic
लोक नृत्य loknritya *n.* folk dance
लोकप्रिय lokpriya *adj.* popular
लोकप्रियता lokpriyatā *n.*
  popularity
लोकसभा lok sabhā *n.* lower house
  of Indian parliament
लोक सेवा आयोग lok sewā āyog
  n. public service commission
लोक समिति loksamiti *n.* popular
  consent
लोग्ने logne *n.* husband
लोकनृत्य loknritya *n.* folk dance
लोचन locan *n.* eye
लोप हुनु lop hunu *v.* disappear
लोभ lobh *n.* greed
लोभी lobhi *adj.* greedy
लौकिक laukik *adj.* secular
ल्याप्चे lyapce *n.* thumbprint
ल्वाँङ lwāng *n.* clove

व

वन्दना vandanā *n.* prayer

वकील vakil *n.* lawyer

वकालत vakālat *n.* pleading

वक्रता vakratā *n.* curve

वक्र vakra *n.* bend

वक्तव्य vaktabya *n.* speech

वक्ता vaktā *n.* speaker

वखत vakhat *n.* time

वर्ग varg *n.* square

वर्ग varg *n.* class

वर्ग किलोमिटर varga kilomitar *n.* square kilometer

वर्ग विभाजन varga division *n.* class division

वर्ग सङ्घर्ष varga sangharsha *n.* class struggle

वर्गाकार vargākār *adj.* square

वर्गीकरण गर्नु argirkaran garnu *v.t.* classify

वचन vacan *n.* speech; word

वचन दिनु vacan dinu *v.t.* undertake; give word

वर्जित varjit *adj.* forbidden

वज्रयान vajrayān *n.* sect in Buddhism practiced by Tibetans

वजन vajan *n.* weight

वतन vatan *n.* address

वडा wadā *n.* ward

वन van *n.* forest

वनस्पति vanaspati *n.* vegetation

वनभोज vanbhoj *n.* picnic

वन्य उत्पादन vanya utpādan *n.* forest product

वन्यजन्तु vanya jantu *n.* wild animals

वफादार vafādār *adj.* loyal

वयस्क vyask *n.* adult

वर var *n.* boon

वरदान vardān *n.* boon

वरिष्ठ varistha *adj.* senior

वरिष्ठ नागरिक varistha nāgarik *n.* senior citizen

वरिष्ठ अधिवक्ता varistha adhivakta *n.* senior advocate

वर्णमाला varnamālā *n.* alphabet

वर्णन varnan *n.* description

वर्णनात्मक varnanātmak *adj.* descriptive

वर्णन गर्नु varnan garnu *v.t.* narrate

वर्णनीय varnaniya *adj.* worthy of description

वर्तमान vartamān *n./adj.* present

वर्दी vardi *n.* uniform

वस्त्र vastra *n.* dress

वरिपरि varipari *adv.* around

वसंत vasant *n.* spring (season)

वसंत पंचमी vasant pancami *n.* spring festival celebrated in Nepal in late February

वस्तु vastu *n.* object

वस्तुगत vastugat *adj.* objective

वस्तु भाउ vastu bhāu *n.* cattle

वस्तुस्थिति vastusthiti *n.* state of affairs

वस्तुत vastut *adj.* virtual

वसीयत vasiyat *n.* will

वश मा गर्नु vas mā garnu *v.t.* control, subdue

वर्षा varshā *n.* rainy season

वहाँ vahān *adv.* yonder

वांछनीय vāncniya *adj.* desirable

वाइरस vāiras n. virus
वाउचर vāucar n. voucher
वाक्य vākya n. sentence
वाक्यांश vākyāns n. phrase
वाक्यविन्यास vākyavinyās n. syntax
वाचा vācā n. vow
वाटिका vātikā n. small garden
वाणी vāni n. speech
वाट vāt n. watt
वाणिज्य vānijy n. commerce
वातावरण vātāvaran n. environment
वाद-विवाद vād-vivād n. controversy
वादक vādak n. player
वादा vādā n. promise
वादा गर्नु vādā garnu v.t. promise
वादी vādi n. suitor
वान्ता vāntā n. vomiting
वानर vānar n. monkey
वाम vām adj. left
वामपन्थी vāmpanthi adj. leftist
वायलिन vāylin n. violin
वायविय vāyviy adj. aerial
वायु vāyu n. air
वायुमंडल vāyumandal n. atmosphere
वायु सेना vāyu sena n. air force
वायु सेवा vāyu sevā n. air service
वायुयान vāyuyān n. airplane
वारंट vārant n. warrant
वारनिश vārnis n. varnish
वारिस vāris n. heir, legal representative
वारिसनामा varisnāmā n. power of attorney
वार्ता vārtā n. negotiation
वार्तालाप vārtālāp n. conversation
वासना vāsana n. smell
वार्षिक varsik adj. yearly

वार्षिक परिक्षा vārsik pariksā n. annual examination
वार्षिक प्रतिवेदन vārsik prativedan n. annual report
वार्षिक सभा vārsik sabha n. annual function
वार्षिकोत्सव vārsikotsav n. anniversary
वाल्व vālv n. valve
वासस्थान vāsasthān n. residency
वासी vāsi n. resident
वास्तव मा vāstav mā adv. indeed, in fact
वास्तविक vāstavik adj. actual
वास्तविकता vāstaviktā n. reality
वास्ता vāstā n. concern
वास्तुकला vāstukalā n. architecture
वास्तुकार vāstukār n. architect
वास्तुशिल्पीय vāstusilpiy adj. architectural
वाहक vāhak n. transporter
वाहन vāhan n. transport
वाहियात vāhiyāt n. nonsense
विकर्ण vikarn adj. diagonal
विकट vikat adj. inaccessible
विकल्प vikalpa n. alternative
विकलांग viklāng adj. handicapped
विकसित गर्नु viksit garnu v.t. develop
विकल्प vikalpa n. option
विकल्परहित vikalpa rahit adj. without alternative
विकास vikās n. development
विकसित vikasit adj. developed
विकासशील vikāssil adj. developing
विकेन्द्रीकरण vikendrikaran n. decentralization
विकासमूलक vikāsmulak adj. interested in development

विकृत गर्नु vikrit garnu *v.t.* distort

विक्री vikri *n.* sale

विक्रीकर vikrikar *n.* sales tax

विक्रेता vikretā *n.* seller

विखण्डन vikhandan *n.* fragmentation

विख्यात vikhyāt *adj.* famous

विघटन vighatan *n.* dissolution

विचलन vicalan *n.* deviation

विचार vicār *n.* thought

विचारक vicārak *n.* thinker

विचार गर्नु vicār garnu *v.t.* consider

विचार-विमर्श vicār-vimars *n.* discussion

विचारगोष्ठी vicar-gosthi *n.* seminar

विचाराधीन vicarādhin *adj.* under consideration

विचरण vicāran *n.* trial

विचारणीय vicāraniya *adj.* thought provoking

विचित्र vicitra *adj.* strange, unusual

विच्छेद vicchod *n.* separation

विच्छेदन vicchedan *n.* amputation

विजय vijay *n.* win

विजय सिद्धि vijay siddhi *n.* victory column

विजया दशमी vijayā dasami *n.* Dasain festival celebrated in Nepal in October

विजयी हुनु vijay hunu *v.t.* conquer

विजयी vijayi *adj.* victorious

विजेता vijetā *n.* winner

विज्ञ vigya *n./adj.* learned

विज्ञप्ति vigyapti *n.* announcement

विज्ञापन vigyāpan *n.* advertisement, commercial

विज्ञान vigyān *n.* science

भिटामिन vitāmin *n.* vitamin

वित्त मन्त्री vitta mantri *n.* minister of finance

वित्त vitta *n.* finance

वित्तिय vittiya *adj.* financial

वितरक vitarak *n.* distributor

वितरण vitaran *n.* distribution

वितरण गर्नु vitaran garnu *v.t.* distribute

विडम्बना vidambanā *n.* irony

विदुषक vidusak *n.* clown

विद्या vidyā *n.* learning

विद्यालय vidyālay *n.* school

विद्यावारिधि vidyabaridhi *n.* doctorate

विद्यार्थी vidyārthi *n.* student

विद्यार्थी संगठन vidyarthi sangathan *n.* student union

विद्युत vidyut *n.* electricity

विधुत धारा vidhut dhārā *n.* (electric) current

विधवा vidhvā *n.* widow

विधुर vidhur *n.* widower

विघ्न-डाल्नु vidhn-dālnu *v.t.* hinder

विरुद्ध viruddh *adj.* contrary

विद्रोह virodh *n.* revolt

विद्रोह गर्नु vidroh garnu *v.i.* label

विद्रोही vidrohi *n.* insurgent

विदेश vides *adv.* abroad, overseas

विदेशी videsi *adj.* foreigner

विदेशी videsi *n.* alien

विदेशीमुद्रा videsi mudrā *n.* foreign currency

विदेशी लगानी videsi lagāni *n.* foreign investment

विद्धान vidvān *adj.* learned

विद्ववातवृत्ति vidwatvritti *n.* fellowship

विधिसम्मत vidhisammat *adj.* lawful

विधवा vidhwa *n.* widow

विधान vidwatvritti *n.* bylaws

विधानसभा vidhān sabhā *n.* legislature

विधायक vidhāyak *n.* legislator

विधवा विवाह vidwā vivāh *n.* re-marriage of a widow

विधुर vidhur *n.* legislator

विनाश vinās *n.* disaster, ruin

विनायक vināyak *n.* Hindu god Ganesh

विनिमय vinimay *n.* exchange

विनियम viniyam *n.* bylaws

विनित vinit *adj.* humble

विनम्र vinamra *adj.* polite

विनोदी vinodi *adj.* witty

विनोद vinod *n.* entertainment

विपत्ति vipatti *n.* distress

विपक्ष vipaksa *n.* opposite

विपक्षी vipaksi *n.* opponent

विपत्ती vipatti *n.* disaster

विपरीत viparit *adj.* opposite

विभाग vibhāg *n.* department

विभागीय vibhāgiya *adj.* departmental

विभाजन vibājan *n.* partition

विभाजित vibhajit *adj.* divided

विभिन्न रुप vibājan rup *n.* variation

विभिन्न vibhinna *adj.* separate

विभिन्नता vibhinnata *n.* difference

विमत vimat *n.* different option

विमान vimān *n.* airplane

विमानशाला vimānsala *n.* hangar

विमान स्थल vimān sthal *n.* airport

विमोचन vimocan *n.* making public

विराम virām *n.* pause

विराचित viracit *adj.* written

विरामचिन्ह लगाउनु virāmcinh lagāunu *v.t.* punctuate

विरामचिन्ह-विधान virāmcinh-vidhān *n.* punctuation

विरोध virodh *n.* opposite

विरोध गर्नु virodh garnu *v.t.* oppose, resist, object

विरोधी virodhi *adj.* resistant

विरुद्ध viruddha *adj.* against

विलाप vilāp *n.* crying

विलम्ब vilamba *n.* delay

विलम्व शुल्क vilamba sulka *n.* delay penalty

विलय vilaya *n.* merger

घुल्ने vilāyak *n.* solvent

विलास vilās *n.* pleasure

विकासी vilāsi *adj.* luxurious

विवरण vivaran *n.* description

विवाद vivād *n.* dispute

विवादग्रस्त vivādgrasta *adj.* controversial

विवाह vivāh *n.* marriage

विवाह विच्छेद vivāh vicched *n.* divorce

विवाहित vivāhit *adj.* married

विविध vividh *adj.* separate

विवेक vivek *n.* wisdom

विवेकी viveki *adj.* discriminating

विवेकशील viveksil *adj.* rational

विशद visad *adj.* vivid

विशिष्ट visista *adj.* special

विशाटश्रेणी visistasreni *n.* special class

विशाल visāl *adj.* immense

विशुद्ध visudhd *adj.* neat

विशेष vises *adj.* special, particular

विशेषण visesan *n.* adjective

विशेषता visestā *n.* trait

विशेषता visestā *adj.* characteristic

विशेषज्ञ visesagya *n.* specialist

विशेषाधिकार visesādhikār *n.* privilege

विश्लेषण vislesan *n.* analysis

विक्षेषण गर्नु vislesan garnu *v.t.* analyze

विश्व viswa *n.* universe

विश्व खाद्य कार्यक्रम viswa khādya kāryakram *n.* world food program

विश्व जलवायु विज्ञान संस्था viswa jalbāyu vigyan samstha *n.* World Meterological Organization

विश्व बैंक viswa bank *n.* World Bank

विश्वकोश viswakos *n.* encyclopedia

विश्वविख्यात viswavikhyāt *adj.* world famous

विश्वविद्यालय viswavdyālaya *n.* university

विश्वव्यापी viswavyāpi *adj.* worldwide

विश्व-संवन्ध viswa sambandha *n.* global relations

विश्व-संबंधी viswa-sambandhi *adj.* global

विश्वस्त visvasta *adj.* trustworthy

विश्व स्वास्थ्य संगठन viswa swāstha sangathan *n.* World Health Organization

विश्वसनीय visvāsniy *adj.* faithful

विश्वास visvās *n.* faith, trust

विश्वसनीय visvasniya *adj.* trustworthy

विश्वासघात गर्नु visvāsghāt garnu *v.t.* betray

विश्वासघाती visvāsghāti *n.* traitor

विश्वास गर्नु visvās garnu *v.t.* believe, trust

विश्वास दिलाउनु visvās dilāunu *v.t.* assure

विश्राम vistām *n.* rest

विश्राम-कक्ष visrām-kaksa *n.* lounge

विषमता visamtā *n.* contrast

विषय visay *n.* subject

विषयवस्तु visayvastu *n.* content

विषयक्षेत्र visaykestra *n.* scope

विषाक्त visākt *adj.* septic

विषाणु visānu *adj.* viral

विषाक्त हुनु visākt hunu *adj.* septic

विषुवत रेखा visukt rekhā *n.* equator

विस्तार vistār *n.* extension

विस्तारित vistārit *adj.* spread out

विस्तृत vistrit *adj.* large

विस्मय vismaya *n.* astonishment

विस्मयकारी vismaykāri *adj.* amazing

विहार vihār *n.* walking for pleasure, strolling

विस्फोट visphot *n.* explosion

विस्फोटक visphotak *n.* explosive

विस्फोटन हुनु visphotan hunu *v.* explode

विस्मय vismaya *n.* surprise

विज्ञान vigyān *n.* science

विज्ञापन vigyāpan *n.* commercial

विज्ञापन गर्नु vigyāpan garnu *v.t.* advertise

वीज vij *n.* seed

वीजा visā *n.* visa

वीणा vinā *n.* harp

वीरता virata *n.* heroism

विर्य virya *n.* semen

वीर vir *n.* hero

वृक्ष vriksa *n.* tree

वृक्षारोपण vriksāropan *n.* planting of trees

विरोचित virocit *adj.* heroic

वृतान्त vrittanta *n.* detailed description

वृद्ध vriddha *adj.* elderly

वृहत vrihat *adj.* large

वेचैन vecain *adj.* impatient

वेद veda *n.* Veda *(a sacred Hindu scripture)*

वेदना vednā *n.* anguish

वेदान्त vedānta *n.* study of the Vedas (Hinduism)

वेदी vedi *n.* altar

वेधशाला vedhsālā *n.* observatory

वेबसाईट vecsāit *n.* website

वेश्या vecsyā *n.* prostitute

वेष ves *n.* disguise

वैकल्पिक vaikalpik *adj.* optional

वैवाहिक vaivāhik *adj.* matrimonial

वैदिक vaidik *n./adj.* related to Vedas

वैशिष्ट्य vaisistya *n.* speciality

वैशाख vaisākh *adj.* first month of Nepali calendar beginning in mid-April

वैज्ञानिक vaigyānik *n.* scientist

वैद्य vaidy *n.* physician

वैध vaidha *adj.* legitimate

वैधता vaidhtā *n.* legitimacy

वैधानिक vaidhānik *adj.* constitutional

वैमनस्य vaimanasya *n.* enmity, hostility toward someone

वैनिला vainilā *n.* vanilla

वोट दिनु vot dinu *n./v.i.* vote

वोल्ट volt *n.* volt

व्यक्ति vyakti *n.* person, individual

व्यग्र vyagra *adj.* distraction

व्यक्तिगत vyaktigat *adj.* individual, personal, private

व्यक्तित्व vyaktitva *n.* personality, individuality

व्याकरण vyākaran *n.* grammar

व्याख्या vyākhyā *n.* explanation

व्याख्यान vyākhān *n.* lecture

व्यंग्य vyagy *n.* irony, satire

व्यंग्यात्मक vyangyātmak *adj.* ironic

व्यंजन vyanjān *n.* consonant

व्यवहार vyavyahār *n.* treatment

व्यवहारिक vyavahārik *adj.* practical

व्यवहारकौशल vyavahārkausal *adj.* tactful

व्यवहारकुशल vyavahārkusal *adj.* tactful

व्यवस्थान vyabasthān *n.* management

व्यवस्थापक vyabasthapāk *n.* manager

व्यवस्थित vyavasthit *adj.* systematic

व्यवस्थित गर्नु vyavasthit garnu *v.t.* arrange

व्यवसाय vyavasāy *n.* profession

व्यवसायी vyavasayi *n.* businessman

व्यभिचार vyabhicār *n.* bad character

व्यभिचारी vyabhicāri *adj.* having bad character

व्यस्त vyast *adj.* busy

व्यस्तता vyastatā *n.* engagement

व्यय vyaya *n.* expenditure

व्याख्या vyākhyā *n.* explanation

व्याधि vyādhi *n.* disease

व्यापक vyāpak *adj.* widespread

व्यापार vyāpāir *n.* business, trade

व्यापार गर्नु vyāpār garnu *v.t.* trade

व्यापारिक संस्था vyāpārik samstha *n.* commercial organization

व्यापारी vyāpāri *n.* merchant

व्यापारी माल vyāpāri māl *n.* merchandise

व्यायाम vyāyām *n.* exercise

व्यायामशाला vyāyāmsālā *n.* gymnasium

व्यायामी vyāyāmi *n.* athlete

व्यावसायिक vyāvasāyik *adj.*
  professional

व्यवहारिक vyāvahārik *adj.*
  practical

व्यास vyās *n.* diameter

व्रत vrat *n.* fast; vow

व्रत लिनु vrat linu *v.t.* vow

श

शक्ति sakti *n.* power, energy

शक्तिशाली saktisāli *adj.* powerful

शटल गाडी satal gāri *n.* shuttle

शताब्दी satābdi *n.* century

शतपद satpad *n.* centipede

शत्रु satru *n.* enemy

शत्रुता satrutā *n.* enmity

शात्रिक sāstrik *n.* jellyfish

शनिवार sanivār *n.* Saturday

शपथ sapath *n.* oath

शपथग्रहण sapathgrahan *n.* taking oath

शब्द sabd *n.* word

शब्दकोश sabdkos *n.* dictonary

शब्दावली sabdāvali *n.* vocabulary

शम्बूक sambuk *n.* scallop

शरण saran *n.* refuge, shelter

शरणार्थी sarnārthi *n.* refugee

शरणार्थी शिविर sarnārthi sibir *n.* refugee camp

शरण-स्थान saran-sthān *n.* sanctuary

शरबत satbat *n.* sweet drink

शरद sarad *n.* autumn

शरम saram *n.* shyness

शराब sarāb *n.* liquor

शराबी sarābi *n.* alcoholic

शरीर sarir *n.* body

शरीर विज्ञान sarir vigyān *n.* physiology

शर्त sart *n.* bet

शर्त लगाउनु sart lagāunu *v.t.* bet

शव sav *n.* dead body

शव-कक्ष sav-kaks *n.* vault

शव-परीक्षा sav-pariksā *n.* autopsy

शल्यचिकित्सा salycikitsā *n.* surgery

शल्यचिकित्सक salyacikitsak *n.* surgeon

शस्त्र sāstra *n.* weapon

शस्त्रागार sastragār *n.* armory

शस्त्रधारी sastradhāri *adj.* armed

शहर sahar *n.* city

शहरीया sahariyā *n.* urban dweller

शहीद sahid *n.* martyr

शहीद दिवस sahid diwas *n.* martyr's day in late January

शहीद स्मारक sahid smārak *n.* martyr's memorial

शाकाहारी sākākāri *n./adj.* vegetarian

शाकाहार sākākār *n.* vegeterian food

शाखा sākha *n.* section

शाखा अधिकृत sakhā adhikrit *n.* section officer

शानदार sāndār *adj.* magnificent

शान्त sānt *adj.* sedated

शान्ति sānti *n.* peace

शान्ति क्षेत्र sānti ksetra *n.* zone of peace

शन्तिपूर्वक santi purvak *adv.* peacefully

शान्तिपूर्ण sāntipurn *adj.* peaceful

शान्तिप्रिय santipriya *adj.* peace loving

शान्तिसन्धी sāntisandhi *n.* peace treaty

शान्तिवार्ता santivārtā *n.* peace talks

शाप दिनु sāp dinu *v.t.* curse
शाब्दिक sābdik *adj.* verbal
शाम sām *n.* evening
शामिल गर्नु sāmil garnu *v.t.* include
शायद sāyad *adv.* perhaps
शारीरिक sāririk *adj.* physical
शायर sāyar *n.* poet
शाल sāl *n.* shawl
शावर sāvar *n.* shower
शारिरिक saririk *adj.* concerning human body
शासक sāsak *n.* administrator
शासन sāsan *n.* regime, administrator
शासन गर्नु sāsan garnu *v.t.* rule, govern
शाश्वत sāswat *adj.* eternal
शासनपत्र sāsanpatra *n.* charter
शास्त्र sāstra *n.* book on religion
शास्त्रार्थ sastrartha *n.* discussion
शास्त्रीय sāstriy *adj.* classical
शाही sāhi *adj.* royal
शाही घोषणा sāhi ghosanā *n.* royal proclamation
शाही परिवार sāhi parivār *n.* royal family
शाही आयोग sāhi āyog *n.* royal commission
शिकार sikār *n.* victim
शिकारी sikāri *n.* hunter
शिकायत sikāyat *n.* grievance
शिक्षा siksā *n.* education
शिक्षाध्यक्ष siksādaksa *n.* rector
शिक्षा मन्त्रालय siksā mantrālaya *n.* Education Ministry
शिक्षा मन्त्री siksā mantri *n.* Education Minister
शिक्षा दिनु siksā dinu *v.t.* instruct
शिक्षा-संबन्ध siksā-sambandh *adj.* educational

शिक्षित siksit *adj.* educator
शिक्षक siksak *n.* school teacher
शिक्षण siksan *n.* teaching
शिक्षण अस्पताल siksan aspatāl *n.* teaching hospital
शिखर sikhar *n.* summit
शिखर सम्मेलन sikhar sammelan *n.* summit conference
शिखा sikhā *n.* crest
शिथिल sithil *adj.* weak, loose
शिल्प silpa *n.* craft
शिव Siva *n.* Hindu god Siva (*aka* Shiva)
शिवपुरी sivpuri *n.* mountain
शिवरात्री sivarātri *n.* Siva's birthday (*festival celebrated in February*)
शिवलिक Sivālik *n.* Himalayan southern hills
शिर Sir *n.* head
शिरोमणि siromani *n.* crown jewel
शिल्पी slip *n.* handicraft
शिलन्यास silānyās *v.* lay the foundation of a building
शिला लेख silā lekh *n.* inscription
शिल्पकृति silpi *n.* craftsman
शिविर sivir *n.* camp
शिविर राख्नु sivir rākhnu *v.i.* camp
शिशु sisu *n.* child
शिरीश sirish *n.* mimosa flower
शिष्ट sist *adj.* polite
शिष्टता sistata *n.* politeness
शिष्टाचार sistācār *n.* courtesy
शिष्टमंडल sistmandal *n.* mission
शिष्य sisya *n.* student, disciple
शीतदंश sitadans *n.* frostbite
शीतल sital *adj.* cool
शीतलहरी sitalahari *n.* cold wave
शीशा sisā *n.* glass
शीशी sisi *n.* vial
शीर्ष sirs *adj.* topmost

शीर्षक sirsak *n.* headline
शीर्षस्थ sirsastha *adj.* topmost
शुक्रवार sukrvār *n.* Friday
शुक्राणु sukrānu *n.* semen
शुद्ध suddh *adj.* pure
शुद्धि suddhi *n.* purity
शुद्ध गर्नु suddh garnu *v.t.* purify
शुद्धिकरण suddhikaran *n.* purification
शुरु suru *n.* beginning
शुरु हुनु suru hunu *v.i.* commence
शुरु गर्नु suru garnu *v.i.* begin
शुभ subh *adj.* auspicious, lucky
शुभकामना subhkāmnā *n.* good wishes
शुभचिन्तक subhacintak *n.* wellwisher
शुभारंभ subhārambha *n.* good beginning
शुभेच्छा subheecha *n.* best wishes
शुल्क sulk *n.* fee
शुष्क suska *adj.* dry
शून्य sunya *num./adj.* zero, void
शून्य स्थान sunya sthān *n.* vacuum
शून्यता sunyatā *n.* vaccum, void
शूद्र sudra *n.* lowest class
शूरता suratā *n.* courage
शूरवीर survir *adj.* valiant
शेयर दलाल seyar dalāl *n.* stockbroker
शेयर बजार seyar bāzār *n.* stock market
शेष ses *adj.* remaining
शेष ses rakhnu *n./adj.* remainder
शेष राख्नु ses rakhnu *v.i.* remain
शैक्षिक saksik *adj.* educational
शैक्षिक भ्रमण saisik bhraman *n.* educational tour
शैंपू saimpu *n.* shampoo
शैतान saitān *n.* devil

शैली saili *n.* style
शोक sok *n.* sorrow
शोक काव्य sok kavya *n.* tragedy
शोक पुस्तिका sok pustikā *n.* condolence book
शोक सभा sok sabhā *n.* condolence visit
शोक मनाउनु sok manāunu *v.i.* remain
शोच soc *n.* thinking
शोध sodh *n.* research
शोध कर्ता sodhkarta *n.* researcher
शोध गर्नु sodh-garnu *v.t.* research
शोध-प्रबन्ध sodh-prabandh *n.* thesis
शोषक sosak *adj.* exploiter
शोषण sosan *n.* exploitation
शोषित sosit *adj.* exploited
शोभा sobha *n.* beauty
शौचालय saucālay *n.* latrine
शौकीन saukin *n.* yearning, desire
शौकीन saukin *adj.* fashionable
श्रेणी sreni *adj.* graded
श्रोता srotā *n.* listener
श्रोतागण srotāgan *n.* audience
श्रद्धांजली sraddhānjali *n.* tribute
श्रद्धालु sraddhālu *adj.* believing
श्रम sram *n.* labor
श्रम विभाग sram bibhāg *n.* Department of Labor
श्रमविभाजन sram bibhājan *n.* division of labor
श्रमिक sramik *n.* laborer
श्रमिक संघ sramik sangh *n.* union
श्रवण sravan *n.* hearing
श्रव्य sravya *adj.* audible
श्रद्धा sraddhā *n.* devotion
श्राद्ध srāddha *n.* ceremony honoring the dead in Hinduism and Newar Buddhism
श्रद्धान्जली sradānjali *n.* tribute

श्री sri honorific title used before
  a name

श्रीमती srimati Mrs.

श्रीमान srimān *n.* mister, sir

श्रेणी sreni *n.* line, class

श्रोणी sroni *n.* pelvis

श्रोत srot *n.* source

श्रवण sravan *adj.* auditory

श्रय sreya *n.* good fortune

श्रेष्ठ srestha *adj.* best

श्रोता srotā *n.* audience

श्वासनली-शोथ svāsnali-soth *n.*
  bronchitis

श्वासनली svāsnli *n.* trachea

श्वासयंत्र svasyantra *n.* respirator

श्वास निकालनु svās nikālnu *v.i.*
  exhale

ष

षडयंत्र sadyantra *n.* plot
षडयंत्र गर्नु sadyantra racanā *v.t.*
   plot

स

साँस तान्नु sams tānnu *v.t.* inhale

संकुचित sankucit *n.* narrow

संकट sankat *n.* difficulty, crisis

संकटकाल sankatkāl *n.* emergency

संकेत sanket *n.* signal, crisis

संकल्प sannkalp *n.* determination

संकलन sankakan *n.* collection

संकोची sankoci *adj.* shy

संक्रमित हुनु sankramit hunu *v.t.* infect

संकेत sanket *n.* hint

संकेत गर्नु sanket garnu *v.i.* hint

संकेतक sanketak *n.* indicator

संबंध sambandh *v.t.* link, relation

संबोधित गर्नु sambodhan garnu *v.t.* direct

संक्षेपण sanksepan *n.* abbreviation

संक्षेप sanksepan *n.* resume; summary

संक्षिप्त sanksipt *adj.* concise

संक्षिप्त गर्नु sanksipt garnu *v.t.* abbreviate

संख्या sankhyā *n.* number

संगठन sangathan *n.* organization

संगठित गर्नु sangathit garnu *v.t.* organize

संग sanga *adv./adj.* together

संगत sangat *adj.* compatible

संगम sangam *n.* junction

संगमरमर sangmarmar *n.* marble

संगति sangati *n.* companionship

संगीतकार sangitkār *n.* musician

संगीत समारोह sangit samāroh *n.* concert

संग्रह sangraha *n.* collection

संग्रह गर्नु sangrah garnu *v.t.* collect

संग्रह क्रिया sangrah kriyā *n.* collection

संग्रहण sangrahan *n.* storage

संग्रहालय sangrāhalaya *n.* museum

संग्रहणीय sangrahaniya *adj.* to be collected

संघ sangha *n.* union

संघीय sanghiya *adj.* federal

संघर्ष sanghars *n.* struggle

संचय sancaya *n.* collection

संचय कोष sancaya kos *n.* provident fund for employees in an organization (government or private)

संचार मंत्री sancār mantri *n.* Minister of Communication

संचार sancar *n.* communication

संचालक sanchâlak *n.* conductor, operator

संचालन sancâlan *n.* navigation

संचालन गर्नु sancâlan garnu *v.t.* guide, conduct

संचित sancit *adj.* collected

संत Sant *n.* saint

संतुष्टि santusti *n.* satisfaction

संतुष्ट santust *adj.* satisfied

संतुलन santulan *n.* balance

संतोष santos *n.* satisfaction

संतोषी santoshi *n.* satisfied

संतोषजनक santosjanak *adj.* satisfactory

संत्रास santrās *n.* horror

सदस्य sadasya n. member

सदस्यता sadasyata adj. membership

संदिग्ध sandigdha adj. doubtful

संदेश sandes n. errand

संदेशवाहक sandesvāhak n. messenger

संदेहजनक sandehjanak adj. suspicious

संदेह sandeh n. doubt

संदेह गर्नु sandeh garnu v.t. doubt

संदेशबाहक sandesbāhak n. messenger

संधि sandhi n. treaty

संज्ञा sangyā n. noun

संपन्न sampanna n./adj. affluent

संपर्क spars n. contact

संपत्ति sampatti n. property

संपादक sampādak n. editor

संपादन गर्नु sampādan garnu v.t. edit

संपादित sampādit adj. edited

संपूर्ण sanpurna adj. total, entire

संप्रदाय sampradāya n. religious or ethnic group

संबंध sambandh n. relationship

संबंध गर्नु sambandh garnu v.t. associate

संबंध हुनु sambandh hunu v.t. relate, concern

संबन्धित sambandhit adj. related

संबोधन sanbodhan n. address

संवर्द्धक samvardhak n. promoter

संभव sambhav adj. possible

संभावना sambhāvnā n. possibility

संभार sambhār n. maintenance

संभावित sambhābit adj. possible

संयम samyam n. restraint

संयुक्त sanyukta adj. united

संयुक्त परिवार sanyukta parivār n. joint family in which parents live with children

संयुक्त राष्ट्र sanyukt rāstra n. United Nations

संयुक्त राष्ट्र वालकोष samyukta rastra bal kos n. UNICEF

संयुक्त खाता samyukta khāta n. joint account

संयुक्त विज्ञासी samyukta vigyapti n. joint communique

संयुक्त राज्य sanyukta rājya n. United States of America

संयोग sanyog n. combination

संयोजक sanyojak adj. convener, someone convening a meeting or movement

संयोजन sanyonjan n. addition

संयम samyam n. restraint

संयमी sanyami n. temperature

संवैधानिक अदालत sambhaidhānik ādālat n. constitutional court

संवैधानिक राज्यतन्त्र sambhaidhanik rājtantra n. constitutional monarchy

संवैधानिक उपचार sambaidhanik upacār n. constitutional remedy

संरचना sanracanā n. structure

संरक्षण sanranksan n. conservation

संरक्षणविद् sanraksanvid n. conservationist

संरक्षक sanraksak n. patron

संरक्षित sanrakshit adj. protected

संवत् samvat n. year

संलग्न samlagna adj. involved

संवाद sambād n. dialogue

संवाददाता sambāddātā n. reporter

संवाददाता सम्मेलन sambāddātā sammelan n. press conference

संविधान sanvihān n. constitution

संविधान सभा sambidhān sabhā *n.* constitutional assembly

संवैधानिक sambaidānik *adj.* constitutional

संविधान सभासद sambidān sabhāsad *n.* constitutional assembly member

समवेदना sanvednā *n.* condolence

संशोधन sansodhan *n.* amendment

संशोधित sansodhit *adj.* revised

संसद sansad *n.* parliament

संसदीय sansadiy *adj.* parliamentary

संसार sansār *n.* world

संस्कार sanskār *n.* crermony, rite

संस्करण sanskaran *n.* edition

संस्कृत sanskrit *n.* Sanskrit

संस्कृति sanskriti *n.* culture

संस्था sansthā *n.* association

संस्थान sansthān *n.* institute

संस्थापक sansthāpak *n.* founder

संस्मरण sansmaran *n.* memoir

संहार sanhār *n.* destruction

सकनु saknu *v. aux.* can, be able to

सकल sakal *n.* all

सकली sakali *n.* true copy

सकस sakas *n.* difficulty

सकिनु sakinu *v.i.* be finished

सकारात्मक विभेद sakāratmak bibhed *n.* affirmative action

सकारात्मक sakārātmak *adj.* positive

सक्रिय sakriya *adj.* active

सक्रियता sakriyatā *n.* activity

सगोल sagol *adj.* joint

सघन saghan *adj.* dense

सघनता saghantā *n.* density

सघाउ saghāu *n.* help

सचित्र गर्नु sacitra garnu *v.t.* illustrate

सचिव sachiv *n.* secretary

सचिवालय sachivālaya *n.* secretariat

सचेत sacet *adj.* conscious

सचेतक sachetak *n.* whip

सच्चा saccā *adj.* earnest

सच्चाई saccāi *n.* truth

सच्याउनु saccāunu *v.* correct

सच्चाई saccāi *n.* truth, fact

सजग sajag *adj.* vigilant

सजगता sajagatā *n.* vigilance

सजाय sajāya *n.* punishment

सजाउनु sajāunu *v.* decorate

सर्जन sarjan *n.* surgeon

सजाउनु sajāunu *v.t.* decorate

सजावट sajāvat *n.* decoration

सजिलो sajilo *adj.* easy

सजीव sajiv *adj.* lively

सज्जन sajjan *n.* gentleman

सज्जित sajjit *adj.* decorated

सडक sarak *n.* road, street

सड्नु sadnu *v.i.* rot, decay

सडाउनु sadāunu *v.t.* cause to rot

सडेको sadedko *adj.* rotten

सतह satah *n.* surface

सतही sathi *adj.* superficial

सतर्क satark *adj.* watchful

सतर्कता satarkatā *n.* caution

सताउनु satāunu *v.t.* pester

सतार satar *n.* ethnic group

सत्कार satkār *n.* hospitality

सत्कारशील satkārsil *adj.* hospitable

सत्तल sattal *n.* inn for pilgrims

सत्तरी sattari *num.* seventy

सत्ता sattā *n.* power

सत्तारुढ sattarudh *adj.* ruling

सत्तारुढ दल sattārudhdal *n.* ruling party

सत्यानाश satyānās *n.* wreck

सत्याग्रह satyāgraha *n.* civil disobedience

सत्यानाश satyānash *n.* total destruction

सत्यवादी satyavādi *adj.* truthful

सत्य satya *n.* truth

समुद्र पारी samudra pāri *adv.* overseas

सत्र sarak *n.* session

सत्र satra *num.* seventeen

सत्रहौं satrahaun *adj.* seventeenth

सदन sadan *n.* house

सदर sadar *n.* acceptance

सदरमुकाम sadarmukm *n.* district headquarters

सदस्य sadsya *n.* member

सदस्यता sadasyatā *n.* membership

सदुपयोग sadupayog *n.* good use *(such as charity)*, worthwhile cause

सदा sadā *adv.* forever

सदाचार sadācār *n.* good conduct

सधैंको लागि sadhain ko lāgi *adv.* forever

सनक sanak *n.* fad

सनकी sanki *adj.* eccentric

सनाखत sanākhat *n.* identification

सनातन sanātan *adj.* existing from old days

सद्भावना sadbhāvana *n.* goodwill

सधै sadhain *adv.* always

सनक sanak *n.* whim

सनकी sanaki *adj.* whimsical

सन्नाटा sannātā *n.* dead silence

सन्यासी sanyāsi *n.* Hindu holy man

सन्त santa *n.* devotee

सन्तति santati *n.* family

सनातन sanātan *n.* eternal

सन्चो sanco *adj.* well

सन्तुष्ट santusta *adj.* satisfied

सन्तुष्टि santusti *n.* satisfaction

सन्ध्या sandhyā *n.* evening

सन्दर्भ sandharva *n.* context

सन्देश sandesh *n.* message

सन्देह sandeh *adj.* suspicious

सन्धि sandhi *n.* treaty

सपना sapnā *n.* dream

सपरिवार saparivār *adj.* with family (bringing my family along)

सर्प sarpa *n.* snake

सस sapta *num.* seven

ससकोसी saptakosi *n.* seven tributaries of Kosi River

ससाह saptaha *n.* week

ससाहांत saptāhānt *n.* weekend

सप्लाई saplāi *n.* supply

सप्लाई गर्नु saplāi garnu *v.t.* supply

सप्रमाण sapramān *adj.* proven, indisputable

सफलता saphaltā *n.* success

सफलतापूर्वक saphaltāpurvak *n.* accomplishment

सफलतापूर्वक पूरा गर्नु saphaltāpurvak purā garnu *v.t.* accomplish

सफा safā *adj.* clean

सफाई safāi *n.* plea

सफाई को safāi ko *adj.* sanitary

संबन्ध sambandha *adj.* relationship

सब sab *n.* all

सबै sabai *pron.* everything

सब ठाउँ sab thau *adv.* everywhere

सबभन्दा असल sab bhandā asal *adj.* best

सबूत sabut *n.* proof

सब्जी sabzi *n.* vegetable

सभ्य sabhyatā *adj.* civilized

सभापति sabhāpati *n.* chairman

सभा sabhā *n.* assembly, club

सभासद sabhāsad *n.* member of assembly

सभागृह sabhāgriha *n.* assembly hall

सभामुख sabhāmukh *n.* speaker

सभ्यता sabhyatā *n.* civilization

सभ्य sabhya *adj.* civilized

समकक्ष बनाउनु samkaks banāunu *v.t.* coordinate

समकालीन samakālin *adj.* contemporary

समग्र samagra *adj.* entire, all

समझ samajh *n.* understanding

समझदार samajhdār *n.* understanding

समझदारी samajhdāri *n.* understanding

समझौता samjhautā *n.* agreement, settlement, treaty, compromise

समन्वय samanbaya *n.* coordinated

समता samatā *n.* equality

समतल samtal *adj.* smooth

समन samanvaya *n.* summons to court

समर्पण samarpan *n.* dedication

समर्पण गर्नु samarpan garnu *v.t.* dedicate

समर्पित samarpit *adj.* dedicated

समर्थ samarth *adj.* competent

समर्थक samarthak *n.* supporter

समर्थन samarthan *n.* support

समलिंगी samlaingi *n.* homosexual

सम्धी samdhi *n.* father of daughter-in-law or son-in-law

सम्मान sammān *n.* regard

सम्मानजनक sammānjanak *adj.* honorary

सम्मोहन sammohan *n.* fascination; hypnotism

सम्पादक sampādak *n.* editor

सम्पादकीय sampādakiya *n.* editorial

सम्पादित गर्नु sampādit garnu *v.t.* edit

समय samaya *n.* time

समय सरिणी samay sārini *n.* timetable

समयावधि samayābadhi *n.* duration

समय भन्दा अघि samay bhandā aghi *n.* early

समयानुकुल samayanukul *adj.* timely

समन्बय samanvaya *n.* coordination

समर्थक samarthak *n.* supporter

समर्थन samarthan *n.* support

समलैंगिक samalaingik *adj.* gay

समवयस्क samavayaska *adj.* contemporary *(belonging to same age group)*

समवेदना samavedāna *n.* condolence

समस्या samasyā *n.* problem

समस्यामूलक samasyāmulak *adj.* difficult

समाचार samāchār *n.* news

समाचारदाता samācardātā *n.* correspondent

समाचारपत्र samāchārpatr *n.* newspaper

समाचारस्रोत samācarsrot *n.* source of news

समाज samāj *n.* association

समाजवाद samājvād *n.* socialism

समाजवादी samājvādi *n.* socialist

समाजशास्त्र samajsāstra *n.* social sciences

समाधान samādhān *n.* solution

समाधि samādhi *n.* profound meditation

समान samān *adj.* alike, equal

समान बनाउनु samān banāunu *v.t.* equalize

सामान राख्नु samān rakhnu *v.t.* stock

समानता samāntā *n.* similarity

समास गर्नु samāpth garnu *v.t.* consume

समानुपातिक samānupātik *adj.* proportionate

समापन samāpan *n.* conclusion

समापन समारोह samāpan samāroh *n.* concluding ceremony

समास हुनु samāpt hunu *v.i.* terminate

समासि samāpti *n.* completion

समारोह samāntar *adj.* parallel

समानान्तर samānantar *adj.* parallel

समालोचक samālocak *n.* critic

समालोचना samālocanā *n.* criticism

समायोजन samāyojan *n.* integration

समायोजित गर्नु samāyojit garnu *v.t.* adjust

समावेश samābes *v.* include

समावेशी samābesi *adj.* inclusive

समावेशीकरण samābesikaran *n.* inclusiveness

समाविष्ट गर्नु samābist garnu *v.t.* comprise

सम्राट samrāt *n.* emperor

समिति samiti *n.* committee

समीकरण sanikaran *n.* equation

समीप samip *adj.* near

समीपता samiptā *n.* nearness

सम्मिलित गर्नु sammilit garnu *v.t.* include

समीक्षा samiksā *n.* review

समीक्षक samiksak *n.* reviewer

समीक्षालय samiksālaya *n.* review room

समुदाय samudaya *n.* community

समुचित samucit *adj.* proper

समृद्ध samrird *adj.* prosperous

समुद्र samundra *n.* sea

समुद्र जल samundra jal *n.* seawater

समुद्र तट samundra tat *n.* seacoast

समुद्र-पत्तन samundra-pattan *n.* seaport

समुद्री samundri *adj.* marine

समुद्री डाकू samundri dāku *n.* pirate

समुद्री माछा samundri macha *n.* seafood

समुद्री यात्रा गर्नु samundri yātra garnu *v.t.* navigate

समुद्री लहर samundri lahar *n.* surf

समूह samuha *n.* group

सम्झना samjhanā *n.* memory

सरकार sarkār *n.* government

सरकारी sarkāri *adj.* governmental

सरकारी कर्मचारी sarkāri karmacāri *n.* government employee

सरकस sarkas *n.* circus

सरसापट sarsāpat *n.* borrowing and lending

सरल saral *adj.* simple

सरल बनाउनु saral banāunu *v.t.* simplify

सरसल्लाह sarsallāh *n.* consultation

सरस्वती saraswati *n.* Hindu
Goddess of Learning

सरलीकरण saralikaran *n.*
simplification

सराप sarāp *n.* curse

सराहना sarāhnā *v.t.* appreciate

सराय sarāy *n.* inn

सराहनीय sarāhaniya *adj.* admirable

सरुवा saruwā *n.* transfer

सरोकार sarokār *adj.* concern

सरोकारवाला sarokārwālā *n.*
stakeholder

सय saya *num.* hundred

सर्वसम्मति sarvasammati *adj.*
universal

सलाद salād *n.* salad

सल्लाह sallāha *n.* advice

सल्लाहकार sallāhkār *n.* advisor

सल्लाह दिनु sallāh dinu *v.t.*
advise

सवार savār *n.* rider

सवारी savāri *n.* travel

सवारी कर savāri kar *n.* travel tax

सवारी चालक savāri calak *n.*
driver

सवाल savāl *n.* question

सवाल जवाफ savāl jawāph *n.*
answer (to a question)

सवाल गर्नु savāl garnu *v.t.*
question

सर्वतोमुखी sarvatomukhi *adj.*
versatile

सर्वनाम sarvanām *n.* pronoun

सराप sarāp *n.* curse

सशक्त sasakta *adj.* powerful

सशुल्क sasulka *adj.* paying a fee
for using certain facility

ससुरो sasuro *n.* father-in-law

सासु sāsu *n.* mother-in-law

ससुराली sasurāli *n.* in-laws' house

सस्तो sasto *adj.* inexpensive

सहअस्तित्व sahaastitwa *n.*
coexistence

सहकारी sahakari *adj.* cooperative

सहज sahaj *adj.* feasible

सहनु sahanu *v.* tolerate

सशस्त्र sasatra *adj.* armed

ससुराली sasurāli *n.* in-law's house

सहनशील sahansil *n.* enduring

सहनशीलता sahansiltā *n.* tolerance

सहकर्मी sahakarmi *n.* co-worker

सहपाठी sahpāthi *n.* schoolmate

सहभागिता sahbhāgita *n.*
participation

सहभागी sahabhāgi *adj.* participant

सहमति sahmati *n.* consent

सहमत हुनु sahamat hunu *v.t.*
agree

सहयोग sahyog *n.* collaboration

सहयोग दिनु sahyog dinu *v.t.*
contribute

सहयोग गर्नु sahyog garnu *v.i.*
cooperate

सहयोगी sahayogi *n.* associate

सहानुभूति sahānubhuti *n.*
sympathy

सहानुभूति जताउनु sahānubhuti
jatāunu *v.i.* sympathize

सहर sahar *n.* city

सहरी sahari *adj.* urban

सहारा sahāra *n.* supporter

सहारा दिनु sahāra dinu *v.t.*
support

सहायक sahāyak *n.* lieutenant

सहायक प्रशासक sahāyak prasāsak
n. assistant administrator

सहायक प्राध्यापक sahayāk
pradhyāpak *n.* assistant
professor

सहायक मन्त्री sahāyak mantri *n.*
assistant minister

सहायक रथी sahayāk rathi *n.*
  brigadier general
सहायता sahāyatā *n.* assistance,
  aid
सहायता दिनु sahāyatā dinu *v.t.*
  aid, accommodate
सहायता गर्नु sahāyata dinu *v.t.*
  assist
सहरी sahari *adj.* urban
सहारा sahāra *n.* support
सहिष्णु sahisnu *adj.* tolerant
सही sahi *adj.* true
सहीछाप sahicap *n.* signature
सहुलियत sahuliyat *n.* facility
सर्वत्र sarvattra *adj.* all over
सक्षम saksam *adj.* competent
सांविधिक sānvidhik *adj.* statutory
सांस्कृतिक sānskrtik *adj.* cultural
साँघुरो sānghuro *adj.* narrow
साँचो sānco *adj.* true
साच्चै sancai *adv.* really
सांझ sanjh *n.* evening
साझा sājha *adj.* common
साझा आय sājha āya *n.* common
  revenue
साझा शासन sājhā sāsam *n.*
  shared rule
साँप sānp *n.* snake
साँढे sāndhe *n.* bull
साइकिल चलाउनु sāikil calāunu
  v.t. cycle
सारी sāri *n.* sari *(women's clothing)*
साठी sāthi *num.* sixty
सात sāt *num.* seven
सातौं sataun *adj.* seventh
साथ sāth *adv.* by, together
साथ काम गर्नु sāth kām garnu
  v.i. collaborate
साथी sāthi *n.* friend
साथै sāthai *adv.* together with

सादृश्य sādrsya *n.* analogy,
  resemblance
साधारण sādhāran *adj.* usual,
  regular
साधन sādhan *n.* resource
साधु sādhu *n.* Hindu holy man
सान्त्वना sāntwanā *n.* consolation
सफा saphā *adj.* clean
साबुन sābun *n.* soap
साभार sābhār *adv.* with courtesy
साइत sāit *n.* auspicious occasion
सापट sāpat *n.* loan
सामाजिक sāmājik *adj.* social
सामाजिक वन sāmājik van *n.*
  social forest
सामना sāmanā *n.* encounter
सामन्त sāmanta *adj.* feudal
सामन्तवाद sāmantavād *n.*
  feudalism
सामरिक sāmarik *adj.* strategic
सामान sāmān *n.* luggage
सामान्य sāmānya *adj.* normal
सामान्यतः sāmānyatah *adv.*
  generally
सामीप्य sāmipya *n.* closeness
साम्राज्य sāmrājya *n.* empire
सामग्री sāmagri *n.* stuff
सामना गर्नु sāmnā garnu *v.t.*
  withstand, face
सामुदायिक sāmudayik *adj.*
  community
सामुदायिक वन sāmudayik van *n.*
  communally-managed forest
सामुदायिक विकास sāmudayik
  vikās *n.* community development
सांप्रदायिक sāmpradāyik *adj.*
  communal
सामुदायिक sāmudāyik *adj.*
  pertaining to a community
संभ्रान्त sāmbhrānta *adj.* feudal

सामुद्रिक sāmudrik *n.* seagull
साम्यवाद samyavād *n.* communism
साम्यवादी sāmyavādī *n.* communist
साम्राज्य sāmrājya *n.* empire
साम्राज्यवाद sāmrājyabād *n.* imperialism
सार sāririk *n.* essence
सारा sārā *adj.* entire
सारांश sārāmsha *n.* abstract
सारजेंट sārjent *n.* sergeant
सारस sāras *n.* crane (bird)
सारिणीकरण sārinkaran *n.* tabulation
साला sālā *n.* brother-in-law
सावधान sāvdhān *adj.* careful
सावधानी sāvdhāni *n.* caution
सार्वजनिक sārvjanik *adj.* public
सार्वभौम sāarbabhaum *adj.* sovereign
सार्वभौमिकता sārbabhaumiktā *n.* sovereignty
साल sāl *n.* year
सालाखाला sālākhālā *n.* average
सालिक sālik *n.* statue
सालिन्दा sālindā *adv.* yearly
साली sāli *n.* wife's younger sister
सालो sālo *n.* wife's younger brother
सासु sāsu *n.* mother-in-law
सावधान sāvadhān *adj.* careful
सावधानी sāvadhani *n.* caution
साहस sāhās *n.* courage; dare
साहस गर्नु sāhās garnu *v.t.* dare
साहसिक sāhasik *adj.* daring
साहसिलो sāhasilo *adj.* brave
साहित्य sāhity *n.* literature
साहित्यिक sāhityik *adj.* literary
साहित्यकार sāhityakār *n.* author
साहु sāhu *n.* merchant
साह्रै sāhrai *adv.* very much

सिंचाई sincāi *n.* irrigation
सिंदूर sindur *n.* red vermillion
सिंदूरी sinduri *adj.* scarlet
सिँढी sindhi *n.* stairs
सिंह sinha *n.* lion
सिंहासन sihāsan *n.* throne
सिंहावलोकन sinhāvalokan *n.* retrospect, review
सिक्का sikkā *n.* coin
सिकाउनु sikāunu *v.t.* teach
सिकिस्त sikista *adj.* ill
सिक्नु siknu *v.* learn
सिकारी sikari *n.* hunter
सिकर्मी sikarmi *n.* carpenter
सिख sikh *n.* Sikh
सिगार sigār *n.* cigar
सिक्री sikri *n.* chain
सिङ्ग sing *n.* horn
सिगरेट sigaret *n.* cigarette
सित sita *prep.* with
सितंबर sitambar *n.* September
सितार sitar *n.* musical instrument
सिद्ध siddha *adj.* proved
सिद्धांत siddhānt *n.* principle, theory
सिद्धांतसंबंधी siddhāntsambandhi *adj.* theoretical
सिद्धार्थ siddhārtha *n.* Buddha
सिनेमा sinemā *n.* cinema
सिपालु sipālu *adj.* expert
सिपाही sipāhi *n.* soldier
सिफारिश sifāris *v.t.* recommendation
सिफारिश गर्नु sifāris garnu *v.t.* recommend
सिमसार simsār *n.* wetland
सिवालिक पहाड siwalik pahād *n.* Siwalik range *(the southernmost Himalayan hill range)*
सिमाना simāna *n.* boundary
सिमी simi *n.* bean

सिर sir *n.* head

सिरप sirap *n.* syrup

सिलसिला silsilā *n.* series

सिलाई silāi *n.* sewing

सिलाई गर्नु silāi garnu *n.* tailor

सिसी sisi *n.* bottle

सिंग sing *n.* horn

सिक्नु siknu *v.t.* learn

सीटी siti *n.* whistle

सीटी बजाउनु siti bajāunu *v.t.* whistle

सीढी sirhi *n.* stair

सीधा sidhā *adj.* direct

सीधासाधा sidhā sāda *adj.* simple

सीमा simā *n.* limit

सीमावर्ती simāvarti *adj.* bordering

सीमा शुल्क simā sulk *n.* customs duty

सीमित गर्नु simit garnu *v.t.* restrict

सीमित simit *adj.* limited

सीमेंट siment *n.* cement

सीरम siram *n.* serum

सील माछा sil machā *n.* seal *(zoo.)*

सीसा sisā *n.* lead *(metallic)*

सीसा कलम sisākalam *n.* pencil

सुङ्गुरको मासु sungur ko māsu *n.* bacon, pork

सुकिलो sukilo *adj.* clean

सुकुमवासी sukumbāsi *adj.* homeless

सुकुमेल sukumel *n.* cardamom

सुकुटी sukuti *n.* dried meat

सुक्नु suknu *v.i.* dry

सुकर्म sukarma *n.* good work

सुख sukh *n.* enjoyment

सुखी sukhi *adj.* happy

सुखद sukhad *adj.* pleasing

सुखकर sukhkar *adj.* pleasant

सुखान्त sukhānt *n.* comedy

सुगन्ध sugandha *n.* perfume

सुगम sugam *adj.* accessible

सुगन्धित sugandhit *adj.* perfumed

सुगा sugā *n.* parrot

सुङ्गुर sungur *n.* pig

सुन sun *n.* gold

सुचारु suchāru *adj.* satisfactory

सुजीकार sujikār *n.* tailor

सुझाव दिनु sujhāv dinu *v.t.* suggest

सुझाव sujhāv *n.* suggestion

सुत्केरी sutkeri *n.* woman who has given birth to a child

सुत्नु sutnu *v.* sleep

सुदर sudur *adj.* far off

सुदृढ sudridh *adj.* very strong

सुदृढिकरण sudridhikaran *n.* strengthening

सुन्तला suntalā *n.* orange, tangerine

सुन्दर sundar *adj.* pretty

सुन्दरी sundari *n.* pretty woman

सुन्दरता sundaratā *n.* beauty

सुद्धिनु suddhinu *v.* be purified

सुधार sudhār *n.* reclamation

सुधारक sudhārak *adj.* reformed

सुधार्नु sudhārnu *v.t.* improve

सुधार हुनु sudhār hunu *v.i.* improve

सुनवाई sunvāi *n.* hearing

सुन्नु sunnu *v.t.* hear

सुनाउनु sunāunu *v.t.* relate

सुनियोजित suniyojit *adj.* well-planned

सुनुवाई sunuwāi *n.* hearing

सुनार sunār *n.* goldsmith

सुनौलो sunaulā *adj.* golden

सुपरबाजार suparbāzār *n.* supermarket

सुपारी supāri *n.* betel nut

सुपरिवेक्षक pariveksak *n.* superintendent

सुपुर्द गर्नु supurd garnu *v.t.* refer

सुवर्ण suvarna *n.* gold

सुविस्ता subistā *n.* comfort

सुविस्ताजनक subistājanak *adj.* comfortable

सुरुंग surung *n.* tunnel

सुरुंगपथ surangpath *n.* subway

सुर sur *n.* tune of a musical instrument

सुरा sura *n.* alcohol

सुराकी surāki *n.* informer

सुरु suru *n.* beginning

सुरुवाल suruwāl *n.* trousers

सुरक्षा suraksā *n.* safety

सुरक्षित suraksit *adj.* secure

सुरक्षित गर्नु suraksit garnu *v.t.* ensure

सुरक्षित राख्नु suraksit rākhnu *v.t.* preserve

सुविधा suvidhā *n.* convenience

सुविधाजनक suvidhājanak *adj.* comfortable

सेकुवा sekuwā *adj.* roasted

सुशासन susāsan *n.* good governance

सुसमाचार susamācar *n.* good news

सूचना sucanā *n.* information

सोमवार somvār *n.* information

सोझो sojho *adj.* simpleminded

सुव्यवस्थित suvyavsthit *adj.* methodical

सौतेनी आमा sauteni āmā *n.* stepmother

सौतेनी बाबु sauteni bābu *n.* stepfather

सौतेनी छोरा sauteni chora *n.* stepson

सौतेनी छोरी sauteni chori *n.* stepdaughter

सौभाग्य saubhagya *n.* good luck

सौभाग्यवश saubhāgyabas *adv.* fortunately

सौर saur *adj.* solar

सौर्य उर्जा saurya urjā *n.* solar energy

सौर्य प्रविधि saurya prabidhi *n.* solar technology

सौर्य विकिरण saurya vikiran *n.* solar radiation

स्की ski *n.* ski

स्कूटर skutar *n.* motorbike

स्कूले केटो skule keto *n.* school boy

स्कूले केटी skule keti *n.* school girl

स्केट sket *n.* skate

स्टाफ stāf *n.* staff

स्टाल stāl *n.* stall, stand

स्टार्च stārc *n.* starch

स्टीरियो stiriyo *n.* stereo

स्टीमर stimar *n.* steamship

स्टूल stul *n.* stool

स्ट्रेचर strecar *n.* stretcher

स्टेडियम stediyam *n.* stadium

स्टेपल stepal *n.* staple

स्टेथस्कोप stethāskop *n.* stethoscope

स्टेशन stesan *n.* station

स्तंभ stambha *n.* column, shaft

स्तनपायी stanpāyi *n.* mammal

स्तर star *n.* standard

स्नायु-रोगी snāyu-rogi *adj.* neurotic

स्त्री stri *n.* female

सृष्टि sristi *n.* creation

स्रोत strot *n.* source

स्रोत नियन्त्रण srot niyantran *n.* source control

स्थगित गर्नु sthagit garnu *v.t.* postpone

स्थल sthal *n.* site

स्थापित गर्नु sthāpit garnu *v.t.* establish

स्थायित्व sthāvitva *n.* permanence

स्थान sthān *n.* place, post

स्थायी sthāyi *n.* permanent

स्थायी आदेश sthāyi ādes *adj.* standing

स्थिर sthir *adj.* stable

स्नान snān *n.* bath

स्नान गर्नु snān garnu *v.i.* bathe

स्नातक snātak *n.* graduate

स्नातक हुनु snātak hunu *v.i.* graduate

स्नेही snehi *adj.* affectionate

स्पंज spanj *n.* sponge

स्पष्ट spasta *adj.* evident, clear

स्पष्ट गर्नु spast garnu *v.t.* explain

स्पर्श sparsa *n.* feel, touch

स्फटिक spatik *n.* crystal

स्लाइड slāid *n.* slide

स्लेटी ढुंगा sleti dhungā *n.* slate

स्लीपर slipar *n.* slipper

स्वयं svayam *pron.* itself, myself

स्वर्ण svarna *n.* gold

स्वर्ण जयन्ती svarna jāyanti *n.* golden jubilee

स्वयंसेवक svayam sevak *n.* volunteer

स्वयं-सेवा svayam-sevā *n./adj.* self-service

स्वचालित svacālit *adj.* automatic

स्वेटर svetar *n.* sweater

स्वत svatah *adj.* spontaneous

स्वतंत्र svatantra *adj.* independent

स्वतंत्रता svatantratā *n.* independence

स्वदेशी svadesi *adj.* indigeneous

स्वशासित svasāsit *adj.* autonomous

स्वच्छता svacchatā *n.* sanitation

स्वशासन svasāsan *n.* autonomy

स्वत्व svatva *n.* possession

स्वर svar *n.* tone

स्वर को svar ko *n.* voice

स्वर्ग svarga *n.* heaven

स्वस्थ svastha *adj.* healthy

स्वास्थ्य swāsthya *n.* health

स्वागत svāgat *n.* reception

स्वागतम svāgatam *n.* welcome

स्वागत गर्नु svāgat garnu *v.t.* welcome

स्वाद svād *n.* flavor, taste

स्वादिष्ट svādist *adj.* savory

स्वभाव svabhāv *n.* nature *(personal)*

स्वाभिमान svābhimān *n.* self-respect

स्वावलम्बन svāvalamban *n.* self-sufficiency

स्वामिनी svāmini *n.* mistress

स्वामी svāmi *n.* lord, master

स्वायत svāyatta *adj.* autonomous

स्वास्नी svāsni *n.* wife

स्वास्थ्य svāsthya *n.* health

स्वास्थ्यकर svasthyakar *adj.* healthy

स्वायत्तता svāyattatā *n.* autonomy

स्वायत शासन svāyatta sasan *adj.* autonomous

स्वीकार गर्नु svikār garnu *v.t.* accept

स्वीकृत svikrit *adj.* accepted

स्विच svic *n.* switch

स्विच खोल्नु svic kholnu *v.t.* switch

स्थिति sthiti *n.* situation

स्थिर sthir *adj.* steady

ह

हक hak *n./adj.* right

हैंड ब्याग haindbaig *n.* handbag

हैंगर haingar *n.* hanger

हजार hajār *num.* thousand

हजारौं hajāraun *adj.* thousandth

हजुर hajur *pron.* you

हटनु hatnu *v.i.* shift

हटाउनु hatāunu *v.i.* eliminate

हटाउनु hatāunu *v.t.* move, shift, withdraw

हठ hath *n.* stubbornness

हड्डी haddi *n.* bone

हडबडी harbari *n.* rush

हडताल hartāl *n.* strike

हडताली hartāli *n.* striker

हडप्नु hadapnu *v.* embezzle

हडवड harwar *n.* haste

हतकडी hatkadi *n.* handcuff

हताहत hatāhat *n.* casualty

हतार hatār *n.* haste

हताश गर्नु hatās garnu *v.t.* disappoint

हतोत्साहित हुनु hatotsāhit hunu *adj.* frustrated

हत्या hatyā *n.* murder

हत्याकाण्ड hatyā kānd *n.* massacre

हत्यारा hatyārā *n.* murderer

हथौडा hathauda *n.* hammer

हद had *n.* limit

हर्निया harniyā *n.* hernia

हर har *n.* every

हर एक (हरेक) har ek *adj.* each

हरियो hariyo *adj.* green

हप्ता haftā *n.* week

हब्शी habsi *n.* black man

हमला hamalā *n.* attack

हमला गर्नु hamalā garnu *v.t.* attack

हमेशा hamesā *adv.* always

हरदम hardam *adv.* always

हरित क्रान्ति harit krānti *n.* green revolution

हरियाली hariyāli *n.* greenery

हरियो hariyo *n.* green

हरियो मल hariyo mal *n.* green manure

हराउनु harāunu *v.t.* defeat

हर्ष harsa *n.* delight

हल hal *n.* solution

हलुवाबेद haluwābed *n.* persimmon

हलो halo *n.* plow

हल्लिनु hallinu *v.i.* shake

हल गर्नु hal garnu *v.t.* solve

हल्लनु halanu *v.i.* shake

हल्का नास्ता halkā nāstā *n.* appetizer

हल्ला hallā *n.* rumor

हवाई अड्डा havāi addā *n.* airport

हवाई डाक havāi dāk *n.* airmail

हवाई चित्र havai citra *n.* aerial photo

हवाई जहाज havāi jahāz *n.* airplane

हवाई कम्पनी havāi kampani *n.* airline

हवेली haveli *n.* mansion

हस्ताक्षर गर्नु hastāksar garnu *v.i.* subscribe

हाकिम hākim *n.* boss

हाब्रे hābre *n.* red panda

हामी hāmi *pron.* we

हाम्रो hāmro *pron.* our

हाकी hāki *n.* hockey

हात hāt *n.* hand

हातपात hātpāt *n.* molestation

हात्ती hātti *n.* elephant

हात्ती दाँत hātti dānt *n.* ivory

हार्दिक hārdik *adj.* hearty

हानि hāni *n.* harm

हानि सहनु hāni sahanu *v.t.* sacrifice

हानिकर hānikar *adj.* harmful

हान्नु hānnu *v.t.* strike

हाफपैंट hāphpaint *n.* shorts

हाम्रो hāmro *pron.* our

हार मान्नु hār mānnu *v.t.* submit

हार hār *n.* defeat

हावापानी परिवर्तन hāwāpāni parivartan *n.* climate change

हार्दिक रुप ले hārdik rup le *adv.* cordially

हार्दिकता hārdiktā *n.* sincerity

हाल को hāl ko *adj.* recent

हालत hālat *n.* state

हावा hāwa *n.* air

हिडनु hidnu *v.i.* walk

हालै halai *adv.* lately

हास्य hāsya *n.* humor

हास्यास्पद hāsyaspad *adj.* ridiculous

हास्यकर hāsyakar *adj.* funny

हिडाई hindāi *n.* walk

हिंसक himsak *adj.* violent

हिंसा himsā *n.* violence

हिंसापूर्ण himsāpurna *adj.* violent

हिंसात्मक himsātmak *adj.* bloody

हिचकिचाहट hickicāhat *n.* hesitation

हिच्की hicki *n.* hiccup

हिचकिचाउनु hickicāunu *v.t.* hesitate

हिजो hijo *n.* yesterday

हिज्जे गर्नु hijje garnu *v.t.* spell

हित hit *n./adj.* good

हितकर hitkar *adj.* wholesome

हितैषी hitaisi *adj.* benevolent

हिउँ him *n.* snow

हिमालय himālaya *n.* Himalayas

हिमाली himali *adj.* alpine

हिम्मत himmat *n.* courage

हिम्मती himmati *adj.* courageous

हीनता hinata *n.* inferiority

हिउँ hiun *n.* snow

हिउँ चितुवा hiun chitwā *n.* snow leopard

हिउँद hiund *n.* winter

हिउँ पहिरो hiun pahiro *n.* avalanche

हिन्दी hindi *n.* Hindi

हिन्दू hindu *n./adj.* Hindu

हिन्दुस्थान hindustān *n.* India

हिमनदी himanadi *n.* glacier

हिमरेखा himrekhā *n.* snow line

हिमताल himtāl *n.* glacial lake

हावापानी hāwāpāni *n.* climate

हिउँद hiund *n.* winter

हिंडनु hindnu *v.i.* walk

हिमनदी himanadi *n.* glacier

हिउँ hiun *n.* snow

हिउँ पहिरो hiunpahiro *n.* avalanche

हिरन hiran *n.* deer

हिरासत hirāsat *n.* custody

हिलसा hilsā *n.* herring

हिलो hilo *n.* mud

हिसाब hisāb *n.* calculation

हिसाब गर्नु hisāb garnu *v.t.* calculate

हिस्सा hissā *n.* share

हिस्सेदार hissedār *n.* partner

हीनता hinatā *n.* inferiority

हीटर hitar *n.* heater

हीरक जयन्ती hirak jayanti *n.*
diamond jubilee

हीरा hirā *n.* diamond

हुकुम hukum *n.* command

हुनु hunu *v.i.* become

हुन दिनु huna dinu *v.t.* let

हुन सक्ने huna sakne *v. aux.* may

हुन सम्म huna samma *adv.* to
the extent possible

हेतु hetu *n.* motive, purpose

हुरी huri *n.* storm

हुर्कनु hurkanu *v.i.* grow up

हुलिया huliya *n.* appearance

हुल्याहा hulyāhā *n.* gangster

हुल hul *n.* crowd

हृदय hridāya *n.* heart

हृदयघात hridaya ghāt *n.* heart
attack

हेमन्त hemant *n.* winter season

हेम hem *n.* gold

हेर्नु hernu *v.* look

हेलिकॉप्टर helikāptar *n.*
helicopter

हेलमिट helmit *n.* helmet

हैजा haijā *n.* cholera

हैरान गर्नु hairān garnu *v.t.* bother

हो ho *adv.* yes

होटल hotel *n.* hotel

होश hos *n.* wit

हो-हल्ला ho-hallā *n.* riot

हौसला hausalā *n.* morale

ENGLISH-NEPALI
DICTIONARY

A

a.d. इस्वी सन् ísaví san

a.m *adj.* दिउँसो बाह्र बजेपछि diuso barha bajepachhi

abandon *v.t.* छोड्नु chhodnu

abandoned *adj.* छोडिएको chodiyeko

abbreviate *v.t.* संक्षिस गर्नु sankshipta garnu

abbreviation *n.* संक्षेपण sanksepan

abdomen *n.* पेट pet

abduct *v.* अपहरण गर्नु apaharan garnu

ability *n.* योग्यता yogyatā, सामर्थ्य smarthya

able *adj.* योग्य yogya

abnormal *adj.* असामान्य asāmanya

aboard *adj* चढेको chadheko

abode *n.* घर ghar

aboriginal *n.* आदिवासी ādivāsi

abortion *n.* गर्भपात garbhpāt

about *adv.* लगभग lagbhag

above *adv.* माथि mathi

above all *adv.* सर्वोपरि sarvopari

abroad *adv.* विदेशमा bidesmā

abrupt *adj.* एकाएक ekāek

abscess *n.* पीप भरेको घाउ pip bhareko ghāu

absence *n.* अनुपस्थिति anupasthiti, गयल gayal

absent *adj.* अनुपस्थित anupasthit, गयल gayal

absolute *adj.* पूर्ण purna

absorb *v.* सोस्नु sosnu

abstain *v.* निष्पक्ष हुनु nispaksa hunu

abstract *adj.* संक्षेप sankchep

absurd *adj.* वाहीयात wāihiyāt

abundance *n.* वाहुल्य vāhulya

abundant *adj.* प्रचुर prachur

abuse *n.* दुरुपयोग durupyog; *v.t.* दुरुपयोग गर्नु durupyog garnu

abusive *adj.* अपमानजनक apmānjanak

academic *adj.* प्राज्ञिक pragyik

academy *n.* प्रज्ञा प्रतिष्ठान pragyā pratisthān

accelerate *v.i.* चाल बढाउनु chāl badhāunu

accent *n.* उच्चारण uchhāran

accept *v.t.* स्वीकार गर्नु svikār garnu

acceptance *n.* स्वीकृति swikriti

access *n.* प्रवेश pravesh

accessible *adj.* सजिलै पुगिने sajilai pugne

accessory *n.* सहायक sahāyak

accident *n.* दुर्घटना durghatnā

accidental *adj.* आकस्मिक akasmik

acclamation *n.* मौखिक स्वीकृति maukhik swikriti

accommodation(s) *n.* आवास āvās

accompany *v.t.* साथ जानु sāth jānu

accomplice *n.* सहायक sahāyak

accomplish *v.t.* सफलतापूर्वक पूरा गर्नु saphalatāpurbak purā garnu

accomplishment *n.* उपलब्धि upalabdhi

accord *n.* समझौता samjhautā

according to *prep.* को अनुसार ko anusār

account *n.* खाता khātā

accountant *n.* लेखापाल lekhāpāl

accounting *v.t.* लेखा lekhā

accumulate *v.t.* जम्मा गर्नु jammā garnu

accuracy *n.* शुद्धता suddhatā

accurate *adj.* ठीक theek

accusation *n.* अभियोग abhiyog

accuse *v.t.* दोष लगाउनु dos lagāunu

accustom *v.i.* अभ्यस्त बन्नु abhyastha bannu

ace *n.* एक्का ekkā

ache *n.* दुख्ने dukhne

achieve *v.t.* सम्पादित गर्नु sampādit garnu

achievement *n.* कार्य सम्पादन kāryasampadan

acid *n.* अम्ल amla

acidic *adj.* अम्लीय amliya

acidity *n.* अम्लता amlatā

acknowledge *v.t.* मान्नु mānnu

acknowledgement *n.* प्राप्ति सूचना prāpti suchana

acquaint *v.t.* परिचित हुनु parichit hunu

acquaintance *n.* परिचय parichaya

acquire *v.t.* प्राप्त गर्नु prapta garnu

acquisition *n.* प्राप्ति prāpti

across *adv.* पार pār, पारी pāri

act *n.* कार्य kārya; *v.* कार्य गर्नु kārya garnu

active *adj.* सक्रिय sakirya

activity *n.* क्रिया kriyā

actor *n.* अभिनेता abhinetā

actual *adj.* वास्तविक vāstavik

actuary *n.* बीमा संबन्धी काम गर्ने bimā sambandhi kām garne

ad (advertisement) *n.* विज्ञापन vigyāpan

adapt *v.t.* अनुकूल गर्नु anukul garnu

add *v.t.* थप्नु thapnu

addict *n.* दुर्व्यसनि durbyabasani

additional *adj.* अतिरिक्त atirikta

address *n.* ठेगाना thegaana

adequate *adj.* पर्याप्त paryāpt

adhere *v.i.* मान्नु mānnu

adhesive *adj.* गूँद gund

adjacent *adj.* निकटवर्ती nikatvartí, नजिकको najikko

adjective *n.* विशेषण visesan

adjoin *v.i.* आसन्न हुनु āsanna honu

adjust *v.t.* समायोजित गर्नु samāyojit garnu, मिलाउनु milaunu

adjustment *n.* समायोजन samāyojan

administer *v.t.* प्रबन्ध गर्नु prabandh garnu

administration *n.* प्रशासन prashāsan

administrative *adj.* प्रशासकीय prashāshikiya

admirable *adj.* प्रशंसनीय prasansníya

admire *v.t.* प्रशंसा गर्नु prasansā garnu

admission *n.* प्रवेश praves

admit *v.t.* प्रवेश दिनु praves dinu

admittance *n.* प्रवेश prabes

adolescent *n.* किशोर kisor

adopt *v.* धर्मपुत्र लिनु dharmapautra linu

adore *v.* धेरै मान्नु dherai mānnu

adult *n.* वयस्क vayask

adulterate *v.* खाद्यमा मिलावट khadyamā milāwat

adultery n. विवाह नभएको बीच यौन vivah nabhaeko bic yaun

advance n. प्रगति pragati

advance v.t. प्रगति गर्नु pragati garnu

advantage n. फाइदा phaida

adventure n. साहस sāhas

adversary n. विरोधी virodhi

advertise v.t. विज्ञापन गर्नु vigyāpan garnu

advertisement n. विज्ञापन vigyāpan

advice n. सल्लाह sallah, सल्लाह दिनु sallah dinu

adviser/advisor n. सल्लाहकार salāhakār

advocate n. अधिवक्ता adhivaktā

aerial photo n. हवाई चित्र hawāi citra

aesthetic adj. सौन्दर्य संबन्धी saundarya sambandhi

affair n. मामला māmlā

affect v.t. प्रभावित गर्नु prabhāvit garnu

affection n. अनुराग anurāg

affectionate adj. स्नेही snehi

affinity n. नाता nāta, संबन्ध sambandha

affirmation n. निश्चित nischit

afflict v.t. दुःख दिनु dukh dinu

affliction n. दुःख dukh

affluence n. संपन्नता sampannatā

affluent n. संपन्न sampanna

afford v.t. खर्च गर्न सक्नु kharcha garna saknu

afraid adj. डराएको darāyeko

Africa n. अफ्रिका afrikā

African n./adj. अफ्रिकी afriki

after adj. त्यसपछि tespachhi

aftereffect n. धेरै पछिको असर dherai pachi ko asar

afternoon n. दिउँसो diuso

afterward adj. पछि pachhi

again adj. फेरि pheri

against prep. को विरुद्ध ko biruddha

age n. उमेर umer

aged adj. बुढो budho

agency n. संस्था sāmstha

agenda n. कार्यसूची kāryasuchi

agent n. दलाल dalal

aggravate v. झन खराब बान्नु jhan kharab bannu

aggression n. आक्रमण akraman

aggressive adj. आक्रमक ākramak

agnostic n. अविश्वासी aviswāsi

ago adv. पहिले pahile

agony n. घोर व्यथा ghor vyathā

agree v.t. सहमत हुनु sahamat hunu

agreeable adj. मनोहर mahohar

agreement n. सहमति sahamati

agribusiness n. कृषि व्यापार krisi byāpār

agricultural adj. खेतको khetko

agriculture n. कृषि krishi, खेतीपाती khetipaati

agroforestry n. कृषिवन krisivan

agronomy n. बालीविज्ञान bālivigyān

ahead adv. अगाडि agādi

aid n. सहायता sahāyatā

aide de camp (ADC) n. अङ्गरक्षक angaraksak

aide n. सहायक sahāyak

aids n. एड्ज edz

aim n. लक्ष्य lakshya

air n. हावा hāwā

air force n. वायु सेना vāyu senā

air pollution n. वायु प्रदुषण vāyu pradusan

air-conditioning n. ए.सी. e.si.

aircraft n. वायुयान vāyuyān

airline *n.* हवाई कम्पनी havāi kampani

airmail *n.* हवाई डाक havāi dāk

airplane *n.* हवाई जहाज havāi jahāz

airport *n.* हवाई अड्डा havāi addā

alarm *n.* चेतावनी, chetāvani; अलार्म घडी alārm ghari

alcohol *n.* रक्सी raksi

alcoholic *adj.* मादक पदार्थ पिउने mādak padartha piune; *n.* रक्सीवाज raksibāj

ale *n.* बियर biyar

alert *adj* सचेत sachet; *n.* चेतावनी chetāvani; *v.t.* चेतावनी दिनु chetāvani dinu

algebra *n.* बीजगणित vijganit

alibi *n.* बहाना bahānā

alien *n./adj.* विदेशी videsi

align *v.t.* सिधा मिल्नु sidhā milnu

alike *adj.* समान samān

alimony *adj.* माना चामल mānācāmal

alive *adj.* बाँचेको bacheko

all *adj.* सब sab

all right *adv.* ठीक thik

allergic *adj.* एलर्जी सम्बन्धी elarji sambadhi

allergy *n.* एलर्जी elarji

alley *n.* गल्ली galli

alliance *n.* गठबन्धन gathabandhan

allocate *v.* बाँड्नु bāndnu

allocation *n.* बाँडफाड bāndphānd

allow *v.t.* अनुमति दिनु anumati diu

ally *n.* मित्र mitra

almanac *n.* पात्रो pātro

almighty *adj./n.* सर्वशक्तिमान (ईश्वर) sarvaaktimān

almond *n.* बदाम badāam

almost *adv.* लगभग lagbhag

alone *adj.* एक्लै eklai

along *adv.* साथसाथ sāth sāth

aloud *adv.* जोरसँग jor sang

alphabet *n.* वर्णमाला varnamālā

already *adv.* पहिलेदेखि pahile dekhi

alright *n.* ठिक thik

also *adv.* पनि pani

alter *v.t.* बदलि दिनु badali dinu

alteration *n.* परिवर्तन parivartan

alternate *n.* पालो गरी हुने pālo gari hune

alternative *n.* विकल्प vikalp

although *conj.* हुन त huna tā

altitude *n.* ऊँचाई uchai

altogether *adv.* पूरै purāi

aluminum *n.* एलुमिनियम aluminium

alumnus *n.* पूर्व विद्यार्थी purva-vidhyārthi

always *adv.* सँधै sadhain

amateur *adj.* शौकिन sāukin

amateur *n.* अव्यवसायी avyavasāyi

amaze *v.t.* हैरान पार्नु hairān parnu

amazing *adj.* अचम्म लाग्ने achamma lagne

ambassador *n.* राजदूत rājdut

ambiance *n.* माहौल māhaul

ambiguous *adj.* अनेकार्थक anekārthak

ambition *n.* महत्वाकांक्षा mahatvākānksā

ambitious *adj.* महत्वाकांक्षी mahatwākānchhi

ambulance *n.* अस्पतालको गाडी aspatālko gādi

amend *v.* बदल्नु badalnu

amendment *n.* संशोधन sansodhan

amenities *n.* सुविधा subidha

America *n.* अमेरिका america

American *n./adj.* अमेरिकी ameriki

amicable *adj.* मित्रबत mitrabat

amid *prep.* बीचमा bichma

ammonia *n.* अमोनिया amoniyā

ammunition *n.* हतियार hatiyār

amnesty *n.* आम माफी ām māphi

among *prep.* मध्ये madhye

amount *n.* जम्मा रकम jammā rakam

ample *adj.* पर्यास paryaptā

amplify *v.* विस्तार गर्नु vistār garnu

amputate *v.* काट्नु kātnu

amuse *v.* मन बहलाउनु man bahālāunu

amusement *n.* मनोरञ्जन manorajnan

analogy *n.* साद्दश्य sādrsya

analysis *n.* विश्लेषण vislesan

analyze *v.* विश्लेषण गर्नु vislesan garnu

anarchy *n.* अराजकता arājaktā

ancestor *n.* पूर्वज purvaj

anchor *v.t.* लंगर langar, लंगर हाल्नु langar hālnu

ancient *adj.* प्राचीन prāchin

and *conj.* र ra

anecdote *n.* किस्सा kissā

angel *n.* देवदूत devdut

anger *n.* रिस ris; *v.i.* रिस उठाउनु ris uthāunu

angle *n.* कोण kon

angora *n.* एक प्रकारको खरायो ek prakār ko kharāyo

angry *adj.* रिसाएको risayeko

anguish *n.* वेदना vedna

animal *n.* जनावर janāvar

animal husbandry *n.* पशुपालन pasupālan

annex *n.* उपभवन upbhavan

anniversary *n.* जयन्ती jayanti

announce *v.t.* घोषणा गर्नु ghosanā garnu

announcement *n.* घोषणा ghosanā

annoy *v.t.* दुःख दिनु dukhā dinu

annual *adj.* वार्षिक varsik

annul *v.t.* रद्द गर्नु radda garnu

anonymous *adj.* गुमनाम gumnam

another *adj.* अर्को arko

answer *n.* जवाफ javāph; *v.t.* जवाफ दिनु javāb dinu

ant *n.* कमिला kamilā

antenna *n.* ऐन्टेना aintenā

anti- *pref.* विपरित viparit

anticipate *v.t.* अपेक्षा गर्नु apeksha garnu

anticipation *n.* अपेक्षा apaksha

antique *n.* पुरानो चीज purano cheej

antiquity *adj.* प्राचीन समय prācin samay

antisocial *adj.* मिलनसार नभएको milansār nabhaeko

anxiety *n.* चिन्ता chintā

anxious *adj.* चिन्तित chintit

any *adj.* कोही koi

anybody *pron.* कोही पनि koi pani

anyone *pron.* कोही पनि koi pani

anything *pron.* जे पनि je pani

anytime *adv.* जहिले पनि jahile pani

anyway *adv.* जे भए पनि je bhae pani

anywhere *adv.* जहाँ पनि jahan pani

apart *adv.* अलग alag

apartment *n.* अपार्टमेन्ट āpartment

apathetic *adj.* उदासीन udasin

apologize *v.i.* क्षमा माग्नु ksamā māagnu

apology *n.* क्षमा-याचना ksamā-yāchnā

apostate *n.* धर्म छाडने dharma chādne

apostle *n.* क्राइस्टका चेलाहरु kraist ka cela haru

apparatus *n.* उपकरण upkaran

apparel *n.* कपडा kapadā

apparent *adj.* स्पष्ट spast

appeal *v.i.* मन पर्नु man parnu

appear *v.i.* देखिनु dekhinu

appearance *n.* दर्शन darsan

appendix *n.* परिशिष्ट parisist

appetite *n.* भोक bhok

appetizer *n.* हल्का नास्ता halkā nāstā

applaud *v.t.* थपडी बजाउनु thapadi bajāunu

applause *n.* स्याबासी syābāsi

apple *n.* स्याउ syāu

appliance *n.* घरायसी कामको सामान gharayasi kām ko sāmān

applicant *n.* आवेदनकर्ता abedankartā

application *n.* आवेदन पत्र āvedan patra

application *n.* उपयोग upyog

apply *v.t.* आवेदन गर्नु āvedan garnu

appoint *v.t.* नियुक्त गर्नु niyukti garnu

appointment *n.* नियुक्ति niyukti

appraisal *n.* मूल्यांकन mulyankan

appraise *v.* मूल्यांकन गर्नु mulyānkan garnu

appreciate *v.t.* सराहना गर्नु sarāhanā garnu

apprehension *n.* नराम्रो भविष्यको पर्खाई narāmro bhavisya ko parkhāi

approach *n.* नजिकिनु najikinu, पहुँच pahunch

appropriate *adj.* ठीक thik

approval *n.* मञ्जुरी manjuri

approve *v.t.* मञ्जुर manjur

approximate *n.* लगभग lagbhag

apricot *n.* खुर्पानी khurpāni

aptitude *n.* झुकाव jhukab, रुचि ruchi

aquatic *adj.* जलचर jalchar, पानीमा बस्ने panima basne

Arab *n.* अरब arab

Arabic *(language) n.* अरबी Arabi

arable *adj.* खेतीयोग्य khetiyogya

arbitrary *adj* मन-माना man-mānā

archaeological *adj.* पुरातत्वीय purātatviy

archaeology *n.* पुरातत्व purātattva

archipelago *n.* टापुसमूह tāpusamuha

architect *n.* वास्तुकार vāstukār

architectural *adj.* वास्तुशिल्पीय vāstsilpiy

architecture *n.* वास्तुकला vāstukalā

archive *n.* अभिलेख abhilekh

Arctic *adj.* उत्तर ध्रुवीय uttardhruviya

Arctic Circle *n.* आर्कटिक वृत ārktik vrtt

Arctic Ocean *n.* आर्कटिक महासागर ārktik mahāsāgar

area *n.* क्षेत्र chetra, इलाका ilāqā

argue *v.t.* बहस गर्नु bahas garnu

argument *n.* बहस bahas

arid *adj.* सुख्खा sukkhā

arise *v.* जाग्नु jāgnu

arithmetic *n.* अंकगणित ankganit

arm *n.* बाहु bāhu

armchair *n.* बाँहदार कुर्सी bāmhadār kursi

armed *adj.* सशस्त्र sasastra

armed force *n.* सेना senā

armpit *n.* बगल bagal

army *n.* सेना sena

aroma *n.* सुगन्ध sugandh

around *adv.* आसपास ās-pās

arrange *v.t.* व्यवस्थित गर्नु vyasthit garnu

arrangement *n.* बन्दोबस्त bandobasta

arrest *n.* गिरफ्तार giraftar; *v.t.* गिरफ्तार गर्नु giraftar garnu

arrival *n.* आगमन āgman

arrive *v.t.* आइपुग्नु aāipugnu

arrogance *n.* घमन्ड ghamanda

arrogant *adj.* घमन्डी ghamandi

arrow *n.* वाण bāan

arsenal *n.* शास्त्रगार sastragār

art *n.* कला kalā

artery *n.* नसा nasāa

article *n.* लेख lekh

articulate *adj.* राम्रोवक्ता rāmrovakta

artifact *n.* शिल्पकृति silpakriti

artificial *adj.* नक्कली nakkali

artisan *n.* कालिगढ kaligadh

artist *n.* कलाकार kalākār

artistic *adj.* कलात्मक kalātmak

as *adv.* जस्तो jasto, जब कि jab ki

asbestos *n.* आस्वेस्टस āsbestas

ascertain *v.* पत्ता लगाउनु pattā lagāunu

ascetic *adj.* त्यागी tyāgi

ash *n.* खरानी kharāni

ashamed *adj.* लज्जित lajjit

aside *adj.* एउटा अरु eutā aru

ask *v.t.* सोध्नु sodhnu

asleep *adj/adv.* सुतेको suteko

asparagus *n.* कुरिलो kurilo

aspect *n.* पहेलु pahalu

aspiration *n.* आकांक्षा ākānsā

aspire *v.* इच्छा गर्नु icchā garnu

ass *n.* गधा gadhā

assassin *n.* हत्यारा hatyāra

assassination *n.* हत्या hatyā

assault *n.* आक्रमण ākraman; *v.t.* हमला गर्नु hamlā garnu

assemble *v.t.* एकत्र हुनु ekatra hunu

assembly *n.* सभा sabhā

assemblyman *n.* सभासद sabhāsad

assert *v.t.* प्रभाव पार्नु prabhav pārnu

assertion *n.* दावा dāvā

asset *n.* सम्पत्ती sampati

assign *v.t.* निश्चित गर्नु nischit garnu

assimilate *v.t.* सम्मिलित हुनु sammilit hunu

assist *v.t.* सहायता गर्नु sahāyatā garnu

assistance *n.* सहायता sahāyatā

assistant *n.* सहायक sahāyak

associate *n.* सहयोगी sahayogi; *v.t.* सम्बन्ध गर्नु sambadha garnu

association *n.* संस्था sanstha

assume *v.t.* मान्नु mānnu

assumption *n.* अनुमान anumān

assurance *n.* आश्वासन āsvāsan

assure *v.t.* विश्वास दिलाउनु visvās dilāunu

asthma *n.* दम dam

asthmatic *adj.* दमको रोगी damko rogi

astonish *v.t.* विस्मृत गर्नु vismrit garnu

astrologer *n.* ज्योतिषी jyotisi

astrology *n.* फलित-ज्योतिष phalit-jyoti

astronomy *n.* गणित-ज्योतिष ganit-jyoti

astute *adj.* चतुर chatur

asylum *n.* शरण saran

at *prep.* मा maa

atheism *n.* नास्तिकता nastikatā

atheist *n.* नास्तिक nāstik

athlete *n.* व्यायामी vyāyāmi

athletics *n.* खेलकूद khelkud

atmosphere *n.* वातावरण vātavāran

atom *n.* परमाणु parmānu

atomic energy *n.* आणविक उर्जा ānabik urjā

attach *v.t.* लगाउनु lagāunu, टाँसिनु tāsinu

attack *n.* हमला hamalā; *v.t.* हमला गर्नु hamlā garnu

attempt *n.* प्रयत्न prayatna; *v.t.* कोशिस kosis

attend *v.t.* उपस्थित हुनु upasthit hunu

attendance *n.* उपस्थिति upsthiti

attendant *n.* नोकर nokar

attention *n.* ध्यान dhyān; pay ~ *v.t.* ध्यान दिनु dhyan dinu

attentive *adj.* सावधान sāvdhān

attic *n.* बुइँगल buigal

attitude *n.* मनोवृत्ति manovrtti

attorney general *n.* महान्यायधिवक्ता maha-nyāyādhibakta

attorney *n.* न्यायधिवक्ता nyadhibaktā

attract *v.* आकर्षित गर्नु akarsit garnu

attraction *n.* आकर्षण ākarsan

attractive *adj.* आकर्षक ākarshak

attribute *n.* गुण gun

auction *n.* लिलाम lilām; *v.t.* लिलाम गर्नु lilām garnu

audience *n.* श्रोता srotā

audit *n.* लेखा पतिक्षण lekhā pariksan

auditor *n.* लेखा पतिक्षक lekhā pariksak

augment *v.t.* बढाउनु badhāunu

August *n.* अगस्त agast

aunt *n.* काकी kāki (father's brother's wife); फुपु phupu (father's sister); माइजु maiju (mother's brother's wife); सानिमा sanima (mother's sister)

authentic *adj.* प्रमाणिक pramānik

authenticity *n.* प्रमाणिकता pramāniktā

author *n.* लेखक lekhak

authority *n.* प्राधिकरण prādhikaran

authorization *n.* अनुमोदन anumodan

authorize *v.t.* अनुमोदन गर्नु anumodan garnu

autobiography *n.* आंत्मकथा atmakathā

automatic *adj.* स्वचालित svachālit

automation *n.* स्वचलन svachalan

automobile *n.* गाडी gādi, मोटर motar

autonomous *adj.* स्वायत्त svāyatt

autonomy *n.* स्वायत्तता svāyattatā

autopsy *n.* शव-परीक्षा sav-parāksa

autumn *n.* शरद sarad

availability *n.* प्राप्तता prapyatā

available *adj.* प्राप्य prāpya

avenge *v.* वदला लिनु badalā linu

avenue *n.* मार्ग mārg

average *n.* औसत ausat

aviation *n.* हवाई hawāi

avoid *v.t.* हटाउनु hataunu

await *v.* पर्खनु parkhanu

awake *v.i.* जाग्नु jāgnu

award *n.* इनाम दिनु inām dinu; पुरस्कार puraskar

aware *adj.* जानकार jānkār

away *adv.* टाढा tāadhāa

awful *adj.* भयानक bhayānak

awkward *adj.* बेढङ्गी bedhangi

ax(e) *n.* बन्चरो bancāro

B

b.c. (before Christ) ईसापूर्व isāpurv

baby n. बच्चा bacā

babysit v. बच्चा हेर्नु bacā hernu

babysitter n. बच्चा हेर्नु bachā herne

bachelor n. स्नातक snātak, अविवाहित abibāhit

back n. पछाडि pachhādi

backbite v. कसैलाई पछाडि गाली गर्नु kasailai pachādi gāli garnu

backbone n. मेरुदण्ड merudanda

backer n. समर्थक samarthak

background n. पृष्ठभूमि pristhabhumi

backward adj. पछाडि परेको pachhādi pareko

bacon n. सुँगुरको मासु sungurko masu

bacteria n. जीवाणु jivānu

bacterial adj. जीवाणु सम्बन्धी jivānu sambadhi

bad adj. खराब kharāb

badge n. बिल्ला billā

badly adv. खराबसित kharābsita

badminton n. बैडमिन्टन baidmintan

bag n. थैलो thailo

baggage n. सामान sāmān

bail n. जमानत jamānat

bait n. चारा chārā

bake v. पकाउनु pākaunu

bakery n. बेकरी bekari

balance n. तराजु tarāju

balcony n. कौसी kausi

bald adj. खल्वाट khalbāt

ball n. बल bal, भकुण्डो bhakundo

balloon n. गुब्बारा gubbārā

ballot n. मतपत्र matpatra

bamboo n. बाँस bāns

bamboo shoots n. तामा tāmā

ban v. रोक लगाउनु rok lagāunu

banal adj. साधारण sadhārān

banana n. केरा kerā

band n. बैण्ड bānd

bandage n. पट्टी patti

bandit n. डाँकु daanku

bangle n. चुरा curā

banish v. देशनिकाला deshnikāla garnu

bank n. बैंक bank

bankrupt adj. टाट उल्टेको tāt ulteko

banner n. झण्डा jhandā

banquet n. भोज bhoj

banyan tree n. बरको रुख barko rukh

baptism n. बपतिस्मा baptism

bar n. बार bār; v. रोक लगाउनु rok lagāunu

barbarian n./adj. असभ्य asabhya

barbecue n. घर बाहिर पकाएको मासु ghar bāhira pakāeko māsu

barber n. नाउ nau

barbershop n. नाउको पसल nāu ko pasal

barbiturate n. लागु पदार्थ lāgu padārtha

bare adj. नाङ्गो nāngo

barefoot adj. नाँङ्गो खुट्टा nāngo khuhttā

bargain n. सौदा saudā

bark *v.i.* भुक्नु bhuknu
barley *n.* जौ jau
barrack *n.* छाउनी chhauni
barrel *n.* पीपा pipā
barren *adj.* बन्जर bañjar
barricade *n.* अवरोध abarodh
barrier *n.* अवरोध abarodh
barter *n.* साटासाट गर्नु satasāt garnu
base *n.* अड्डा addā, आधार adhār
baseball *n.* बेसबल besbāl
basement *n.* तहखाना tahkhānā
basic *adj.* मूल mul
basin *n.* चिलमची cilmaci
basis *n.* आधार ādhār
basket *n.* डलिया daliyā, टोकरी tokari
basketball *n.* बास्केट बल bāsket bāl
bastard *n.* अवैध सन्तान abaidh santān
bat *(zoo.) n.* चमेरो chamero
batch *n.* टोली toil
bath *n.* स्नान snān, नुहाउनु nuhāunu
bathe *v.i.* नुहाउनु nuhāunu; *v.t.* स्नान गर्नु snān garnu
bathroom *n.* बाथरुम bāthroom
bathtub *n.* स्नान टब snān tab
battery *n.* ब्याटरी battri
battle *n.* लडाइँ ladai, युद्ध yuddha
battle *v.t.* लडाइँ ladai
battlefield *n.* युद्धस्थल yuddhasthal
battleship *n.* युद्धपोत yuddhapot
bay *n.* खाडी khādi
be *v.i.* हुनु hunu
beach *n.* समुद्र तट samudra tat
beak *n.* चुच्चो chuchho
beam *n.* किरण kiran
bean *n.* सिमी simi

bear *n.* भालु bhālu
beard *n.* दारी dāri
beast *n.* पशु pasu
beat *v.t. (hit/strike)* पिट्नु pitnu; *v.i.* धड्कनु dhadkanu; *n.* धड्कन dhadkan, ताल tāl
beatnik *n.* हिप्पि hippy
beautiful *adj.* सुन्दर sundar
beautify *v.* सुन्दर बनाउनु sundar banāunu
beauty *n.* सुन्दरता sundartā
because *conj.* किनभने kinabhane
become *v.t.* हुनु hunu
becoming *adj.* योग्य yogya
bed *n.* बिछ्यौना bichhauna, विस्तरा bistarā
bedbug *n.* उड्डुस udus, उपिया upiyan
bedridden *adj.* थला परेको thalā pareko
bedroom *n.* सुत्ने कोठा sutne kothā
bedtime *n.* राती सुत्ने बेला rāti sutne belā
bee *n.* माहुरी māhuri
beef *n.* गाईको मासु gaiko māsu
beer *n.* बियर biyar
before *adv./prep.* पहिले pahile
befriend *v.* साथी बनाउनु sāthi banāunu
beg *v.i.* भिक्षा माग्नु bhikshā magnu
beggar *n.* माग्ने māgne
begin *v.i.* शुरु गर्नु suru garnu
beginner *n.* भर्खर सिक्न लागेको varkhar sikna lāgeko
beginning *n.* शुरु suru
behalf *n.* तर्फबाट tarphabata
behave *v.i.* व्यवहार गर्नु byavahār garnu
behavior *n.* व्यवहार byavahār

behind *prep./adj.* पछाडि pachhādi

behold *v.i.* देख्नु dekhanu

belief *n.* विश्वास biswās

believe *v.t.* विश्वास गर्नु biswās garnu

belittle *v.* अपमान गर्नु apmān garnu

bell *n.* घन्टी ghanti

bellhop *n.* होटेलको भरिया hotel ko bhariyā

belly *n.* पेट pet

bellyache *n.* पेट दुख्नु pet dukhnu

belong *v.i.* को हुनु ko hunu

belonging *n.* सामान sāmān

beloved *adj.* प्रिय priya

below *adv./prep.* तल tala

belt *n.* पेटी peti

bench *n.* बेन्च bench

bend *v.t.* झुकाउनु jhukāunu

beneath *prep.* को तल ko tala

benefactor *n.* उपकारी upakāri

beneficial *adj.* लाभदायक lābhadāyak

beneficiary *n.* लाभान्वित हुने lābhānuit hune

benefit *n.* लाभ labh; *v.t.* लाभ पुर्याउनु lābh puryaunu

bent *adj.* बाङ्गिएको bāngiyeko

berry *n.* बयर bayer

beside *prep./adj.* को छेउमा ko chheuma

best *adj.* सबभन्दा असल sabbhandā asal

bestial *adj.* जंगली jangali

bet *n.* शर्त लगाउनु sart lagāunu

betray *v.t.* विश्वासघात गर्नु biswasghāt garnu

better *adj.* झन् राम्रो jhan rāmro

between *prep.* बीचमा beechmā

beverage *n.* पिउने पदार्थ piune padārtha

beware! *interj.* खबरदार khabardār

beyond *prep.* भन्दा पारी bhandā pāri

biannual *adj.* अर्धवार्षिक semi-annual

biannual *adj.* द्विवार्षिक dwi bārsik

bible *n.* बाइवल bāibal

bibliography *n.* पुस्तकको तालिका pustak ko talika

bicameral *adj.* दुई सदनको dui sadanko

bicycle *n.* साइकल saikal

bifurcate *v.* दुई टुक्रा पार्नु dui tukrā pārnu

big *adj.* ठूलो thulo

bigamy *n.* दुई पत्नी संग विवाह dui patnisanga bibāh

bigot *n.* असहनशील asahansil

bilateral *adj.* द्विपक्षिय dwipaksiya

bilingual *adj.* दुई भाषा जान्ने dui bhasā jānne; *adj.* दुई भाषा बोल्ने dui bhasa bolne

bill *n.* बिल bil

billiards *n.* बिलियर्ड biliyard

billion *n.* विलियन biliyan

bimonthly *adj.* द्वैमासिक dwaimāsik

bind *v.t.* बाँध्नु bāndhnu

binocular *n.* दुरवीन durbin

biography *n.* जीवनी jivani

biological *adj.* जैविक jaivik

biology *n.* जैविक विज्ञान jaivik bigyān

bird *n.* चरा charā

birth *n.* जन्म janma

birthday *n.* जन्मदिन janma din

biscuit *n.* बिस्कुट biscuit

bit *n.* टुक्रा tukrā

bitch *n.* कुकुरनी kukkurni

bite *n.* टोक्नु toknu

bitter *adj.* कटु katu

biweekly *adj.* हप्तामा दुई पटक haptāmā dui patak

black *adj.* कालो kālo

black market *n.* कालो बजार kālo bajār

black sheep *n.* कसैसंग नमिल्ने kasai sanga namilne

blackmail *n.* धुत्नु dhutnu

blackout *n.* केहिबेर बेहोस हुनु kehiber behos hunu

blacksmith *n.* कामी kāmi

blame *n.* दोष दिनु dos dinu

blanket *n.* कम्बल kambal

blasphemy *n.* इश निन्दा ish nindā

blast *n.* धमाका dhamakā

blaze *n.* आगोको ज्वाला āgoko jwālā

bleak *adj.* निराशापूर्ण nirāsāpurna

bleed *v.i.* रगत आउनु ragat āunu

blend *v.* मिसाउनु misāunu

bless *v.t.* आशीर्वाद दिनु asirvād dinu

blessing *n.* आशीर्वाद asirvād

blind *adj.* अन्धो andho

blindness *n.* अन्धोपन andhopān

blink *v.i.* आँखा झिम्काउनु ankhā jhimkaaunu

blond *adj.* पहेलो कपाल pahelo kapāl

blood *n.* रगत ragat

blood pressure *n.* रक्तचाप raktachāp

blood relation *n.* रगतको नाता ragat ko nātā

bloom *v.i.* फूल्नु phulnu

blouse *n.* व्लाउज blāus

blow *v.t.* उडाइदिनु udai dinu

blow up *v.* पड्किनु padkinu

blue *adj.* नीलो nilo

bluff *v.* झूठा कुरा गरी धोका दिनु jhuto kurā gari dhokā dinu

blunder *n.* ठूलो भूल thulo bhul

blush *v.* लाजले रातो हुनु lājle rāto hunu

board *n.* कार्य समिती karya samiti

boarder *n.* छात्रवास वस्ने chatrāvās basne

boarding school *n.* छात्रावास chātrāvās

boast *v.* गर्व संग बोल्ने garb sanga bolne

boat *n.* नाउ nau, डुंगा dungā

boating *n.* नौकाविहार naukāvihār

bodily *adj.* शारिरिक sāririk

body *n.* शरीर sarir

bodyguard *n.* अंगरक्षक angaraksak

bogus *adj.* नक्कली nakkali

boil *n.* उमाल्नु umālnu

boiled *adj.* उमालेको umāleko

bold *adj.* बहादुर bahādur

bomb *n.* बम खसाल्नु bomb khasālnu

bombard *v.* बमले हमला गर्नु bamle hamlā garnu

bond (*personal*) *n.* सम्बन्ध sambandha

bone *n.* हाड hād

bonus *n.* बोनस bonus

book *n.* पुस्तक pustak, किताब kitab

bookcase *n.* पुस्तकको दराज pustak ko darāj

booking *n.* अग्रिम आरक्षण agrim āraksan

bookkeeping *n.* खाता र लेनदेनको हिसाब khātā ra lendenko hisāb

booklet *n.* सानो पुस्तक sāno pustak

bookstore *n.* पुस्तकको पसल pustak pasal

bookworm *n.* किताबी किरा kitābi kirā

boomerang *n.* फर्कर आउनु pharkera āunu

boon *n.* बरदान bardān

boorish *adj.* बदमास badtamij

boot *n.* बूट but

booty *n.* लूट loot

border *n.* सीमा simā

borderline *n.* सीमा रेखा simārekhā

boredom *n.* बोरदिक्क हुनु dikka hunu

born *adj.* जन्मजात janamjāt

borough *n.* शहरको एक भाग saharko ek bhāg

borrow *v.* सापट लिनु sāpat linu

boss *n.* मालिक mālik

botany *n.* विरुवाको विज्ञान biruwā ko bigyān

both *adj.* दुवै dubai

bother *v.* दुख दिनु dukh dinu

bottle *n.* बोटल botal

bottleneck *n.* बाधा bādha

bottom *n.* तल tala

boulder *n.* ठूलो ढुंगा thulo dhungā

bounce *v.* फर्कर आउनु pharkera āunu

bounty *n.* सरकारी इनाम sarkāri inām

bourgeois *n.* मध्यमवर्गीय madhyam bargiya, पूंजीपति punjipati

boutique *n.* सानो पसल sāno pasal

bow *v.* निहुरनु nihuranu

bowel *n.* पेट pet

box *n.* बाकस bākas; सन्दुक sanduk

boxing *n.* मुक्केबाजी mukkebāzi

boy *n.* केटा ketā

boycott *n.* बहिष्कार bahiskār

boyfriend *n.* प्रेमी premi

brag *v.* बढाई कुरा गर्नु badhāi kurā garnu

brahmin *n.* बाहुन bāhun

brain *n.* मगज magaj

brainwashing *n.* मानिसको विचार वदल्ने mānisko bicār badalne

brake *n.* ब्रेक brek

branch *n.* हांगा nāngā

brandnew *adj.* एक दम नयाँ ekdam nayā

brave *adj.* बहादुर bahādur

breach *n.* भंग गर्ने काम bhangā gārne kāam

bread *n.* रोटी roti

breadth *n.* चौडाई caudai

break *n.* बेरक; *v.i.* भाँच्चिनु bhāchinu

breakdown *n.* बिग्रनु bigranu

breakfast *n.* बिहानको खाजा bihānko khāja

breast *n.* आईमाईको छाती स्तन āimāi ko chāti?

breath *n.* सास sās

breathe *v.* सास फेर्नु sas phernu

brewery *n.* बीयर बनाउने ठाँउ biiyar banāune thaun

bribe *n.* घुस ghus; *v.t.* घुस दिनु ghus dinu

brick *n.* ईंटा intā

bricklayer *n.* डकर्मी dararmi

bride *n.* दुलही dulahi

bridegroom *n.* दुलहा dulahā

brief *adj.* संक्षिप्त sanksipta

briefcase *n.* ब्रिफकेस brifkes

brigand *n.* डाकू dānku

bright *adj.* चम्किलो chamkilo

brilliant *adj.* चम्किलो chamkilo

bring *v.i.* ल्याउनु lyāunu

Britain *n.* ब्रिटेन biten

British *adj.* अंगेजी angreji; *n.* अंगेज angre

brittle *adj.* सजिलै सँग भाँचिने sajilai sanga bhancine

broad *adj.* चौडा caudā

broadcast *v.* प्रसारण prasāran
broccoli *n.* ब्रोकाउली kāuli
broken *adj.* भाचेँको bhānceko
broker *n.* दलाल dalāl
brokerage *n.* दलाली dalāli
bronchitis *n.* ब्रोङकाइटिस bronkaitis
bronze *n.* पित्तलको pittalko
broom *n.* कुचो kucho
brothel *n.* वेश्यालय veshyālaya
brother *n.* भाइ bhāi
brother-in-law *n.* *(wife's younger brother)* सालो sālo; *(wife's older brother)* जेठान jethan; *(husband's elder brother)* जेठाजु jethāju; *(husband's younger brother)* देवर dewar
brotherhood *adj.* भाई चारा bhāi cara
brush *n.* ब्रस bras
brutal *adj.* क्रूर krur
bubble *n.* फोका phokā
bucket *n.* बाल्टिन bāltin
bud *n.* कोपिला kopilā
Buddhism *n.* बुद्ध धर्म buddha dharma
buddy *n.* असल साथी asal sāthi
budget *n.* बजेट bajet
buffalo *n.* भैंसी bhainsi
buffet *n.* बूफे bufe
bug *n.* किरा kirā
build *v.* बनाउनु banāunu
building *n.* घर ghar, भवन bhawan
built *adj.* बनाएको banāeko
bulb *n.* बल्ब balb
bulk *n.* धेरै जसो dherai jaso
bullet *n.* गोली goli
bulletin *n.* बुलेटिन buletin
bullock *n.* गोरु goru

bum *n.* गुण्डा gundā
bundle *n.* बन्डल bandal
bungalow *n.* वैंगला bungalā
bunker *n.* बङकर bankar
burden *n.* भार bhar
bureau *n.* कार्यालय kāryālay
bureaucracy *n.* लालफिताशाही lāl fita sahi
bureaucrat *n.* कर्मचारी karmachāri
burglar *n.* चोर cor
burglarize *v.* चोरी गर्नु cori garnu
burn *n.* जल्नु jālnu, बल्नु balnu
bury *v.t.* गाइनु gādnu
bus *n.* बस bas
business *n.* व्यापार byāpār
busy *adj.* व्यस्त byasta
but *conj.* तर tara
butcher *n.* कसाइ kasai
butter *n.* मक्खन makkhan
butterfly *n.* पुतली putali
buttermilk *n.* मही mahi
button *n.* टाँक tānk
buy *v.t.* किन्नु kinnu, खरिद गर्नु kharid garnu
buyer *n.* खरिददार kharidadār
by *prep.* बाट bāta
by-gone *adj.* वितिसकेको bitisakeko
by-law *n.* संस्थाको नियम samsthāko niyam

C

cabbage *n.* बन्दगोभी bandāgobhi

cabin *n.* कोठा kothā

cabinet *n.* मन्त्रीमण्डल mantrimandal

cable *n.* तार tār

cadaver *n.* मुर्दा murdā

cafe *n.* जलपानगृह jalpāngriha

cafeteria *n.* क्याफिटेरिया cafiteria

cage *n.* पिंजरा piñjarā

cake *n.* केक kek

calamity *n.* आपतको कारण āpat ko kāran

calculate *v.t.* हिसाब गर्नु hisāb garnu

calculator *n.* गणक ganak

calendar *n.* तिथि पत्र tithi-patra

calf *(zoo.)* *n.* बाच्छो bāchho

call *n.* फोन गर्नु phon garnu; *v.* बोलाउनु bolāunu

calm *adj.* शान्त sānt; *v.i.* शान्त हुनु sānt hunu

camel *n.* ऊँट unt

camera *n.* क्यामेरा kyāmerā

camp *n.* शिविर sivir; *v.i.* शिविर राख्नु sivir rākhnu

campaign *n.* अभियान abhiyān

campus *n.* कलेज भवन kalej bhawan

can *v. aux.* सक्नु saknu

canal *n.* नहर nahar

cancel *v.t.* रद्द गर्नु radd garnu

cancer *n.* क्यान्सर kyansar

candid *adj.* सरल saral

candidate *n.* उम्मेदवार ummedbar

candle *n.* मैनबत्ती mainbatti

candy *n.* मिठाई mithāi

cane *n.* बेत bet

cannon *n.* तोप top

canoe *n.* डुङ्गा dungā

canteen *n.* क्यान्टिन kāntin

cantonment *n.* छाउनी chāuni

cap *n.* टोपी topi

capable *adj.* समर्थ sāmartha

capacity *n.* सामर्थ्य sāmarthya

cape *n.* अन्तरिप antarip

capital *(fin.)* *n.* पूँजी punji

capitalism *n.* पूँजीवाद punjibād

capitol *n.* राजधानी rajdhāni

capitulate *v.* आत्मसमर्पण गर्नु atmā samarpan garnu

captain *n.* कप्तान kaptān

captivity *n.* कैद kaid

car *n.* गाडी gāri

caravan *n.* कारवाँ caraban

carbon *n.* कार्वन kārban

care *v.i.* देख-रेख dekh–rekh; परवाह गर्नु parvah garnu

careful *adj.* सावधान sāvdhān

careless *adj.* लापरवाह lāparavāh

cargo *n.* कारगो kārgo

caricature *n.* व्यङ्ग vyanga

carnage *n.* हत्याकाण्ड hatyā kānd

carnival *n.* आनन्दोत्सव ānandotsav

carnivorous *adj.* मांसाहारी māmsāhāri

carpenter *n.* सिकर्मी sikarmi

carpet *n.* गलैंचा galainca

carrot *n.* गाजर gāzar

carry *v.t.* लैजानु laijānu

cart *n.* ठेला thela

cartoon *adj.* कार्टून kārtun

cartridge *n.* कारतूस kārtus
case *n.* मुद्दा muddā
cash *n.* नगद पैसा nagad paisā
cashew *n.* काजु kāju
cashier *n.* खन्चाजी khanchāji
casino *n.* कसिनो kasino
caste *n.* जात jāt
castle *n.* कोट cot, जात jāt
casual *adj.* आकस्मिक ākasmik
casualty *n.* हताहत hatāhat
cat *n.* बिरालो birālo
catalog *n.* सूचीपत्र suchipatrā
cataract *n.* आँखाको रोग āankhā
 ko rog
catastrophe *n.* ठूलो विपत्ती thulo
 bippati
catch *n.* समात्न samātnu; *v.* समात्नु
 samatnu
category *n.* किसिम kisim
caterpillar *n.* झुसिलकीरा jhusilkirā
cathedral *n.* इसाईहरूको पूजास्थल
 isāiharuko pujāsthal
Catholic *adj.* क्याथोलिक kyatholok
Catholicism *n.* क्याथोलिक धर्म
 kyatholok dharma
cattle *n.* गाईवस्तु gāibastu
cauliflower *n.* फुलगोभी gobhi
cause *n.* कारण kāran
caution *n.* सावधानी sāvdhani
cautious *adj.* सावधान sāvadhan
cavalry *n.* घुघोडसवार सेना
 ghudsawār senā
cave *n.* गुफा gufa
cavern *n.* ठूलो गुफा thulo gufā
cease *v.i.* बन्द हुनु vanda hunu
cedar *n.* देवदार devdār
celebrate *v.t.* मनाउनु manāunu
celebration *n.* समारोह samāroh
celebrity *n.* प्रसिद्ध व्यक्ति
 prasiddha vyakti
cell *n.* कोठरी kothāri

cellar *n.* तहखाना tahkhānā
cement *n.* सिमेन्ट siment
cemetery *n.* कब्रिस्तान kabristaan
censor *v.* सेन्सर गर्नु sensar garnu
centenarian *n.* सयवर्ष वाँच्नु
 sayavarsa bachnu
centenary *n.* शताब्दी satābdi
center *n.* केन्द्र kendra
centimeter *n.* सेन्टीमीटर
 sentimitar
central *adj.* केन्द्रीय kendriya
centralization *n.* केन्द्रीकरण
 kendrikaran
century *n.* शताब्दी satābdi
ceramic *adj.* माटोको mātoko
cereal *n.* अनाज anāj
ceremonial *adj.* आलंकारिक
 ālankārik
ceremony *n.* समारोह samāroh
certain *adj.* निश्चित niscit
certificate *n.* प्रमाणपत्र pramān-
 patrā
certified check *n.* बैंकले ग्यारेन्टी
 दिएको चेक bankle gyaranti
 diyeko cek
certify *v.t.* प्रमाणित गर्नु pramanit
 garnu
chair *n.* कुर्सी kursi
chairman *n.* सभापति sabhāpati
challenge *n.* चुनौती cauunauti;
 v.t. चुनौती दिनु cunauti dinu
chamber *n.* कोठा kothā
champagne *n.* श्याम्पेन syampen
champion *n.* बिजेता vijetā
chance *n.* संयोग sanyog
chancellor *n.* कुलपति kulpati
change *v.i.* परिवर्तन गर्नु
 parivartan garnu
changeable *adj.* परिवर्तनीय
 parivartaniya
channel *n.* चैनल cainal

chaos *n.* अव्यबस्था abyabasthā

chaotic *adj.* गडबड garbar

chapel *n.* प्रार्थनालय prathnālaya

chapter *n.* अध्याय adhyaya

character *n.* चरित्र caritra

characteristic *n.* विशेषता visesta

charcoal *n.* कोइला koilā

charge *(leg.) v.t.* अभियोग लगाउनु abhiyog lagāunu; *n.* अभियोग abhiyog

chariot *n.* रथ rath

charism *n.* करिश्मा karismā

charity *n.* दान dān

charm *n.* आकर्षण ākarsan

chart *n.* मानचित्र māncitra

charter *n.* शासनपत्र sāsanpatra

chase *v.* लखेट्नु lakhetnu

chat *n.* कुराकानी kurākāni; *v.i.* कुरा गर्नु kurākani garnu

chauffeur *n.* डाइभर dāibhar

cheap *adj.* सस्तो sasto

cheat *v.* ठग्नु thagnu

check *v.t.* चेक cek; जाँच गर्नु jānc garnu

check-in *n.* होटेलमा रजिस्टर गर्नु hotel mā rajistar garnu

check-out *n.* होटेलमा बिल तिरी निस्कनु hotel mā bil tiri niskanu

cheek *n.* गाला gālā

cheerful *adj.* खुशी हुनु khusi hunu

cheese *n.* पनिर panir

chemical *adj.* रसायनिक rasāynik

chemist *n.* रसायनिक सास्त्री rasāynik sāstri

chemistry *n.* रसायन शास्त्र rasāyan shāstra

cherish *v.t.* मान्नु mānnu

chess *n.* बुद्धिचाल buddhichāl

chest *(anat.) n.* छाती chāti

chestnut *n.* कटुस katus

chew *v.t.* चपाउनु chapāunu

chicken *n.* कुखुरा kukhurā

chief *n.* मुख्य mukhya

child *n.* बालक bālak

childhood *n.* बाल्यावस्था bālyabasathā

childish *adj.* केटाकेटी जस्तो ketāketi jasto

childlike *adj.* बच्चा जस्तो baccā jasto

chill *n.* चिसो chiso

chilly *adj.* ठण्डा thandā

chin *n.* चिउँडो chiudo

China *n.* चीन cin

Chinese *adj./n.* चीनीया ciniyā

chip *n.* चिप cipp; *v.t.* काट्नु katnu

chocolate *n.* चकलेट caklet

choice *n.* चुनाव cunāv

choir *n.* गायक-मण्डल gāyak-mandal

choke *v.t.* घाँटी थिच्नु ghāti thichnu

cholera *n.* हैजा jaihā

cholesterol *n.* कोलेस्ट्रोल kolesterol

choose *v.t.* छान्नु chānnu

chop *v.t.* काट्नु kātnu

Christian *n./adj.* ईसाई isāi

Christianity *n.* ईसाई धर्म isāi dharma

Christmas *n.* क्रिसमस krismas

chronic *adj.* पुरानो purāno

church *n.* गिर्जाघर girjāghar

chutney *n.* चटनी catni

cigar *n.* सिगार sigār

cigarette *n.* चुरोट churot

cinema *n.* सिनेमा sinemā

cinnamon *n.* दालचिनी dālcini

circle *n.* गोलो golo

circuit *n.* चक्कर cakkar

circulate *v.t.* प्रचारित गर्नु pracārit garnu

circulation *n.* प्रचार pracār

circumference *n.* घेरा gherā, परिधि paridhi

circumstance *n.* परिस्थिति paristhiti

circus *n.* सरकस sarkas

cite *v.t.* उद्धरण दिनु udhdaran dinu

citizen *n.* नागरिक nāgarik

citizenship *n.* नागरिकता nāgariktā

city *n.* सहर sahar

civil rights *n.* नागरिक अधिकार nāgarik adhikar

civil service *n.* निजामती सेवा nijāmati sevā

civil war *n.* गृहयुद्ध griha yuddha

civilization *n.* सभ्यता sabhyatā

civilized *adj.* सभ्य sabhya

claim *n.* दावा dāvā; *v.t.* दावा गर्नु dāvā garnu

clandestine *adj.* गोप्य gopya

clap *v.t.* ताली बजाउनु tāli bajāunu

clarify *v.* स्पष्ट गर्नु spasta garnu

class *n.* कक्षा kaksā

classical *adj.* शास्त्रीय sāstriy

classify *v.t.* वर्गीकरण गर्नु vargikaran garnu

classroom *n.* कक्षाकोठा kaksā kothā

claw *n.* पञ्जा panjā

clay *n.* माटो mitti

clean *v.t.* सफा गर्नु safā garnu

clear *adj.* स्पष्ट spasta

clemency *n.* माफी māphi

clergy *n.* पादरी वर्ग pādri varg

clergyman *n.* पादरी pādri

clerical *adj.* कारिन्दा बारे kārinda bāre

clerk *n.* कारिन्दा kārinda

clever *adj.* चलाख chalakh

client *n.* ग्राहक grāhak

cliff *n.* चट्टान cattān

climate *n.* जलवायु jalvāyu

climax *n.* पराकाष्ठा parākāstā

climb *n.* चढाई chadhāi; *v.t.* चढ्नु chadhnu

cling *v.i.* टाँस्सिनु tāssinu

clinic *n.* चिकित्सालय cikitsālay

clip *n.* प्याला pyālā

clock *n.* घडी ghadi

close *adj.* नजिक najik; *v.t.* बन्द गर्नु band garnu

closed *adj.* बन्द band

closet *n.* कोठरी kothari

cloth *n.* कपडा kapadā

clothe *v.t.* कपडा पहिराउनु kapadā pahiraunu

clothing *n.* कपडा kapadā, लुगा luga

cloud *n.* बादल bādal

cloudy *adj.* बदली bādali

clove *n.* ल्वाङ lwāng

cloves *n.* ल्वाङ lwāng

club *(group) n.* क्लब kalab; सभा sabhā

clue *n.* सूत्र sutra

cluster *n.* समूह sanuha

coach *n.* डिब्बा dibbā

coal *n.* कोइला koilā

coalition *n.* गठबन्धन gathabandhan

coarse *adj.* मोटो moto

coast guard *n.* तट रक्षक raksak

coast *n.* किनारा kinārā

coat *n.* कोट kot

cobra *n.* कोब्रा kobrā

cobweb *n.* जालो jālo

cock *n.* कुखुरा kukhurā

cockroach *n.* साङलो sānglo

cocoa *n.* कोको koko

coconut *n.* नरिवल nariwal

code *n.* संकेत sanket

code of conduct *n.* आचार संहिता acār samhitā

coerce *v.* कर गर्नु kar garnu

coffee *n.* कफी kāfi

coffee shop *n.* कफी गृह kāfi griha

coffin *n.* कफिन kafin

cohabit *v.* विवाह नगरी सँगै वस्नु vivah nagari sangai basnu

coil *n.* कुण्डली kundali

coin *n.* सिक्का sikkā

coincide *v.i.* एकै पटक हुने ekaipatak hune

coincidence *n.* संयोग sanyog

coincidental *n.* आकस्मिक ākasmik

cold *n./adj.* चिसो chiso

colic *n.* शूल sul

collaborate *v.i.* सँगै काम गर्नु sangai kām garnu

collaboration *n.* सहयोग sahayog

collect *v.t.* जम्मा गर्नु jammā garnu

collection *n.* संग्रह sangrah

college *n.* कलेज kalej

collide *v.i.* ठक्कर लाग्नु thakkar lāgnu

collision *n.* ठक्कर thakkar

colloquial *adj.* बोलिने भाषा boline bhāsā

colon *n.* आन्द्रा āndrā

colonel *n.* कर्नेल karnel

colonialism *n.* उपनिवेशवाद upaniveshvād

colony *n.* उपनिवेश upnives

color *n.* रङ्ग rang

column *n.* स्तम्भ stamb

columnist *n.* स्तंभकार stambhakār

comb *n.* काँगियो kāngiyo

combat *v.* लड्नु ladnu

combatant *n.* लडाकु ladāku

combination *n.* संयोग sanyog

combine *v.t.* मिलाउनु milāunu

come *v.i.* आउनु āunu

comedy *n.* हास्य hāsya

comet *n.* धूमकेतु dhumketu

comfort *n.* आराम ārām

comfortable *adj.* आरामदायक ārāmdāyak

comic *n.* हास्यकार hāsyakar

comma *n.* अल्प विराम alp virām

command *n.* आदेश ādes; *v.t.* आदेश दिनु ades dinu

commence *v.i.* शुरु हुनु suru hunu

comment *n.* टिप्पणी tippani; *v.t.* टिप्पणी गर्नु tippani garnu

commentary *n.* टीका भाषा tikā bhāsā

commerce *n.* वाणिज्य vānijy

commercial *adj.* व्यापारिक vyāpārik; *n.* विज्ञापन vigyāpan

commission *n.* आयोग āyog

commit *v.* काम गर्नु kām garnu

committee *n.* समिति samiti

common *adj.* सामान्य sāmāny

common market *n.* साझा बजार sājha bajār

commonwealth *n.* राष्ट्रमण्डल rastra mandal

communal *adj.* सांप्रदायिक sāmpradayik

communicable *adj.* सर्ने sarne

communicate *v.t.* सूचना दिनु suchana dinu

communication *n.* सम्पर्क samparka, सूचना suchanā

communism *n.* साम्यवाद sāmyavād

communist *n./adj.* साम्यवादी sāmyavādi

community *n.* समुदाय samudaya

commute *v.* काम गर्ने आफ्नो सहरबाट बाहिर जानु kām garna aphno sahar bāta bāhira jānu

compact disc (CD) *n.* कम्प्याक्ट डिस्क kampakt disk

companion *n.* साथी sāthi

companionship *n.* संगति sangati

company *n.* कम्पनी campani

comparable *adj.* तुलनायोग्य tylanāyogya

compare *v.t.* तुलना गर्नु tulnā garnu

comparison *n.* तुलना tulnā

compartment *n.* उपखण्ड upkhand

compass *n.* दिकसूचक diksucak

compassion *n.* करुणा karunā

compatible *adj.* संगत sangat

compel *v.* जवर्जस्ती काम गराउनु jawarjasto kām garāunu

compensate *v.* क्षतिपूर्ति दिनु ksatipurti dinu

compensation *n.* क्षतिपूर्ति ksatipurti

compete *v.* प्रतिस्पर्धा गर्नु pratispardha garnu

competence *n.* योग्यता yogyatā

competent *adj.* समर्थ samarth

competition *n.* प्रतियोगिता pratiyogita

competitive *adj.* प्रतियोगी pratiyogi

complaint *n.* उजुर ujur

complete *adj.* पूर्ण purna; *v.t.* पूरा गर्नु purā garnu

complicate *v.t.* जटिल बनाउनु jatil banāunu

complicated *adj.* जटिल jatil

complication *n.* जटिलता jatilatā

compliment *n.* प्रशंसा prasnsā; *v.t.* अभिनन्दन गर्नु abhinandan garnu

comply *v.i.* पालना गर्नु palanā garnu

compose *v.t.* रचना गर्नु racnā garnu

composition *n.* रचना racnā

comprehend *v.* बुझ्नु bujhnu

comprehensive *adj.* व्यापक vyāpak

comprise *v.t.* समाविष्ट गर्नु samāvist garnu

compromise *n.* सम्झौता samjhautā; *v.* सम्झौता गर्न samjhauta garnu

compulsion *n.* बाध्यता vadhyatā

compulsory *adj.* अनिवार्य anivārya

computer *n.* कम्प्यूटर kampyutar

conceal *v.t.* लुकाउनु lukāunu

conceit *n.* अहंकार ahankār

conceive *v.* गर्भवती हुनु garbhavati hunu

concentrate *v.i.* एकत्र गर्नु ekatra garnu

concept *n.* धारणा dhāranā

concern *n.* चिन्ता cintā; *v.t.* चासो राख्नु chaso rākhnu

concerned *adj.* चिन्तित cintit

concert *n.* संगीत समारोह sangit samāroh

concession *n.* सहुलियत sahuliyat

concise *adj.* संक्षिप्त sanksipt

conclude *v.* समाप्त गर्नु samapta garnu

conclusion *n.* समाप्ति samāpati

concubine *n.* रखैल rakhail

condemn *v.t.* निन्दा गर्नु ninda garnu

condition *n.* शर्त sart

condolence *n.* समवेदना samvedanā

condom *n.* कण्डम kondom

conduct *n.* आचरण ācaran; *v.t.* सञ्चालन गर्नु sancālan garnu

conductor *n.* सञ्चालक sañcālak

conference *n.* सम्मेलन sammelan

confess *v.t.* मान्नु mannu. स्वीकार गर्नु swikār garnu

confession *n.* स्वीकृति swikriti
confidence *n.* विश्वास visvās
confidential *n.* गोप्य gopya
confirm *v.t.* पक्का गर्नु pakkā garnu
confirmation *n.* पुष्टिकरण pustikaran
confiscate *v.* अधिग्रहण गर्नु adhigrahan garnu
conflict *n.* संघर्ष sanghars
confuse *v.t.* भ्रमित हुनु bhramit hunu
confusion *n.* भ्रम bhram
congratulate *v.t.* बधाई दिनु badhāi dinu
congratulation *n.* बधाई badhāi
congress *n.* महासभा mahāsabhā
conjecture *n.* अनुमान anumān
conjunction *n.* मेल mel
connect *v.t.* जोड़िनु jodnu
connection *n.* सम्बन्ध sambandh
conquer *v.t.* विजय गर्नु viyay garnu
conquest *n.* विजय viyay
conscience *n.* विवेक vivek
conscientious *adj.* इमान्दार imāndār
conscious *adj.* जानकार jānkār
consensus *n.* सर्वसम्मति sarvasammati
consent *n.* सहमति sahamati; *v.t.* सहमति दिनु sahamati dinu
consequence *n.* परिणाम parinām
conservation *n.* संरक्षण samraksan
conservative *adj.* अनुदार anudār
conserve *v.t.* संरक्षण गर्नु samraksan garnu
consider *v.t.* विचार गर्नु vicār garnu
considerable *adj.* निकै nikai
consideration *n.* विचार vicār
consist *v.i.* को हुनु ko hunu

consolation *n.* सान्त्वना sāntwanā
console *v.t.* सान्त्वना दिनु sāntwanā dinu
consolidate *v.* एकरूपता दिनु elrupatā dinu
conspiracy *n.* षडयन्त्र sadyantra
constant *adj.* स्थिर sthir
constipation *n.* कब्जियत kabijiyat
constituency *n.* निर्वाचन क्षेत्र nirvācan ksetra
constituent assembly *n.* संविधान सभा sambidhān sabhā
constitute *v.t.* बनाउनु banāunu
constitution *n.* संविधान samvidhān
constitutional *adj.* संवैधानिक sambaidhānik
construct *v.t.* बनाउनु banaunu
construction *n.* निर्माण nirmān
consul *n.* वाणिज्य दूत vanijyadut
consulate *n.* दूतावास dutāvās
consult *v.i.* सल्लाह लिनु sallah linu
consultant *n.* परामर्शदाता parāmarsdātā
consume *v.t.* उपभोग गर्नु upbhog garnu
consumer *n.* उपभोक्ता upabhoktā
consumption *n.* उपभोग upabhog
contact *n.* स्पर्श spars; *v.t.* सम्पर्क sampark
contagious *adj.* सर्ने sarne
contain *v.t.* समावेश गर्नु samāves garnu
contaminate *v.t.* दुषित गर्नु dusit garnu
contempt *n.* तिरस्कार tiraskār, अपमान apmān
content *adj.* सन्तुष्ट santust; *n.* विषयवस्तु visayvastu
contest *n.* प्रतियोगिता pratiyogitā; *v.t.* मुकाबिला गर्नु mukavila garnu

contestant *n.* प्रतियोगी pratiyogi

context *n.* संदर्भ sandarbha

continent *n.* महाद्वीप mahādvip

continue *v.t.* चालु गर्नु chalu garnu

continuity *n.* निरन्तरता nirantartā

continuous *adj.* निरन्तर nirantar

contraceptive *adj./n.* निरोधक nirodhak

contract *n.* अनुबन्ध anubandh, करार karār, ठेक्का thekkā

contrary *adj.* विरुद्ध viruddha

contrast *v.t.* विषमता visamtā

contribute *v.* योगदान गर्नु yogadān garnu

contribution *n.* चन्दा candā

control *n.* नियन्त्रण गर्नु niyantran garnu

controller *n.* नियन्त्रक niyantrak

controversial *n.* विवादास्पद vivādaspad

controversy *n.* विवाद vivādh

convene *v.t.* आयोजना गर्नु āyojanā garnu

convenience *n.* सुविधा suvidhā; *v.* विश्वास दिलाउनु biswās dilāunu

convent *n.* मठ math

convention *n.* अभिसन्धी abhisandhi; सम्झौता samjhautā

converge *v.* विवाद vivād

conversation *n.* बातचित bātcit, कुराकानी kurākāni

convert *v.t.* परिवर्तन गर्नु parivartan garnu

convey *v.t.* भन्नु bhannu

convict *v.* दोषी ठहर गर्नु dosi thahar garnu

convince *v.* चित्त बुझाउनु citta bujhāunu

cook *n.* पकाउनु pakāunu; *v.* पकाउनु pakaunu

cookie *n.* बिस्कुट biskut

cool *adj.* शीतल sital; *v.t.* चिसो गर्नु chiso garnu

cooperate *v.i.* सहयोग गर्नु sahayog garnu

coordinate *v.t.* समन्वय गर्नु samnwaya garnu

coordination *n.* समन्वय samanvaya

cop *n.* पुलिस pulis

copper *n.* तामा tāmā

copy *n.* प्रतिलिपि pratilipi

copyright *n.* प्रतिलिपि अधिकार pratilipi adhikār

coral *n.* मुगा mugā

cordially *adv.* हार्दिक रूपले hārdik ruple

core *n.* सार sār

cork *n.* डाट dāt

corn *n.* मकै makāi

corner *n.* कुना kunā

cornerstone *n.* आधारशिला ādhārsilā

coronary *adj.* मुटु संबन्धि mutu sambandhi

coronation *n.* राज्यभिषेक rājyābhiksek

corporation *n.* निगम nigam, संस्थान sansthān

corpse *n.* लास lās

correct *adj.* ठीक tik; *v.t.* ठीक गर्नु tik garnu

correction *n.* संशोधन sansodhan

correspond *v.i.* पत्र व्यवहार गर्नु patra vyavahār garnu

correspondence *n.* पत्र व्यवहार patra vyavahār

correspondent *n.* पत्र लेखक patra lekhak; संवाददाता sambadātā

corrupt *adj.* भ्रष्ट bhrst; *v.t.* खराब गर्नु kharāb garnu

corruption *n.* भ्रष्टाचार bhrastācār

cost *n.* दाम dām, मोल mol

costume *n.* पोशाक posāk

cot *n.* खाट khāt

cottage *n.* कुटी kuti

cotton *n.* कपास kapās

couch *n.* सोफा sofā

cough *n.* खकार khakār

could *v. aux.* सक्नु saknu

council *n.* परिषद parisad

count *n.* गणना gananā; *v.t.* गन्नु gannu

counter *n.* काउन्टर kauntar

counterfeit *adj.* नक्कल nakkali

country *n.* देश des

county *n.* जिल्ला zilā

couple *n.* दम्पती dampati

courage *n.* साहस sāhas

courageous *adj.* साहसी sāhasi

course *n.* पाठ्यक्रम pātyakram

court *n.* अदालत adālat

court martial *n.* सैनिक अदालत sainik adālat

courtesan *n.* उच्चस्तरीय बेश्या ucastariya vesyā

courtesy *n.* शिष्टाचार sistācār

courtyard *n.* आँगन āngan

cousin *n.* काकाको छोरा kakako chhorā; काकाको छोरी दिदी बहिनी kakako chhori didi bahini; मामाको छोरा mamako chhorā; मामाको छोरी दिदी बहिनी mamako chhori didi bahini

cover *n.* ढक्कन dhakkan; *v.t.* ढाक्नु dhāknu

coverup *n.* ढाकछोप dhākchop

cow *n.* गाई gāi

coward *n.* कायर kāyar

cowboy *n.* गोठालो gothalo

crab *n.* गँगटो gangato

cracker *n.* बिस्कुट biskut

cradle *n.* पालना palnā

craft *n.* शिल्पकला silpakalā

craftsman *n.* शिल्पी silpi

crane *(zoo.) n.* सारस sāras

crash *n.* धमाका dhamākā; *v.* धमाका गर्नु dhamaka garnu

crawl *v.i.* घस्रिनु ghasrinu

crazy *adj.* पागल pāgal, बहुला bahulā

cream *n.* मलाई malāi

create *v.t.* बनाउनु banāunu

creation *n.* सृष्टि srsti

creative *adj.* सिर्जनशील sirjanshil

creature *n.* प्राणी prāni

credit *n.* जम्मा गर्नु jama garnu

creditor *n.* साहू sāhu

cremation *n.* दाह संस्कार dāh sanskār

crest *n.* शिखा sikhā

crew *n.* कर्मीदल karmidal

crime *n.* अपराध aprādh

criminal *adj.* आपराधिक āpradhik; *n.* अपराधी aprādhi

crisis *n.* संकट sankat

critic *n.* आलोचक ālocak

criticism *n.* आलोचना ālocanā

criticize *v.t.* आलोचना गर्नु ālocanā garnu

crocodile *n.* गोही gohi

crook *n.* वदमाश badmās

crooked *adj.* बाङ्गो bāngo

crop *n.* फसल phasal

cross *n.* सूली suli; *v.t.* विरोध गर्नु virodh garnu

crosseye *n.* डेढो dedo

crow *n.* काग kāg

crowd *n.* भीड bhir

crowded *adj.* भीड भएको bhir bhayeko

crown *n.* मुकुट mukut, श्रीपेच sripech

crown prince *n.* युवराज yubrāj

crucial *adj.* निर्णायक महत्त्वको nirnāyak mahatwako

crude *adj.* कच्चा kaccā

cruel *adj.* क्रूर krur

crumb *n.* टुक्रा tukarā

crush *v.t.* कुल्चिनु kulchinu

crutch *n.* बैशाखी baisākhi

cry *n.* चिच्याहट cicāhat; *v.* रुनु runu

crypt *n.* चिहान cihān

crystal *n.* स्फटिक spatik

cube *n.* घन ghan

cuckold *n.* जार jar

cuckoo *n.* कोइली koili

cucumber *n.* काँक्रो kānkro

culprit *n.* दोषी doshi

cultivate *v.* खेती गर्नु kheti garnu

cultivation *n.* खेती kheti

cultural *adj.* सांस्कृतिक sānskritik

culture *n.* संस्कृति sanskriti

cunning *adj.* धूर्त dhurta

cup *n.* प्याला pyālā

cupboard *n.* आलमारी ālmāri, दराज darāj

curb *n.* प्रतिबन्ध pratibandh; *v.t.* दबाब दिनु dabāb dinu

curd *n.* दही dahi

cure *n.* रोगमुक्ति rogmukti; *v.t.* निको पार्नु niko hunu

curfew *n.* कर्फ्यू carfyoo

curiosity *n.* कौतुहल kautuhal

curious *adj.* उत्सुक utsuk

curly *adj.* घुम्रिएको ghumrieko

currency *n.* सिक्का sikkā

current *adj.* चालु cālu

curse *n.* श्राप srāp; *v.* श्राप दिनु sarap dinu

curtain *n.* पर्दा pardā

cushion *n.* गद्दी gaddi, तकिया takiyā

custom *n.* चलन calan, रिवाज rivāz

customer *n.* ग्राहक grāhak

cut *n.* घात ghat; *v.t.* काट्नु kātnu

cycle *n.* साइकल saikal; *v.t.* साइकल चलाउनु saikal calāunu

cynical *adj.* कपटी kapti

D

dad(dy) *n.* पिता pita, बुबा buwā
dagger *n.* छुरा churā
daily *adj.* दैनिक dainik
dairy *n.* डेरी deri; *adj.* दूधबाट बनेको dudhbata baneko
dam *n.* बाँध bāndh
damage *n.* क्षति ksati; *v.t.* बिग्रनु bigranu
damn *v.t.* निन्दा गर्नु nindā garnu
damp *adj.* ओसिएको osiyeko
dance *n.* नाच nāc; *v.i.* नाच्नु nācnu
dandruff *n.* चाया cayā
danger *n.* खतरा khatarā
dangerous *adj.* खतरनाक khatarnāk
dare *n.* साहस sāhas; *v.i.* साहस गर्नु sāhas garnu
daring *adj.* साहसी sāhasi
dark *adj.* अँध्यारो andhyāro
darken *v.t.* अन्धकारमय बनाउनु andhkārmaya banāunu
darkness *n.* अँध्यारो āndhyāro
darling *n.* प्रिय priya
darn *v.t.* रफू गर्नु raphu garnu
dash *n.* ठक्कर thakkar
data *n. pl.* आधार सामग्री ādhar sāmagri; तथ्याङ्क tathyānka
date *n.* खजूर khajur; तारिख tārikh
daughter *n.* छोरी chhori
daughter-in-law *n.* बुहारी buhāri
dawn *n.* उषाकाल usākāl
day *n.* दिन din
dead *adj.* मुर्दा murdā, मरेको mareko

deadline *n.* समयसीमा samayasimā
deaf *adj.* बहिरो bahiro
deal *n.* सौदा saudā
dealer *n.* व्यापारी vyapari
dealing *n.* व्यवहार vyabahār
dear *adj.* प्रिय priya
death *n.* मृत्यु mritu
deathbed *n.* मृत्युशैया mrityu saiyā
debate *n.* बहस bahas; *v.t.* बहस गर्नु bahas garnu
debt *n.* कर्जा karjā
debtor *n.* सापट दिनु sāpat dinu
decade *n.* दशक dasak
decay *v.i.* सड्नु sadnu
deceit *n.* धोका dhokā
deceive *v.t.* धोका दिनु dkhokā dinu
December *n.* दिसेम्बर disembar
decent *adj.* पर्याप्त paryāpta
decentralization *n.* विकेन्द्रीकरण vikendrikaran
deception *n.* धोका dhokā
decide *v.t.* निर्णय गर्नु nirnay garnu, निश्चय गर्नु niscay garnu
decimal *adj.* दशमिक dasmik
decipher *v.* अर्थ लगाउनु artha lagāunu
decision *n.* निर्णय nirnaya
decisive *adj.* निर्णायक nirnāyak
declaration *n.* घोषणा ghosanā
declare *v.t.* घोषणा गर्नु ghosanā garnu
decline *v.i.* नमान्नु namānnu
decompose *v.* सड्नु sadnu
decorate *v.t.* सजाउनु sajāunu

decoration *n.* सजावट sajāvat

decrease *v.t.* घटाउनु ghatāunu

dedicate *v.t.* समर्पण गर्नु samarpan garnu

dedication *n.* समर्पण samarpan

deduct *v.* घटाउनु ghatāunu

deduction *n.* घटाउ ghatāu

deed *n.* कार्य kārya; दस्तावेज datāvez

deem *v.t.* सम्झना samjhanā

deep *adj.* गहिरो gahiro

deer *n.* मृग mriga, हरिण harin

default *n.* चूक cuk

defeat *n.* हार hār; *v.t.* हराउनु harāunu

defect *n.* त्रुटि truti

defective *adj.* त्रुटि भएको truti bhaeko

defend *v.t.* रक्षा गर्नु raksa garnu

defendant *n.* प्रतिवादी prativādi

defense *n.* सुरक्षा suraksā

defer *v.t.* स्थगित गर्नु sthagit garnu

deficit *n.* घाटा ghātā

define *v.t.* परिभाषा दिनु paribhāsā dinu

definite *adj.* निश्चित niscit

definition *n.* परिभाषा paribhāsā

definitive *adj.* निश्चायक niscāyak

deflate *v.t.* हावा निकाल्नु havā nikālnu

defy *v.t.* अवज्ञा गर्नु avagyā garnu

degree *n.* उपाधी upadhi

dehydrated *adj.* निर्जलित nirjalit

deity *n.* देवता devatā

delay *n.* अबेर गर्नु aber garnu

delegate *n.* प्रतिनिधि pratinidhi

delete *v.t.* काट्नु kātnu

deliberate *adj.* जानी जानीकन jāni jānikan

deliberation *n.* छलफल chalphal

delicacy *n.* स्वादिष्ट swādista

delicate *adj.* कोमल komal

delicious *adj.* स्वादिष्ट swādista

delight *n.* हर्ष hars

deliver *v.t.* पुर्‍याउनु puryāunu

delivery *n.* सुत्केरी sutkeri

demand *n.* माग māg; *v.t.* माग्नु māgnu

dementia *n.* मानसिक रोग mānasik rog

democracy *n.* लोकतन्त्र loktantra

democratic *adj.* लोकतान्त्रिक loktāntrik

demography *n.* जनसंख्या बारे janasankhyā bare

demon *n.* राक्षस rāksyas

demonstrate *v.t.* प्रदर्शन गर्नु pradarsan garnu

demonstration *n.* प्रदर्शन pradarsan

dengue fever *n.* एक सरुवा रोग ek saruwā rog

denomination *n.* धार्मिक समूह dharmik samuha

dense *adj.* सघन saghan

density *n.* सघनता saghantā

dent *n.* खाडल khādal

dental *adj.* दाँतको dāntako

dentist *n.* दन्त चिकित्सक dantacikitsak

deny *v.t.* अस्वीकार गर्नु asvikār garnu

depart *v.i.* प्रस्थान गर्नु prasthān garnu

department *n.* विभाग vibhāg

departure *n.* प्रस्थान prasthān

depend *v.i.* निर्भर हुनु nirbhar hunu

dependable *adj.* भरपर्दो bhar pardo

dependent *adj.* निर्भर nirbhar; *n.* आश्रित āsrit

depict *v.t.* चित्रण गर्नु citran garnu

deport *v.t.* निर्वासित गर्नु nirvāsit garnu

deposit *v.* जम्मा गर्नु jammā garnu

depress *v.t.* दबाउनु dabāunu

depressed *adj.* उदास udās; खिन्न khinn

depression *n.* उदासी udāsi; खिन्नता khinntā

deprive *v.t.* वञ्चित गर्नु vancit garnu

depth *n.* गहिराइ gahirāi

deputy *n.* उप upa

derive *v.t.* प्राप्त गर्नु prāpta garnu

dermatologist *n.* चर्मरोग विशेषज्ञ carmarog bisesagya

descend *v.i.* तल झर्नु tala jharnu

descent *n.* उतार utār

describe *v.t.* वर्णन गर्नु varnan garnu

description *n.* वर्णन varnan

desert *n.* मरुभूमि marubhumi

deserve *v.t.* योग्य हुनु yogya hunu

design *n.* परिकल्पना parikalpnā; *v.t.* परिकल्पना गर्नु parikalpanā garnu

designate *v.t.* नमूना बनाउनु namuna banāunu

designer *n.* डिजाइन बनाउने dizāin banāune

desirable *adj.* वाञ्छनीय vāncniy

desire *n.* इच्छा icchā; *v.t.* चाहना cāhanā

despair *n.* निराशा nirāsā; *v.i.* निराश हुनु nirās hunu

desperate *n.* अतिनिराश atiniras

despise *v.* मन नपराउनु man naparāunu

despite *prep.* यसो हुदा पनि yaso hundā panii

despot *n.* निरंकुश शासक nirankus sāsak

dessert *n.* डिजर्ट dizart

destination *n.* गन्तव्य gantavya

destiny *n.* भाग्य bhagya

destroy *v.t.* नाश गर्नु nās garnu

destruction *n.* विनास vinās

detach *v.t.* अलग गर्नु alag garnu

detail *n.* विस्तृत विवरण vistrit vivaran

detain *v.t.* बन्दी बनाउनु bandi banāunu

detect *v.t.* पत्ता लगाउनु pattā lagāunu

detection *n.* खोज khoj

detective *n.* गुप्तचर guptcar

detergent *n.* सावुन sabun

determination *n.* संकल्प sankalp

determine *v.t.* निर्धारित गर्नु nirdharit garnu

determined *adj.* निश्चित niscit

detest *v.* घृणा गर्नु ghrinā garnu

develop *v.t.* विकसित गर्नु viksit garnu

development *n.* विकास vikās

deviant *adj.* मापदण्डवाट फरक māpdanda bāta pharak

deviation *n.* विचलन vicalan

device *n.* युक्ति yukti

devil *n.* शैतान saitān

devise *v.t.* सोच निकाल्नु soc nikālnu

devolve *v.* अरुलाई दिनु aru lai dinu

devoted *adj.* समर्पित samarpit

devotion *n.* भक्ति bhakti

devour *v.* लोभ लागी खानु lobh lāgi khānu

devout *adj.* भक्त bhakt

dew *n.* ओस os

diabetes *n.* मधुमेह madhumeh
diabetic *adj./n.* मधुमेही madhumehi
diagnosis *n.* निदान nidān
dial *n.* डायल deyal; *v.t* टेलिफोन गर्नु telifon garnu
dialect *n.* बोली boli
dialogue *n.* संवाद sanvād
diameter *n.* व्यास vyās
diamond *n.* हीरा hirā
diarrhea *n.* दिसा लाग्ने disā lāgnu
diary *n.* डायरी dāyari
dictate *v.t.* लेखाउनु lekhāunu
dictator *n.* एकाधिनायक ekādhināyak, तानाशाह tanasah
dictionary *n.* शब्दकोश sabdkos
die *v.i.* मर्नु marnu
diesel *n.* डिजल dijal
diet *n.* आहार āhār
dietician *n.* आहार विशेषज्ञ āhār visesagya
differ *v.i.* बेग्लै मत राख्नु beglai mat rākhnu
difference *n.* फरक pharak
different *adj.* फरक pharak
differentiate *v.* देखाउनु dekhāunu
difficult *adj.* कठिन kathin
difficulty *n.* कठिनाई kathināi
dig *v.t.* खोद्नु khodnu
digest *v.t.* पचाउनु pacāunu
digestion *n.* पाचन pācan
dignified *adj.* प्रतिष्ठित pratisthit
dignity *n.* प्रतिष्ठान pratisthā
diligent *adj.* मेहनती mehanati
dim *adj.* धमिलो dhamilo
dimension *n.* आयाम āyām
diminish *v.t.* कम गर्नु kam garnu
dine *v.i.* भोजन गर्नु bhojan garnu
dining room *n.* भोजनकक्ष bhojankaks

dinner *n.* रातीको खाना rātiko khānā
dinosaur *n.* डाइनोसोर dainosor
dip *v.t.* डुबाउनु dubāunu
diploma *n.* प्रमाणपत्र prāman patra
diplomat *n.* कुटनीतिज्ञ kutnitigya
diplomatic *adj.* कुटनीतिक kutnitik
diptheria *n.* घाँटीको रोग ghānti ko rog
direct *adj.* सीधा sidhā; *adv.* व्यतिगत रुपमा vyaktigat rupmā; *v.t.* सम्बोधित गर्नु sambodhit garnu
direction *n.* दिशा disa
director *n.* निर्देशक nirdesak
directory *n.* निर्देशिका nirdesikā
dirt *n.* फोहर phohar
dirty *adj.* धुलो dhulo
disagree *v.i.* असहमत हुनु asahamat hunu
disagreement *n.* असहमति asahamati
disappear *v.i.* हराउनु harāunu
disappoint *v.t.* निराश गर्नु nirās garnu
disappointment *n.* निराशा nirāsā
disarmament *n.* निशस्त्रिकरण nisastrikaran
disaster *n.* विनाश vinās
disbelief *n.* अविश्वास abiswās
discharge *v.* निकाल्नु nikālnu
disciple *n.* चेला celā
discipline *n.* अनुशासन anusāsan
disco *n.* नाट्यशाला nātyasālā
discount *n.* छूट chut
discourage *v.* निरुत्साहित गर्नु nirutsāhit garnu
discover *v.t.* पत्ता लगाउनु patta lagaunu

discovery *n.* खोज khoj
discreet *adj.* विवेकी viveki
discretion *n.* तजवीज tajbij
discriminate *v.i.* भेदभाव गर्नु bhedbhav garnu
discuss *v.t.* विचार गर्नु vicār garnu
discussion *n.* विचार–विमर्श vicār-vimars
disease *n.* रोग rog
disgrace *n.* बदनामी badnami
disguise *n.* भेष बदलेको bhes badaleko
disgust *n.* खीझ khiijh
disgusting *adj.* घृणा योग्य grinā yogya
dish *n.* थाली thāli
dishonest *adj.* बेइमान beimān
dishonesty *n.* बेइमानी beimāni
disinfect *v.t.* रोगाणु नष्ट गर्नु rogānu nast garnu
disinfectant *n./adj.* रोगाणुनाशक rogānunāsak
disintegrate *v.* टुक्रिनु tukrinu
disinterested *adj.* अभिरुचि नभएको abhiruci nabhaeko
disk *n.* डिस्क disk
dislike *v.t.* मन नपराउनु man naparāunu
dismiss *v.t.* पदच्युत गर्नु padcyut garnu
dismount *v.* ओर्लनु orlanu
disobey *v.t.* आज्ञा भङ्ग गर्नु āgyā bhang garnu
dispensary *n.* चिकित्सालय cikitsālaya
display *v.* प्रदर्शन pradarsan; *v.t.* प्रदर्शित गर्नु pradarsit garnu
displease *v.t.* अप्रसन्न गर्नु aprasann garnu
disposable *adj.* उपलब्ध upalabdha
dispose *v.i.* क्रमले राख्नु kramle rākhnu

dispute *n.* विवाद vivād
disregard *n.* अनादर anādar; *v.t.* उपेक्षा गर्नु upeksā garnu
disrepute *n.* बेइजत beijjat
disrupt *v.* वाधा डाल्नु vādhā dālnu
dissatisfaction *n.* असन्तोष asantos
dissimilar *adj.* असमान asamān
dissolution *n.* विघटन vighatān
dissolve *v.* घोल्नु gholnu
distance *n.* दूरी duri
distant *adj.* टाढाको tādhāko
distinct *adj.* भिन्न bhinn
distinction *n.* अन्तर antar
distinguish *v.t.* भेद गर्नु bhed garnu
distinguished *adj.* विशिष्ट visista
distort *v.t.* विकृत गर्नु vikrit garnu
distract *v.t.* ध्यान भंग गर्नु dhyān bhang garnu
distress *n.* विपत्ती vipatti
distribute *v.t.* बाध्नु bādnu
distribute *v.t.* वितरण गर्नु vitran garnu
distribution *n.* वितरण vitran
distributor *n.* वितरक vitarak
district *n.* जिल्ला jillā
distrust *n.* अविश्वास avisvās; *v.t.* अविश्वास गर्नु avisvās garnu
disturb *v.* वाधा डाल्नु vādhā dālnu
ditch *n.* खाडल khādal
dive *n.* गोता gotā
diverse *adj.* भिन्न–भिन्न bhinna-bhinna
diversity *n.* विविधता vividhatā
divide *v.t.* भाग लगाउनु bhag lagāunu
dividend *n.* लाभांश lābhāns
divine *adj.* दैविक daibik
division *n.* विभाजन vibhajan
divisive *adj.* विभाजनकारी vibhājankāri

divorce *n.* तलाक talak; *v.i.* तलाक हुनु talak hunu; *v.t.* तलाक दिनु talak dinu

divorced *adj.* तलाक गरेको talak gareko

dizziness *n.* रिंगटा ringata

do *v.t.* गर्नु garnu

doctor *n.* डाक्टर dāktar

document *n.* दस्तावेज dastābej

dog *n.* कुकुर kukur

doll *n.* खेलौना khelaunā

dollar *n.* डलर dalar

domain *n.* क्षेत्र kshetra

dome *n.* गुम्बद gumbad

domestic *(household affairs) adj.* घरेलु gharelu

domestic pet *n.* घर पलुवा ghar paluvā

domicile *n.* निवासी niwāsi

dominate *v.t.* शासन गर्नु sāsan garnu

domination *n.* शासन sāsan

donate *v.t.* दानमा दिनु dānma dinu

donation *n.* दान dān

donkey *n.* गधा gadhā

door *n.* ढोका dhokā

dose *n.* मात्रा mātrā

dossier *n.* फाइल file

dot *n.* थोपा thopā

double *adj.* दुगुना dugunā

doublecross *n.* विश्वासघात visvāsghāt

doubt *n.* सन्देह sandeh; *v.* शंका गर्नु sanka garnu

doubtful *adj.* सन्देहजनक sadehajanak

doughnut *n.* डोनट donat

dove *n.* ढुकुर dhukur

down *adv.* तल tal

downfall *n.* पतन patan

dowry *n.* दाइजो dāijo

dozen *n.* दर्जन darjan

draft *n.* मस्यौदा masyaudā

drag *v.t.* खिंच्नु khicnu

dragon *n.* उड्ने सर्प udane sarpa

drain *n.* नाली nāli

drama *n.* नाटक nātak

dramatist *n.* नाटककार nātakkār

draw *v.t.* तान्नु tānnu

drawing room *n.* बैठक baithak

dread *n.* त्रास trās; *v.t.* डराउनु darāunu

dream *n.* सपना sapnā; *v.i.* सपना देख्नु sapnā dekhnu

dress *n.* लुगा lugā; *v.i.* लुगा लगाउनु lugā lagāunu

drift *n.* बहाव bahāv; *v.i.* बहनु bahanu

drill *n.* बरमा barmā; *v.t.* प्वाल पार्नु pwāl pārnu

drink *n.* पेय pey; *v.t.* पिउनु piunu

drive *v.t.* चलाउनु calāunu

driver *n.* ड्राइभर drāivar

drizzle *v.i.* बूँदावाँदी हुनु bundāvādi hunu

drop *v.t.* गिराउनु girāunu

drought *n.* सुख्खा sukkhā

drown *v.t.* डुब्नु dubnu

drug *n.* औषधि ausadhi

drum *n.* ढोल dhol

drunk *adj.* नशामा चूर nasāma cur

dry *adj.* सुक्नु suknu; *v.t.* सुख्खा sukhhā

dryer *n.* लुगा सुकाउनु lugā sukāunu

dubious *adj.* शंकास्पद sankāspad

duck *n.* हाँस hāns

due *adj.* देय dey

dull *adj.* मन्दबुद्धि madbudhhi

dumb *adj.* लाटो lāto

dung *n.* गोबर gobar

during *prep.* को बेला kobelā

dust *n.* धुलो dhulo

dusty *adj.* धुलोले भरिएको dhulo le bhariyeko

duty *n.* कर्तव्य kartabya

dwell *v.i.* रहनु rahanu

dwelling *n.* निवास nivās

dye *n.* रङ्ग rang; *v.t.* रंगाउनु rangāunu

dying *adj.* मर्न लागेको marna lageko

dynamic *adj.* गतिशील gatisil

E

each *adj./adv.* हरेक harek
eager *adj.* उत्सुक utsuk
eagle *n.* चील cil
ear *n.* कान kān
earache *n.* कान दुख्नु kān dukhnu
early *adj.* समय भन्दा पहिले samay bhandā pahile
earn *v.i.* कमाउनु kamāunu
earnest *adj.* सच्चा saccā
earnings *n.* कमाई kamāi
earring *n.* कानपासा kānpāsā
earth *n.* पृथ्वी prithvi
earthquake *n.* भूकम्प bhukamp, भूइँचालो bhuinchalo
east *adj.* पूर्व purv
eastern *adj.* पूर्वी purvi
easterner *n.* पूर्वीया purviya
easy *adj.* सजिलो sajilo
eat *v.t.* खानु khānu
eccentric *adj.* सनकी sanki
echo *n.* प्रतिध्वनि pratidhvani
eclipse *n.* ग्रहण grahan
economical *adj.* किफायती kifāyati
economics *n.* अर्थशास्त्र arthsāstra
economist *n.* अर्थशास्त्री arthsāstri
economy *n.* अर्थव्यवस्था arthvyavasthā
eczema *n.* चर्मरोग carmarog
edge *n.* किनारा kinārā
edible *adj.* खान योग्य khana yogya
edit *v.t.* सम्पादन गर्नु sampādan garnu
edition *n.* संस्करण sanskaran
editor *n.* सम्पादक sampādak
editorial *n.* सम्पादकीय sampādakiya

educate *v.t.* शिक्षा दिनु siksā dinu
education *n.* शिक्षा siksā
educational *adj.* शिक्षा–सम्बन्धी siksā-sambandhi
effect *n.* परिणाम parinām
effective *adj.* प्रभावकारी prabhavkāri
efficient *adj.* योग्य yogya
effort *n.* प्रयास prayās
egalitarian *adj.* समतामूलक samatāmulak
egg *n.* फूल phul, अन्डा andā
eggplant *n.* भन्टा bhantā
Egypt *n.* मिश्र misra
eight *num.* आठ āth
eighteen *num.* अठार athāra
eighteenth *adj.* अठारौं athārau
eighth *adj.* आठौं athuan
eighty *num.* अस्सी assi
either *conj.* दुइटामा एक duitamā ek
eject *v.* निकाल्नु nikālnu
elastic *n.* इलास्टिक ilāstik
elbow *n.* कुइनो kuino
elderly *adj.* प्रौढ praudh
eldest *n.* जेठो jetho
elect *v.t.* चुन्नु chunnu
election *n.* चुनाव cunāv
electorate *n.* निर्वाचक nirvacak
electric *adj.* बिजुलीको bijuliko
electrician *n.* बिजुलीको काम गर्ने bijuliko kām garne
electricity *n.* बिजुली bijuli
electrocute *v.* बिजुली लागेर मृत्यु bijuli lāgera mritu
electronic *adj.* इलेक्ट्रोनिक ilektrānik

elegant *adj.* मनोरम manoram

element *n.* तत्त्व tattva

elementary *adj.* प्राथमिक prāthmik

elephant *n.* हात्ती hātti

elevator *n.* लिफ्ट lift

eleven *num.* एघार eghāra

eleventh *adj.* एघारौं eghārau

eligible *adj.* योग्य yogya

eliminate *v.t.* हटाउनु hatāunu

elite *n.* प्रवुद्धवर्ग prabuddha

else *adj.* अन्य anya

elsewhere *adv.* अन्यत्र anyatra

emancipate *v.* मुक्त गराउनु mukta garāunu

emancipation *n.* मुक्ति mukti

embark *v.t.* जहाजमा चढ्नु jahājmā chadhnu

embarrass *v.t.* लज्जित पार्नु lajjit pārnu

embassy *n.* दूतावास dutāvās

embezzle *v.* हिनामिना गर्नु hināminā garnu

emblem *n.* प्रतीक pratik

embrace *n.* आलिंगन ālingan; *v.* मान्नु mannu, आलिंगन गर्नु ālingan garnu

embroider *v.t.* बुट्टाको कटाई गर्नु buttāko katai garnu

embroidery *n.* कसिदाकारी kasidākāri

emerald *n.* पन्ना pannā

emerge *v.i.* निस्कनु niskanu

emergency *n.* आपत्काल āpātkāl

emigrant *n.* प्रवासी pravāsi

emigrate *v.i.* परदेश जानु pardes jānu

emigration *n.* प्रवास pravās

eminent *adj.* प्रतिष्ठित prastisthit

emit *v.t.* निकाल्नु nikālnu

emotion *n.* भावना bhāwanā

emperor *n.* सम्राट samrāt

emphasis *n.* ध्यान दिनु dhyān dinu

emphasize *v.t.* बल दिनु bal dinu

empire *n.* साम्राज्य sāmrājya

employ *v.t.* काम लगाउनु kām lagānunu

employee *n.* कर्मचारी karmachāri

employer *n.* मालिक mālik

employment *n.* रोजगारी rojgāri

emporium *n.* ठूलो पसल thulo pasal

empty *adj.* खाली khāli; *v.t.* खाली गर्नु khāli garnu

enable *v.t.* योग्य बनाउनु yogya banāunu

encircle *v.* घेर्नु ghernu

enclose *v.t.* बन्द गर्नु band garnu

enclosure *n.* घेरा gherā

encounter *n.* भिडन्त bhirant; *v.t.* सामना गर्नु samnā garnu

encourage *v.t.* प्रोत्साहन दिनु protsāhan dinu

encouragement *n.* प्रोत्साहन protsāhan

encroach *v.* अतिक्रमण गर्नु atikraman garnu

encyclopedia *n.* विश्वकोष visvakos

end *n.* अन्त ant; *v.i.* अन्त गर्नु ant garnu

endanger *v.* खतरा पार्नु khatarā parnu

endeavor *n.* प्रयत्न prayatna

ending *n.* अन्त anta

endless *adj.* अल्तहीन antahin

endorse *v.t.* समर्थन गर्नु samarthan garnu

endorsement *n.* समर्थन samarthan

endurance *n.* सहनशीलता sahansiltā

endure *v.i.* सहनु sahnu

enemy *n.* शत्रु shatru

energetic *adj.* बलवान् balbān, सक्रिय sakriya

energy *n.* शक्ति sākti

enforce *n.* लागु गर्नु lāgu garnu

engagement *n.* सगाई sagāi

engagement ring *n.* सगाईको औंठी sagāiko aunthi

engine *n.* इन्जिन injin

engineer *n.* इन्जीनियर injiniyar

England *n.* ईंग्लैंड ingland

English *n./adj.* अंग्रेजी angreji

Englishman *n.* अंग्रेज angrej

engrave *v.t.* खोद्नु khodnu

enjoy *v.t.* आनन्द लिनु ananda linu

enjoyment *n.* सुख sukh, आनन्द ananda

enlarge *v.t.* ठूलो गर्नु thulo garnu

enmity *n.* शत्रुता satrutā

enormity *n.* ज्यादै ठूलो jyadai thulo

enormous *adj.* विशाल visāl

enough *adj./adv.* प्रशस्त prasasta

enquire *v.t.* बुझनु bujhnu

enrich *v.* धनी बनाउनु dhani banāunu

enroll *v.* भर्ना हुनु bharnā hunu

enslave *v.* दास बनाउनु dās banāunu

ensure *v.t.* पक्का गर्नु pakkā garnu

enter *v.i.* प्रवेश गर्नु praves garnu

enterprise *n.* उद्यम udyam

entertain *v.t.* मनोरञ्जन गर्नु manoranjan garnu

entertainer *n.* मनोरञ्जनकर्ता manoranjankarta

entertaining *adj.* मनोरञ्जक manoranjak

entertainment *n.* मनोरञ्जन manoranjan

enthusiasm *n.* उत्साह utsāh

entire *adj.* सम्पूर्ण sampurna

entourage *n.* सहयोगको समुह sahayog ko samuh

entrance *n.* प्रवेश praves

entrust *v.t.* सुम्पनु sumpanu

entry *n.* प्रवेश praves

enumerate *v.* गन्नु gannu

envelop *v.t.* ढाक्नु dhāknu

envelope *n.* खाम khām

envious *adj.* ईर्ष्यालु isyaryālu

environment *n.* वातावरण vātāvaran

environs *n.* आसपास āspās

envisage *v.* बनाउन खोज्नु bahāuna khojnu

envoy *n.* राजदूत rājdoot

envy *n.* ईर्ष्या irsyā; *v.t.* ईर्ष्या गर्नु irsyā garnu

eon *n.* युग yug

epic *n.* महाकाव्य mahākavya

epicenter *n.* भूकम्पको केन्द्र bhupampako kendra

epidemic *adj.* सङ्क्रामक sankramak; *n.* महामारी māhāmāri

epilogue *n.* रचनाको अन्तमा लेखिने racanako antama lekhine

episode *n.* घटना ghatanā

epoch *n.* युग yug

equal *v.t.* समान बनाउनु samān banāunu

equality *n.* बराबरी barābari

equalize *v.* बराबर पार्ने barabar parne

equalized *adj.* समान samān

equate *v.* बरावर मान्नु barābar mānnu

equation *n.* समीकरण samikaran

equator *n.* भूमध्य रेखा bhumadhy rekha

equidistant *adj.* समदुरी samaduri

equip v. सामान राख्नु sāmān rākhnu

equipment n. सामान sāmān

equity n. निष्पक्षता nispaksata

equivalent adj. बराबर barābar

era n. युग yug

eradicate v. उन्मूलन गर्नु unmulan garnu

eradication n. उन्मूलन unmulan

erase v.t. मेटाउनु metāunu

eraser n. रबर rabar

erect adj. सीधा sidhā; v.t. निर्माण गर्नु nirmān garnu

erode v. खिईनु khienu

erosion n. खुर्किनु khurkinu

erotic adj. यौनसम्बन्धि yaun sambandhi

errand n. सन्देश sandes

error n. गल्ती galti, भूल bhool

erstwhile adj. पूर्व purva

escape n. पलायन palāyan; v.t. भाग्नु bhāgnu

escort n. रक्षक raksak; v.t. रक्षक साथ जानु raksārth sāth jānu

eskimo n. उत्तरी ध्रुव निवासी uttari dhruv nivāsi

especially adv. विशेष किसिमले bises kisimle

espionage n. जासूसी jāsusi

essay n. निबन्ध nibandh

essence n. सार sār

essential adj. आवश्यक āvasyak

establish v.t. स्थापित गर्नु sthāpit garnu

estate n. सम्पत्ति sampatti

estimate n. अनुमान anumān; v.i. अनुमान लगाउनु anumān lagāunu; v.t. अनुमान गर्नु anumān garnu

et cetera n. इत्यादि ityādi

eternal adj. नित्य nitya

ethical adj. नीतिपरक nitiparak

ethnic adj. जातीय jātiya

ethnicity n. जातीयता jātiyatā

ethnology n. नृवंश शास्त्र nribamshasāstra

euphoria n. ठूलो खुशी thulo khusi

Europe n. यूरोप yurop

European adj. यूरोपिय yuropiya; n. यूरोपियन yuropiyan

evacuate v.t. खाली गराउनु khāli garāunu

evacuation n. निकास nikas

evaluate v. मूल्याङ्कन गर्नु mulyānkan garnu

evaluation n. मूल्याङ्कन mulyānkan

eve n. पूर्व दिन purv din

even adj. बराबर barābar; v.t. बराबर गर्नु barābar garnu

evening n. साँझ sānjh

event n. घटना ghatnā

eventual adj. भविष्यको घटना bhavisyako ghatnā

ever adv. सँधै sadhai

everlasting adj. सदावहार sadābahār

every adj. हर har

everybody pron. सबै जना sabai janā

everyday adj. हरेक दिन hareko din

everyone pron. हरेक harek

everything pron. सबथोक sabthok

everywhere adv. सबै ठाउँमा sabai thaunmā

evict v. निकाल्नु nikālnu

evidence n. गवाही gavāhi, प्रमाण pramān

evident adj. स्पष्ट spasta

evil n. खराब kharāb

evolution n. खुदाई गर्नु khudai garnu

exact adj. ठीक thik

exactly *adv.* ठीक thik

exaggerate *v.t.* अतिरञ्जन गर्नु atiranjan garnu

exaggeration *n.* अतिशयोक्ति atisayokti

examination *n.* परीक्षा pariksā

examine *v.t.* जाँच गर्नु janc garnu

example *n.* उदाहरण udāharan

excavation *n.* खुदाई khudāi

exceed *v.t.* बढ्दै जानु badhāi jānu

excellent *adj.* अत्युत्तम atyuttam

except *prep.* लाई छोडेर lai choder

exception *n.* अपवाद apvād

excess *n.* अधिकता adhiktā

exchange *n.* विनिमय vinimay; *v.t.* विनिमय गर्नु vinimay garnu

excise *n.* अन्तः शुल्क antasulka

excite *v.t.* उत्तेजित गर्नु uttejit garnu

excitement *n.* उत्तेजना uttejnā

exclaim *v.t.* चिच्याउनु cicyāunu

exclude *v.t.* निकाल्नु nikālnu

excursion *n.* छोटो यात्रा choto yātrā

excuse *n.* माफी māfi; *v.t.* माफ गर्नु māf garnu

execute *v.t.* पूरा गर्नु pura garnu

executive *n.* कार्यकारिणी karyākārini

exempt *v.t.* छुट दिनु chut dinu

exemption *n.* छुट chut

exercise *n.* व्यायाम vyāyām

exhale *v.i.* श्वास निकाल्नु svās nikālnu

exhaust *n.* निकास नली nikās nali; *v.t.* थाक्नु thaknu

exhibit *n.* प्रदर्शन pradarsan; *v.t.* प्रदर्शन गर्नु pradarsit garnu

exhume *v.* चिहान सार्नु sihān sārnu

exile *n.* निर्वासन nivārsan; *v.t.*

निर्वासन गर्नु nivārsit garnu

exist *v.i.* अस्तित्व राख्नु astitva rākhnu

existence *n.* अस्तित्व astitva

exit *n.* निकास nikās

exorbitant *adj.* ज्यादै धेरै jyādai dherai

expand *v.t.* फैलाउनु phailāunu

expansion *n.* फैलाव phailāv

expect *v.t.* आशा गर्नु āsā garnu

expectation *n.* आशा āsā

expel *v.t.* निकालि दिनु nikāli dinu

expense *n.* खर्च kharc

expensive *adj.* महँगो mahango

experience *n.* अनुभव anubhav; *v.t.* अनुभव गर्नु anubhav garnu

experiment *n.* प्रयोग prayog

expert *n.* विशेषज्ञ visesagyā

expertise *n.* विशेष शीप vises sip

expire *v.* मर्नु marnu

explain *v.t.* स्पष्ट गर्नु spast garnu

explanation *n.* व्याख्या vyākhyā

explode *v.t.* फुट्नु phutnu

exploit *v.* शोषण गर्नु sosan garnu

explore *v.t.* छानबिन गर्नु chān-bin garnu

explosion *n.* धमाका dhamākā

explosive *adj.* विस्फोटक visphotak

export *n.* निर्यात गर्नु niryāt garnu; *v.t.* निर्यात niryāt

expose *v.t.* खोल्नु kholnu

exposure *n.* दिखावा dikhāvā

express *adj.* छिटो chito; *v.t.* प्रकट गर्नु prakat garnu

extemporaneous *adj.* पहिले तयार नगरेको pahile tayr nagareko

extend *v.t.* तान्नु tānnu

extension *n.* विस्तार vistār

extensive *adj.* धेरै फैलेको dherai phaileko

extent *n.* मात्रा matrā

exterminate *v.* संहार गर्नु samhar garnu

extermination *n.* सम्हार samhar

external *adj.* बाहिरी bāhari, विदेशी videsi

extinguish *v.t.* निभाउनु nibhāunu

extort *v.* धुत्नु dhutnu

extra *adj.* बढी badhi; *n.* अतिरिक्त atirikta

extract *n.* निचोड nicor; *v.t.* निचोड्नु nicornu

extradite *v.t.* प्रत्यर्पित गर्नु pratyarptit garnu

extramarital *adj.* विवाह देखि वाहिर vivāh dekhi bāhira

extraordinary *adj.* निराला nirālā

extravagant *adj.* फजूलखर्ची phajulkharchi

extreme *adj.* परम param

extremist *n.* अतिवादी atibādi

extrovert *n.* वहिर्मुखी bahirmurkhi

eye *n.* आँखा ānkhā

eyebrow *n.* आँखीभुइँ ānkhibhuin

eyesore *n.* आँखाको कसिङ्गर ankhāko kasingar

eyewitness *n.* प्रत्यक्षदर्शी pratyaksa darsi, चश्मादीद गवाह chasmadid gabah

F

fable *n.* कथा kathā
fabric *n.* कपडा kapā
fabricate *v.* बनाउनु banāunu
facade *n.* मुहरा muharā
face *n.* मुख much
facial *adj.* मुखको mukhko
facilitate *v.t.* सरल बनाउनु saral banāunu
facility *n.* सुविधा suvidā
fact *n.* सच्चाई saccāi, तथ्य tathya
faction *n.* समूह samuha, टुक्रा tukra
factory *n.* फैक्टरि faiktari, कारखाना karkhānā
factual *adj.* वास्तविक vāstavik
fad *n.* सनक sanak
fade *v.* फीका बन्नु phikā bannu
fail *v.i.* असफल हुनु asaphal hunu
failure *n.* असफलता asaphaltā
faint *adj.* बेहोश behos; *v.* बेहोश हुनु behos hunu
fair *adj.* उचित ucit; *n.* मेला melā
fairly *adv.* उचित तरिकाबाट ucit tarikā bāta
fairy *n.* परी pari
fait accompli *n.* भएको कुरा bhaeko kurā
faith *n.* विश्वास visvās
faithful *adj.* विश्वसनीय visvāsniy
fake *adj.* नक्कली nakkali
fall *n.* खस्नु khasnu
false *adj.* झूठो jhutho
falsify *v.t.* झूठो बनाउनु jhuto banāunu
fame *n.* नाम nām
familiar *adj.* परिचित paricit

familiarity *n.* परिचय paricaya
familiarize *v.* चिनाउनु cināunu
family *n.* परिवार parivār
famine *n.* अनिकाल anikāl
famous *adj.* प्रसिद्ध prasiddh
fan *n.* पंखा pankhā
fanatic *n.* कट्टर kattar
fanaticism *n.* कट्टरपन्थ kattarpantha
fancy *adj.* रंगी-विरंगी rangi-virangi
fantasy *n.* काल्पनिक kālpanik
far *adj.* टाढा tadha; **as far as known** *n.* थाहा भए सम्म thāha bhae samma; **far away** *adj.* धेरै टाढा dherai tādhā
far-reaching *adj.* धेरै प्रभावपार्ने dherai prabhav parne
farm *n.* खेत khet
farmer *n.* किसान kisān
farmhouse *n.* किसानको घर khet mā kisān ko ghar
farsighted *adj.* दूरदर्शी durdarsi
farther *adv.* धेरै टाढा dherai tadhā
fascinate *v.t.* मोहित हुनु mohit hunu
fascination *n.* सम्मोहन sammohan
fascism *n.* तानाशाही tānā sāhi
fashion *n.* फैशन phaisan
fashionable *adj.* शौकीन saukin
fast *adj.* छिटो chito; *n.* व्रत vrat
fast food *n.* छिटो खाना पकाउने chito khānā pakāune
fasten *v.t.* बाँधनु bāndhnu
fasting *v.* व्रत बस्नु vrat basnu
fat *adj.* मोटो moto

fatal *adj.* घातक ghātak

fatalism *n.* भाग्यवाद bhāgyavād

fateful *adj.* प्रभावकारी prabhav kāri

father *n.* पिताजी pitāji

father-in-law *n.* ससुरा sasura

fatigue *n.* थकावट thakāwat

fatty *adj.* चिल्लो भएको chillo bhaeko

fault *n.* गलती galti

faulty *adj.* खराब kharāb

fauna *n.* जनावर janāwar

favor *n.* अनुग्रह aungrah

favorable *adj.* फाइदा हुने phaidā hune

favorite *adj.* मनपरेको manpareko

favoritism *n.* पक्ष लिने paksa line

fear *n.* डर dar; *v.t.* डराउनु darāunu

feasible *adj.* सहज sahaj, संभाव्य sambhābya

feast *n.* भोज bhoj

feather *n.* प्वाँख pwaankh

feature *n.* आकार ākār, लेख lekh

February *n.* फरवरी farvari

feces *n.* दिसा disā

federal *adj.* संघीय sanghiya

federalism *n.* संघीयता sanghiyatā

fee *n.* शुल्क sulk

feeble *adj.* दुब्लो dublo

feed *n.* चारा cārā; *v.t.* खुवाउनु khuwāunu

feedback *n.* पढेर दिएको प्रतिक्रिया जवाफ padhera dieko pratikriya, jawāf

feel *n.* स्पर्श sparsa; *v.t.* स्पर्श गर्नु sparsa gārnu

feeling *n.* भावना bhāvnā

felicitate *v.* वधाइ दिनु badhāi dinu

felicitation *n.* बधाई badhāi

fellow *n.* साथी sāthi

fellowship *n.* छात्रवृति chatrabritti

felon *n.* अपराधी aparādhi

felony *n.* अपराध aparādh

female *n.* स्त्री stri

feminine *adj.* जनाना zanānā

fence *n.* बार bār

ferry *n.* नाउ nāu

fertile *adj.* उ ब्जाउ upjāu

fertilizer *n.* उर्वरक urbarak, मल mal

festival *n.* उत्सव utsav

festive *adj.* रमाइलो ramāilo

feud *n.* झगडा jhagadā

feudal *adj.* सामन्त sāmanta

feudalism *n.* सामन्तवाद sāmanta–bād

fever *n.* ज्वरो jaro

few *adj.* केही kehi

fiasco *n.* पूरा असफल purā asaphal

fiction *n.* कल्पना kalpanā

fictitious *adj.* काल्पनिक kālpanik

fidelity *n.* इमानदारी imān-dari

field *n.* खेत khet

field marshal *n.* अतिर थी atirathi

fiend *n.* राक्षस rāksyas

fierce *adj.* खूँखार khunkhār

fiesta *n.* उत्सव utsav

fifteen *num.* पंध्र pandrah

fifteenth *adj.* पन्द्रहाँ pandhraun

fifth *adj.* पाचौं pānchaun

fiftieth *adj.* पचासौं pacasaun

fifty *num.* पचास pacās

fig *n.* अंजीर añjir

fight *v.t.* लडनु ladnu

fighter *n.* लडाकु ladāku

figure *n.* चित्र citra; *v.t.* हिसाब hisāb

figurehead *n.* नाम मात्रको nām matra ko, शक्तिहिन saktihin

file *n.* फाइल phāil

fill *v.t.* भर्नु bharnu

filling *n.* भराई bharāi

film *n.* फिल्म film
filter *n.* फिल्टर filtar
filth *n.* फोहर phohar
filthy *adj.* फोहरी phohari
final *adj.* अंतिम antim
finality *n.* अन्तिमता antimata
finalize *v.* पूरा गर्नु purā garnu
finance *n.* अर्थ artha
finance minister *n.* अर्थ मन्त्री artha mantri
financial *adj.* आर्थिक ārthik
find *n.* खोज khoj; *v.t.* पाउनु pāunu
finding *n.* पाएको कुरा pāeko kurā
fine *n.* जरिवाना jariwanā
finger *n.* औँला aunlā
fingerprint *n.* ल्यापचे lyāpce
finish *n.* अंत गर्नु anta garnu; परिष्कार pariskār; *v.* परिष्कार गर्नु pariskar garnu; सक्नु saknu
fire *n.* आगो āgo
firearm *n.* वन्दुक banduk
fireproof *adj.* आगो नलाग्ने āgo nalagne
firewood *n.* दाउरा dāurā
firm *adj.* निश्चल पक्का pakkā; *n.* फर्म farm
first *adj.* पहिले देखि pahile dekhi; *adj.* पहिलो pahilo
first aid *n.* आकस्मिक सहायता ākasmik sahāyatā
firstborn *n.* जेठो jetho
fisherman *n.* माछा मार्ने machā mārne
fishing *n.* माछा मार्नु macha marnu
fist *n.* मुक्का mukkā
fit *n.* दौरा daurā; *adj. (appropriate)* उपयुक्त upyukta; *v.t.* ठीक हुनु thik hunu
fitness *n.* अनुकूलता anukultā
five *num.* पाँच panc (pānch)
fix *v.t.* ठीक गर्नु thik gārnu

flag *n.* झण्डा jhandā
flame *n.* ज्वाला jvālā
flamenco *n.* स्पेनको नाच spenko nāc
flash *n.* चमक camak; *v.i.* चम्कनु camaknu
flat *adj.* सम्म samma
flatter *v.t.* खुशामद गर्नु khusāmad gārnu
flattering *adj.* खुशामदी khusāmadi
flavor *n.* स्वाद svād
flaw *n.* दोष dos
flea *n.* उपियाँ upiyān
flee *v.i.* भाग्नु bhāgnu
flesh *n.* मासु māsu
flexibility *n.* लचक lacak
flexible *adj.* लचकदार lacakdār
flight *n.* उडान uṛān
flirt *n.* चुलबुली culbuli; *v.t.* जिस्किनु jiskinu
flock *n.* दल dal
flood *n.* बाढी bāṛh
flood plain *n.* नदी वरिपरि भुमि nadi waripari bhumi
floor *n.* भुंई fars
flora *n.* बनस्पति vanaspati
florist *n.* माली mali
flour *n.* आटा ātā
flow *n.* बहाव bahāv; *v.* वह्न bahanu
flower *n.* फूल phul
flu *n.* रुघाखोकी rughākhoki
fluent *adj.* धाराप्रवाह dhārāpravāh
fluid *n./adj.* तरल taral
flute *n.* बाँसुरी bānsuri
fly *v.* उड्नु udnu; *n.* माखा makha
foam *n.* फिज jhāg
focus *n.* केन्द्र kendra
focus *v.t.* केन्द्रित गर्नु kendrit gārnu
fog *n.* कुहिरो kuhiro, हुस्सु hussu
foggy *adj.* कुहिरोमय kuhiromaya

fold *n.* तह taha; *v.* बेर्नु bernu

folder *n.* पुस्तिका pustikā

folk *n.* जनता janāta

folk dance *n.* लोक नृत्य lok sangit

folk music *n.* लोक संगीत lok sangit

folklore *n.* लोक कथा lok katha

follow *v.i.* पछाडि लाग्नु pachadi lagnu

follower *n.* अनुयायी anuyāyi

following *adj.* त्यसपछि tyaspachi

fond *adj.* स्नेही snehi

food *n.* खाना khāna

Food and Agriculture Organization *n.* खाद्य कृषि संगठन khādya krishi sangathān

fool *n.* मूर्ख mukha

foolish *adj.* बेवकुफ bevkuf

foot *n.* खुट्टा khuttā

football (soccer) *n.* फुटबल phutbāl

foothill *n.* सानो पहाड sāno pahād

footnote *n.* पादटिप्पणि pād tippani

footprint *n.* पद चिन्ह pad cinh

for *prep.* को लागि ko lāgi

forbid *v.t.* निषेध गर्नु nisedh gārnu

forbidden *adj.* निषेधित nisedit, वर्जित varjit

force *n.* बल bal; *v.t.* जबरजस्ती गर्नु jabardasti gārnu

forcible *adj.* बलपूर्वक balpurbak

forecast *n.* पूर्वानुमान purvāumān

forefather *n.* पुर्खा purkhā

forehead *n.* निधार nidhār

foreign *adj.* विदेश vides

foreigner *n.* विदेशी videsi

foresight *n.* दूरदर्शिता durdarsitā

forest *n.* वन van

forestry *n.* वन शास्त्र vansāstra

forever *adv.* सधैं को लागि sādāi ko lāgi

foreword *n.* प्रस्तावना prastāwanā

forget *v.t./v.i.* विर्सनु birsanu

forgive *v.t.* क्षमा गर्नु ksamā garnu

fork *n.* काँटा kāntā

form *n.* रुप rup

formal *adj.* औपचारिक aupcārik

former *adj.* पहिलेको pahileko

formidable *adj.* जित्न गाह्रो jitna gāharo

formula *n.* सूत्र sutra

fornication *n.* अविवाहितको वीच करणी avivāhit ko bic karni

forsake *v.* छाडनु chadnu

fort *n.* किल्ला killa

forthcoming *adj.* आगामि āgāmi

fortieth *adj.* चालिसौं chalisaun

fortnight *n.* पक्ष paksac

fortress *n.* गढ garh

fortunate *adj.* सौभाग्यशाली saubhāgyasāli

fortunately *adv.* सौभाग्यवश saubhāgyavas

fortune *n.* भाग्य bhāgya

forty *num.* चालीस cālis

forum *n.* छलफल गर्ने ठाउँ chalphal garne thāun

forward *adv.* अगाडि agādi

foster *v.t.* बढावा दिनु badhāwa dinu

foul *adj.* फोहर phohar

found *v.t.* पाउनु pāunu

foundation *n.* आधार ādhar

foundation *n.* जग jag

founder *n.* संस्थापक sansthāpak

four *num.* चार cār

four score *adj.* चार वीस(अस्सी) carbisa(assi)

fourteen *num.* चौदह caudha

fourteenth *adj.* चौधौं chaudhaun

fourth *adj.* चौथो cautho

fox *n.* फ्याउरो phyauro

fraction *n.* टुक्रा tukda

fragile *adj.* कमजोर kamjor

frame *n.* चौखटा caukhta

frank *adj.* खुल्ला khulā

frantic *adj.* उत्तेजित uttejit

fraud *n.* छल chāl

free *adj.* नि:शुल्क nisulkā, सित्तैमा sittaimā

freedom *n.* स्वतंत्रता svāntratā

freeze *v.i.* जम्नु jamnu; *v.t.* जमाउनु jamāunu

freight *n.* भाडा bhārā

French *n./adj.* फ्रान्सेली franseli

frequency *n.* आवृत्ति avrtti

frequent *adj.* अकसर aksar

frequently *adv.* बारंबार bārambār

fresh *adj.* ताजा tāzā

Friday *n.* शुक्रबार sukravār

fried *adj.* तारेको tāreko

friend *n.* मित्र mitra, साथी sathi

friendly *adj.* मित्रबत् mitrābat

friendship *n.* दोस्ती dosti, मित्रता mitrātā

fright *n.* भय bhaya

frighten *v.t.* डराउनु darāunu

frightening *adj.* भयंकर bhayankar

frog *n.* भ्यागुतो bhāguto

from *prep.* देखि dekhi

front *adj.* अगाडिको agādi ko

frontier *n.* सीमा simā

frost *n.* तुषारो tusāro

frostbite *n.* शीतदंश sitadans

frozen *adj.* जमेको jameko

frugal *adj.* मितव्यती mitavyayi

fruit *n.* फल phal

fruitful *adj.* परिणाममुखी parināmmukhi

frustrate *v.t.* निराश गर्नु nirās gārnu

frustrated *adj.* हतोत्साहित हुनु hatotsāhit hunu

frustration *n.* निराशा nirasā

fry *v.t.* तार्नु tārnu

frying pan *n.* कराहि karāhi

fuel *n.* पेट्रोल petrol

fugitive *adj.* भागेको bhāgeko; *n.* भगौडा bhagauda

fulfill *v.* पूरा गर्नु purā garnu

full *adj.* पूर्ण purna, पूरा pura

full moon *n.* पूर्णिमा purnimā

fully *adv.* पूरा तौरले purā taurle

fun *n.* मजा majā

function *n.* समारोह samāroh; *v.i.* काम गर्नु kām gārnu

functional *adj.* कार्यशील kāryasil

fund *n.* कोष kosh; *v.t.* कोस मा राख्नु kosh ma rākhnu

fundamental *adj.* मूल mul

funeral *n.* अन्तिम संस्कार Antim sanskār

funny *adj.* हास्यकारी hāsyakari

fur *n.* रोवा rovā

furious *adj.* अतिक्रुध्द atikruddh

furnace *n.* भट्टी bhatti

furnish *v.t.* जुटाउनु jutāunu

furniture *n.* फर्नीचर farnicar

further *adv.* अरु अगाडि aruagādi

futile *adj.* निरर्थक nirarthak

future *n./adj.* भविष्य Bhavisya

G

gain n. लाभ lābh; v.t. प्राप्त गर्नु prāpt gārnu

gainful adj. लाभप्रद lābhprad

gall n. पित्त pitta

gallbladder n. पिट्टको थैली pittako thaili

gallery n. गैलरी gailari

gallon n. गैलन gailan

gallop n. छलाँग chalāng; v.i. छलाँग लगाउनु chalāng lāgāunu

gallstone n. पित्तको पत्थरी pittā ko pāttari

gamble v. जुवा खेल्नु juwā khelnu

game n. खेल khel

gang n. टोली toli

gangster n. अपराधी aparādhi

gap n. प्वाल pwāl

garage n. गैरज gairaj

garbage n. रद्दी raddi

garden n. बगैंचा bagainchā

gardener n. बगैंचे bagainche

gargle v.i. कुल्ला गर्नु kullā gārnu

garland n. माला mālā

garlic n. लसुन lasun

garment n. कपडा kapdā

gas n. गैस gais

gasoline n. पेट्रोल petrol

gate n. ढोका dhokā

gatecrasher n. अनिमन्त्रित व्यक्ति animantri vyakti

gather v.i. जम्मा हुनु jammā hunu; v.t. जम्मा गर्नु jammā gārnu

gay (homosexual) n./adj. समलिङ्गी samalingi; adj. समलैंगिक samalaingik; (happy) adj. सुखी sukhi

gear n. साज-सामान sāj-sāmān

gem n. रत्न ratna

gender n. लिंग linga

general n. (mil.) जनरल janaral; adj. आम ām, साधारण sadhāran

generally adv. सामान्यतः sāmānyatā

generate v.t. उत्पन्न गर्नु utpann gārnu

generation n. (familial) पुस्ता pustā; उत्पादन utpādan

generous adj. उदार udār

genetic adj. उत्पत्ति utpatti; सम्बन्धित sambandhit

genital adj. जननेन्द्रीय jananendriya

genitals n. pl. जननांग jananānga

genius n. प्रतिभाशाली pratibhāsāli

genocide n. जनसंहार jansamhār

gentle adj. भलो bhalo

gentleman n. सज्जन sajjan

gentry n. उच्च वर्ग uccavarga

geography n. भूगोल bhugol

geology n. भूविज्ञान bhuvignan

geometry n. रेखागणित rekhā ganit

germ n. जिवाणु jivānu

German n. जर्मन jarman

Germany n. जर्मनी jarmani

germicide n. कीटनाशक kitnāsak

gesture n. चेष्टा cestā

get v.t. प्राप्त गर्नु prāpt gārnu

get ahead v. सफल हुनु saphal hunu

ghost n. भूत bhut

giant adj. ठूलो thulo; n. भीमकाय bhimakāy

gift n. उपहार uphār

gigolo n. पुरुष वेश्या purush vesyā

gild v.t. सुनको जलफ लगाउनु sunko jalaph lagaunu

gin *n.* जिन jin

ginger *n.* अदुवा aduwā

giraffe *n.* जिराफ jirāph

girl *n.* केटी keti

girlfriend *n.* प्रेमिका premikā

give *v.t.* दिनु dinu

give up *v.* छोड्नु chodnu

glad *adj.* प्रसन्न prasanna

glamour *n.* मोहकता mohktā

glance *n.* सरसरी नजर sarsari nazar; *v.i.* झलकाउनु jhalkāunu

glare *n.* चमक camak; *v.i.* चम्किनु camkinu

glass *n.* शीशा sisā

glasses (eyeglasses) *n.* चश्मा casmā

glaucoma *n.* आँखाको रोग ānkhāko rog

glimpse *n.* झलक jhalak

glimpse *v.t.* झल्काउनु jhalkāunu

global *adj.* विश्व-सबंधी visv-sambandhi

globe *n.* ग्लोब glob

globetrotter *n.* यायावर yāyāvar

gloom *n.* अँध्यारो andhyaro

gloomy *adj.* धमिलो dhamilo

glorify *v.* गौरवन्वित गर्नु gaurabāvit garnu

glory *n.* गौरव gaurab

glove *n.* पंजा panjā

glow *v.i.* उल्लासित हुनु ullasit hunu

glue *n.* गुँद gund

go *v.i.* जानु jānu

goal *n.* लक्ष्य laksya

goat *n.* बोका bokā

god *n.* भगवान bhagavān

godchild *n.* धर्मपुत्र dharmaputra

goddaughter *n.* धर्मपुत्री dharmaputri

goddess *n.* देवी devi

godfather *n.* धर्मपिता dharmapitā

godlike *adj.* ईश्वरजस्तो iswājasto

godmother *n.* धर्ममाता dharmamātā

godson *n.* धर्मपुत्र dharmaputra

gold *n.* सुन sun

golden *adj.* सुनौलो sunaulo

goldsmith *n.* सुनार sunār

golf *n.* गोल्फ golf

gonorrhea *n.* गर्नेरिया gonoria

good *adj.* असल asal

good-bye! *interj.* नमस्ते namaste

goods *n.* माल māl

goose *n.* हाँस Hāns

gospel *n.* उपदेश upadesh

gossip *n.* गफ gaph; *v.i.* गफ गर्नु gaph gārnu

gout *n.* वात bāt

govern *v.t.* शासन गर्नु sāsan gārnu

government *n.* सरकार sarkār

governmental *adj.* सरकारी sarkāri

governor *n.* राज्यपाल rājyapal

grab *v.* समात्नु samātnu

grace *n.* मनोहरता manohartā

graceful *adj.* मनोहर manohar

gracious *adj.* कृपालु kripālu

grade *n.* श्रेणी sreni; *v.t.* क्रमअनुसार राख्नु kramānusār rākhnu

gradual *adj.* क्रमिक krāmik, बिस्तारै bistāri

graduate *n.* स्नातक snātak; *v.i.* स्नातक हुनु snātak hunu

grain *n.* अनाज anāj

gram *n.* चना canā

grammar *n.* व्याकरण vyākaran

grand *adj.* मुख्य mukhya

grandchild *n.* नाती nāti

granddaughter *n.* नातिनि nātini

grandfather *n.* बाजे bāje

grandmother *n.* बजै bajai

grandparents *n.* बाजे बजै baje bajai

grandson *n.* नाती nāti

granite *n.* ग्रेनाइट grenāit

grant *n.* अनुदान anudān; *v.t.* प्रदान गर्नु pradān gārnu

grape *n.* अंगूर angur

grapefruit *n.* भोगटे bhogate

graph *n.* रेखाचित्र rekhācitra

graphic *adj.* आलेखी ālekhi

grasp *v.t.* कसेर समात्नु kasera samatnuo

grass *n.* घास ghās

grateful *adj.* आभारी abhāri

gratitude *n.* आभार abhār

grave *adj.* गंभीर gambhir; *n.* चिहान chihān

gravity *n.* गुरुत्वआकर्षण gurutwa akarshan

gray *adj.* खैरो khairo

great *adj.* महान् mahān

greatness *n.* महानता mahānata

Greece *n.* यूनान yunān

greed *n.* लोभ lobh

greedy *adj.* लोभी lobhi

Greek *n./adj* यूनानी yunāni

green *n./adj* हरियो hariyo

greenhouse *n.* विरुवाघर biruwāghar

greet *v.t.* नमस्कार गर्नु namaskār gārnu

greeting *n.* अभिवादन abhibādān; नमस्कार namaskār

grenade *n.* विस्फोटक bisphotak

grief *n.* दुख dukh

grievance *n.* शिकायत sikāyat

grieve *v.t.* दुख पाउनु dukh pāunu

grill *v.t.* सेकेको sekeko

grind *v.t.* पिस्नु pisnu

grip *n.* पकड pakaṛ; *v.t.* पकड्नु pakaṛnu

groan *n.* कराउनु karāunu

grocer *n.* तरकारी tarkāri, फल विक्रेता phal bikreta

grocery *n.* तरकारी tarkāri, फल पसल phal pasal

groom *n.* दुलाहा dulāhā

ground *n.* जमीन jamin

groundwater *n.* भूमिगत जल bhumigat jal

groundwork *n.* आधार कर्म ādhār karm

group *n.* समूह samuh

grow *v.t.* उमन्नु umrānu, बढ्नु badnu

grown-up *n.* बालिग bālig

growth *n.* बुद्धि briddhi

growth rate *n.* वृद्धिदर briddi dar

guarantee *n./v.t.* गारंटी gāranti

guard *n.* रक्षा raksā; *v.t.* रक्षा गर्नु raksā gārnu

guarded *adj.* संरक्षित samraksit

guardian *n.* संरक्षक samraksak

guava *n.* अम्बा ambā

guerilla *n./adj.* छापामार chāpamār

guess *n.* अनुमान anumān; *v.i.* अनुमान गर्नु anumān gārnu

guest *n.* अतिथि atithi

guide *n.* पथप्रदर्शक padapradarsan

guidebook *n.* पथप्रदर्शक पुस्तक pathapradarsak pustak

guilt *n.* दोष dos

guilty *adj.* दोषी dosi

guitar *n.* गितार gitār

gulf *n.* खाडी khādi

gum *n.* गुँद gund

gun *n.* बंदुक banduk

gust *n.* झोंका jhoṅkā

gutter *n.* नाली nāli

guy *n.* जवान javān

gymnasium *n.* व्यायामशाला vyāyāmsālā

gymnastics *n.* व्यायाम vyāyam

gynecologist *n.* आइमाइ को डाक्टर aimāi ko dāktar

gypsy *n.* जिप्सी Jipsi

H

habit *n.* बानी bani

habitable *adj.* वस्न योग्य basna yogya

habitat *n.* बस्ने ठाँउ basne thāun

hair *n.* कपाल kapāl

haircut *n.* कपाल काट्नु kapāl kātnu

hairdresser *n.* नाउ nāu

half *adj.* आधा ādhā

half brother *n.* सौतेनी भाई sauteni bhāi

half sister *n.* सैतेनी बहिनी sauteni bahini

half-breed *n.* वर्णशंकर sarna sankar

halfhearted *adj.* मन नलागी man nalāgi

half-moon *n.* अष्टमी asthami

half-truth *n.* आधा सांचो ādhā sānco

halfway *adj.* आधावाटो adhā bāto

hall *n.* हाल hāl

hallucination *n.* भ्रम bhram

ham *n.* सुङ्गुरको मासु sungurko māsu

hammer *n.* हथौडा hathaurā

hamper *v.* बाधा पुर्याउनु bādh dālnu

hand *n.* हात hāt

handbag *n.* हैंडबैग hainnbyag

handbook *n.* पुस्तिका pustikā

handcuff *n.* नेल nel

handful *n.* केही kehi

handicap *n.* वाधा badhā

handicapped *adj.* विकलांग viklāng

handicraft *n.* शिल्प silp

handkerchief *n.* रुमाल rumāl

handmade *adj.* हातले बनाएको hāt le banāeko

handout *n.* गरीवलाई दिएको दान gariblāi dieko dān

handshake *n.* हात मिलाउनु hāt milāunu

handsome *adj.* सुन्दर sundar

handwriting *n.* हस्तक्षर hastaksar

handy *adj.* दक्ष saks; सजिलो सँग पाइने sajilo sanga pāine

hang *v.t.* झुन्डाउनु jhunudāunu

hang up *n.* टेलिफोन वार्ता सकिनु telephone vartā sakinu

hangar *n.* विमानशाला vimansala

hanger *n.* हैंगर haingar

hangover *n.* रक्सी खाए पछि टाउको दुखाई raksi khaye pachi tauko dukhne

hapless *adj.* अभागी abhāgi

happen *v.i.* हुनु hunu

happening *n.* घटना ghatanā

happiness *n.* खुशी khusi

happy *adj.* सुखी sukhi

harass *v.t.* दुःख दिनु dukh dinu

harassment *n.* परेशानी paresāni

harbor *n.* बंदरगाह bardargāh

hard *adj.* कडा karā

hard cash *n.* नगद nagad

hard drug *n.* लागु पदार्थ lāgu padārtha

harden *v.i.* कडा बनाउनु kada banāunu

hardly *adv.* मुश्किल muskil

hardness *n.* कडापन karāpan

hardship *n.* कष्ट kasta

hardware *n.* फलाम को सामान falam ko sāmān

hare *n.* खरायो kharāyo

harlot *n.* रन्डी randi

harm *n.* हानि hāni; *v.t.* कष्ट दिनु kast dinu

harmful *adj.* हानिकर hānikar

harmless *adj.* अहानिकर ahānikar

harp *n.* वीणा vinā

harsh *adj.* रुखो rukho

harvest *n.* फसल fasal

hashish *n.* गाँजा gānjā

hassle *n.* दुख dukha

haste *n.* चाँडै chāndai

hasten *v.* हतपत साथ hatpat sāth

hat *n.* टोप top

hatch *v.* भूत लाग्नु bhut lāgnu

hate *n./v.* घृणा गर्नु ghrinā gārnu

hatred *n.* अति घृणा ati ghrina

haul *n.* घिसार्नु ghisārnu

haunt *v.* भूत लाग्नु bhut lāgnu

have *v.t.* साथ हुनु sāth hunu

have-not *n.* केही नभएको kehi nabhaeko

hawk *n.* चील chil

hay *n.* सुकेको घाँस sukeko ghāns

hazard *n.* दुर्घटना durghatanā

haze *n.* कुहिरो kuhiro

hazy *adj.* कुहिरो लागेको kuhiro lāgeko

he *pron.* उ U, उनि uni

head *n.* टाउको tāuko

headache *n.* टाउको दुख्ने tāuko dukhne

headdress *n.* श्रीपेच sripech

heading *n.* शीर्षक sirsak

headlight *n.* अगाडिको वत्ती agādiko batti

headline *n.* शीर्षक sirsak

headmaster *n.* प्रधान अध्यापक pradhān adhyāpak

headquarters *n. pl* मुख्यालय mukhyālay

heal *v.i.* ठीक हुनु thik hunu; *v.t.* ठीक गर्नु thik gārnu

health *n.* स्वास्थ swāsthya

healthy *adj.* स्वस्थ svasth

heap *n.* थुप्रो thupro

hear *v.t.* सुन्नु sunnu

hearing *n.* सुनाई sunāi

hearing aid *n.* कान सुन्ने यन्त्र kān sunne yantra

heart *n.* मुटु mutu

heart attack *n.* हृदयघात hridaya ghāt

hearth *n.* चुलो chulo

hearty *adj.* हार्दिक hārdik

heat *n.* गरमी garmi

heater *n.* हीटर hitar

heathen *n.* असभ्य asabhya

heating *n.* तापन tāpan

heatstroke *n.* लू loo

heaven *n.* स्वर्ग svarg

heavy *adj.* भारी bhāri

Hebrew *n.* हिब्रु hibru

heed *v.* ध्यानले सुन्नु dhyānle sunnu

hegemony *n.* नियन्त्रण niyantran

height *n.* ऊँचाई uncāi

heir *n.* वारिस vāris

heir apparent *n.* उत्तराधिकारी uttarādhikāri

heirloom *n.* खानदानी संपत्ति khādāni sampatti

helicopter *n.* हेलिकाप्टर helikāptar

hell *n.* नरक narak

hello *n.* नमस्कार namaskār

helmet *n.* हेलमिट helmit

help *n.* मदत madad, सहायता sahāyatā; *v.t.* मदत गर्नु madad gārnu

helper *n.* सहायक sahāyak

helpful *adj.* उपयोगी upyogi

helpless *adj.* परनिर्भर paranirbhar

hemisphere *n.* गोलार्ध golārdha

hemorrhage *n.* धेरै रगत आउनु dherai ragat āunu

hen *n.* कुखुरा kukhurā

hence *adv.* यसकारणले yas kāranle

herb *n.* औषधीको विरुवा ausadhi ko biruwā

herd *n.* बथान bathāṅ

here *adv.* यहाँ yahān

hereby *adv.* यसबाट yasbāta

herewith *adv.* यसैसंग yasai sanga

heritage *n.* परम्परा parampāra

hermit *n.* जोगी jogi

hernia *n.* हर्निया harniyā

hero *n.* वीर vir

heroic *adj.* वीरताको viratāko

herpes *n.* एक किसिमको योन रोग ek kisim ko yaun rog

herring *n.* हिलसा hilsā

hers *pron.* उसको usko, उनको unko

herself *pron.* उनी आफै uni aphai

hesitate *v.t.* हिचकिचाउनु hickicānu

hestitation *n.* हिचकिचाहट hickicāhat

heterosexual *adj.* इतरलिंगी itarliṅgi

heyday *n.* लोकप्रियताको दिन lokpriyatā ko din

hiccup *n.* बाडुली hikkā; *v.i.* बाडुली लाग्नु hikkā linu

hidden *adj.* गुप्त gupta, लुकेको lukeko

hide *v.t.* लुकाउनु lukāunu

hideaway *n.* लुकेको ठांउ lukeko thāun

high *adj.* अग्लो aglo

high school *n.* माध्मिक विद्यालय mādhyamik vidyālaya

high-class *adj.* उच्चवर्गीय ucca vargiya

high-rise *adj.* धेरै अग्लो भवन dherai aglo bhawan

highway *n.* राजपथ rājpath

hijacking *n.* अपहरण apaharan

hike *n.* घुम्नु ghumnu; *v.i.* पैदल घुम्नु paidāl ghumnu

hiker *n.* पैदल यात्री paidāl yatri

hiking *n.* पदयात्रा गर्नु padyātrā gārnu

hill *n.* पहाडी pahāṛi

hillock *n.* सानो पहाड sāno pahār

hilltop *n.* पहाडको शिखर pahār ko sikhar

hilly *adj.* पहाडी pahāṛi

him *pron.* उसलाई uslāi

Himalayas *n.* हिमालय himālaya

himself *pron.* आफै āphai

hinder *v.t.* वाधा हाल्नु bādhā hālnu

Hindi *n.* हिन्दी hindi

hindrance *n.* वाधा bādhā

Hindu *n./adj.* हिन्दू hindu

Hinduism *n.* हिन्दू धर्म hindu dharma

hint *n.* संकेत sanket; *v.i.* संकेत गर्नु sanket gārnu

hip *n.* चाक cāk

hippie *n.* हिपी hipi

hire *v.t.* भर्ना गर्नु bhārnā gārnu

his *pron.* उसको usko, उनको unko

historian *n.* इतिहासकार itihāskār

historical *adj.* ऐतिहासिक atihāsik

history *n.* इतिहास itihās

hit *v.i.* पिटनु pitnu

hit and run *adj.* दुर्घटना गरी भाग्ने डाइभर durghatana gari vagne divar

hitherto *adv.* अहिलेसम्म ahile samma

hive *n.* महघारी mahaghāri

hoarse *adj.* भारी bhāri

hoax *n.* ठगी thagi

hobby *n.* सोख sokh

hockey *n.* हाकी hāki

hoist *v.t.* उठाउनु uthāunu

hold *n.* पकड pakar; *v.t.* समात्नु samātnu

holdup *n.* डकैती dakaiti

hole *n.* प्वाल pwāl

holiday *n.* छुट्टी chutti, विदा bidāa

hollow *adj.* खोक्रो khokro

holocaust *n.* ठूलो नोक्सानी thulo noksāni

holy *adj.* पवित्र pavitra

holy day *n.* पुण्य दिवस punya divas

holy land *n.* पवित्रभूमि pavitra bhumi

homage *n.* श्रद्धांजली sraddhānjali

home *n.* घर ghar

home economics *n.* गृह विज्ञान griha vigyān

homeland *n.* जन्म-भूमि janm-bhumi

homemade *adj.* घरमा बनाएको gharmā banaeko

homemaker *n.* गृहस्थ grihastha

homesick *adj.* गृह-वियोगी grha-viyogi

homesickness *n.* गृह-वियोग grha-viyog

hometown *n.* गृह नगर grha-nagar

homework *n.* गृह-कार्य grha-kārya

homicide *n.* हत्या hatyā

homosexual *n./adj* समलिंगी samalingi

honest *adj.* ईमानदार imāndār

honesty *n.* ईमानदारी imāndāri

honey *n.* मह maha

honeymoon *n.* मधुमास madhumās

honor *n.* सम्मान sammān; *v.t.* सम्मानित गर्नु sammānit gārnu

honorable *adj.* माननीय mānaniya

honorarium *n.* पारिश्रमिक pārisramik

hook *n.* काँटा kāntā

hope *n.* आशा āsā; *v.t.* आशा गर्नु āsā gārnu

hopeful *adj.* आशाजनक āsājanak

hopeless *adj.* निराशाजनक nirāsājanak

horizon *n.* क्षितिज ksitij

horn *n.* सिंग siṅg

horrible *adj.* भयंकर bhayaṅkar

horror *n.* संत्रास santrās

hors-d'oeuvre *n.* हल्का नाश्ता halkā nāstā

horse *n.* घोडा ghoṛā

horseman *n.* घोडसवार ghodsavār

horticulture *n.* फलोद्यान phalodhyān

hospitable *adj.* सत्कारशील satkārsil

hospital *n.* अस्पताल aspatāl

hospitality *n.* अतिथिसत्कार atithi satkār

host *n.* अतिथेय ātitheya

hostage *n.* बन्धक bandhak

hostel *n.* छात्रावास chātrāvās

hostess *n.* अतिथेय atitheya

hostile *adj.* विरोधी virodhi

hot *adj.* तातो tāto

hotel *n.* होटल hotal

hour *n.* घंटा ghantā

hourly *adj.* प्रति घंटा prati ghantā

house *n.* घर ghar

household *n.* गृहस्थी grhasthi

housekeeper *n.* नोकर nokar

housewarming *n.* नव गृह प्रवेश nava griha praves

housewife *n.* गृहस्वामिनी grhasvāmini

housing *n.* निवास niwās

how *adv.* कसरी kasari

however *adv.* तै पनि tai pani

hub *n.* केन्द्र kendra

hug *v.t.* अंगालो मार्नु angalo mārnu

huge *adj.* विशाल visāl

human *adj.* मानवीय mānviy

human rights *n.* मानवधिकार mānav adhikār

humane *adj.* मानवोचित mānvocit

humanitarian *n.* मानवतावादी mānabtā bādi

humanity *n.* मानवता mānvatā

humble *adj.* विनीत vinit

humid *adj.* ओसिलो osilo

humidity *n.* ओस os

humiliate *v.* अपमान गर्नु apamān garnu

humiliation *n.* अपमान apmān

humor *n.* हास्य hāsya

humorist *n.* हास्यव्यङ्गकार hasyavyangakār

hunch *n.* पूर्वाभास purvabās

hunchback *n.* कुप्रो kupro

hundred *Num.* सय saya

hundredth *adj.* सयौं saiyaun

hunger *n.* भोक bhok

hungry *adj.* भोको bhoko

hunt *n.* शिकार sikār; *v.* सिकार खेल्नु shikar khelnu

hunter *n.* शिकारी sikāri

hurdle *n.* बाधा bādhā

hurray! *interj.* हुरे hure!

hurricane *n.* आँधी āndhi

hurry *n.* चाँडो chādo; *v.t.* चाँडो गर्नु chādo gārnu

hurt *n.* चोट cot; *v.t.* चोट लाग्नु cot lāgnu

husband *n.* पति pati, लोग्ने logne

hush *n.* चूप हुनु cup hunu

hut *n.* झोपडी jhopadi

hybrid *n.* जातीय मिश्रण jtiya misran

hydro-electricity *n.* जलविद्युत jal vidyut

hydrogen *n.* हाइड्रोजन haidrojan

hygeine *n.* स्वास्थ विज्ञान swāsthya bigyān

hymn *n.* भजन bhajan

hyphen *n.* योजक चिन्ह yojak cinh

hypnosis *n.* सम्मोहन sammohan

hypocrisy *n.* पाखण्ड pākhanda

hysteria *n.* मानसिक रोग mānasik rog

I

I *pron.* म ma
ice *n.* बरफ barf
ice cream *n.* आइसक्रीम āiskrim
icon *n.* प्रतिमा pratimā
iconoclast *n.* स्थापित मान्यता विरोधी sthapit manyata virodhi
icy *adj.* बरफीलो barfilo
idea *n.* विचार vicār
ideal *n./adj* आदर्श ādars
idealism *n.* आदर्शवाद āsarsavād
identical *adj.* दुरुस्त उही durusta uhi
identification *n.* पहिचान pahicān
identify *v.t.* चिन्नु cinnu
idiom *n.* मुहावरा muhāvarā
idiot *n.* मुर्ख murkha
idle *adj.* अल्छी alchi
idol *n.* मूर्ति murti
idolatry *n.* मूर्तिपूजा murtipujā
if *conj.* यदि yadi
ignite *v.* आगो लगाउनु āgo lagāunu
ignition *n.* ज्वलन jvalan
ignorance *n.* अज्ञान agyān
ignorant *adj.* अज्ञानी agyāni
ignore *v.t.* उपेक्षा upeksā
ill *adj.* विरामी birāmi
illegal *adj.* गैर-कानूनी gair-kānuni
illegible *adj.* अस्पष्ट aspast
illegitimate *adj.* अवैध abaidh
illicit *adj.* अवैध abaidh
illiterate *adj.* अनपढ anpaṛh
illness *n.* बिमारी bimāri
illuminate *v.* उज्यालो बनाउनु ujyālo banāunu
illumination *n.* प्रदीप pradipt
illusion *n.* भांति bhrānti

illustrate *v.t.* सचित्र गर्नु sacitra gārnu
illustration *n.* चित्र citra
image *n.* मुर्ति murti
imaginary *adj.* काल्पनिक kālpanik
imagination *n.* कल्पना kalpanā
imagine *v.t.* कल्पना गर्नु kalpanā gārnu
imitate *v.t.* नकल गर्नु nakal gārnu
imitation *n.* अनुकरण anukaran
immaterial *adj.* केही फरक नपर्ने kehi pharak na parne
immature *adj.* अपरिपक्व aparipakwa
immeasurable *adj.* नाप्नै नसक्ने napnai nasakne
immediate *adj.* तुरुन्त turunta
immediately *adv.* तुरुन्त turunta
immense *adj.* विशाल visāl
immerse *v.* डुवाउनु dubāunu
immigrant *n.* आप्रवासी āprabāsi
immigrate *v.* बसाई सराई गर्नु basāi sarāi garnu
immoral *adj.* अनैतिक anaitik
immortal *adj.* अमर amar
immortalize *v.* अमर बनाउनु amar banāunu
immovable *adj.* अचल achal
immune *adj.* असर नपर्ने asar naparne
impact *n.* प्रभाव prabhāb
impartial *adj.* निष्पक्ष nispaksha
impartiality *n.* निष्पक्षता nispaksyatā
impasse *n.* गतिरोध gātirodh
impatient *adj.* बेचैन becain

impeachment *n.* महाअभियोग mahā abhiyog

impediment *n.* वाधा vādhā

imperfect *adj.* अपूर्ण apurna

imperialism *n.* साम्राज्यवाद sāmrājyabād

imperil *v.* खतरा पुर्याउनु khatarā puryāunu

impertinent *adj.* असान्दर्भिक asāndarvik

implement *n.* औजार aujār; *v.* कार्यान्वयन गर्नु kāryanvayan garnu; *v.t.* लागु गर्नु lāgu gārnu

implementation *n.* कार्यान्वयन kāryānvayan

imply *v.t.* अर्थ राख्नु arth rākhnu

impolite *adj.* अशिष्ट asist

import *n.* आयात āyāt; *v.t.* आयात गर्नु āyāt gārnu

importance *n.* महत्व mahatva

important *adj.* महत्वपूर्ण mahatvapurna

impose *v.t.* लगाउनु lagāunu

impossible *adj.* असंभव asambhav

impostor *n.* ठग thag

impotent *adj.* नपुंसक napunsak

impoverish *v.* गरीव वनाउनु garib banāunu

impracticable *adj.* अव्यावहारिक avyāvaharik

impress *v.t.* प्रभाव पार्नु prabhav pārnu

impressive *adj.* प्रभावशाली prabhāsāli

imprint *v.t.* अंकित गर्नु ankit gārnu

imprison *v.t.* कैद गर्नु kaid gārnu

improper *adj.* अनुचित anuchit

improve *v.i.* सुधार हुनु sudhār hunu; *v.t.* सुधार्नु sudhārnu

improvement *n.* सुधार sudhār

impulse *n.* अंतप्रेरणा antprernā

impunity *n.* दण्डहीनता dandahintā

impure *adj.* अपवित्र apavitra

in *prep.* मा mā

inability *n.* असमर्थता asamarthatā

inaccessible *adj.* अगम्य agamya

inaccurate *adj.* अंशुद्ध assuddha

inactive *adj.* निष्क्रिय niskriya

inadequate *adj.* अपर्याप्त aparyāpta

inadvisable *adj.* गर्न नहुने garna nahune

inalienable *adj.* नैसर्गिक naisargik

inapplicable *adj.* लागु नहुने lāgu nahune

inappropriate *adj.* बेठीक bethik

inaugurate *v.t.* उद्घाटन गर्नु udgātan gārnu

inauguration *n.* उद्घाटन udgātan

inauspicious *adj.* अशुभ asubh

in-born *adj.* जन्मजात janmajāt

incalculable *adj.* गन्नै नसकिने gannai nasakine

incapable *adj.* असमर्थ asamartha

incarnation *n.* अवतार avatār

incense *n.* अत्तर attar

incentive *n.* प्रेरणा preranā

incest *n.* हाडनाता करणी hād nālā karani

inch *n.* इंच ińc

inclination *n.* झुकाव jhukāv

incline *n.* ढाल dhāl; *v.i.* झुक्नु jhuknu, ढल्कनु dhalkanu

include *v.t.* समावेश गर्नु samābesh gārnu

income *n.* आय āya

incomparable *adj.* अतुलनीय atulaniya

incompetence *n.* नालायकी nālāyaki

incompetent *adj.* अक्षम aksam

incomprehensible *adj.* बुझ्नु नसक्ने bujhna nasakne

inconsiderable *adj.* सानो sāno

inconvenience *n.* असुविधा asubidhā

inconvenient *adj.* असुविधाजनक asubidhājanak

incorrect *adj.* अशुध्द asuddha

incorruptible *adj.* भ्रष्ट नभएको bhrasta nabhaeko

increase *n.* बढती barhti

incredible *adj.* अविश्वसनीय abiswasniya

increment *n.* वृद्धि briddhi

incurable *adj.* निको नहुने niko nahune

indecision *n.* अनिर्णय anirnaya

indeed *adv.* वास्तवमा vāstavmā

independence *n.* स्वतंत्रता svatantratā

independent *adj.* स्वतंत्र svatantra

indescribable *adj.* अवर्णनीय avarnaniya

indestructible *adj.* नाश नहुने nas nahune

index *n.* अनुक्रमिका anukramikā; *v.* अनुक्रमिका बनाउनु anukramikā banāunu

India *n.* भारत bhārat

indicate *v.t.* सूचित गर्नु sucit gārnu

indicative *adj.* सूचनीय sucaniya

indifferent *adj.* उदासीन udāsin

indigeneous *adj.* आदिवासी ādhivāsi

indigestion *n.* अपच pac

indignation *n.* रोष ros

indirect *adj.* अप्रत्यक्ष apratyaks

indiscriminate *adj.* भेदभाव रहित bhedbhav rahit

indispensible *adj.* नभई नहुने nabhai nehune

indistinguishable *adj.* छुट्टयाउन नसकिने chuttayuna nasakine

individual *adj.* व्यक्तिगत vyaktigat; *n.* व्यक्ति vyakti

indivisible *adj.* अविभाज्य abibhājya

indoor *adj.* भित्र bhitra

indulgent *adj.* उदार udār

industrial *adj.* औद्योगिक audhyogik

industrious *adj.* उद्योगी udyogi

industry *n.* उद्योग udyog

ineffective *adj.* असरदार नभएको asardār nabhaeko

inefficient *adj.* अयोग्य ayogya

ineligible *adj.* अयोग्य ayogya

inequality *n.* असमानता asamāntā

inestimable *adj.* अनुमान गर्न नसक्ने anumān garna nasakne

inevitable *adj.* नभईनहुने nabhai nahune

inexhaustible *adj.* नथाक्ने nathakne

inexpensive *adj.* सस्तो sasto

infamous *adj.* कुख्यात kukhyat

infant *n.* शिशु sisu

infantile *adj.* वालकीय bālakiya

infeasible *adj.* असम्भाव्य asambhāvya

infect *v.t.* संक्रमित गर्नु sankramit garnu

infection *n.* संदूषण sandusan

infectious *adj.* संक्रमण sankraman

inferior *adj.* कमसल kamsal

infidel *n.* नास्तिक nāstik

infiltrate *v.* पस्नु pasnu

infirmary *n.* सानो अस्पताल sāno aspatāl

inflamed *adj.* सुन्निएको sunniyeko

inflammable *adj.* ज्वलनशील jvalansil

inflammation *n.* सुन्निएको sunnieko

inflation *n.* मुद्रा-स्फीति mudrā-sphiti

inflexible *adj.* लचकदार नभएको lacakdār nabhaeko

influenza *n.* प्रभाव prabhāv

influenza *n.* रुघाखोकी rughākhoki

inform *v.t.* सूचना दिनु sucnā dinu

informal *adj.* अनौपचारिक anaupacārik

information *n.* सूचना sucnā

infrequent *adj.* कहिले काहिँ kahile kāhin

infringe *v.t.* उल्लंघन गर्नु ullaṅghan gārnu

ingenious *adj.* चतुर catur

ingredient *n.* घटक ghatak

inhabit *v.t.* बस्नु basnu

inhabitant *n.* निवासी niwāsi

inhale *v.t.* सासले तान्नु sasle tānnu

inhaler *n.* श्वासयंत्र savāsyantra

inherit *v.t.* दाय पाउनु dāy pāunu

inheritance *n.* दाय dāy

inhospitable *adj.* मित्रवद् नभएको mitrāvan nabhaeko

inhuman *adj.* अमानवीय amānaviya

inhumane *adj.* करुणाहीन karunāhin

inimical *adj.* शत्रुतापूर्ण satrutāupurna

initial *adj.* प्रारंभिक prārambhik; *n.* शुरुको shuruko

initiate *v.* शुरु गर्नु suru garnu

initiative *n.* नेतृत्व netratva

inject *v.t.* सुई लगाउनु sui lagāunu

injection *n.* सुई sui

injure *v.t.* चोट लगाउनु chot lagāunu

injured *adj.* घायल ghāyal

injury *n.* चोट cot

injustice *n.* अन्याय anyāya

ink *n.* मसी masi

inland *adj.* भुमिभित्र bhumi bhitra

in-law *n.* विहेको नातो biheko nāto

inn *n.* सराय sarāy, होटेल hotel

inner *adj.* भित्री bhitri

inner city *n.* सहरको केन्द्र saharko kendra

innocent *adj.* निर्दोष nirdos

innovate *v.* आविष्कार गर्नु āviskār garnu

innumerable *adj.* असंख्या asnkhya

inoculate *v.i.* खोप लगाउनु khop lagāunu

inoculation *n.* खोप khop

inpatient *n.* अस्पतालमा बस्ने रोगी asparālmā basne rogi

inquire *v.* सोध्नु sodhnu

inquiry *n.* जाँच बुझ jaṁc bujh

inquisitive *adj.* जान्न उत्सुक jānna utsuk

insane *adj.* पागल pagāl

inscribe *v.* लेख्नु lekhnu

insect *n.* किरा kirā

insecticide *n.* किरा मार्ने औषधी kirā marne ausadhi

insecure *adj.* असुरक्षित asuraksit

inseparable *adj.* अभिन्न abhinna

insert *n.* घुसाउनु ghusāunu

inside *adv.* भित्र bhitrā; *prep.* मा ma

insider *n.* भित्रिया bhitriyā

insight *n.* अन्तर्दृष्टि antardrsti

insignificant *adj.* सानो sāno

insincere *adj.* हार्दिक नभएको hārdik nabhaeko

insist *v.i.* आग्रह गर्नु agrah garnu

insistence *n.* आग्रह anidrārog

insoluble *adj.* नघोलिने nagholine

insomnia *n.* अनिद्रारोग anidrārog

inspect *v.t.* जाँच-पडताल jānc-partāl gārnu

inspection *n.* निराक्षण niriksan

inspector *n.* निराक्षक niriksak

inspiration *n.* प्रेरणा prernā

inspire *v.t.* प्रेरणा दिनु prernā dinu

install *v.t.* लगाउनु lagāunu

installation *n.* अधिस्थापन adnisthāpan

instance *n.* उदाहरण udāharan

instant *n.* छिटो chito

instantly *adj.* तुरंत turant

instead *adv.* को ठाउँ मा ko thau mā

instinct *n.* भित्री धारना vitri dharana

institute *n.* संस्थान sansthān

institutionalize *v.* संस्थागत गर्नु samsthagar garnu

instruct *v.t.* शिक्षा दिनु siksā dinu

instruction *n.* पढाइ padhāi

instructor *n.* शिक्षक shikshak

instrument *n.* यंत्र yantra

insubordinate *adj.* कसैलाई नमान्ने kasailāi namānne

insufficient *adj.* अपर्यास aparyāpt

insulate *v.t.* बेग्लै गर्नु beglai gārnu

insulation *n.* पृथक्करण prathakkaran

insult *n.* अपमान apmān; *v.* अपमान गर्नु apmān garnu

insurance *n.* बिमा bimā

insure *v.t.* बिमा गर्नु bimā gārnu

insured *n.* बिमा गरेको व्यक्ति bimā gareko byakti

insurgency *n.* विद्रोह vidroha

insurgent *n.* विद्रोही vidrohi

insurmountable *adj.* समाधान गर्न नसक्ने samādhān garna nasakne

insurrection *n.* क्रान्ति krānti

intact *adj.* पूरा purā

integral *adj.* संपूर्ण sampurna

integrate *n.* मिलाउनु milāunu

intellectual *adj.* बुद्धिजीवि buddhijivi

intelligence *n.* बुद्धि buddhi

intelligent *adj.* बुद्धिमान buddhimān

intend *v.t.* ईच्छा गर्नु icchā gārnu

intense *adj.* तेज tej

intensify *v.* झन चर्को हुनु jhan carko hunu

intention *n.* इच्छा iccha, चाख cakh

intentional *adj.* जानी जानीकन jāni jāni kana

interact *v.* अन्तर्कृया गर्नु antarkriyā garnu

interaction *n.* अन्तर्कृया antarkriyā

intercourse *n.* करणी karani

interest *n.* आभिरुचि abhiruchi; चाख cakh; *v.t.* दिलचस्पी लिनु dilcaspi linu

interesting *adj.* दिलचस्प dilcasp

interfere *v.* हस्तक्षेप गर्नु hastakshep garnu

interference *n.* हस्तक्षेप hastakshap

interior *adj.* भित्री bhitri; *n.* भित्र bhitra

internal *adj.* भित्री bhitri

international *adj.* अंतरराष्ट्रीय antarrāstriy

interpret *v.* अर्थ बताउनु artha batāunu

interpreter *n.* दोभासे dubhāsiyā

interrogate *v.* पूछताछ गर्नु puctāc garnu

interrupt *v.t./v.i.* रोक्नु roknu

interruption *n.* बाधा bādhā

interval *n.* मध्यांतर madhyāntar

intervene *v.i.* हस्तक्षेप गर्नु hastakshup gārnu

interview *n.* अन्तर्वार्ता antarbartā

intestines *n.* आन्द्रा āndrā

intimate *adj.* घनिष्ठ ghanisth

intimidate *v.* तर्साउनु tarsāunu

into *prep.* मा mā

intolerable *adj.* असहनीय asahaniya

introduce *v.t.* परिचय दिनु paricay dinu

introduction *n.* परिचय paricay, भूमिका bhumikā

introvert *n.* अतर्मुखी antarmukhi

invade *v.t.* हमला गर्नु hamalā gārnu

invalid *n.* विकलाङ्ग vikalānga

invasion *n.* हमला hamalā

invent *v.t.* आविष्कार गर्नु āviskār gārnu

invention *n.* आविष्कार aviskār

inventory *n.* तालिका tālikā

invest *v.* लगानी गर्नु lagāni garnu

investigate *v.t.* पत्ता लगाउनु pattā lagāunu

investigation *n.* जाँच-पडताल jānc-partāl

investment *n.* लगानी lagāni

invisible *adj.* अदृश्य adṛsya

invitation *n.* निमन्त्रणा nimantrana, निम्ता nimtā

invite *v.t.* निम्ताउनु nimtāunu

invoice *n.* बीजक bijak; *v.t.* बीजक बनाउनु bijak banāunu

involve *v.t.* संलग्न गराउनु sanladna garāunu

inward *adj.* भित्र पटि्ट bhitra patti

iron *n.* *(metal)* फलाम phalām; *v.t.* इस्तरी istari

ironic *adj.* व्यंग्यात्मक vyangyātmak

irony *n.* विडम्वना bidamwanā

irregular *adj.* अनियमित aniyamit

irrelevant *adj.* अप्रासंगिक aprāsangik

irremovable *adj.* हटाउन नसकिने hatāuna nasakne

irreparable *adj.* मरम्मत नहुने marammat nahune

irresponsible *adj.* अनुत्तरदायी anuttardāi

irrigation *n.* सिंचाई sincāi

irritation *v.t.* सिंचाइ sińcāi

Islam *n.* इस्लाम islām

Islamic *adj.* इस्लामी Islāmi

island *n.* टापू tāpu

isolate *v.t.* अलग alag

Israel *n.* इजराइल isrāil

Israeli *adj.* इजराइली isrāili

issue *n.* मुद्दा muddā; *v.t.* निकालनु nikālnu

it *pron.* यो yo, उ u, उनि uni

Italian *n.* इटालीको निवासी Italyko niwāsi

itch *n.* चिलाइ chilāi; *v.i.* चिलाउनु chilāunu

item *n.* विषय visay

itinerary *n.* यात्राको वाटो yātrā ko bāto

its *pron.* यसको yasko

itself *pron.* त्यही tyahi

ivory *n.* हस्तिदाँत hastidānt

ivy *n.* लहरा laharā

J

jack *n.* गुलाम gulām

jackal *n.* स्याल syāl

jacket *n.* जाकट jāket

jade *n.* पहेँलो रत्न pahelo ratna

jail *n.* जेल jel

jam *n.* मुरब्बा murabbā

janitor *n.* द्वारपाल dvārpāl

January *n.* जनवरी janvari

Japan *n.* जापान Jāpān

Japanese *n./adj* जापानी Jāpāni

jargon *n.* कुनै समूहको विशेष भाषा kunai samuhako bises bhāsā

jasmine *n.* चमेली cameli

jaundice *n.* कमल पित्त kamal pitta

jaw *n.* जबडा jabrā

jealous *adj.* ईर्ष्यालु isyaryālu

jealousy *n.* ईर्ष्या irshyā

jeep *n.* जीप jip

jelly *n.* जेली jeli

jeopordize *v.* बिगार्नु bigārnu

jeopordy *n.* खतरा khatarā

Jesuit *n.* इसाइको संप्रदाय isāiko sampraday

jet *n.* जेट jet

Jew *n.* यहूदी yahudi

jewel *n.* मणि mani

jeweler *n.* जौहरी jauhari

jewelry *n.* जवाहरात javāharāt

Jewish *adj.* यहूदी yahudi

jigsaw puzzle *n.* टुक्रा-टुक्रा tukrā-tukra

job *n.* नौकरी naukari, काम kam

jog *v.* दौडनु daudanu

join *v.t.* मिलाउनु milāunu

joint *n.* जोड jor

joke *n.* ठट्टा thattā; *v.t.* ठट्टा गर्नु thattā gārnu

joker *n.* जोकर jokar

journal *n.* पत्रिका patrikā

journalism *n.* पत्रकारिता patrakāritā

journalist *n.* पत्रकार patrakār

journey *n.* यात्रा yātrā; *v.i.* यात्रा गर्नु yātrā gārnu

joy *n.* आनंद ānand

jubilation *n.* आनन्दोत्सव anandotsav

judge *n.* न्यायधिश nyāyādish

judgment *n.* फैंसला faisalā

judicial *adj.* न्यायिक nyāyik

judiciary *adj.* न्याय पालिका nyaypālika

jug *n.* जग jag

juice *n.* रस ras

July *n.* जुलाई julāi

jumble *n.* गड्डमड्ड gaddmaḍḍ; *v.t.* गड्डमड्ड गर्नु gaddmaḍḍ gārnu

jump *v.t.* उफ्रिनु uphrinu

junction *n.* संगम sangam

June *n.* जून jun

jungle *n.* जंगल jangal

junior *adj.* सानो sano

junk *n.* कबाड kabār

jurisdiction *n.* क्षेत्राधिकार kshetrādhikār

jury *n.* पंच समिति panc samiti

just *adj.* न्यायप्रिय nyaypriya; *adv.* केवल keval

justice *n.* न्याय nyāya

justification *n.* औचित्य aucitya

justify *v.t.* न्यायसंगत सिद्ध गर्नु
  nyāyasangat siddh gārnu
jute *n.* सनपाट sanpāt
juvenile *adj.* बाल bāl; *n.* किशोर
  kisor

K

kangaroo *n.* कंगारु kaṅgāru
keen *adj.* उत्साही utsāhi
keep *v.t.* राख्नु rakhnu
keeper *n.* रक्षक raksak
kerosene *n.* मट्टितेल mattitel
kettle *n.* कितली ketali
key *n.* चाबी cābi, साँचो sanco
khaki *n./adj.* खाकी khāki
kick *n.* ठक्कर thakar; *v.t.* लाति हान्नु lātti hānnu
kid *v.* ठट्टा गर्नु thattā garnu; *v.t.* बालक bālak
kidnap *v.t.* अपहरण गर्नु apaharan gārnu
kidney *n.* मिर्गौला mirgaula
kill *v.t.* मार्नु mārnu
kilogram *n.* किलोग्राम kilogrām
kilometer *n.* किलोमीटर kilomitar
kind *adj.* दयालु dayalu; *n.* किसिम kisim
kindergarten *n.* शिशु स्कुल sisu skul
kindhearted *adj.* दयालु dayālu
kindle *v.t.* जलाउनु jalāunu
kindness *n.* दया dayā
king *n.* राजा rājā
kingdom *n.* अधिराज्य adhirājya
kiss *n.* चुम्बन cumban; *v.t.* म्वाई खानु mwaikhānu
kit *n.* किट kit
kitchen *n.* भान्छा bhanchā
kitchenware *n.* भान्छाको भाँडाकुँडा bhansāko bhandakuda
kite *n.* चङ्गा cangā
kitten *n.* बिरालोको बच्चा biralo ko bachha

knapsack *n.* झोला jholā
knee *n.* घुँडा ghudā
kneel *v.i.* घुँडा टेक्नु ghuda teknu
knife *n.* चक्कु chakku
knit *v.t.* बन्नु bannu
knock *n.* ढकढकाउनु dhakdhakaunu
knot *n.* गाँठो gāntho; *v.t.* गाँठो बाँध्नु gāntho badhnu
know *v.t.* चिन्नु chinnu
know-how *n.* शीप seep
knowing *v.t.* जान्नु jānnu
knowledge *n.* ज्ञान Gyān

L

label *n.* नामपत्र ṅåmpatra
labor *n.* मजदूर majduri
laboratory *n.* प्रयोगशाला prayogsālā
laborer *n.* मजदूर majdoor
labyrinth *n.* भुलभुलैया bhulbhulaiyā
lace *n.* फीता phittā
lack *n.* कमी kami; *v.t.* कमी हुनु kami hunu
ladder *n.* भरेङ bhareng
lady *n.* महिला mahilā
lag *v.i.* पछाडि पर्नु pachadi parnu
lake *n.* ताल tāl
lamb *n.* बाख्रो bākhro
lame *adj.* लँगडो langaṛo
lament *v.* दुखित हुनु dukhit hunu
lamp *n.* बत्ती batti
lamppost *n.* बत्ती को खंभा batti ko khambhā
land *n.* भूमि bhumi
land tax *n.* मालपोत mālpot
landing *n.* अवतरण avtaran
landlocked *adj.* भूपरिवेष्ठित bhu-parivesthit
landlord *n.* घरपति gharpati
landmark *n.* सीमाचिन्ह simācihn
landscape *n.* भू-दृश्य bhu-dṛsya
landslide *n.* पहिरो pahiro
lane *n.* गली gali
language *n.* भाषा bhāsā
lantern *n.* लालटेन lālten
lap *n.* काख kākh
lapse *n.* भूल bhul
laptop *n.* सानो कप्युटर sano computer, ल्यापटप lyaptop
larceny *n.* चोरी cori
lard *n.* सुंगुर को बोसो sungur ko boso
large *adj.* ठूलो thulo
largely *adv.* धेरै जसो dherai jaso
largess *n.* उदारता udāratā
laser *n.* लेजर lejar
lash *n.* कोर्रा korrā
last *adj.* अन्तिम antim
lasting *adv.* धेरै समयरहने dherai samaya rahane
lastly *adv.* आखिरमा ākhirmā
latch *n.* छेसकीनी cheskini
late *adj.* अवेर awer
lately *adv.* हालै halai
latent *adj.* गुप्ता gupta
Latin *n./adj.* लैटिन laitin
Latin America *n.* लैटिन अमेरिका laitin ameika
latitude *n.* अक्षांश aksāns
latrine *n.* शौचालय saucālay, चर्पी charpi
latter *adj.* पछिल्लो pachilo
laugh *n.* हँसी hamsi; *v.i.* हाँस्नु hāsnu
laughable *adj.* हाँस्नु लायक hasnu lāyak
laughter *n.* हँसी hamsi
launch *n.* लांच lānc; *v.t.* छोड्नु chornu
laundry *n.* लुगा धुने ठाँउ luga dhune thau
lavatory *n.* चर्पी carpi
lavish *adj.* खर्चिलो kharchilo
law *n.* कानून kānun
lawful *adj.* विधिसम्मत vidhisammat

lawless *adj.* कानून विहिन kanun bihin

lawn *n.* मैदान maidān

lawsuit *n.* नालिश nālish

lawyer *n.* वकील vakil

lay *v.t.* बिछाउनु bichānu

layer *n.* तह taha

lazy *adj.* अल्छी alchi

leach *n.* जुका juka

lead *n.* सीसा sisā; *v.t.* लैजानु laijānu

leader *n.* नेता netā

leadership *n.* नेतृत्व netāgiri

leaf *n.* पात pāt

leaflet *n.* पर्चा parcā

leak *v.i.* चुहिनु chuhinu

lean *adj.* दुबलो dublo; *v.i.* झुक्नु jhuknu

leap *n.* उछाल uchāl; *v.i.* उफ्रनु uphranu

learn *v.t.* सिक्नु siknu

learned *adj.* विद्वान vidwān

lease *n.* पट्टा pattā; *v.t.* पट्टी मा दिनु patte mā dinu

leash *n.* पट्टा pattā

least *n.* अलिकति alikati; *adv.* कम-से कम kam-se kam

leather *n.* छाला chālā

leave *n.* छुट्टी chutti; *v.t.* छोड्नु chodnu

lecture *n.* व्याख्यान vyākhyān

ledge *n.* कगार kagār

leech *n.* जुका jukā

left *adj.* बायाँ bāyān

left-handed *adj.* बायाँ हातले काम गर्ने bāyān hātle kām garne

leftist *n.* वामपन्थी bāmpanthi

leftover *adj.* वाँकी रहेको bānki raheko

leg *n.* खुट्टा khuttā

legacy *n.* परम्परा paramparā

legal *adj.* कानूनी kānuni

legality *n.* वैधता vaidhtā

legation *n.* दुतावास dutabas

legend *n.* कथा kāthā

legible *adj.* पढन सकिने padhna sakine

legislation *n.* कानून kānun

legislative *adj.* व्यवस्थापिका वारे baidhatā bare

legislature *n.* व्यवस्थापिका vyabasthapikā

legitimate *adj.* वैध vaidhtā

leisure *n.* अवकाश avkās

lemon *n.* कागती kāgati

lend *v.t.* सापट दिनु sāpat dinu

length *n.* लंबाई lambāi

lengthen *v.t.* लामो गर्नु lāmo gārnu

lengthy *adj.* लामो lāmo

lenient *adj.* उदार udār

lens *n.* लेन्स lens

lentil *n.* दाल dāl

leopard *n.* चितुवा chitwā

leper *n.* कोढी kodhi

leprosy *n.* कुष्ठ रोग kusthā rog

lesbian *n.* महिला समालंगी mahilā samalingi

less *adv.* कम kam

lessee *n.* भाडामा बस्ने bhāsāmā basne

lesson *n.* पाठ pāth

lessor *n./adj.* भाडामा दिने bhādā dine, घरपति gharpati

let *v.t.* हुन दिनु huna dinu

lethal *adj.* खतरनाक khatatnāk

letter *n.* (*note*) चिट्ठी citthi, पत्र patra; (*alphabet*) अक्षर akshyar

lettuce *n.* सलाद पत्ता salād pattā

leukemia *n.* रगत क्यान्सर ragat cancer

level *adj.* समतल samtal

lever *n.* कलेजो kalejo

liability *n.* खर्च kharcha

liable *adj.* जिम्मेवार jimmevār

liaison *n.* संपर्क samparka

liar *n.* झूटो बोल्ने jhuto bolne

libel *n.* अपमान-लेख apmān-lekh, चितुवा chitwa; *v.t.* अपमान-लेख लेख्नु apmān-lekh lekhnu

liberal *adj.* उदार udār

liberate *v.* छुटाउनु chutaunu

liberation *n.* मुक्ति mukti

liberty *n.* स्वतंत्रता svarantratā

librarian *n.* पुस्तकालयाध्यक्ष pustākālayādhyaksa

library *n.* पुस्तकालय pustakālaya

license *n.* आज्ञा āgyā

lick *v.* चाटनु catnu

lid *n.* ढक्कन dhakkan, बिर्को birko

lie *n.* झूठो jhutho; *v.i.* झूठो बोल्नु jhutho bolnu

lieutenant *n.* लप्टन laptan; सहायक sahāyak

life *n.* जिन्दगी jindagi, जीवन jivan

life insurance *n.* जीवन वीमा jivan bimā

lifeboat *n.* रक्षा-नौका raksā-naukā

lifeless *adj.* निर्जीव nirjiv

lifelong *adj.* बाँचुन्जेल bāchunjel

lifetime *n.* जीवन काल jivan kāl

lift *n.* लिफ्ट lift; *v.t.* उठनु uthnu

light *n.* प्रकाश prakās, वत्ती batti; *v.t.* बल्नु balnu

lighten *v.t.* बाल्नु bālnu

lighthouse *n.* प्रकास गृह prakās grha

lightning *n.* बिजुली bijuli

likable *adj.* आकर्षक ākarsak

like *adj./adv.* समान samān; *v.t.* मन पराउनु man parāunu

likelihood *n.* सम्भावना sambhāvanā

likely *adv.* संभावित sambhāvit

likewise *adv.* यसै गरी yasai gari

liking *n.* मन पराई man parāi

limb *n.* अंग ang

lime *n.* कागती kāgati

limelight *n.* ध्यानाकर्षण dhyānākarsan

limestone *n.* चुन ढुङ्गा chun dhunga

limit *n.* सीमा simā

limited *adj.* सीमित simit

limousine *n.* लामो बस lāmo bas

limp *v.i.* लंगडाउनु langaraunu

line *n.* लाइन lāin; *v.t.* पंक्तिबद्ध गर्नु panktibaddh gārnu

lineage *n.* बंशज vamsaj

linen *n.* सनका कपडा san ko karā

liner *n.* लाइनर lāinar

lingua franca *n.* संपर्क भाषा samparka bhāsa

linguist *n.* भाषाशास्त्री bhāsāsāstri

linguistics *n.* भाषाशास्त्र bhāsāsāstra

lining *n.* अस्तर astar

link *n.* कडी kari; *v.t.* संबंध sambandh

linkage *n.* जोडाइ jodi

lion *n.* सिंह sinha

lip *n.* ओठ oth

lipstick *n.* लिपस्टिक lipstik

liqueur *n.* मदिरा madirā

liquid *adj.* तरल पदार्थ taral padārtha; *n.* द्रव drav

liquidate *v.* सखाप पार्नु sakhāp pārnu

liquor *n.* मादक पदार्थ mādak padārtha

list *n.* सूची suci; *v.t.* सूची बनाउनु suci banāunu

listen *v.* ध्यान दिएर सुन्नु dhyān diyera sunnu

listener *n.* श्रोता srotā

literacy *n.* साक्षरता sākshartā

literary *adj.* साहित्यिक sāhityik

literate *adj.* साक्षर sākshar

literature *n.* साहित्य sāhitya

litigation *n.* मुद्दा मामला muddā māmalā

litter *n.* फोहोर kurā-kacarā

little *adj.* अलिकति alikati

livable *adj.* बस्न लायक basna lāyak

live *adj.* जीवित jiwit; *v.i.* वाँच्नु bāchnu

livelihood *n.* जीविका jivikā

lively *adj.* क्रियाशील kriyāsil, जीवन्त jiwanta

liver *n.* कलेजो kalejo

livestock *n.* गाईवस्तु gai bāstu

living *adj.* वाँचेको bānceko

living room *n.* बैठक baithak

lizard *n.* पल्ली palli

load *n.* भार bhār; *v.t.* लादनु lādnu

loaf *n.* पाउरोटी pauroti

loan *n.* सापटी sāpati, उधार udhār; *v.t.* उधार udhār

lobster *n.* समुन्द्री माछा samundri mācā

local *adj.* स्थानीय sthāniya

locale *n.* ठाँउ thāun

locate *v.* पत्ता लगाउनु pattā lagāunu

lock *n.* ताल्चा talca; *v.t.* ताल्चा लगाउनु tālchā lagaunu

locker *n.* लाकर lākar

lockjaw *n.* धनुष्टंकार dhanustankār

locomotive *n.* इंजन injan

locust *n.* सलह salah

lodge *n.* झुप्रो jhupro, सानो होटेल sano hotel, होटेल hotel

lodging *n.* आवास āvās

log *n.* लट्ठा lattā

logging *n.* काठ काट्ने kāth kātne

logic *n.* तर्कशास्त्र tarksāstra

logical *adj.* तर्कसंगत tarksangat

lone *adj.* एक्लो eklo

lonely *adj.* एक्लो eklo

long *adj.* लामो lāmo

long distance *n.* लामो दूरी lāmo duri

longevity *n.* दीर्घजीवन dirghajivi

longing *n.* आकांक्षा ākānsyā

longitude *n.* देशांतर desāntar

look *n.* दृश्य drsya; *v.i.* देखनु dekhnu

loom *n.* करघा karghā

loop *n.* फन्दा phandā

loose *adj.* खुला khulā

loosen *adj.* खुकुलो पार्नु khukolo pārnu

loot *n.* युद्धकालमा लुटिएको yuddhākālmā lutiyeko

lord *n.* प्रभु prabhu; स्वामी svāmi

lose *v.t.* हराउनु harāunu

loss *n.* नोक्सानी noksāni

lost *adj.* हराएको harāeko

lottery *n.* चिठ्ठा citthā

lotus *n.* कमल kamal

loud *adj.* ठूलो आवाज thulo āwaj

loudmouth *n.* बकवके bakbake

loudspeaker *n.* लाउडस्पीकर lāuḍspikar

lounge *n.* प्रतीक्षालय pratiksālāya; विश्राम-कक्ष visrām-kaksa

lousy *adj.* खराब kharāb, नराम्रो narāmro

love *n.* प्रेम prem; *v.t.* प्रेम गर्नु prem gārnu

lovely *adj.* मनोहर manohar

lover *n.* *(m.)* प्रेमी premi; *(f.)* प्रेमिका premika

loving *adj.* प्रिय priya

low *adj.* तल tala

lower *adj.* तल्लो tallo

loyal *adj.* वफादार vafādār

lucid *adj.* राम्ररी बुझिने rāmrari bujhine

luck *n.* भाग्य bhāgya
lucky *adj.* भाग्यशाली bhāgyasāli
lucrative *adj.* फायदा हुने phāyadā
  hune
ludicrous *adj.* हास्यास्पद
  hāsyaspad
luggage *n.* सामान sāmān
lumber *n.* काठ kāth
lunar *adj.* चन्द्रमा संवन्धि
  chandrama sambandhi
lunatic *adj.* पागल pāgal
lunch *n.* दिन को खाना din ko
  khānā
lung *n.* फोक्सो phokso
lure *v.* लोभ्याउनु lobhyāunu
lust *n.* बासना vāsanā
luxurious *adj.* विलासी vilāsi
luxury *n.* विलास vilās

M

machine *n.* मेशीन mesin

machinery *n.* यंत्र yantra

mad *adj.* पागल pāgal

madam *n.* मैदम maiḍam

madhouse *n.* गडबड भएको ठाउं gadbad bhaeko thāun

madness *n.* रिस ris

mafia *n.* अपराधी संस्था aparādhi samsthā

magazine *n.* पत्रिका patrikā

magic *n.* जादू jādu

magical *adj.* जादुई jadui

magician *n.* जादूगर jādugar

magistrate *n.* मजिस्ट्रेट majistret

magnanimous *adj.* उदार udār

magnet *n.* चुंबक cumbak

magnetic *adj.* चुम्बकीय cumbakiya

magnificent *adj.* शानदार sāndār

magnify *v.t.* वढाउनु badhāunu

magnitude *n.* मात्रा mātrā

maid *n.* कुमारी kumāri, काम गर्ने महिला kām garne mahilā

maiden *n.* विवाह गर्नु अघिको vivah garnu aghiko

mail *n.* हुलाक hulāk

mailman *n.* हुलाकी hulāki

main *adj.* मुख्य mukhya

mainland *n.* मुख्य भू-भाग mukhya bhu-bhāg

mainly *adv.* मुख्य रुपले mukhya ruple

mainstream *n.* मध्यधार madhyadhār

maintain *v.t.* बनाइ राख्नु banai rākhnu

maintenance *n.* सँभार sambhār

maize *n.* मकै makai

majestic *adj.* राजसी rājsi

majesty *n.* प्रताप pratāp

major *n.* (*college ~*) मेजर mejar

majority *n.* बहुमत bahumat

make *n.* निर्माण nirmān; *v.t.* बनाउनु banāunu

maker *n.* बनाउने banāune

make-up *n.* बनावट banāvat

malady *n.* रोग rog

malaria *n.* औलो aulo

male *adj.* पुरुष purush

malice *n.* नोक्सान पुर्याउने noksān puraune

malignant *adj.* अहितकर ahitkar

malnourished *adj.* कुपोषित kuposit

malnutrition *n.* कुपोषण kuposan

malpractice *n.* लापरवाही lāparbāhi

mammal *n.* स्तनपायी stanpāyi

man *n.* मानिस mānis

manage *v.t.* प्रबंध गर्नु prabandh gārnu

management *n.* प्रबंध prabandh

manager *n.* मैनेजर mainejar

mandate *n.* जनादेश janādesh

mandatory *adj.* अनिवार्य anivārya

manhood *n.* पुरुषत्व purusatva

maniac *n.* पागल pāgal

manifest *adj.* देखिनु dekhinu

manifestation *n.* प्रदर्शन pradarsan

manifesto *n.* घोषणापत्र ghosanāpatra

manifold *n.* विविध vividh

manipulate *v.t.* चलाउनु calunu

mankind *n.* मानव जाति mānav jāti

manmade *adj.* मानव निर्मित mānav nirmit

mannequin *n.* पुतली putli

manner *n.* ढंग dhang

manpower *n.* जनशक्ति jansakti

mansion *n.* हवेली haveli

manufacture *n.* निर्माण nirmān; *v.t.* निर्माण गर्नु nirmān gārnu

manufacturing *n.* निर्माण nirmān

manure *n.* मल mal

manuscript *n.* हस्तलिपि hastlipi

many *adj.* धेरै dherai

Maoism *n.* माओवाद māobad

Maoist *adj.* माओवादी māobādi

map *n.* नक्शा naksā

marathon *n.* लामो दौड lāmo daud

marble *n.* संगमरमर saṅgmarmar

march *n.* मार्च mārc

mare *n.* घोडी ghodi

margin *n.* किनारा kinārā

marginalized *adj.* सिमान्तिकृत simāntikrit

marigold *n.* सयपत्री sayapatri

marijuana *n.* भाँग bhāng

marine *(mil.) n.* जहाजी बेडा jahāji berā

marital *adj.* विवाह संबन्धी vivāh sambandhi

mark *n.* चिन्ह cihn

market *n.* बजार bājār

marketable *adj.* बेच्न सक्ने bechna sakine

marketing *n.* बजारमा लैजानु bajar mā laijānu

marmalade *n.* मुरब्बा murbbā

maroon *adj.* चकलेट रंगको cāklet rang ko

marriage *n.* विवाह vivāha

married *adj.* विवाहित vivāhit

marry *v.t.* विहे गर्नु bihe gārnu

marsh *n.* दलदल daldal

marshal *n.* मार्शल mārsal

martial *adj.* मार्शल mārsal

martial law *n.* सैनिक शासन sainik sāsan

martyr *n.* शहीद sahid

martyrdom *n.* शाहादत sahādat

marvelous *adj.* आश्चर्यजनक āscaryajanak

Marxism *n.* माक्र्सवाद marxvād

Marxist *adj.* माक्र्सवादी marxvādi

masculine *adj.* पुलिंग pullinga; मरदाना mardānā

mask *n.* मुखौटा mukhautā, नकाब nakāb; *v.t.* नकाब लगाउनु naqāb lagāunu

mason *n.* मिस्त्री mistri, डकर्मी dakarmi

mass *adj.* सामूहिक sāmuhik; *n.* राशिक rāsik

massacre *n.* हत्याकाण्ड hatyā kānd

massage *n.* मालिश mālis

massive *adj.* भारी bhāri

mast *n.* मस्तूल mastul

master *n.* स्वामी swāmi

mastermind *n.* आयोजना बनाउने āyojanā banāune

mastery *n.* आधिपत्य ādhipatya

masturbation *n.* हस्त मैथुन hasta maithun

mat *n.* चटाई catāi

match *n.* जोड jor

matchmaker *n.* लमी lami

mate *n.* साथी sāthi

material *n.* सामान sāmān

maternal *adj.* आमा तर्फको āmā tarphako

mathematician *n.* गणीतज्ञ ganitagya

mathematics *n.* गणित ganit

matriarch *n.* परिवारको मुख्य महिला parivār ko mukhy mahilā

matrimonial *adj.* विवाह सबन्धी vivāh sambandhi

matrimony *n.* विवाह vivah

matter *n.* बात bāt

mattress *n.* चटाई chatai

mature *adj.* प्रौढ praudh

maturity *n.* परिपक्त्ता paripakvatā

mausoleum *n.* ठूलो चिहान thulo cihān

maverick *n.* स्वतन्त्र विचारक swatantra vicarak

maximum *adj.* अधिकतम adhikatam

May *n.* मई mai

may *v.* हुन सक्नु huna saknu

maybe *adv.* शायद sāyad

mayonnaise *n.* सलादको मसाला salād ko masālā

mayor *n.* मेयर meyar, महापौर mahāpaur

maze *n.* भूल-भूलैया bhul-bhulaiya

me *pron* मलाई malai, म ma

meadow *n.* चौर chaur

meager *adj.* अल्प alpa

meal *n.* खाना khānā

mealtime *n.* खाने वेला khanebelā

mean *adj.* कंजूस kanjus; *n.* बीचको बाटो bic ko bato

meaning *n.* अर्थ artha

means *n.* उपाय upāy, साधन sādhan

meantime *adv.* यसै बीच yasai bic; *n.* यतिमा yetima

measles *n.* दादुरा dādurā

measure *n.* नाप nāp; *v.* नाप्नु napnu

measurement *n.* नापी nāpi

meat *n.* मासु māsu

mechanic *n.* मैकेनिक maikenik

mechanism *n.* संयन्त्र samyantra

medal *n.* पदक padak

meddle *v.* हस्तक्षेप गर्नु hastakshep garnu

mediate *v.* मध्यस्थता गर्नु madhyasthā garnu

medical *adj.* डाक्टरी ḍāktari

medicament *n.* औषधी ausadhi

medicate *v.* औषधी गर्नु ausadhi garnu

medicine *n.* औषधी ausadhi

medieval *adj.* मध्यकालीन mādhyakālin

mediocre *adj.* साधारण sādhāran, मामूली māmuli

medium *n.* माध्यम mādhyam

meet *v.t.* भेटाउनु bhetaunu

meeting *n.* भेटनु bhetnu

melancholy *adj.* दुखी dukhi

melon *n.* खरबुजा kharbuja

melt *v.i.* पग्लनु paglanu

member *n.* सदस्य sadsya

membership *n.* सदस्यता sadasyatā

membrane *n.* झिल्ली jhilli

memoir *n.* संस्मरण sansmaran

memorandum *n.* टिप्प णी tippani

memorial *n.* स्मारक smārak

memorize *v.t.* संझनु samjhaunu

memory *n.* स्मरण smaran

menace *n.* खतरा khatra

mend *v.t.* मर्मत गर्नु marammat gārnu

menial *adj.* सेवकले गर्ने काम sewakle garne kām

mensuration *n.* रजस्वला rajaswalā, पर सर्ने para sarne

mental *adj.* मानसिक mānasik

mentality *n.* मनोवृति manovritti

mention *n.* उल्लेख ullekh; *v.t.* उल्लेख गर्नु ullekh gārnu

mentor *n.* गुरु guru, शिक्षक siksak

menu *n.* मेन्यू menyu

mercantile *adj.* व्यापार संबन्धि vyāpār sambandhi

mercenary *adj.* विदेशी सेनामा काम

गर्ने सैनिक videsi senāmā kām garne sainik

merchandise *n.* व्यापारी माल vyāpāri māl

merchant *n.* व्यापारी vyāpāri, साहू महाजन sāhu mahājan

merciful *adj.* दयालु dayālu

merciless *adj.* निर्दयी nirdayi

mercury *n.* पारो pāro

mercy *n.* दया dayā

mere *adj.* मात्र mātra

merely *adv.* केवल keval

merge *v.t.* मिल्नु milnu

merit *n.* गुण gun

meritorious *adj.* प्रशंसा योग्य prasansā yogya

merry *adj.* प्रसन्न prasanna

mesh *n.* छिद्र chidra

mesmerize *v.* सम्मोहन गर्नु sammohan garnu

mess *n.* खाना खाने ठाउँ khāna khāne thāu, गडवड gadbad

message *n.* संदेश sandes

messenger *n.* संदेश वाहक sandes bāhak

metal *n.* धातु dhātu

metallurgy *n.* धातु शास्त्र dhātu sāstra

meteor *n.* उल्का ulkā

meteoric *adj.* उल्का जस्तो ulkā jasto

method *n.* तरीका tarikā

methodical *adj.* सुव्यवस्थित suvyavsthit

Methodist *n.* इसाई संप्रदाय isāi sampradaya

meticulous *adj.* अति सावधान ati sāvadhān

metropolis *adj.* महानगरपालिका mahānagarpālikā

microphone *n.* माइक māik

microscope *n.* सूक्ष्मदर्शी suksamdarsi

midday *n.* दिउँसो diunso

middle *adj.* मध्यम madhyam

Middle Ages *n.* मध्ययुग madhya yug

middle class *n.* मध्यमवर्ग madhyam varga

middle-aged *adj.* प्रौढ praudh

midnight *n.* मध्यरात्रि madhyarāti

midst *n.* बीचमा bicmā

midwife *n.* सूडिनी sudini

might *v. aux.* सकनु sakanu

mighty *adj.* शक्तिशाली shaktishali

migrant *n.* आप्रवासी āprabāsi

migrate *v.i.* बसाई सर्नु basāi sarnu

mild *adj.* मृदुल mridul

mile *n.* माइल māil

milestone *n.* मील-पत्थर mil-patthar

militant *adj.* लडाकु laṛāku

military *n.* सेना Senā

milk *n.* दूध dudh

mill *n.* चक्की cakki

miller *n.* चक्कीवाला cakkivālā

millimeter *n.* मिलीमीटर milimitar

million *n.* दस लाख das lākh

mind *n.* मन man

mindful *adj.* सावधान sāvdhān

mindless *adj.* तर्कहीन tarkhin

mine *n.* खानी khāni; *pron.* मेरो mero

mineral *n.* खनिज पदार्थ khanij padartha

mingle *v.i.* सित मिल्नु sita milnu

miniature *n.* सानो sāno

minimal *adj.* सबभन्दा कम sabbhandā kam

minimize *v.* सवभन्दा कन गर्नु sabbhandā kam garnu

minimum *n.* न्यनतम kamsekam

mining *n.* खन्नेकाम khannekām

minister *n.* मंत्री mantra

ministry *n.* मंत्रालय mantrālay

minor *adj.* अल्प alpa; *n.* नाबालिग nābālig

minority *n.* अल्पसंख्यक alpsankhyak

mint *n.* टकसार taksār

minus *prep.* बिना binā

minuscule *adj.* धेरै सानो dherai sāno

minute *n.* मिनट minat

miracle *n.* चमत्कार camatkār

miraculous *adj.* चमत्कारी camatkāri

mirage *n.* मृगतृष्णा mrigatrsna

mirror *n.* ऐना ainā, दर्पण darpan

misadventure *n.* अनिष्ट anist

misapprehend *v.* नबुझ्नु nabujhnu

misappropriate *v.* हिनामिना गर्नु hināminā garnu

misbehave *v.* दुर्व्यवहार गर्नु durbhavahār garnu

miscall *n.* गलत नम्बर salat number

mischief *n.* उपद्रव upadrab

mischievous *adj.* उपद्रवी upadravi

misdeed *n.* दुष्कर्म duskarma

misery *n.* दुख dukha

misfortune *n.* दुर्भाग्य durbhagya

mishap *n.* दुर्घटना durghatanā

misinform *v.* गलत सूचना दिनु galt sucanādinu

misplace *v.t.* गलत ठाँउमा राख्नु gahan thau ma rākhnu

miss *n.* गल्ती galti; *(girl)* कुमारी kumāri; *v.* भुल्नु bhulnu

missile *n.* प्रक्षेपास्त्र praksepāstra

missing *adj.* हराएको harāeko

mission *n.* शिष्टमंडल sistmadal

missionary *n.* मिशनरी misnari

misspell *v.* गलत हिज्जे लेख्नु galt hijje lekhnu

misstep *n.* गलत कदम galt kadam

mist *n.* कुहिरो kuhiro

mistake *n.* भूल bhul; *v.t.* भूल हुनु bhul hunu

mistaken *adj.* गलत galat

mister *n.* श्रीमान srimān

mistress *n.* स्वामिनी svāmini, उप-पत्नी upapatni

mistrust *v.t.* अविश्वास avisvās

misunderstand *v.* राम्ररी नबुझ्नु rāmrari nabujhnu

misunderstanding *n.* गलतफहमी galatfahami

misuse *n.* गलत उपयोग galat upayog

mix *n.* मिश्रण misran; *v.t.* मिलाउनु milāunu

mixture *n.* मिश्रण misran

moan *n.* कराई karāi

mob *n.* भीड bhid

mobile *adj.* एक ठाउँवाट अर्को ठाँउमा जाने ek thāun bata arko thāun ma jāne

mode *n.* ढंग ḍhang

model *n.* नमुना modal

modem *n.* मोडेम moḍem

moderate *adj.* मध्यममार्गी madhyam margi

moderator *n.* मध्यस्थ madhyastha

modern *adj.* आधुनिक ādhunik

modest *adj.* साधारण sādhāran

modification *n.* परिवर्तन parivartan

modify *v.t.* परिवर्तन गर्नु parivartan gārnu

module *n.* मापांक māpānk

moist *adj.* नरम naram

moisten *v.t.* नरम गराउनु naram garāunu

moisture *n.* नमी nami

mole *(med.) n.* कोठी kothi

molest *v.* दुख दिनु dukha dinu

mom *n.* आमा āmā

moment *n.* क्षण kshyan

momentary *adj.* क्षणिक kshanik

monarch *n.* राजा rājā

monarchy *n.* राजतन्त्र rājā sambandhi

monastery *n.* मठ math, विहार bihār

Monday *n.* सोमबार somvār

money *n.* पैसा paisā

money order *n.* धनादेश dhanādesh

mongoose *n.* न्याउरीमुसा nyāuri musā

monied *adj.* पैसावाल paisāwāl

monitor *n.* मानीटर mānitar

monitoring *n.* अनुगमन anugaman

monk *n.* महन्त mahanta, साधु sādhu

monkey *n.* बाँदर bandar

monogamy *n.* एक पति या एक पत्नी विवाह ek pati ya ek patni vivāh

monologue *n.* लामो भाषण lāmo bhāsan

monopoly *n.* एकाधिकार ekādhikār

monotonous *adj.* एकसुरे eksure

monsoon *n.* वर्षाकाल varsākāl

monster *n.* राक्षस raksas

monstrous *adj.* भीमाकार bhimākār

month *n.* महीना mahina

monthly *adj.* प्रति महिना prati mahinā

mood *n.* मिजाज mijāj

moon *n.* चन्द्रमा candramā

moonlight *n.* जुन jun

mop *v.t.* कुचो kucho

moral *n./adj.* नैतिक naitik

morale *n.* हौसला hausalā

morality *n.* नैतिकता naitikatā

morbidity *n.* अशक्तता asaktatā

more *adj./adv.* बढी badhi

moreover *adv.* यसको अतिरिक्त yasko atiriktā

morgue *n.* मुर्दाघर murdāghar

morning *n.* विहान bihāna

mortal *adj.* ज्यानको खतरा jyān ko khatarā

mortgage *n.* बंधकी bandhaki

mosque *n.* मस्जिद masjid

mosquito *n.* लामखुट्टे lāmkhutte

moss *n.* झार jhār

most *adj.* अधिकतम adhikatam; *adv.* सब भन्दा बढी sab bhandā badi

mostly *adv.* धेरै जसो dherai jaso

motel *n.* सराय sarāy

mother *n.* आमा āmā

mother-in-law *n.* सासु sāsu

motherland *n.* मातृभूमी matri bhumi

motion *n.* गति gati

motionless *adj.* गतिहिन gatihin

motivate *v.t.* प्रेरित गर्नु prerit gārnu

motivation *n.* प्रेरणा prernā

motive *n.* प्रेरणा preranā

motor *n.* मोटर motar

motorbike *n.* स्कूटर skutar

motorcycle *n.* मोटर साइकल motor sāikil

motorist *n.* मोटर चालक motar calak

mount *v.i.* चढनु caṛhnu, ढिस्को dhisko

mountain *n.* पहाड pahād

mountaineer *n.* पर्वतारोही parwartārohi

mourn *v.i.* शोक मनाउनु shok manaunu

mournful *adj.* शोकपूर्ण sokpurna

mourning *n.* शोक shok

mouse *n.* मुसा musā

mouth *n.* मुख mukh

mouthpiece *n.* प्रवक्ता pravakta

move *n.* चेष्टा cestā; *v.i.* चलनु calnu; *v.t.* हटनु hatnu

movie *n.* फिल्म film
Mr. *n.* श्रीमान srimān
Mrs. *n.* श्रीमती srimati
much *adj.* धेरै dherāi
mud *n.* हिलो hilo
muddy *adj.* हिलाम्य hilāmya
mug *n.* प्याला pyālā; *v.t.* लुट्नु lutnu
muggy *n.* गरम र आर्द्र garam ra ārdra
mule *n.* खच्चड khaccad
multifarious *adj.* बहुआयामिक bahuāyāmik
multiplication *n.* गुणा gunā
multiply *v.t.* गुणा गर्नु gunā gārnu
municipality *n.* नगरपालिका nagarpālika
murder *n.* हत्या hatyā; *v.t.* हत्या गर्नु hatyā gārnu
murderer *n.* हत्यारा hatyārā
muscle *n.* मांसपेशी mānspesi
museum *n.* संग्रहालय sangrāhalaya
mushroom *n.* च्याउ cyāu
music *n.* संगीत sangit
musical *adj.* सांगितिक sangitik
musician *n.* संगीतकार sangitkār
musk deer *n.* कस्तुरी मृग kasturi mriga
Muslim *n.* मुसलमान musalmān; *adj.* मुसलमानी musalmāni
mussel *n.* मसल masal
must *v. aux* अनिवार्य गर्नुपर्ने parnu
mustache *n.* जुङ्गा jungā
mustard *n.* तोरी tori
mute *adj.* लाटो lato
mutineer *n.* विद्रोही vidrohi
mutiny *n.* बगावत bagāvat
mutton *n.* भेडाको मासु bheḍa ko māsu
mutual *adj.* आपसी āpasi

my *pron. (m. sing.)* मेरो mero, *(m. pl.)* मेरो merai; *(f. sing./pl.)* मेरी meri
myopia *n.* आँखाको रोग ānkhā ko rog
myself *pron.* स्वयं svayam, आफैं āfāi
mystery *n.* रहस्य rahasya
mystic *adj.* जोगी jogi
myth *n.* पौराणिक paurānik
mythology *n.* पुराण purān, पुराण संबन्धी purān sambandhi

N

nail *n.* नङ nang

naive *adj.* सीधा-सादा sidhā-sādā

naked *adj.* नंगा nangā

name *n.* नाम nām

nameless *adj.* बेनामी benāmi

namely *adv.* अर्थात arthāt

nap *n.* झपकी jhapki; *v.i.* झपकी लिनु jhapki linu

napkin *n.* नैपकिन naipkin

narcotic *n./adj.* लागु पदार्थ lāgu padārtha

narrate *v.t.* वर्णन गर्नु varnan gārnu

narrator *n.* कथावाचक kathāvācak

narrow *adj.* साँगुरो sānguro

narrowminded *adj.* संकुचित मनोवृत्ति sankucit manovritti

nasty *adj.* खराब kharāb

nation *n.* राष्ट्र rastra

national *n./adj.* राष्ट्रीय rāstriya

national park *n.* राष्ट्रीय निकुंज rāstriya nikunja

nationalism *n.* राष्ट्रवाद rāstravād

nationality *n.* राष्ट्रीयता rāstriyatā

nationalize *v.* राष्ट्रियकरण गर्नु rāstriya karan garnu

nationwide *adj.* राष्ट्रव्यापि rāstravyāpi

native *adj.* जन्मभूमि janm bhumi; देशीय desiya; *n.* मुलवासी mulvāsi

natural *adj.* प्राकृतिक prākrtik

natural balance *n.* प्रकृतिक सन्तुलन prākritik santulan

naturalize *v.* अंगिकृत नागरिक हुनु angrikrit nāgarik hunu

naturally *adv.* स्वभाविक svābhāv

nature *n.* *(flora & fauna)* प्रकृति prakriti; *(personality)* स्वभाव svabhāv

naughty *adj.* खराब kharāb

naval *adj.* नौसैनिक nausainik

navel *n.* नाभि nābhi, नाइटो nāito

navigate *v.t.* समुद्री यात्रा गर्नु samundri yātrā gārnu

navigation *n.* संचालन sācālan

navy *n.* नौ-सेना nau-senā

near *adj.* नजिक najik

nearby *adj.* निकट nikat; *adv.* नजिक बाट najik bāta

nearly *adv.* लगभग lagbhag

nearsighted *adj.* निकटदर्शी nikatdarsi

neat *adj.* सफा saphā

necessarily *adv.* अवश्यमेव avasyameva

necessary *adj.* आवश्यक āvasyak

necessitate *v.* आवश्यक वनाउनु āvasyak banāunu

necessity *n.* आवश्यकता āvasyaktā

neck *n.* गर्दन gardan

necklace *n.* घाँटीको माला ghatiko mālā

necktie *n.* टाई tāi

nectar *n.* अमृत amrit

nectarine *n.* एक प्रकारको आरु ek prakārko āru

need *n.* आवश्यकता āvasyaktā; *v.t.* चाहना cāhanā

needful *adj.* आवश्यक āvasyak

needle *n.* सियो siyo

needless *adj.* अनावश्यक anāvasyak

negation *n.* नकार्नु nakārnu

negative *adj.* नकारात्मक nakārātmak; *n.* नकार nakār

neglect *v.t.* बेवास्ता गर्नु bewasta gārnu

negligence *n.* लापरवाही lāparwāhī

negotiate *v.i.* बातचीत गर्नु bātcit gārnu, वार्ता गर्नु vārtā gārnu

negotiation *n.* वार्ता vārtā

neighbor *n.* छिमेकी chimekī

neighborhood *n.* आसपासको इलाका āspās ko ilākā

neither *adj.* कुनै पनि होइन kunai pani hoina

Nepalese *n.* नेपाली Nepali

nephew *n.* भतिजा bhatijā

nepotism *n.* नातावाद nātāvād

nerve *n.* नसा nasā

nervous *adj.* उत्तेजित uttejit

nest *n.* गुड gund

net *n.* जाल jāl

network *n.* जाल तंत्र jāl tantra; *v.t.* जाल तंत्र बनाउनु jāl tantra banāunu

neurologist *n.* नसा विशेषज्ञ nasā bisesagya

neurology *n.* स्नायु प्रणाली विज्ञान snāyu pranali vigyan

neurosis *n.* मानसिक रोग mānasik rog

neutral *adj.* तटस्थ tatstha

neutrality *n.* तटस्थता tatsthatā

never *adv.* कहिले पनि होइन kahile pani hoina

nevertheless *adv.* तै पनि tai pani

new *adj.* नयाँ nayā

new moon *n.* औंसी aunsi

new year *n.* नयाँ साल nayā sāl

newborn *n./adj.* नवजात navjāt

newly *adv.* भर्खर bharkhar

newlywed *n.* नवविवाहित navavibāhit

news *n.* समाचार samāchār; सूचना sucnā

newsletter *n.* कुनै समूहको समाचार kunai samuhako samācār

newspaper *n.* समाचारपत्र samāchārpatra

newsprint *n.* पत्रिका छाप्ने कागज patrikā chapne kāgaj

next *adj./adv.* संग को sangai ko; *adj./adv./prep.* अर्को arko

nice *adj.* राम्रो rāmro

nickname *n.* उपनाम upnām

niece *n.* भतीजी bhatiji; भान्जी bhānji

night *n.* रात rāt

nightclub *n.* रात्रीक्लव ratriklab

nightmare *n.* कुस्वप्न kusvapna

nightwatchman *n.* रात्री प्रहरी ratri prahari

nine *num.* नौ nau

nineteen *num.* उन्नाईस unnais

nineteenth *adj.* उन्नाइसौं unnaisaun

ninety *num.* नब्बे nabbe

ninth *adj.* नवौं navaun

nitrogen *n.* नाइट्रोजन nāitrajan

no *adj./adv.* हुदैन hudaina, होइन hoina

no one *pron.* कोई होइन koi hoina

noble *adj.* उदार udār

nobody *pron.* कोइ पनि होइन koi pani hoina

noise *n.* हल्ला hallā

noisy *adj.* धेरै हल्ला dherai hallā

nom de plume *n.* लेख्ने नाम lekhne nām

nomadic *adj.* घुमन्ते जातिका मानिस ghumante jātka mānis

nominal *adj.* मामुली māmuli

nominate *v.t.* मनोनित गर्नु maninit gārnu

nomination *n.* मनोनयन manonayan

non-aligned *adj.* असंलग्न asamlangna

none *pron.* कोही पनि होइन kohi pani hoina

nonsectarian *adj.* गैर सांप्रदायिक gair sāmprādayik

nonsense *n.* वाइहात waihāt

nonstop *adj.* नरोकेर narokera

nonviolence *n.* अहिंसा ahimsā

noodle *n.* नूडल nuḍal

noon *n.* मध्यदिन madhyadin

nor *conj.* अरु न aru na

normal *adj.* सामान्य sāmānya

normality *n.* सामान्यता sāmānyatā

normally *adv.* साधारण तया sādhārntaya

north *n.* उत्तर uttar

northeast *n./adj.* उत्तर-पूर्व utar-purva

northerly *adj.* उत्तर तिर uttar tira

northern *adj.* उत्तरी uttari

northward *adv.* उत्तरतर्फ uttar tarpha

northwest *n./adj.* उत्तर-पश्चिम utar-pascim

nose *n.* नाक nāk

nosebleed *n.* नाकवाट रगत आउनु nāk bāta ragat āunu

nostalgia *n.* पुरानो कुरा संझेर purāno kurā samjhera

nostril *n.* नाथ्रो nāthro

not *adv.* होइन hoina

notable *adj.* संझन लायक samjhana lāyak

notary pubic *n.* लेखक प्रमाणक lekhya pramānak

note *n.* नोट not; *v.t.* उल्लेख गर्नु ullekh gārnu

notebook *n.* कापी kāpi

noteworthy *adj.* हेर्नेयोग्य herna yogya

nothing *pron.* केही पनि होइन kehi pani hoina

notice *n.* नोटिस notis; *v.t.* देख्नु dekhnu

noticeable *adj.* सुस्पष्ट suspast

notification *n.* सूचना sucnā

notify *v.t.* सूचना दिनु sucnu dinu

notion *n.* धारणा dhārnā

notorious *adj.* कुख्यात kukhyāt

noun *n.* संज्ञा sañgyā

nourish *v.t.* पालन पोषण गर्नु palan posan gārnu

nourishing *adj.* पुष्टिकर pustikar

nourishment *n.* आहार āhār

novel *n.* उपन्यास upanyās

novelty *n.* नवीनता navintā

November *n.* नवंबर navambar

now *adv.* अहिले ahile

nowadays *adv.* आजकल ājkal

nowhere *adv.* कहीं पनि होइन kahi pani hoina

noxious *adj.* हानिकर hānikar

nuance *n.* सूक्ष्म भेद suksam bhed

nuclear *adj.* परमाणिक parmānik

nucleus *n.* केन्द्र kendra

nude *adj.* नांगो nāngo

nudity *n.* नग्नता nagantā

nugget *n.* सुनको टुक्रा sunko tukra

nuisance *n.* वाधा badhā

null *adj.* रद्द radda

nullify *v.t.* रद्द गर्नु radd gārnu

numb *adj.* सुन्न sunn

number *n.* संख्या sankhyā

numerous *adj.* धेरै संख्यामा dherai sankhya mā

nun *n.* भिक्षुणी bhikshuni, मठवासिनी mathvāsini

nurse *n.* नर्स nars; *v.t.* दूध पिलाउनु dudh pilāunu

nursery *n.* नर्सरी narsari
nursing *n.* स्याहार सुसार
  syāhārsusār
nut *n.* सुपारी supāri
nutrition *n.* पोषण posan
nutritious *adj.* पोषक posak
nylon *n.* नाइलन nāilan

O

oasis *n.* मरुभूमिमा बगैंचा marubhumimā bagaica

oat *n.* जौ jau

oath *n.* शपथ sapath

oatmeal *n.* जौको दाल jau ko dāl

obedience *n.* आज्ञापालन āgyāpālan

obedient *adj.* आज्ञाकारी āgyākāri

obese *adj.* धेरै मोटो dherai moto

obey *v.t.* आज्ञा को पालन agyā ko pālan

obituary *n.* मृत्युको खवर mrityu ko khabar

object *n.* वस्तु vastu; *v.t.* विरोध गर्नु virodh gārnu

objection *n.* आपत्ति āpatti

objectionable *adj.* आपत्ति जनक āpatti janak

objective *adj.* वस्तुगत vastugat

obligation *n.* बाध्यता bādhyatā

obligatory *adj.* अनिवार्य anivārya

oblige *v.t.* बाध्य गर्नु bādya gārnu

oblong *adj.* आयताकार āyatākār; *n.* आयत āyāt

obscene *adj.* अश्लील aslil

obscure *adj.* अस्पष्ट aspasta

observance *n.* अवलोकन abalokan

observation *n.* अवलोकन abalokan

observatory *n.* वेधशाला vedhsālā

observe *v.t.* अवलोकन गर्नु abalokan gārnu; मान्नु mannu

obsession *n.* अति चिन्ता ati cintā

obsolete *adj.* काम नलाग्ने kām nalāgne

obstacle *n.* बाधा bādhā

obstetrician *n.* प्रसूति-विशेषज्ञ prasiti bisheshagya

obstinate *adj.* ढिपि गर्नु dhipi garnu

obstruct *v.t.* बाधा डाल्नु bādhā dalnu

obstruction *n.* बाधा bādhā

obtain *v.t.* पाउनु pāunu

obtainable *adj.* प्राप्त prapya

obvious *adj.* स्पष्ट spast

occasion *n.* अवसर avsar

occasional *adj.* कहिले कांहि kahile kāhin

occult *adj.* गुप्त gupta

occupancy *n.* भोग गर्ने bhog garne

occupant *n.* दखल dakhal

occupation *n.* पेशा pesā

occupy *v.t.* अधिकार गर्नु adhikār gārnu

occur *v.i.* घटनु ghatnu

occurrence *n.* घटना ghatnā

ocean *n.* महासागर mahāsāgar

oceanography *n.* समुद्र विज्ञान samundra vigyān

o'clock *adv.* बजे baje

October *n.* अक्टूबर aktubar

octopus *n.* अष्टभुज astbhuj

odd *adj.* अनौठो anautho

oddity *n.* अनौठोपन anauthopan

odor *n.* गंध gandh

odorless *adj.* गन्धहीन gandhhin

of *prep.* को ko

offend *v.t.* अपराध गर्नु aprādh gārnu

offense *n.* अपराध aprādh

offensive *adj.* अपमानजनक apmānjanak

offer *n.* दिनु dinu

offering *n.* दान dān

office *n.* कार्यालय kāryālaya

officer *n.* पदाधिकारी padādhikāri

official *adj.* अधिकारिक adhikārik; *n.* अधिकारी adhikāri

officiating *adj.* कार्यवाहक karyavāhak

offset *v.t.* क्षतिपूर्ति गर्नु ksatipurti

often *adj.* अक्सर avsar

oil *n.* तेल tel; *v.t.* तेल निकाल्नु tel nikālnu

oily *adj.* तेल जस्तो tel jasto

ointment *n.* औषधी ausadhi

OK! *interj.* ठीक छ thik cha

old *adj.* पुरानोङ purāno, बूढो budho

old maid *n.* बूढी कन्या budhi kanyā

old-fashioned *adj.* पुरानो चाल को purāno cāl ko

oligarchy *n.* निरंकुश शासन nirankus sāsan

olive *n.* जैतून jaitun

olympic *adj.* ऑलम्पिक ālampik

olympics *n.* ऑलम्पिक खेल ālampik khel

omelet(te) *n.* आम्लेट āmlet

omission *n.* छूट chut

omit *v.t.* नराख्नु narākhnu

omnipotent *adj.* सर्वशक्तिमान् sarvasaktimān

on *prep.* माथि māthi

once *adv.* एक पटक ekpatak

one *num.* एक ek

one-sided *adj.* एक तर्फी ektarphi

one-way *adj.* एक तर्फी वाटो ek tarphi bāto

onion *n.* प्याज pyāj

onlooker *n.* तमाशे tamāse

only *adj.* केवल kewal

onward *adv.* अग्रगामी agragāmi

opaque *adj.* अपारदर्शी apārdarsi

open *adj.* खुला khulā; *v.i.* खुल्नु khulnu; *v.t.* खोल्नु kholnu

opening *n.* प्रारंभ prāpambh

opera *n.* गीति-नाटय giti-nitya

operable *adj.* शल्यकृया गर्न सकिने salyakriya garna sakine

operate *v.t.* चलाउनु calāunu

operation *n.* शल्यक्रिया salyakriyā

ophthalmic *adj.* आँखा संबन्धी ānkhā sambandhi

ophthalmology *n.* आँखाबारे विज्ञान ānkhā bāre vigyān

opinion *n.* राय rāy

opinionated *adj.* विचार नवदल्ने vichār nabadalne

opponent *n.* प्रतिद्वन्दि prātidwandi; प्रतिवादी prātiwādi

opportunist *n.* अवसरवादी avsarvādi

opportunity *n.* मौका maukā

oppose *v.t.* विरोध virodh gārnu

opposite *adj.* विपरीत viparit; *n.* अगाडिको agadiko

opposition *n.* विरोध virodh gārnu

oppress *v.t.* दमन गर्नु daman garnu

oppression *n.* दमन daman

oppressive *adj.* अत्याचार atyācāri

optical *adj.* आँखा सबन्धी ānkhā sambandhi

optician *n.* चश्मा बनाउने casmā banaunewālā

optimist *n.* आशावादी āsāvādi

optimistic *adj.* आशान्वित asānvit

option *n.* विकल्प vikalpa

optional *adj.* वैकल्पिक vaikalpik

or *conj.* या yā

oral *adj.* मौखिक maukhik

orange *n./adj.* सुन्तला suntalā

orchard *n.* बगैंचा phalodyān

orchestra *n.* अकिष्ट्रा vādyā-vrt

orchid *n.* गाभा gābha

order *n.* आदेश ādes; *v.t.* आदेश दिनु ādes dinu

orderly *adj.* सुव्यवस्थित suvyavasthit

ordinance *n.* अध्यादेश adhyādes

ordinary *adj.* साधारण sādhāran

ore *n.* कच्चा धातु kacca dhātu

organ (*anat.*) *n.* अङ्ग anga

organic *adj.* जीवंसबन्धी jibsambandhi

organization *n.* संगठन sangathan

organize *v.t.* संघटित saṅghatit

orgasm *n.* यौन आनन्द yaun ānand

Orient *n.* पूर्व purva

Oriental *adj.* पूर्वी purvi

origin *n.* उदभव udbhav

original *n./adj.* मूल mul

originally *adv.* शुरूदेखि suru dekhi

orinthology *n.* चरा अध्ययन carā adhyayan

ornament *n.* गहना gahanā

orphan *n.* अनाथ anāth

orphanage *n.* अनाथालय ānāthālaya

orthodox *adj.* कट्टर kāttar

oscillate *v.i.* डोल्नु dolnu

ostracism *n.* निवासन nivarsan

other *adj.* अर्को anya, अन्य arko

otherwise *adv.* अन्यथा anyathā, नत्र भने natra bhane

ought *v.* हुनु पर्ने hunu parne

our *pron./adj.* हाम्रो hāmro

ours *pron.* हाम्रो hāmro

ourselves *pron.* हामी आफैं hāmi aphai

oust *v.* निकाल्नु nikālnu

out *adv.* बाहर bāhar

out-of-date *adj.* पुरानो purāno

outcast *n.* बहिष्कृत bahiskrit

outcome *n.* परिणाम pariṅām

outdoors *n.* बाहिरी bāhiri

outer *adj.* बाहिरी bāhiri

outermost *adj.* सब भन्दा बाहिर sabbhandā bāhira

outline *n.* रुपरेखा ruprekhā

outline *v.t.* रुपरेखा बनाउनु ruprekhā bānaunu

outrage *n.* अति रिस ati ris

outrageous *adj.* अपमानजनक apmānjanak

outright *adv.* पूरा तवरले purā tawarle

outside *adj.* बाहिरी bāhiri; *adv./prep.* बाहिर bāhira; *n.* बाहिर bāhira

outsider *n.* बाहिरिया bāhiriyā

outskirts *n.* किनारा kinārā

outstanding *adj.* विशिष्ट visist

outward *adj.* बाहिर bāhira

oval *n./adj.* अंडाकार andākār

oven *n.* चुलो chulo

over *adv.* माथि māthi

overall *adj.* संपूर्ण sampurna; *adv.* सबै मिलाएर sabāi milāerā

overcast *adj.* बादल छाएको bādāl chāeko

overcoat *n.* ओभरकोट overkot

overdue *adj.* धेरै अवेर भएको dherai aber vayeko

overlook *v.t.* नदेरक्षु nadekhnu

overnight *adv.* रात भर rāt bhar

overseas *adj.* विदेश vides; *adv.* समुद्रमा samundramā

overtake *v.t.* उछिन्नु agadi niklanu

overtime *n.* वढी समय badhi samaya

overweight *adj.* ज्यादै मोटो jyadai moto

owe *v.t.* लिनु पर्ने linu parne
owl *n.* लाटोकोसेरो lātokosero
own *adj.* आफ्नो afno
owner *n.* मालिक mālik
ox *n.* वयल bayal, साँडे sāde
oxygen *n.* आक्सीजन āksijan
ozone *n.* ओजोन ozon

P

p.m. *n.* मध्यरात्र सम्म madyarat samma
pace *n.* गति gati
Pacific Ocean *n.* प्रशान्त महासागर prasant mahasagar
pack *v.t.* पैक गर्नु paik garnu
package *n.* पैकेज paikej
pact *n.* सन्धी sandhi
pad *n.* गद्दी gaddi; *v.t.* गद्दी लगाउनु gaddi lagāunu
paddy *n.* धान खेत dhānkhet
pagan *n.* गैर-ईसाई gair-isāi, गैर-मुस्लिम gair-muslim
page *n.* पाना pānā
pagoda *n.* पगोडा pagodā
pain *n.* दुःख dukha; *v.t.* दुःख दिनु dukha dinu
painful *adj.* दुखदायी dukhadayi
painless *adj.* पीडाहीन pidāhin
paint *n.* पेंट pent; *v.i.* रङ्ग लगाउनु rang lagāunu; *v.t.* तस्वीर बनाउनु tasvir banāunu
painter *n.* चित्रकार citrakār
painting *n.* चित्र citra
pair *n.* जोडा jorā
pajamas *n. pl.* पाजामा pājāmā
pal *n.* साथी sāthi
palace *n.* दरवार darbār, महल mahal
palatial *adj.* दरवार जस्तो darbār jasto
pale *adj.* हल्का halkā
pall *n.* आवरण āvaran
pallet *n.* रंगपट्टिका rañg-pattikā
palm *(anat.)* *n.* हत्केला hatkelā
palm tree *n.* ताडको रुख tār ko rukh

palmistry *n.* हस्तरेखा विज्ञान hastarekhā vigyan
palpitation *n.* धडकन dharkan
pamphlet *n.* सानो पर्चा sano parchā
pan *n.* तावा tavā
panacea *n.* सबै रोगको औषधी sabai rog ko ausadhi
panaroma *n.* दृश्य drisya
panda *n.* हाब्रे habre
pandemonium *n.* हो हल्ला hohallā
panel *n.* दिलहा dilahā
panic *n.* त्रास ākasmik bhay; *v.i.* छटपटाउनु chatpatāunu
panties *n. pl.* आईमाईको अन्डरवीयर aaimaiko anderwear
pants *n.* पतलून patlun
papaya *n.* मेवा papitā
paper *n.* कागज kāgaj
paperwork *n.* कागजी काम kāgaji kām
parachute *n.* हवाई छाता havāi chatā
parade *n.* परेड pared; *v.t.* परेड गर्नु pared gārnu
paradise *n.* स्वर्ग svarga
paragraph *n.* अनुच्छेद anucched
parallel *adj.* समानान्तर samānantar
paralysis *n.* पक्षघात pakshyaghāt
paralyze *v.i.* पक्षघात हुनु pakshyaghāt hunu
paramedic *n.* डाक्टरको सहायक dāktar ko sahāyak
paramour *n.* विवाहित व्यक्तिको प्रेमी vivahit vyakri ko premi
parasite *n.* परजीवी parjivi
parasitic *adj.* परजीवी parjivi

parcel *n.* पार्सल pārsal

parchment *n.* चर्मपत्र carampatr

pardon *n.* माफ māph; *v.t.* माफ गर्नु māph gārnu

parents *n.* बाबु आमा bābu āmā, माता-पिता mātā-pitā

parish *n.* पैरिश pairis

parity *n.* बराबरी barābari

park *n.* निकुंज nikunj; *v.t.* पार्क गर्नु pārk gārnu

parking lot *n.* गाडी-पार्क स्थान gāṛi-park sthān

parliament *n.* संसद sansad

parliamentary *adj.* संसदीय sansadiya

parole *n.* कैदीलाई चांडै रिहाई kaidilāi cadai rihāi

parrot *adj.* सुगा sugā

part *n.* पुर्जा purjā

part-time *adj.* कम समय काम गर्ने kam samay kām garne

partial *adj.* आंशिक ānsik, केही भाग kehi bhāg

participant *n.* सहभागी sahabhāgi

participate *v.i.* भाग लिनु bhāg linu

particle *n.* कण kan

particular *adj.* विशेष vises

partition *n.* विभाजन vibhājan

partner *n.* हिस्सेदार hissedār

party *n.* दल dal

pass *n.* भंज्याङ bhanjyang

passage *n.* वाटो bāto

passenger *n.* यात्री yātri

passerby *n.* पथिक pathik

passion *n.* मनोभाव manobhāv

passionate *adj.* भावुक bhāvuk

passive *adj.* क्रियाशील नभएको kriyasil na bhaneko

passport *n.* पासपोर्ट pāsport

password *n.* पासवर्ड मेवा gupt sabd

past *n.* वितेको biteko

paste *v.t.* टाँस्नु tānsnu

pasteurize *v.t.* तताएर जीवाणु रहित गर्नु tātayera jiwānu rahit gārnu

pastime *n.* मनोरंजक manorānjāk

pastry *n.* पेस्ट्री pestri

pasture *n.* चरण caran

patch *n.* पैबंद paiband; *v.t.* पैबंद लगाउनु paiband lāgāunu

patent *n.* एकसब eksav

paternal *adj.* पैत्रिक paitrik

paternity *n.* पितृत्व pitritwa

path *n.* पथ path, वाटो bāto

pathetic *adj.* कारुणिक kārunik

patience *n.* धैर्य dhairy

patient *adj.* सहनशील sahansil; *n.* रोगी rogi

patrimony *n.* पैत्रिक संपत्ति paitrik sampatti

patriot *n.* देशभक्त desbhakt

patriotic *adj.* देशभक्तिपूर्ण desbhaktpurna

patrol *n.* गश्ती gasti; *v.i.* गश्ती गर्नु gasti garnu

patron *n.* संरक्षक sanraksak

pattern *n.* नमूना namunā

pauper *n.* ज्यादै गरिव jyadai garib

pause *n.* विराम virām; *v.i.* रोकिनु roknu; *v.t.* रोक्नु roknu

pave *v.t.* कालो पत्र सडक बनाउनु kalo patre sadak banaunu

pavilion *n.* मण्डप mandap

paw *n.* पंजा panjā

pawn *n.* कठपुतली kathputli

pay *v.t.* पैसा दिनु paisa dinu

pay attention *v.t.* ध्यान दिनु dhyān dinu

pay-off *n.* पूरा तलव दिनु purā talab dinu

payable *adj.* तिर्नु पर्ने tirnu parne

payment *n.* भुगतान bhugtān

pea *n.* मटर matar
peace *n.* शान्ति sānti
peaceful *adj.* शान्तिपूर्ण sāntipurn
peach *n.* आरु āru
peacock *n.* मजूर majur
peak *n.* शिखर shikar
peanut *n.* बदाम badām
pear *n.* नासपाती nāspātii
pearl *n.* मोती moti
peasant *n.* किसान kisān, देहाती dehāti
pebble *n.* सानो ढुंगा sāno dhungā
peculiar *adj.* अचम्मको acammako
pedal *n.* पैदल paidal
pedestrian *n.* पदयात्री paddyatri
pediatrician *n.* बालरोग विशेषज्ञ bāl rog visesagya
peel *n.* बोक्रा bokrā; *v.t.* काटनु kātnu
peg *n.* खूँटी khumti
pelvis *n.* श्रेणी sroni
pen *n.* कलम kalam
penalize *n.* दण्ड दिनु danda dinu
penalty *n.* दण्ड danda
pencil *n.* सिसाकलम sisākalam
penetrate *v.t.* छिर्नु chirnu
penicillin *n.* पेन्सलिन pensalin
peninsula *n.* प्रायद्विप prāyadwip
penis *n.* लिंग ling
penitentiary *n.* कारागार kārāgār
penny *n.* पेनी (अमेरिकी एक सेन्ट) peni
penury *n.* अत्यन्त गरिबी atyanta garibi
people *n.* जनता janata
pepper *n.* खुर्सानी khursāni
peppermint *n.* पेपरमिंट peparmint
per capita *adv.* प्रतिव्यक्ति prati vyakti
per diem *n.* प्रतिदिन pratidin

perceive *v.t.* महसूस गर्नु mahsus garnu
percent *n.* प्रतिशत pratisat
percentage *n.* प्रतिशत pratisat
perception *n.* प्रत्यक्ष ज्ञान pratyaks gyān
perch *n.* छतरी chatri
perfect *adj.* पूर्ण purna, विलकुल ठीक bilkul thik
perform *v.i.* पूरा गर्नु purā gārnu
performance *n.* काम गराई kam garai
perfume *n.* सुगन्ध sugandh
perhaps *adv.* शायद sāyad
peril *n.* जोखिम jokhim
period *(time) n.* अवधि abadhi
periodic *adj.* निश्चित अवधिमा nischit awadimā
periodical *n.* पत्रिका patrikā
perish *v.* नाश हुने nās hune
perishable *adj.* नाशहुन सक्ने nāsh huna sakne
perjury *n.* सपथमा झुटो बोल्ने sapath mā jhuto bolne
permanence *n.* स्थायित्व sthāyitva
permanent *adj.* स्थायी sthāyi
permission *n.* अनुमति anumati, इजाजत ijrjat
permit *n.* अनुमति पत्र anumati patra; *v.t.* अनुमति दिनु anumati dinu
perpendicular *adj.* लामो lāmo
persecute *v.* दुर्व्यवहार गर्नु durbyabwhar garnu
persist *v.i.* लागी राख्नु lagi rākhnu
person *n.* व्यक्ति vyakti
personal *adj.* व्यक्तिगत vyaktigat, निजी niji
personality *n.* व्यक्तित्व vyaktitwa
personnel *n.* कर्मचारीगण karamcārigan

perspective *n.* दृष्टिकोण sandars

perspiration *n.* पसीना pasinā

perspire *v.i.* पसीना निक्लनु pasinā nikalnu

persuade *v.t.* मनाउनु manāunu

persuasion *n.* मनाउने प्रक्रिया manāune prākriyā

pertinent *n.* संबन्धित विषय sambandhit visaya

pessimistic *adj.* निराशावादी nirāsāvādi

pester *v.t.* सताउनु sātāunu

pesticide *n.* कीरा मार्ने औषधी kirā mārne ausadhi

pet *n.* पालतू जनावर pāltu janābar

petal *n.* पंखुडी pañkhuḍi

petition *n.* उजुर ujur

petrol *n.* पेट्रोल petrol

petroleum *n.* पेट्रलियम petroliyam

petticoat *n.* पेटिकोट petikot

petty *adj.* छोटो-मोटो choto-moto

phantom *n.* छाया cāyā, भूत bhut

pharmaceutical *adj.* औषधीय ausadhiy

pharmacist *n.* औषधी पसले ausadhi pasle

pharmacy *n.* औषधालय aushadhalaya

phase *n.* अवस्था avasthā

pheasant *n.* कालीज kālij

phenomenon *n.* तथ्य tathya

philanthropy *n.* दान दातव्य dān dātabya

philately *n.* हुलाक टिकट संकलन hulāk tikat sankalan

philosopher *n.* दार्शनिक dārsanik

philosophy *n.* दर्शन शास्त्र darsan sāstra

phone *n.* फोन fon

phonetic *adj.* जे लेखेको त्यही उच्चारण je lekheko tyahi uccharan

phonetics *n. pl.* ध्वनिविज्ञान dhvanivigyān

photocopy *v.* फोटो कपी गर्नु photocapi linu

photograph *n.* फोटो photo; *v.t.* फोटो खिंच्नु photo khiṁnu

photographer *n.* फोटोग्राफर photogrāfar

photography *n.* फोटोग्राफी photogrāfi

phrase *n.* मुहावरा muhāvarā, वाक्यांश vākyāns

physical *adj.* शारीरिक sāririk

physician *n.* चिकित्सक cikitsak, वैद्य vaidya

physicist *n.* भौतिक bhautik

physics *n.* भौतिक विज्ञान bhautik bigyān

physiology *n.* शरीर विज्ञान sarir vigyān

piano *n.* पियानो piyāno

pick *v.t.* छान्नु chānnu

picket *n.* खूँटा khuṁtā

pickle *n.* अचार acār; *v.t.* अचार हाल्नु acār hālnu

pickpocket *n.* जेबकट jebkat

picnic *n.* वनभोज vanbhoj

pictorial *adj.* चित्रले भरेको citrale bhareko

picture *n.* चित्र citra; *v.t.* को चित्र बनाउनु ko citra banāunu

picturesque *adj.* चित्र जस्तो citra jasto

pie *n.* फलफूलको केक phalphul ko kek

piece *n.* टुक्रा tukrā

pierce *v.t.* प्वाल पार्नु pwāl parnu

piety *n.* भक्ति bhakti

pig *n.* सुङ्गुर sungur

pigeon *n.* परेवा parewā

pile *n.* थुप्रो thupro

pilgrim *n.* तीर्थयात्री tirthyātri
pilgrimage *n.* तीर्थयात्रा tirthyātrā
pill *n.* गोली goli
pillage *v.* लुट्नु lutnu
pillar *n.* खंभा khambā
pillow *n.* तकिया takiyā
pillowcase *n.* तकिया को खोल takiyā ko khol
pilot *n.* पायलट pāylat
pimple *n.* डण्डीफोर dandiphor
pin *n.* आलपिन ālpin
pinch *n.* चिमटनु chimatnu
pine (tree) *n.* चीड cir̥
pineapple *n.* भँईकटर bhainkathar
pink *adj.* गुलाबी gulābi
pioneer *n.* अगुआ aguā
pious *adj.* धर्मनिष्ठ dharmnisth
pipe *n.* चिलिम cilam
piper *n.* मुरली बजाउने murli bajaune
pirate *n.* समुद्री डाँकू samudri d̥āku
pistachio *n.* पेस्ता pesta
pistol *n.* पिस्तोल pistual
piston *n.* पिस्टन pistan
pit *n.* खाल्डो khāldo
pitcher *n.* घडा ghar̥ā
pity *n.* दया dayā; *v.i.* दया गर्नु dayā garnu
pizza *n.* पिस्ता pistā
pizzeria *n.* पित्साको पसल pitsāko pasal
place *n.* स्थान sthān; *v.t.* राख्नु rakhnu
plagiarize *v.* अर्काको लेखेको सार्नु ārkāle lekheko sārnu
plain *adj.* सादा sādā; *n.* मैदान maidān
plan *n.* योजना yojnā; *v.t.* योजना बनाउनु yojnā banaunu
plane *n.* हवाईजहाज hawāijahaj
planet *n.* ग्रह graham

plank *n.* तख्ता takhtā
plant *n.* विरुवा biruwā
plastic *adj./n.* प्लास्टिक plāstik
plastic surgery *n.* प्लास्टिक शल्यक्रिया plastik salyakriya
plate *n.* थाली thāli, प्लेट plet
platform *n.* प्लेटफार्म pletfārm
platinum *n.* प्लैटिनम plaitinam
platonic *adj.* आध्यात्मिक ādhyātmik
play *n.* (*theater*) नाटक nātak; *v.t.* खेल्नु khelnu
player *n.* खेलाडी khelāri; वादक vādak
playground *n.* क्रीडास्थल krir̥āsthal, खेल्ने ठाँउ khelne thāun
playwright *n.* नाटककार natakkār
plea *n.* निवेदन nivedan, सफाई safāi
pleasant *adj.* रमाइलो ramāilo; राम्रो rāmro, सुखकर sukhkar
please *v.t.* कृपया kr̥pyā
pleasure *n.* सुख ānand, आनन्द sukh
plebiscite *n.* मतगणना matagananā
pledge *v.* प्रतिज्ञा गर्नु pratigyā garnu
plenipotentiary *adj.* महामहिम mahāmahim
plenty *n.* प्रचुरता prachurtā
plight *n.* कठिन परिस्थिती kathin paristhiti
plot *n.* (*story*) कथानक kathānak; (*scheme*) षडयंत्र sad̥yantra; *v.t.* षडयंत्र गर्नु sad̥yantra garnu
plow *n.* हलो halo; *v.t.* हल चलाउनु halo calaunu
plum *n.* आलुवखडा alubakhadā
plumber *n.* पानीको धाराको मिस्त्री pani ko dhara ko mistri
plume *n.* पंख pankha

plump *adj.* गोल-मटोल gol-matol

plunder *v.* लुटनु lutnu

plunge *v.i.* गोता-लगाउनु gotā lagāunu

plural *n.* बहुबचन bahuvacan

plurality *n.* वहुलता bahulatā

pneumonia *n.* शीत ज्वर sit jvar

pocket *n.* खल्ती khalti; जेब jeb

poem *n.* कविता kavitā

poet *n.* कवि kavi

poetry *n.* काव्य kāvya

poetry festival *n.* काव्य महोत्सव kāvya mahotsav

pogrom *n.* अल्पसंख्यकको सफाया alpasankyak ko saphāyā

point *n.* नोक nok

point of view *n.* दृष्टिकोण dristikon

pointless *adj.* वेकार bekār

poison *n.* विष bish

poisonous *adj.* विषालु bishālu

pole *n.* खंभा khambha

polemic *n.* विवाद vibād

police *n.* पुलिस pulis

policeman *n.* प्रहरी prahari

policy *n.* नीति niti

polio *n.* पक्षपात paksya pāt

polish *n.* पोलिश polis; *v.t.* पालिश गर्नु pālis garnu

polite *adj.* नम्र namra

political *adj.* राजनैतिक rājnaitik

politician *n.* राजनीतिज्ञ rājnitik

politics *n. pl.* राजनीति rājnitigya

polity *n.* सरकारको किसिम sarkārko kisim

poll *n.* मतदान matdān

pollutant *n.* प्रदूषक pradusak

pollute *v.i.* प्रदूषित हुनु pradusit hunu; *v.t.* प्रदूषित गर्नु pradusit garnu

polluted *adj.* प्रदूषित pradusit

pollution *n.* प्रदूषण pradusan

polyclinic *n.* धेरै रोग जाँच्ने क्लिनिक dherai rog jancne klinik

polygamy *n.* बहुपत्नी प्रथा bahupatni prathā

polyglot *n.* बहुभाषाविद bahubhāsavid

pomegranate *n.* अनार anār

pomp *n.* शानदार प्रदर्शन sāndar pradarsan

pond *n.* तलाउ talāu

pony *n.* टट्टू tattu

pool (swimming ~) *n.* तनाउ talāu

poor *adj.* गरीब garib

pop music *n.* पॉप संगीत pāp sangit

popcorn *n.* भुटेको मकै bhuteko makai

pope *n.* पोप, रोमन क्याथोलिक चर्चको मुख्य Pop, Roman catholic carc ko muikhya

popular *adj.* लोकप्रिय lokpriya

popularize *v.* लोकप्रिय बनाउनु lokapriya banāunu

population *n.* जनसंख्या janamsankhyā

porcelain *n.* पोर्सिलेन porsilen

pore *n.* लोम-कूप rom-kup

pork *n.* सुङ्गुरको मासु sungur ko māsu

pornography *n.* अश्लील साहित्य aslil sāhityā

porous *adj.* प्वाल परेको pwāl pareko

porridge *n.* पोरिज porij

port *n.* वन्दरगाह bandargah

portable *adj.* उठाई लैजाने सकिने uthai laijana sakne

porter *n.* कुली kulli

portfolio *n.* पोर्टफोलियो व्याग portfolio bad

portion *n.* भाग bhāg

portrait *n.* चित्र citra

position *n.* स्थिति sthiti

positive *adj.* सकारात्मक sakārātmak

possess *v.t.* को मालिक हुनु ko malik hunu

possession *n.* कब्जा kabjā

possessive *adj.* नियन्त्रण गर्ने ईच्छुक niyantran garna ichuk

possibility *n.* संभावना sambhāvanā

possible *adj.* संभव sambhav

post *n.* स्थान sthān, खंवा khambhā

post office *n.* डाकघर dākghar, हुलाक घर hulāk ghar

postage *n.* महसूल mahsul

postage stamp *n.* डाक टिकट dāk tikat

postcard *n.* पोस्ट-कार्ड post-kārḍ

posterity *n.* सन्तान santān

postgraduate *adj.* स्नातकोत्तर snātakottar

posthumous *adj.* मरणोपान्त maropānt

postman *n.* हल्कारा halkara

postmark *n.* हुलाक छाप hulāk chāp

postmaster *n.* पोस्ट मास्टर post mastar

postmortem *n.* लाशको चिरफार lās ko chirphār

postpaid *adj.* अगाडीनै तिरेको agādi nai tireko

postpone *v.t.* स्थगित गर्नु sthagit garnu

pot *n.* भाँडा bhandā

potable *adj.* पिउन लायक piuna lāyak

potassium *n.* पोटाशियम potasiyam

potato *n.* आलु ālu

potato chip *n.* आलू चिप ālu cip

potential *adj.* संभावना sambhāvanā

pottery *n.* माटो को भाँडो matoko bhāndo

pouch *n.* थैली thaili

poultry *n.* कुखुरा पालन kukhurā pālan

pound *n.* पाउन्ड pāund

pour *v.t.* पोख्नु pokhnu

poverty *n.* गरीवी gaibi

powder *n.* चूर्ण curna

power *n.* शक्ति sakti

power of attorney *n.* अधिकृत वारेसनामा adhikrit wāresnāmā

powerful *adj.* शक्तिशाली saktisāli

powerless *adj.* शक्तिहीन asktihin

practical *adj.* व्यावहारिक vyāvahārik

practically *adv.* व्यावहारिक vyāvahārik

practice *n.* व्यवहार vyavahar; *v.i.* अभ्यास गर्नु abhyās garnu; *v.t.* प्रयोग गर्नु prayog garnu

pragmatic *adj.* व्यवहारिक vyābaharik

praise *n.* प्रशंसा prasansā; *v.t.* सराहना sarāhanā

praiseworthy *adj.* प्रशंसनीय prasansaniya

prawn *n.* प्राउन माछा prāun māchā

pray *v.i.* प्रार्थना गर्नु prarthanā garnu

prayer *n.* प्रार्थना prārthanā

preach *v.i.* प्रवचन गर्नु pravacan garnu; *v.t.* धार्मिक प्रवचन गर्नु dhārmik pravacan garnu

preamble *n.* प्रस्तावना prastāvanā

prearrange *v.* पहिले नै वन्दोवस्त मिलाउनु pahile nai bandobast milāunu

precarious *adj.* अनिश्चित anikscit, अस्थिर asthir

precaution *n.* सतर्कता satarkatā

precede *v.t.* घटित हुनु ghatit hunu

precedent *n.* नजीर najir

preceptor *n.* गुरु guru

precious *n.* वहुमुल्य bahumulya
precipitation *n.* वर्षा bārsa
precise *adj.* ठीक thik
preconceive *v.* अगाडि नै मन्तव्य बनाउनु agādi nai mantabya banāunu
predator *n.* मांसाहारी जनावर māmsāhāri janāwar
predecessor *n.* पूर्ववर्ती purvarti
predicament *n.* हास्यास्पद अवस्था hāsyāspad avasthā
predict *v.t.* भविष्यवाणी गर्नु bhavisyavāni garnu
predominant *adj.* सबभन्दा महत्वपूर्ण sabbhandā mahatwa-purna
preeminent *adj.* सर्वोत्तम sarvottam
preexistent *adj.* पहिले देखि भएको pahile dekhi bhaeko
preface *n.* प्रस्तावना prastavana
prefer *v.t.* बढी मनपराउनु badi manparaunu
preference *n.* मनपराई manparai
prefix *n.* उपसर्ग upsarg
pregnant *adj.* गर्भवती garabhvati
prehistoric *adj.* प्राग्-ऐतिहासिक pragaithāsik
prejudice *n.* पूर्वाग्रह purvāgrah
preliminary *adj.* प्रारंभिक prārambhik
premature *adj.* समयभन्दा पहिले भएको samaya bhandā pahile bhaeko
premeditate *v.* अगाडि देखि सोचेको agādi dekhi soceko
prenatal *adj.* जन्म भन्दा अघि janma bhandā aghi
preparation *n.* तैयारी taiyāri
prepare *v.i.* तैयार हुनु taiyār hunu; *v.t.* तैयार taiyār
preposition *n.* पूर्वसर्ग purvāsarg

prerogative *n.* अधिकार adhikār
prescribe *v.t.* निर्धारित nirdhārit
prescription *n.* नुसखा nuskhā
presence *n.* उपस्थिति upasthiti
present *n./adj.* उपहार uphār; *v.t.* उपस्थित गर्नु upsthit garnu
present-day *adj.* हाल hāl
presentable *adj.* अरुसंग भेट्न योग्य aru sanga bhetna yogya
presentation *n.* प्रस्तुतिकरण prastutikaran
presently *adv.* अहिले भर्खरै ahile bharkharai
preserve *n.* रक्षा rāksha; *v.* सुरक्षित राख्नु surksit rakhnu
president *n.* राष्ट्रपति rāstrapati
press *n.* प्रेस pres; *v.t.* दबाउनु dabāunu
pressure *n.* दवाब dabāb; *v.t.* दबाब डाल्नु dabāb dalnu
prestige *n.* प्रतिष्ठा pratisthā
presume *v.* अनुमान गर्नु anumān garnu
presuppose *v.* अगाडिनै अनुमान गर्नु sgādi nai anumān garnu
pretend *v.* वहाना गर्नु bahānā garnu
pretty *adj./adv.* सुन्दर sundar
pretzel *n.* एक किसिमको विस्कुट ekkisimko biskut
prevail *v.* जित्नु jitnu
prevailing *adj.* प्रबल prabal
prevalent *adj.* प्रचलित pracalit
prevent *v.t.* रोक्नु roknu
prevention *n.* रोकथाम rokthām
preventive *adj.* निवारक nivārak
previous *adj.* पूर्ववर्ती ourvāvarti
prey *n.* शिकार sikār
price *n.* दाम dām
priceless *adj.* अनमोल anmol
pride *n.* गर्व garv

priest *n.* पुजारी pujāri

priestly *adj.* पुरोहितले गर्ने purohitle garne

prima facie *n.* प्रचलित pracalit

primarily *adv.* मुख्य कारण mukhya kāran

primary *adj.* प्राथमिक prāthmik

primary school *n.* प्राथमिक विद्यालय prāthamik vidyālay

prime *adj.* आदिम ādim

prime minister *n.* प्रधान मन्त्री pradhān mantra

primitive *adj.* असभ्य asabhya

prince *n.* राजकुमार rājkumār

princess *n.* राजकुमारी rājkumāri

principal *n.* प्राचार्य pracārya, मुख्य mukhya

principle *n.* सिद्धांत siddhānt

print *v.t.* छाप्नु chāpnu

printable *adj.* छाप्न योग्य chāpna yogya

printer *n.* मुद्रक mudrak

printing *n.* छपाई chapāi

printing press *n.* छापाखाना chapākhānā

prior *n.* पहिलेको pahileko

priority *n.* प्राथमिकता prāthmiktā

prison *n.* जेलखाना jelkhānā

prisoner *n.* कैदी kaidi, बन्दी bandi

prisoner of war *n.* युद्ध बन्दी yuddhā bāndi

privacy *n.* एकांत ekānt

private *adj.* व्यक्तिगत vyāktigat

privilege *n.* विशेषाधिकार visesādhikār

privileged *adj.* विशेषाधिकार सहित visesādhikār sahit

prize *n.* पुरस्कार purskār

probable *adj.* संभावित sambhāvit

probation *n.* नसिहत nasihat

probe *n.* अनुसन्धान anusandhān

problem *n.* समस्या samasyā

problematical *n.* हल गर्न कठिन hal garna kathin

procedure *n.* क्रिया-विधि kriyā vidhi

proceed *v.i.* अगाडि बढनु agadi badnu

proceeds *n.* नाफा nāphā

process *n.* प्रक्रिया prākriyā

procession *n.* जुलुस julus

proclaim *v.* घोषणा गर्नु ghosanā garnu

procrastinate *v.* काम पछि सार्नु kām pachi sārnu

procrastination *n.* काम पछि सार्नु kām pachi sārnu

proctor *n.* स्कूल होस्टेल सुपरिवेक्षक skulmā hostel suparibakshak

procure *v.* प्राप्त गर्नु prāpta garnu

prodigal *adj.* फजुलखर्ची phajul kharci

produce *v.t.* उत्पादन गर्नु utpādan garnu

product *n.* उत्पादन utpādan

profane *adj.* धर्म प्रति अनादर dharma prati anādar

profess *v.* व्यवसाय vyavasāy

profession *n.* पेशा pesā

professional *adj.* व्यावसायिक vyavasāyik

professor *n.* आचार्य ācārya

profile *n.* छोटो विवरण choto vivaran

profit *n.* लाभ lābh, नाफा nāphā; *v.i.* लाभ लिनु lābh linu

profound *adj.* गहिरो gahiro

program *n.* कार्यक्रम kāryakram

programmer *n.* प्रोग्रामर prograimar

progress *n.* प्रगति pragati; *v.i.* प्रगति गर्नु pragati garnu

progressive *adj.* प्रगतिशील pragatisil
prohibit *v.t.* रोक्नु roknu
prohibition *n.* मनाही manāhi
prohibitive *adj.* निषेधात्मक nisedhatmak
project *n.* आयोजना ayojanā
proletarian *n.* मजदूर mājdoor
proliferate *v.* चाँडै वढ्नु cadai badhnu
prologue *n.* भूमिका bhumikā
prolong *v.* लम्ब्याउनु lambyāunu
promenade *n.* घुम्ने ठाउँ ghumne thāu
prominence *n.* विशिष्टता bisistatā
promiscuous *adj.* व्यभिचारी vyavichāri
promise *n.* प्रतिज्ञा pratigya
promising *adj.* राम्रो भविष्य भएको rāmro bhavisya bhaeko
promote *v.* प्रवर्द्धन गर्नु pravardhan garnu
promotion *n.* प्रमोशन pramosan
prompt *adj.* समयमा samayamā
pronoun *n.* सर्वनाम sarvanām
pronounce *v.t.* उच्चारित uccārit garnu
pronunciation *n.* उच्चारण uccaāran
proof *n.* प्रमाण pramān
propaganda *n.* प्रचार pracār
propel *v.t.* ठेल्नु thelnu
proper *adj.* उपयुक्त upyukta
properly *adv.* उचित uchit
property *n.* सम्पत्ति sampatti
prophecy *n.* भविष्यवाणी bhavisyavāni
prophet *n.* देवदूत devdoot
proportion *n.* अनुपात anupāt
proposal *n.* प्रस्ताव prastāv
propose *v.t.* प्रस्ताव गर्नु prastāv garnu

proprietor *n.* मालिक mālik
prorata *n.* अनुपात anupāt
prose *n.* गद्य gadya
prosecute *v.* कारवाही गर्नु kārbāhi garnu
proselytize *v.* धर्म परिवर्तन गराउनु dharma parivartan garāunu
prospective *adj.* अग्रदर्शी agaradarsi
prospectus *n.* संभावना sambhāvanā
prosper *v.i.* उन्नति गर्नु unnati garnu; फूलनु phulnu
prosperity *n.* समृद्धि samriddhi
prosperous *adj.* समृद्ध samriddh
prostate *n.* प्रस्टैट ग्रन्थि prastait granthi
prostitute *n.* रण्डी randi
protagonist *n.* महत्वपूर्ण व्यक्तित्व mahatwapurna vyaktitwa
protect *v.t.* रक्षा गर्नु raksā garnu
protection *n.* रक्षा raksā
protege *n.* संरक्षक samtaksak
protein *n.* प्रोटीन protin
protest *n.* विरोध virodh; *v.i.* विरोध हुनु virodh hunu; *v.t.* विरोध गर्नु virodh garnu
proud *adj.* गर्वित garvit
prove *v.t.* प्रमाणित गर्नु pramānit garnu
proverb *n.* उखान kahāvat
provide *v.t.* दिनु dinu
providence *n.* भाग्य bhāgya
province *n.* प्रदेश prades
provincial *adj.* प्रादेशिक pradesik
provision *n.* रसद rasad
provisional *adj.* अस्थायी asthāyi
provocation *n.* जिस्काउनु jiskāunu
prudence *n.* बुद्धि buddhi
prudent *adj.* बुद्धिमान buddhimān
prune *n.* नासपाती naspati
pseudonym *n.* उपनाम upanām, नक्कलीनाम nakkali nām

psoriasis *n.* सोरायसिस soraysis
psyche *n.* मन man
psychiatrist *n.* मनचकित्सक mansicakitsak
psychic *adj.* साइकिक saikik
psychological *adj.* मनोवैज्ञानिक manovaigyānik
psychologist *n.* मनोवैज्ञानिक विशेषज्ञ manovaigyānik visesagya
psychology *n.* मनोविज्ञान manovigyān
psychosis *n.* मानसिक रोग mānasik rog
public *adj.* सार्वजनिक sārvajanik
public domain *n.* सार्वजनिक क्षेत्र sārvajanik ksetra
public school *n.* सरकारी स्कूल sarkāri school
publication *n.* प्रकाशन prakāsan
publicity *n.* प्रचार pracār
publish *v.t.* प्रकाशित गर्नु prakāsit garnu
publisher *n.* प्रकाशक prakāsak
pudding *n.* खिर khir
pull *v.t./v.i.* तान्नु tānnu
pullover *n.* स्वेटर swetar
pulse *n.* नाडी nāri
pump *n.* पम्प pamp; *v.t.* पम्प गर्नु pamp garnu
pumpkin *n.* फर्सी pharsi
punch *n.* मुक्का mukkā; *v.t.* मुक्का हान्नु mukkā hānnu
punctual *adj.* समयको पाबन्द samayako pāwanda
punctuate *v.t.* विरामचिन्ह लगाउनु virāmcinh lagāunu
punctuation *n.* विराम-चिन्ह virām-cihn
pungent *adj.* कडा गन्ध kadā gandha

punish *v.t.* सजाय दिनु sajāy dinu
punishment *n.* सजाय sajāy
punitive *adj.* दन्डनीय dandaniya
pupil *n.* विद्यार्थी bidyārthi
puppet *n.* कठपुतली kathputali
puppy *n.* कुकुरको बच्चा kukurko bachha
purchase *n.* खरिद kharid; *v.t.* खरिद गर्नु kharid garnu
pure *adj.* शुद्ध suddh
purification *n.* शुद्धिकरण suddhikaran
purify *v.t.* शुद्ध गर्नु suddh garnu
purity *n.* शुद्धता suddhatā
purple *adj.* बैजनी baigani
purpose *n.* प्रयोजन prayojan
purse *n.* पर्स pars
pursuant *adj.* को अनुसार ko anusār
pursue *v.t.* पीछा गर्नु pichā garnu
pus *n.* पीप pip
push *v.t.* धकेल्नु dhakelnu
put *v.* राख्नु rākhnu
puzzle *n.* पहेली paheli
pyramid *n.* पिरामिड piraimid
pyre *n.* चिता chita
python *n.* अजिङ्गर ajingar

Q

quack *(fake doctor) n.* नकली डाक्टर nakali daktar
quadrangle *n.* चतुष्कोण catuskon
quail *n.* बटेर bater
quaint *adj.* अनोखा anokhā
quake *n.* भुकम्प bhukampa
qualification *n.* योग्यता yogyata
qualified *adj.* योग्य yogya
qualify *v.i.* योग्य हुनु yogya hunu
quality *n.* गुण gun
qualm *n.* अशंका asankā
quantitative *adj.* परिमाणिक pārimānik
quantity *n.* परिमाण parimān
quarrel *n.* झगडा jhagṛā; *v.i.* झगडा गर्नु jhagṛā garnu
quarry *n.* ढुंगाको खानी dhunga ko khāni
quart *n.* क्वार्ट kvyārt
quarter *n.* चार खण्डको एक भाग cār khanda ko ek bhāg; चार भागको एक भाग car bhāg ko ek bhāg
quarterly *adj.* त्रैमासिक traimāsik
quartz *n.* क्वार्ट ढुंगा kwarz dhungā, स्फटिक sphatik
queen *n.* रानी rāni
queer *adj.* अजीब ajib
quell *v.* दवाउनु dabāunu
quench *v.* तिर्खो मेटनु tirkha metnu
query *n.* प्रश्न prasna; *v.t.* प्रश्न गर्नु prasan garnu
question *n.* प्रश्न prasna; *v.t.* प्रश्न गर्नु prasn garnu
question mark *n.* प्रश्न चिन्ह prasna cinha

questionable *adj.* प्रश्न सूचक prasna sucak
questionnaire *n.* प्रश्नावली prasnawali
queue *n.* लाइन line
quick *adj.* छिटो chito
quickly *adv.* छिटोसाथ chito sath
quiet *n./adj.* शान्त sānta
quietly *adv.* शान्तिपूर्वक santipurvak
quilt *n.* सिरक sirag
quinine *n.* कुईनिन kwinin
quite *adv.* निकै nikai
quiz *n.* प्रश्न prāsna
quorum *n.* गणपूरक ganapurak
quota *n.* कोटा kotā
quotation *n.* उद्धरण uddharan

R

rabid *adj.* अति बिरोधी ati birodhi

rabies *n.* कुकुरले टोकि हुने रोग kukur le toki hune rog

race *n.* जाति jāti

racial *adj.* जातीय jātiya

racism *n.* जातिय भेद jatiya bhed

radar *n.* रेडार redar

radiation *n.* विकीरण vikiran

radical *adj.* अतिवादि ativādi

radio *n.* रेडियो redio

radio broadcast *n.* रेडियो प्रसारण redio prasāsan

radish *n.* मुला mulā

rag *n.* कपडाको टुक्रा kapadā ko tukrā

ramble *v.* कुनै उदेश्य नलिई घुम्नु kunai uddeshya nalighmnu

ramification *n.* फैलाउनु phailāunu

ramp *n.* ढल्केको वाटो dhalkeko bāto

rampant *adj.* फैलेको phaileko

ranch *n.* ठूलो खेत thulo khet

rancid *adj.* बासी bāsi

random *adj.* छिटपुट chitput

range *n.* जनावर चर्ने ठाँउ jānawar chādne thāu

rank *n.* दर्जा darjā

ranking *adj.* सबभन्दा माथिल्लो दर्जाको sabbhanda māthillo darja ko

ransack *v.t.* विगारेर खोज्नु bigarera khojnu

ransom *v.t.* फिरौती phirauti

rape *n.* बलात्कार balātkāri; *v.t.* बलात्कार गर्नु balātkāri garnu

rapid *adj.* छिटो chito

rapport *n.* संवन्ध sambandha

rapprochement *n.* समझौता samjhauta, पुनर्मिला purnarmilan

rare *adj.* दुर्लभ durlabh

rarely *adv.* कहिले काहि kahile kāhi

rascal *n.* बदमाश badmās

raspberry *n.* ऐंसेलु rāto beri

rat *n.* मुसो muso

rate *n.* दर dar

rather *adv.* बल्कि balki

ratification *n.* अनुमोदन anumodan

ratify *v.* अनुमोदन गर्नु anumodan garnu; *v.t.* अनुमोदन गर्नु anusamarthan

rating *n.* वर्गीकरण bargikaran

ratio *n.* अनुपात anupāt

ration *n.* राशन rāsan

rational *adj.* विवेकशील vivelsil

rationale *n.* प्रमुख कारण pramukh kāran

ravage *n.* विनीश vinās

ravine *n.* साँगुरो गल्छी sānguro galchi

ravioli *n.* डल्लो परेको मासुको परिकार dallo pareko masu ko parikār

raw *adj.* काँचो kāācho

ray *n.* किरण kiran

raze *v.t.* भत्काउनु bhatkāunu

razor *n.* दारी काट्ने ब्लेड dāri kātne bled

re-entry *n.* पुन:प्रवेश punaprabes

reach *n.* पहुँच pahumc; *v.t.* पुग्नु pugnu

react *v.i.* प्रतिक्रिया दिनु pratikriyā dinu

reaction *n.* प्रतिक्रिया pratikriyā

reactionary *adj.* प्रतिक्रयावादी pratikriyābādi

read *v.t.* पढनु padhnu

reader *n.* पाठक pāthak

readily *adv.* तुरुन्त turunta, सजिलो सित sajilo sita

reading *n.* पढ्ने padhne

ready *adj.* तैयार taiyār

ready-made *adj.* पहिले देखि तैयार कपडा pahile dekhi tayar kapadā

real *adj.* वास्तविक bāstabik

real estate *n.* घर जग्गा ghar jaggā

realism *n.* क्षेत्र ksetra

reality *n.* वास्तविकता vāstaviktā

realize *v.t.* पूरा हुनु purā hunu, बुझ्नु bujhnu

really *adv.* साँचै sāncai

reap *v.t.* फलेको वाली काट्नु phaleko bāli kātnu

reappear *v.i.* फेरी देखिनु pheri dekhinu

rear *n./adj.* पछाडि pachāri

reason *n.* कारण kāran; *v.i.* तर्क गर्नु tark garnu

reasonable *adj.* उचित uchit

reassure *v.t.* आश्वासन āsvāsan

rebate *n.* छूट chut

rebel *n.* विद्रोही vidrohi; *v.i.* विद्रोह गर्नु vidroh garnu

rebellion *n.* विद्रोह vidroh

rebellious *adj.* विद्रोहमा सहभागी vidrohma sahabhagi

rebuff *v.t.* नकारी दिनु nakār dinu

rebuke *v.* आलोचना गर्नु ālocanā garnu

recall *v.t.* फर्काउनु pharkaunu, संझनु sanjhanu

recapitulate *v.t.* पुरानो कुरा संझनु purāno kirā samjhanu

recapitulation *n.* फेरी सँझनु pheri samjhanu

recapture *v.* फेरी पक्रनु pheri pakranu

receipt *n.* रसीद rasid

receivable *adj.* पाउन योग्य pāuna yogya

receive *v.* पाउनु pāunu

recent *adj.* हालै को halaiko

reception *n.* स्वागत svāgat, समारोह samāroh

receptionist *n.* स्वागत गर्ने svāgat garne

recess *n.* बन्द banda; लामो छुट्टी lāmo chutti

recession *n.* आर्थिक मन्दी ārthikmandi

recipe *n.* नुसखा nuskhā

reciprocity *n.* आदान-प्रदान ādan-pradān

recital *n.* बादन vādan

recite *v.t.* पढनु padhnu

reckless *adj.* अनियंत्रित aniyantrit

reckon *v.t.* गन्नु gannu

reclaim *v.* जमीन खेतियोग्य बनाउनु jamin khetiyogya banāunu

reclamation *n.* सुधार sudhār

recognition *n.* मान्यता mānyatā, पहिचान pahican

recognizable *adj.* चिन्न सकिने cinna sakine

recognize *v.t.* चिन्नु chinnu

recollect *v.* संझनु samjhanu

recommend *v.t.* सिफारिश गर्नु sifāris garnu

recommendation *n.* सिफारिश sifāris

recompense *n.* इनाम inām; *v.t.* पुरस्कार दिनु purskār dinu

reconcile *v.t./v.i.* मेल मिलाप गर्नु mel-milāp garnu

reconciliation *n.* मेल-मिलाप mel-milāp

reconnaissance *n.* प्रांरभिक सर्भेक्षण prārambhik sarveksan reconsider v. पुनर्विचार गर्नु punarvicār garnu

reconstruct v. पुननिर्माण गर्नु punarnirmān garnu

reconstruction n. पुननिर्माण punarnirmān

record n. अभिलेख abhulekh; v.t. लेख्नु lekhnu

recount v. फेरी गन्नु pheri gannu

recover v.t. विसेक हुनु bisek hunu

recreation n. मनोरंजन manoranjan

recruit n. रंगरुट rangrut; v.t. भरती गर्नु bharti garnu

rectangular adj. आयाताकार āyātākār

rectify v. सुधार गर्नु sudhār garnu

rectum n. चाक chāk

recuperate v.i. विसेक हुनु bisek hunu

recurrence n. फेरि हुनु pheri hunu

recurring adj. आवर्तक āvartak

recycling adj. फेरी उपयोग गर्नु pheri upyog garnu

red adj. रातो rāto

red soil n. रातोमाटो rāto māto

red-handed adv. अपराध गर्दागर्दै पक्रनु aprdh garda gardai i pakranu

redden v. रातो हुनु rāto hunu

reddish adj. केहि रातो kehi rāto

redness n. रातोपन rātopan

reduce v.t. घटाउनु ghataunu

reduction n. घटाव ghatāv

redundant adj. चाहिने भन्दा वढी cāhine bhandā badhi

reef n. समुद्री चट्टान samundri cattān

refer v.t. सिफारिस गर्नु sipharis garnunu

reference n. संदर्भ sandharbha

referendum n. जनमंत संग्रह janamat sangraha

refill v.t. फेरी भर्नु pheri bharnu

refine v.t. शुद्ध गर्नु suddha garnu

refined adj. शुद्ध suddha

refinery n. परिष्करण pariskaran-sālā

refit v.t. दुरुस्त durust

reflect v.t. चिंतन गर्नु cintan garnu

reflector n. परावर्तक parāvartak

reform n. सुधार sudhār; v.i. सुधार गर्नु sudhār garnu

refresh v.t. ताजा हुनु tājā hunu

refreshment n. जलपान jalpān

refrigerate v.t. फ्रिज गर्नु frij garnu

refrigerator n. फ्रिज frij

refuge n. शरण saran

refugee n. शरणार्थी sarnārthi

refund v.t. फर्काउनु pharkāunu

refusal n. अस्विकार inkār

refuse n. कचरा kacrā, काम नलाग्ने कुरा kām nalāgnen kurā; v.t. र अस्विकार गर्नु inkār garnu

regain v. फेरी पाउनु pheri pāunu

regard n. सम्मान sammān; v.t. मान्नु mānnā

regarding prep. को बारे मा ko bāre mā

regardless adj. यसो हुँदा हुंदै yaso hunda hundai

regency n. नायवी nāyavi

regent n. नायब nāyav

regicide n. राजाको हत्या rajāko hatyā

regime n. शासन sāsan

region n. इलाका ilākā

regional adj. प्रादेशिक pradesik

register n. रजिस्टर rajistar

registration n. रजिस्ट्रेशन rajistresan

regret n. खेद khed; v.i. खेद प्रकट गर्नु khed prakat garnu; v.t. पछ्ताउनु pachtāunu

regular *adj.* नियमित niyamit, साधारण sādhāran

regulate *v.* नियम बमोजिम काम गराउनु niyam bamojim kām garāunu

regulation *n.* नियम niyam

rehabilitate *v.* पुनस्थापना punasthāpanā garnu

rehabilitation *n.* पुनर्वास purvārs

rehearsal *n.* पूर्वाभ्यास purvābhyās

rehearse *v.t.* रिहर्सल गर्नु riharshal garnu

reign *n.* राजाले राज्य गरेको rajāle rājye gareko, राज्य rājya

reimburse *v.t.* फिर्ता लिनु phirtā linu

rein *n.* बागडोर bāgḍor

reincarnation *n.* पुनर्जन्म punarjanam

reinforce *v.t.* बढाउनु badhaunu; मजबूत गर्नु mazbut garnu

reinstate *v.* पुरानो पदमा राख्नु purāno pad mā rākhnu

reiterate *v.t.* फेरी भन्नु अथवा गर्नु feri vannu apawa garnu

reject *v.t.* नामंजूर गर्नु nāmanzur garnu

rejection *n.* अस्वीकरण asvikaran

rejoice *v.t.* खुशी हुनु khusi hunu

rejoinder *n.* जवाफ jawāph

relapse *n.* पुनरावर्तन punrāvartan

relate *v.t.* सबंध हुनु sambandh hunu; सुनाउनु sunāunu

related *adj.* संबन्धि sambandhit

relation *n.* नाता nāta

relationship *n.* सबंध sambandh

relative *adj.* प्रासंगिक prāsangik; *n.* नातेदार natedar

relax *v.i.* आराम गर्नु ārām garnu

relaxation *n.* आराम arām, विश्राम bisrām

release *n.* छोडनु chodne; *v.i.* मुक्त गर्नु mukt garnu

relevant *adj.* प्रासंगिक prāsangik

reliable *adj.* विश्वसनीय visvasniy

relief *n.* आराम ārām

relieve *v.t.* आराम दिनु ārām dinu; चिंता बाट मुक्त हुनु cintā bāta mukt hunu

religion *n.* धर्म dharma

religious *adj.* धार्मिक dhārmik

relinquish *v.t.* परित्याग गर्नु parityag garnu, छोडनु chodnu

reluctant *adj.* अनिच्छुक anicchuk

rely *v.i.* माथि भरोसा राख्नु mathi bharosā rakhnu

remain *v.i.* बाँकी रहनु banki rahanu

remainder *n.* बाँकी रहेको bānki raheko

remaining *adj.* बाँकी banki

remains *n.* शेष रहनु ses rahanu

remark *n.* टिप्पणी tippani, भनाई bhanāī

remarkable *adj.* महत्वपूर्ण mahatwapurna

remedial *adj.* सुधारात्मक sudhāratmak

remedy *n.* औषधी ausadhi; *v.t.* प्रतिकार गर्नु pratikār garnu

remember *v.t.* सझन्नु samjhanu

remind *v.t.* याद दिलाउनु yad dilāunu

remit *v.t.* प्रेषित गर्नु, presit garnu, पठाउनु pathāunu

remittance *n.* प्रेषित रुपैया presit rupayā

remnant *n.* बाँकी bānki

remorse *n.* पश्चताप paschātāp, पछुतो pachuto

remote *adj.* दूरवर्ती duravarti, दुर्गम durgām

remove *v.t.* हटाउनु hatāunu

remunerate v.t. न्यायोचित परिश्रमिक दिनु nyayodit pārisramik

renaissance n. पुनर्जागरण punarjāgaram

renal adj. मिर्गौलावारे mirgaulā bāre

renegade n. अपराधी aparādhi

renew v.t. नवीकरण गर्नु navikaran garnu

renewal n. नवीकरण navikaran

renounce v.t. छोडी दिनु chodi dinu

renovate v.t. नयाँ गरिदिनु naya gāridinu

renovation n. नवीकरण navikaran

renown n. प्रसिद्धि prasiddhi

rent n. भाडा bhādā, वहाल bahāl; v.t. वहालमा दिनु bahāl ma dinu

rental n. वहालमा दिएको bahāl mā dieko

renunciation n. त्याग tyaag

reorganize v. पुनर्गठन गर्नु punargathan garnu; v.t. फेरि राख्नु pheri rākhnu

repair n. मरम्मत marammat; v.t. मरम्मत गर्नु marammat garnu

reparation n. क्षतिपूर्ति kshatipurti

repatriation n. घर फिर्ता गर्नु ghar phirtā garnu

repay v. फेरी pheri

repeal v.t. कानुन वदल्नु kanun badalnu

repeat n./v.t. दोहराउनु dohrāunu

repel v.t. फर्काउनु phakāunu

repercussion n. अप्रत्यक्ष असर apratyaksa asar

repetition n. पुनरावृत्ति punarāvṛtti

replace v.t. फिर्ता राखी दिनु phirta rakhi dinu

replenish v.t. फेरी भरी दिनु pheri bhari dinu

replica n. प्रतिलिपि prarilipi

reply n. जवाब javāb; v.i. जवाब दिनु javāb dinu

report n. रिपोर्ट riport, प्रतिवेदन prativedan; v.t. प्रस्तुत गर्नु prastut garnu

reporter n. संवाददाता samvāddātā

repose v. आराम गर्नु ārām garnu

reprehensible adj. दोष दिन योग्य dos dina yogya

represent v.t. प्रतिनिधित्व गर्नु pratinidhitwa garnu

representation adj. प्रतिनिधित्व pratinidhitwa

representative n. प्रतिनिधि pratinidhi

repression n. दमन daman

reprimand n. फटकार phatkār, नसीहत nasihat; v.t. फटकारनु phatkārnu

reprisal n. प्रत्यपकार pratyapakar

reproduce v.t. उत्पन्न गर्नु utpanna garnu

reproduction n. पुनरुत्पादन punrutpādan

reptile n. घस्रने जीव ghasrane jib

republic n. गणतंत्र gantantra

republican n./adj. गणतंत्रवादी gantantravādi

repudiate v.t. अस्वीकार गर्नु aswikār garnu

repulse n. फिर्ता गर्नु phirtā garnu

reputable adj. नाम चलेको nām caleko

reputation n. नाम nām

reputed adj. नाम चलेको nām caleko

request n. निवेदन nivedan, आग्रह āgraha; v.t. निवेदन गर्नु nivedan garnu

require v.t. चाहिने chāhine

requirement n. आवश्यकता āvasyaktā

request adj. आवश्यक ābasyak

rescue n. उद्धार गर्नु uddhār garnu; v.t. बचाउनु bacāunu

research n. अनुसन्धान ānusāndhān; v.t. अनुसन्धान गर्नु ānusāndhān garnu

resemblance n. उस्तै देखिने ustai dekhine

resemble v.t. उस्तै देखिनु ustai dekhinu

resent v.t. खराब मान्नु kharāb mānnu

reservation n. बुकिंग bukin, आरक्षण ārakshan

reserve n./v.t. आरक्षण गर्नु āraksn garnu

reserved adj. आरक्षण गरिएको āraksan garieko

reservoir n. टंकी tanki, जलाशय jalāsaya

reside v.i. रहनु rahanu

residence n. निवास nivās

resident n. निवासी nivāsi

residential adj. आवासीय āvasiya

residual adj. वाकी रहेको bānki rāheko

residue n. अवशेष avses

resign v.i. राजीनामा दिनु rājināmā dinu

resignation n. राजीनामा rājināmā

resilience n. पुरानो रुपमा आउने purāno rupmā āune

resist v.t. विरोध गर्नु virodh garnu

resistance n. विरोध virodh

resistant adj. विरोधी virodhi

resolution n. समाधान samādhan

resolve v.t. समाधान गर्नु samādhān garnu

resort n. अंतिम उपाय antim upāya, पर्यटकीय ठाऊँ paryatakiya thāun

respect n. आदर ādar; v.t. आदर गर्नु ādar garnu

respectable adj. आदरणीय ādarniya

respiration n. सास फेर्नु sās phernu

respond v.i. जवाब दिनु javāb dinu

response n. जवाब Javāb

responsibility n. उतरदायित्व uttardāyitwa

responsible adj. उत्तरदायी uttardayi

rest n. आराम ārām; v.i. आराम गर्नु ārām garnu

restaurant n. रेस्टाराँ restarāṁ

restless adj. बेचैन becain

restoration n. पुननिर्माण punarnirmān

restore v.t. मरम्मत गर्नु maramat garnu

restrain v.t. रोक्नु roknu

restraint n. संयम samyam

restrict v.t. सीमित गर्नु simit garnu

restricted adj. प्रतिबन्धित pratibandhit

restriction n. रोक rok

result n. परिणाम parinām

resume v.t. फेरि शुरु गर्नु pheri suru hunu

resurrect v. पुनर्जीवित गर्नु punarjivit garnu

resurrection n. पुनर्जीवन punarjivan

retail n. फुटकर phutkar

retailer n. फुटकर सामान बेच्ने phutkar sāmān bechne

retain v.t. आफू सँग राख्नु āphu sanga rākhnu

retaliate v. बदला लिनु badlā linu

retarded adj. सुस्त मनस्थिति susta manasthitiko

retina n. आँखाको नानी ānkhā ko nāni

retire v.i. सेवानिवृत्त हुनु sewānibritta hunu

retired *adj.* सेवानिवृत sewānivritta

retort *v.* छिटो जवाफ दिनु chito jawāb dinu

retract *v.* फिर्ता लिनु phirtā linu

retreat *n.* एकान्तवास ekāntabās

retribution *n.* वदला badalā

retroactive *adj.* काम भएको अगाडि kām bhaeko āgadi

retrospect *n.* पुनराबलोकन punaravalokan

return *n.* फर्कनु pharkanu

reunion *n.* पुनर्मिलन punarmilan

reunite *v.t.* जोड्नु joṛnu

reveal *v.t.* प्रकट गर्नु prakat hunu

revelation *n.* प्रकट को प्रकृया prakat ko prakriya

revenge *n.* बदला badlā

revenue *n.* राजस्व rājaswa

reverse *n./adj.* उल्टो ultā; *v.t.* उल्टो गर्नु ultā garnu

review *n.* समीक्षा samiksā; *v.t.* समीक्षा गर्नु samiksā garnu

revise *v.t.* दोहराउनु dohrāunu

revive *v.t.* फेरि उठाउनु pheri uthaunu

revoke *v.* बन्द गर्नु banda garnu

revolt *n.* विद्रोह vidroh; *v.i.* विद्रोह गर्नु vidroh garnu

revolution *n.* क्रांति krānti

revolutionary *adj.* क्रांतिकारी krāntikari

revolutionize *v.* ठूलो परिवर्तन ल्याउनु thulo parivartan lyāunu

revolve *v.t.* परिक्रमा गर्नु parikrama garnu

revolver *n.* बन्दुक banduk

reward *n.* पुरस्कार puraskar

rhinoceros *n.* गैंडा gaindā

rhododendron *n.* गुरास gurāns

rhythm *n.* ताल tāl

rib *n.* पसली pasli

ribbon *n.* फीता fitā

rice *n.* भात bhāt

rich *n./adj.* धनी dhani

rid *v.* छुटकारा पाउनु cutkārā pāunu

riddance *n.* छुटकारा chuhtkārā

riddle *n.* पहेली paheli

ride *n.* सवारी गर्नु savari garnu; *v.t.* चढ्नु carhnu

rider *n.* सवार savār

ridge *n.* सानो पहाड sāno pāhar

ridicule *n.* हाँसो hānso

ridiculous *adj.* हास्यास्पद hasyāspad

rifle *n.* राइफल rāifal

right *adj. (correct)* ठीक thik; *(opp. of left)* दाहिने dāhine

right now *adv.* अहिले ahile

right-hand *adj.* विश्वासी viswāsi

right-handed *adj.* दहिने हाते dāhine hat

rightful *adj.* उचित ucit, बैध vaidh

rigid *adj.* कठोर kathor

rim *n.* किनारा kinārā

ring *n.* औठी authi

ringleader *n.* नाइके nāike

rinse *v.t.* पखाल्नु pakhālnu

riot *n.* दङ्गा dangā; *v.t.* हो-हल्ला गर्नु ho-hallā gārnu

ripe *adj.* पाकेको pākeko

ripoff *n.* चोरी cori

rise *v.t.* उठ्नु utthnu

risk *n.* जोखिम jokhim; *v.t.* जोखिम उठाउनु jokhim uthāunu

rite *n.* धार्मिक चलन dhārmik calan

ritual *n.* रिति रिवाज riti riwāj

rival *n./adj.* प्रतिद्वन्दी pratidvandvi

rivalry *n.* प्रतिद्वन्दिता pratidvanditā

river *n.* नदी nadi

riverside *n.* नदी किनारा nadi kinārā

road *n.* सडक sadak

roadside n. सडक छेउ sadakcheu

roar n. गरज garaj; v. गर्जनु garjanu

roast meat n. सेकेको मासु sekeko māsu

rob v.t. लुटनु lutnu

robber n. डाकु dāku

robbery n. डकैती dakaiti

robe n. पोशाक posāk

robot n. यन्त्रमानव yantramānav

robust adj. बलियो baliyo

rock n. चट्टान cattān

rocket n. रोकेट roket

rocky adj. चट्टानी cattāni

rod n. छड chaṛ

rodent n. मुसा musā

rogue n. बदमाश badmās

role n. भूमिका bhumikā

roll n. मुट्ठा mutthā

romance n. प्रेम-लीला prem-lilā

romantic adj. प्रेमी premi

romanticism n. छायावाद cāyābād

roof n. छाना chānā

roof garden n. छानाको बगैंचा chānā ko bagāicha

room n. कोठा kothā

roomful n. कोठा भरी kothā bhari

roommate n. एउटै कोठामा बस्ने eutai kothāmā basne

roomy adj. धेरै ठाँउ भएको dherai thāun bhaeko

rooster n. कुखुरा kukhurā

root n. जरा jarā

rope n. डोरी dori

rosary n. माला mālā

rose n. गुलाब gulāb

rosebush n. गुलाब को बिरुवा gulāb ko biruwa

rot v.i. सडनु sadnu

rotate v. घुमाउनु ghumāunu

rotation n. घुमाई ghumāi

rote n. कन्ठ गर्ने kanthā garne

rotten adj. सडेको sadeko

rough adj. खस्रो khasro

round adj. गोलो golo

roundtrip adj. ने दोहोरो यात्रा dohoro yātrāaurā

rout n. ठूलो हार thulo hār

routine n. नित्यकर्म nityak aram

row n. पंक्ति paṅkti; v.t. डुंगा चलाउनु dungā chalaunu

rowdy n. बदमाश badmās

royal adj. राजकीय rājkiya

royalist n. राजावादी rajāvādi

royalty n. राजपरिवार rājpariwār

rub v.t. मलनु malnu

rubber n. रबर rabar

rubbish n. काम नलाग्ने kām na lāgne

ruby n. माणिक mānik

rucksack n. रकसैक raksaik

rude adj. असभ्य asabhya

rug n. गलैंचा galaica

ruin n. नास nās; v.t. नास गर्नु nās garnu

rule n. नियम niyam; v.t. शासन गर्नु sāsan garnu

ruler n. शासक sāsak

rum n. रम ram

rumble n. गडगडाहट gargarāhat

ruminate v. सम्झनु samjhanu

rumor n. हल्ला hallā

run n. दौड dauṛ; v.i. दौडनु dauṛnu

run away v. भाग्नु bhagnu

runaway n. भगौडा bhagaudā

rupee n. रुपैया rupaiya

rupture n. फुटनु phutnu

rural adj. ग्रामीण grāmin

rush n. हतपत hatpat

Russia n. रूस rus

Russian n./adj. रूसी rusi

rust *n.* खिया khiya; *v.t.* खिया लाग्नु
  khiya lagnu
rustic *adj.* गाँउमा बस्ने gāun mā
  basne
rustler *n.* गाई वस्तु चोर gāi basti
  cor
rustless *adj.* दयाहीन dayāhin
rusty *adj.* खिया लागेको khiya
  lāgeko
rye *n.* राई rāi

S

sabotage *n.* विगार bigăr

saboteur *n.* विगार गर्नु bigăr garnu

sack *n.* बोरा borā; *v.* खारेज गर्नु khārej garnu

sacred *adj.* पवित्र pavitra

sacrifice *n.* बलिदान balidān

sacrilege *n.* पवित्र वस्तु चोर्ने pavitra vastu corne

sad *adj.* उदास udās

sadden *v.i.* उदास हुनु udās hunu

saddle *n.* काठी kāṭhi

sadism *n.* अर्काको दुखमा खुशी हुनु ārkāko dukhama khusi hunu

sadness *n.* उदासी udāsi

safari *n.* शिकारको लागी अभियान sikāri ko lāgi abhiyān

safe *adj.* सुरक्षित suraksit; *n.* तिजोरी ढुकुटी tijori dhukuti

safe passage *n.* शत्रु इलाकावाट सुरक्षित यात्रा satru ilākābāta suraksit yātrā

safeguard *n.* रक्षा गर्नु raksā garnu

safety *n.* सुरक्षा suraksā

saffron *n.* केसर kesar

sage *n.* मुनि muni

sail *n.* पाल pāl; *v.t.* जलयात्रा गर्नु jalayātrā garnu

sailboat *n.* पाल-नाउ pāl-nāu

sailor *n.* मल्लाह mallāh, माझी mājhi

saint *n.* संत sant

saintly *n.* संत जस्तो sant jasto

sake *n.* खातिर khātir

salable *adj.* बिकाऊ bikāu, बेच्न bechna, सकिने sakine

salad *n.* सलाद salād

salary *n.* तलब talab

sale *n.* बिक्री bikri

salesman *n.* विक्रेता bikretā

salient *adj.* प्रमुख pramukh

saliva *n.* रियाल riyal

salt *n.* नुन nun

salty *adj.* नमकीन namkin

salutation *n.* अभिवादन abhivādan

salute *v.t.* प्रणाम गर्नु praṇām garnu, अभिवादन गर्नु abhibādan garnu

salvation *n.* मुक्ति mukti

same *adj.* उस्तै ustai, उही uhi

sample *n.* नमूना namunā; *v.t.* नमूना लिनु namunā linu

sanctify *v.* शुद्ध गर्नु suddha garnu

sanctuary *n.* पवित्र स्थल pabitra sthal

sand *n.* वालुवा baluwa

sandal *n.* चप्पल cappal

sandalwood *n.* रक्तचन्दन raktacandan

sandwich *n.* स्यान्दविच sandwich

sane *adj.* मानसिक रुपले ठीक mānasik ruple thik

sanitarium *n.* स्वास्थ ठीक गर्ने स्थल swāstha thik garne sthān

sanitary *adj.* स्वास्थकर swāsthakar; *n.* सरसफाई sarsafāi

sanitation *n.* सरसफाई sarsaphāi

Sanskrit *n.* संस्कृत sanskrit

sapling *n.* विरुवा biruwa

sarcasm *n.* व्यङग vyanga

sartorial *adj.* लोग्ने मान्छेको कपडा वारे logne manche ko lugā bāre

Satan *n.* शैतान saitān

satellite *n.* उपग्रह upagraha

satire *n.* व्यङ्ग्य vyanga

satisfaction *n.* सन्तोष santos

satisfactory *adj.* सन्तोषजनक santoshjanak, सन्तोषप्रद santosprad

satisfy *v.* चित्त बुझाउनु citta bujhāunu

Saturday *n.* शनिवार sanivār

savage *adj.* जंगली jangali

save *v.* बचाउनु bacāunu

savings *adj.* बचत bacāt

sawmill *n.* लकडी चिर्ने मिल lakadi cirne mil

saying *n.* भनाइ bhanāi

scabies *n.* दाद dād

scar *n.* दाग dāg

scarce *adj.* अपुग apug

scare *v.* डराउने darāune

scarf *n.* रुमाल rumāl

scenery *n.* दृश्य drishya

scheme *n.* आयोजना āyojanā

scholar *n.* विद्वान vidwān

scholarship *n.* छात्रवृत्ति catrabritti

scientist *n.* वैघानिक vaigyānik

scissors *n.* कैंची kainchi

scold *v.t.* हप्काउनु hakkāunu

scope *n.* विषयक्षेत्र visayksetra

score *n.* प्रासांक prāptānka

scorn *n.* घृणा ghrinā; *v.t.* घृणा गर्नु ghrinā garnu

scorpion *n.* बिच्छी bichhi

scoundrel *n.* बदमाश badmās

scratch *v.t.* कोट्याउनु kotyāunu

scream *v.t./v.i.* चिच्याउनु chichyāunu

screen *n.* परदा pardā

screw *n.* पेच pec; *v.t.* कस्नु kasnu

screwdriver *n.* पेजकस peckas

scribe *n.* लेखक lekhak

script *n.* लिपि lipi

scripture *n.* धार्मिक ग्रन्थ dhārmik grantha

scrutiny *n.* जाँच jāmc

sculptor *n.* मूर्तिकार murtikār

sculpture *n.* मूर्ति murti

sea *n.* समुद्र samudra

sea level *n.* समुद्री तह samudra taha

seacoast *n.* समुद्र तट samudra tat

seafood *n.* समुद्री माछा samudri māchā

seal *n.* सील माछा sil māchā

seam *v.t.* सिलाउनु silāunu

seaport *n.* समुद्री वन्दरगाह samundri bandargah

search *n.* खोज khoj; *v.i.* खोज्न दिनु khojna dinu; *v.t.* खोज्नु khojnu

seaside *n.* समुद्र किनारा samundra kinara

season *n.* मौसम mausam

seasonal *adj.* मौसमी mausami

seat *n.* कुर्सी kursi

seatbelt *n.* कुर्सी को पेटी kursi ko peti

seaward *adv.* समुद्रतर्फ samundratarpha

seawater *n.* समुद्र जल samundra jal

secede *v.* अलगिनु alaginu

seclusion *n.* एकांत ekānt

second *n./adj.* दोस्रो dosro

secondary school *n.* माध्यमिक विद्यालय mādhyamik vidyālaya

secondhand *adj.* पुरानो purāno

secrecy *n.* गुस gopyatā

secret *adj.* गुप्ता gupt; *n.* भेद bhed

secretariat *n.* सचिवालय sachibālaya

secretary *n.* सचिव sachib

sect *n.* सम्प्रदाय sampradaya

sectarian *adj.* सांप्रदायिक sāmpradāyik

section n. भाग bhāg; संप्रदाय sampradāya

secular adj. धर्म निरपेक्ष dharma nirapeksa

secure adj. सुरक्षित suraksit; v.t. सुरक्षित गर्नु suraksit garnu

security n. सुरक्षा suraksā

sedentary adj. घुमफिरत नगर्ने ghumphir nagarne

sedition n. राजद्रोह rājdroha

seduce v.t. फकाउनु phakāunu

seduction n. फकाएको phakāyeko

see v.t. हेर्नु hernu, देख्नु dekhnu

see off v.i. विदा गर्नु bidā garnu

seed n. बीज bij, बिउ biu

seed money n. नयाँ आयोजनाको लागी पैसा nayā āyojanā ko lāgi paisā

seek v.t. खोज्नु khojnu

seem v.i. प्रतीत हुनु pratit hunu

segment n. भाग bhāg

segregate v.t. छुट्याएर राख्नु chuttaera rākhnu

seismograph n. भूकम्प नाप्ने यन्त्र bhukampa napne yantra

seize v.t. समात्नु samātnu, कब्जा गर्नु kabja garnu

seizure n. गिरफ्तारी giraftāri

seldom adv. कहिले काहिँ kahile kahin

select v.t. छान्नु chānnu

selection n. चयन cayan, छनावट chanāwat

self adj. आफै āphai

self-addressed adj. आफै ठेगाना लेखेको aphai thegānā lekheko

self-centered adj. अन्तर्मुखी antamurkhi

self-conscious adj. चेतनशील cetansil

self-control n. आत्म नियंत्रण atmāniyantran

self-defense n. आत्मरक्षा ātmaraksya

self-determination n. आत्मनिर्णय atmanirnaya

self-evident adj. आफै प्रत्यक्ष हुनु aphai pratyaksa hunu

self-explanatory adj. आफै बुझ्न सकिने aphai bujhna sakine

self-government n. स्वायत्त शासन swāyatta sāsan

self-reliance n. आत्म निर्भरता atma-nirbharata

self-respect n. आत्मसम्मान atma-sammān

self-satisfaction n. आत्मसंतुष्टि atma-santusti

self-service n./adj. स्वयं-सेवा svayam-sevā

self-sufficient adj. आत्मनिर्भर atma-nirbhar

selfish adj. स्वार्थी swārthi

sell v.t. बेच्नु becnu

seller n. विक्रेता bikretā

sellout n. सबै संपत्ति वेच्नु sabai sampatti becnu

semen n. बीर्य virya

semiannual adj. अर्ध वार्षिक ardhabarsik

semicircle n. अर्धवृत ardha-vritta

semicolon n. अर्ध-विराम ardh-virām

semimonthly adj. अर्धमासिक ardhamāsik

seminar n. गोष्ठी gosthi

senate n. सेमेट semet

senator n. सीनेटर sinetar

send v.t. पठाउनु pathāunu

sender n. पठाउने pathāune

senile adj. सुद्धि हराएको suddhi haraeko

senior adj. वरिष्ठ baristha; n. जेठो jetho

senior citizen *n.* वरिष्ठ नागरिक baristha nagarik

seniority *n.* वरिष्ठता baristhatā

sensation *n.* अनुभूति anubhuti

sense *n.* होस hos

senseless *adj.* बेहोश behos

sensitive *adj.* संवेदनशील sanvedanasil

sentence *n.* दंड को आदेश dand ko ādes

sentiment *n.* भावना bhāvna

sentimental *adj.* भावुक bhābuk

sentry *n.* पाले pāle

separate *adj.* वेग्लै beglai, अलग alag

separation *n.* विच्छेद vicched, विभाजन bibhājan

seperable *adj.* छुट्याउन सकिने chutyāune sakine

September *n.* सितंबर sitambar

septic tank *n.* मल टैंक mal taink

sequence *n.* सिलसिला silsilā

serene *adj.* शान्त sāntā

serf *n.* दास dās

sergeant *n.* सारजेंट sārjent

series *n. pl.* सिलसिला silsilā

serious *adj.* गंभीर gambhir

sermon *n.* प्रवचन pravacan

serpent *n.* सर्प sarpa

servant *n.* नौकर naukar, सेवक sevak

serve *v.t.* सेवा गर्नु sevā garnu

service *n.* सेवा sevā

servitude *n.* दास dās, कमारो kamāro

session *n.* सत्र satra, वैठक baithak

set *adj.* तैयार taiyār; *n.* सेट set; *v.t.* राख्नु rākhnu

settle *v.i.* मिलाउनु milāunu; *v.t.* बस्नु bāsnu

settlement *n.* समझौता samjhautā, वस्ती basti

seven *num.* सात sāt

seventeen *num.* सत्र satra

seventeenth *adj.* सत्रहौं satrahaun

seventh *adj.* सातौं sātnāu

seventy *num.* सत्तरी sāttāri

sever *v.* काट्नु kātnu

several *adj.* धेरै dherai

severe *adj.* कठोर kathor

sew *v.t./v.i.* सिउनु siunu

sewage *n.* फोहर phohar

sewer *n.* सिउने मानिस siune manis, ढल dhal

sewing *n.* सिलाई silāi

sewing machine *n.* सिलाउने मशीन silāune macine

sex *n.* यौन yaun, लिङ्ग linga

sexism *n.* लिङ्गको आधारमा भेदभाव lingako adharma bhed

sexual *adj.* यौन संवन्धि yaun sambandhi

sexuality *n.* लैंगिकता laingaiktā

sexy *adj.* यौन इच्छा yaun ichā

shabby *adj.* पुरानो काटेको purano kateko

shade *n.* छाया chāyā

shadow *n.* छाया chāyā; *v.* पछि लाग्नु pachi lāgnu

shady *adj.* छायादार chāyādār

shake *v.t.* हल्लाउनु hallaunu

shaky *adj.* असुरक्षित asuraksit

shallow *adj.* कम गहिरो kam gahiro

sham *n.* बनावट banāvat

shaman *n.* झाँकी jhānki

shame *n.* लज्जा lajjā

shameful *adj.* लज्जाजनक lajjājanak

shameless *adj.* निर्लज्ज nirlajja

shampoo *n.* शैंपू saimpu

Shangri-La (*a mythical place*) *n.* पृथ्वी भित्रको स्वर्ग prithvi bhitra ko swarga

shape *n.* रुप rup

share *n.* हिस्सा hissā; *v.t.* बाँडनु bādnu

sharecropper *n.* मोही mohi

shareholder *n.* हिस्सेदार hissedār

shark *n.* शार्कमाछा sārk māchā

sharp *adj.* तीखो tikho

sharpen *v.t.* तीखो पार्नु tikho pārnu

shave *v.t./v.i.* दारी काटनु dāri kātnu

shaving cream *n.* हजामत क्रीम hajāmat krim

shawl *n.* शाल sāl, दोसल्ला dosallā

she *pron.* उ u, उनी uni

sheep *n.* भेडा bheda

sheet *n.* चादर cādar, तन्ना tannā

shelter *n.* शरण saran

shepherd *n.* गोठालो gothālo

sherpa *n.* जातीय समूह jātiya samuh

sherry *n.* रक्सी raksi

shield *n.* ढाल dhāl

shift *n.* पाली pāli; *v.t.* हटनु hatnu, हटाउनु hatāunu

shine *v.t.* चम्कनु chamkanu

Shinto *n.* जापानमा मानिने धर्म japānmā mānine dharma

ship *n.* जहाज jahāz; *v.t.* पठाउनु pathāunu

shipbuilding *n.* जहाज बनाउनु jahāj banāunu

shirt *n.* कमीज kamiz

shish kebab *n.* भुटेको मासु bhuteko māsu

shiva *n.* शिव shiva

shiver *v.i.* काम्नु kāmnu

shock *n.* धक्का dhakkā; *v.t.* बिजुलीको धक्का bijuli ko dhakka

shoe *n.* जुता juttā

shoelace *n.* जुत्ता को फीता juttā ko fitā

shoemaker *n.* सार्की, जुत्ता बनाउने मानिस sārki, juttā banāune mānis

shoot *v.t.* गोली हान्नु goli hannu

shop *n.* पसल pāsal; *v.i.* खरीदारी गर्नु kharidāri garnu

shopkeeper *n.* पसले pasale

shoplifter *n.* पसलको चोर pasal ko chor

shoplifting *n.* पसलबाट चोर्ने pasal bāta chorne

shopping *n.* किनमेल गर्नु kinmel garnu

shore *n.* समुद्र samundra-tat

short *adj.* सानो sano, छोटो choto

short story *n.* लघु कथा laghuu kathā

short-tempered *adj.* चाँडै रिसाउने cadai risāune

short-term *adj.* छोटो अवधि choto awadhi

shortage *n.* कमी kami

shortcut *n.* छोटो वाटो choto bāto

shorten *v.t.* छोटो गर्नु choto garnu

shortening *n.* घटाई ghatāi

shortfall *n.* कमी kami

shortly *adv.* अविलंब avilamb

shorts *n. pl.* हाफपैंट hāfpaint

should *v.i.* चाहिन्छ chāhincha

shoulder *n.* काँध kāndh

show *n.* तमाशा tamāsā; *v.t.* देखाउनु dekhāunu

shower *n.* शावर sāvar, नुहाउने पानी nuhāune pāni

shrewd *adj.* चलाख calākh

shrine *n.* मंदिर mandir

shrink *v.t.* खुम्चिनु khumchinu

shroud *n.* मुर्दालाई बेर्ने कपडा murdalai berna kapadā

shut *v.t.* बंद गर्नु banda garnu

shutter *n.* बन्द गर्ने ढोका banda garne dhoka

shuttle *n.* शटल गाडी satal gāri

shy *adj.* लाज मान्ने lāj manne; संकोची sankoci

sibling *n.* भाइबहिनी bhai-bahini

sick *adj.* विरामी birāmi

sickly *adj.* विरामी जस्तो birāmi jasto

sickness *n.* रोग rog, बीमारी bimāri

side *n.* छेउ chheu

side effect *n.* औषधी खाएर खराब ausadi khaera kharāb

sidewalk *n.* हिडने सडक hindane sadak

sideways *adj./adv.* तेर्सौ terso

siege *n.* घेरा gherā

sigh *n.* सुस्केरा suskerā; *v.i.* सुस्केरा गर्नु suskerā garnu

sight *n.* दृष्टि drsti

sign *n.* संकेत sanket; *v.t.* हस्ताक्षर गर्नु hastāksar garnu

sign language *n.* संकेत भाषा sanket bhasa

signal *n.* संकेत sanket

signature *n.* दस्तखत dastkhat, हस्ताक्षर hastāksar

significance *n.* अर्थ artha

signify *v.t.* सूचित गर्नु sucit garnu

silence *n.* चुप्पी cuppi, मौन maun; *v.t.* चुप गर्नु cup garnu

silent *adj.* चुप cup

silk *n.* रेशम resham

silly *adj.* मूर्ख murkh

silver *n.* चाँदी cāmdi

silver anniversary *n.* रजत जयन्ती rajat jayanti

silverware *n.* चाँदी को भाडा cāmdi ko bhāda

similar *adj.* समान samān

similarity *n.* समानता samāntā

simple *adj.* सरल saral

simplicity *n.* सवलता savalatā

simplify *v.t.* सरल बनाउनु saral banaunu

simply *adv.* सादगी sadgi

simulate *v.t.* अनुकरण गर्नु anukaran garnu

simulation *n.* अनुरुपण anurupan

simultaneously *adv.* एकै पटक ekai patak

sin *n.* पाप pip; *v.i.* पाप गर्नु pap garnu

since *adv.* को पछि ko pachi

sincere *adj.* हार्दिक hārdik

sincerity *n.* हार्दिकता hārdikta

sinew *n.* धागो dhāgo

sing *v.t./v.i.* गाउनु gāunu

singer *n.* गायक gāyak

singing *n.* गायन gāyan

single *adj.* एक्लो eklo

singlehanded *adj.* एकै eklai

sinister *adj.* दुष्ट dust

sink *n.* नाली nāli; *v.t.* डुब्नु dubnu

sip *n.* चुस्कि chuski; *v.t.* चुस्कि लिनु cuski linu

sir *n.* श्रीमान srimān

sister *n.* *(younger)* बहिनी, bahini, *(elder)* दिदी didi

sister-in-law *n.* *(husband's sister)* नन्द nanda; *(brother's wife)* भाउजु bhauju; *(wife's sister)* साली sāli

sit *v.i.* बस्नु basnu

sitar *n.* सितार sitār

site *n.* स्थल sthal

situated *adj.* रहेको raheko

situation *n.* स्थिति sthiti

six *num.* छ cha

sixteen *num.* सोह्र sora

sixteenth *adj.* सोहरौं soharaun

sixth *adj.* छैटौं chaitaun

sixty *num.* साठी sāthi

sizable *adj.* निकै ठूलो nikai thuulo

size *n.* आकार ākār

skate *n.* स्केट sket

skeleton *n.* कंकाल kankāl

skeptic *n.* शंका गर्नु sankā garnu

skeptical *adj.* शंकास्पद sankāspad

sketch *n.* रुपरेखा ruprekhā;
v.t. रुपरेखा बनाउनु ruprekhā banaunu

sketchy *adj.* अपुरो apuro

skid *v.i.* चिप्लनु ciplanu

skill *n.* सीप seep

skillful *adj.* कुशलता kusaltā

skim *v.t.* मलाई उतारनु malāi utarnu

skim milk *n.* मलाई उतारेको दुध malai utāreko dudh

skin *n.* छाला chāla

skinny *adj.* दुव्लो dublo

skip *v.i.* नाघ्नु nāghnu

skirt *n.* घाँघर ghaghar

skull *n.* खोपडी khopari

sky *n.* आकाश ākash

skyscraper *n.* अग्लो भवन aglo bhawan

slack *adj.* ढीलो dhilo

slam *v.t.* जोर सँग वन्द गर्नु jor sanga banda garne

slander *n.* अपमानजनक apamānjanak

slang *n.* वर्ग-बोली varg-boli

slap *n.* थप्पड thappar

slate *n.* स्लेटी ढुङ्गा sleti dhungā

slaughter *n.* हत्या hatyā

slave *n.* दास dās

slavery *n.* दासप्रथा dāsprathā

slay *v.t.* मार्नु mārnu

sleazy *adj.* सस्तो खालको sasto khālko

sleep *n.* निद्रा nidrā; *v.i.* सुत्नु sutnu

sleeping pill *n.* निद्राको गोली nidrako goli

sleepless *adj.* नसुतेको nasuteko

sleepy *adj.* निद्रालु nidrālu

slender *adj.* पातलो pātlo

slice *n.* टुक्रा tukrā

slide *v.i.* स्लाइड slāid

slight *adj.* अलिकति alikati

slim *adj.* दुव्लो पातलो dublo pātlo

slip *n./v.i.* चिप्लनु chiplanu

slippery *adj.* चिप्लन सकने chiplana sakne

slogan *n.* नारा nārā

slope *n.* ढाल dhāl

sloppy *adj.* रद्दी raddi

slow *adj.* विस्तारै bistārāi

slowly *adv.* विस्तारै विस्तारै bistārāi bistārāi

sluggish *adj.* मंद mand

slum *n.* गरीब वस्ती garib basti

small *adj.* सानो sāno

smallpox *n.* विफर biphār

smart *adj.* बुद्धिमान buddhimān

smash *v.t.* टुक्रा टुक्रा गर्नु tukra-tukra garnu

smell *n.* गन्ध ganda

smile *n.* मुस्कराहट muskarāhat;
v.i. मुस्कुराउनु muskurāunu

smith *n.* कामी kāmi

smog *n.* कुहिरो kuhiro

smoke *n.* धुवा dhuām; *v.t.* चुरोट खानु churot khanu

smoky *adj.* धुवाले भरेको dhuanle bhareko

smooth *adj.* समतल samtal

smorgasbord *n.* विभिन्न किसिमको खाना bibhinna kisimko khāna

smuggle *v.t.* तस्करी गर्नु taskari garnu

smuggler *n.* तस्कर taskar

smuggling *n.* तस्करी taskari

snack *n.* नाश्ता nāstā

snake *n.* सर्प sarpa

snapshot *n.* तस्विर snaipsāt

snarl *v.i.* घुर्नु ghurnu

snatch *v.t.* खोस्नु khosnu

sniper *n.* लुकेर गोली हान्ने lukera goli hanne

snob *n.* दंभी dambhi

snobbish *adj.* दंभ-भरेको dambha bhareko

snore *v.i.* घुर्नु ghurnu

snorkel *n.* साँस फेर्नु को लागि sāms ferna ko lagi

snow *n.* हिउँ hiw; *v.i.* हिउँ पर्नु hiw parnu

snowfall *n.* हिउँ परेको hiun pareko

snowshoe *n.* हिउँको जुता hiun ko juttā

snowstorm *n.* हिउँको आँधी hiun ko āndhi

so *adv.* त्यसो हुनाले tyaso hunale

so-called *adj.* तथाकथित tathā kathit

soak *v.i.* भिज्नु bhijnu; *v.t.* भिजाउनु bhijaunu

soap *n.* साबुन sābun; *v.t.* साबुन लगाउनु sābun lagāunu

soar *v.i.* चढ्नु carhnu

soccer *n.* फुटबल phutbāl

sociable *adj.* मित्रवद् mitrāvad

social *adj.* सामाजिक sāmājik

social security *n.* सामाजिक सुरक्षा sāmājik suraksha

socialism *n.* समाजवाद samājvād

socialist *n./adj.* समाजवादी samājvādi

socialize *v.t.* संपर्क राख्नु samparka rākhnu

society *n.* समाज samāj

socioeconomic *adj.* सामाजिक sāmājik, आर्थिक āthik

sociology *n.* समाज शास्त्र samajsāstra

sock *n.* मोजा mojā

socket *n.* साकेट sāket

soda *n.* सोडा sodā

sodium *n.* सोडियम sodiyam

sodomy *n.* गुदामैथुन gudāmaithun

sofa *n.* सोफा sofā

soft *adj.* मुलायम mulāyam, नरम naram

soil *n.* माटो māto

solar *adj.* सौर saur

soldier *n.* सिपाही sipāhi

sole *n.* तला talā, तलवा talvā

solicit *v.* खोजनु khojnu

solid *adj.* ठोस thos

solitary *adj.* एक्लो eklo

solution *n.* हल hal, घोल ghol

solve *v.t.* हल गर्नु hal garnu

somber *adj.* उदास udās, निराशजनक nirāsjanak

some *adj.* केही kehi

somebody *pron.* कोही kohi

someday *adv.* कुनै वेला kunai belā

somehow *adv.* कुनै तरह kunai tarah

someone *pron.* कोई koi

someplace *adv.* कहीं kahin

something *pron.* केही कुरा kehi kurā

sometimes *adv.* कहिले काहि kahile kahin

somewhat *adv.* केही केही kehi kehi

somewhere *adv.* कहीं kahin

son *n.* छोरा chorā

son-in-law *n.* जुवाई juwāin

song *n.* गीत geet

soon *adv.* चाडै chādai

sophisticated *adj.* सभ्य sabhya

sorcerer *adj.* बोक्सो bokso

sorcery *n.* वोक्सी विद्या boksi bidyā

sorrow *n.* दुख dukha

sorry *interj.* माफ गर्नोंस maph garnos

sort *n.* प्रकार prakār; *v.t.* छाँटनु chāntnu

soul *n.* आत्मा ātmā

sound *adj.* ठीक thik; *n.* आवाज āvāj; *v.i.* आवाज गर्नु āvāj garnu

soundproof *adj.* आवाज नपस्ने āvāj napasne

soup *n.* सूप sup

sour *adj.* अमिलो amilo

source *n.* स्रोत strot

south *adj.* दक्षिणी daksini; *n.* दक्षिण daksin

south pole *n.* दक्षिण ध्रुव daksin dhruwa

southeast *n.* दक्षिण-पूर्व daksin-purv

southeastern *adj.* दक्षिण-पूर्वी daksin-purvi

southern *adj.* दक्षिणी daksini

southwest *n.* दक्षिण-पश्चिम daksin-pascim

southwestern *adj.* दक्षिण-पश्चिमी daksin-pascimi

souvenir *n.* निशानी nisāni

sovereign *adj.* सार्वभौम sarbabhaum

sovereignty *n.* सार्वभौमिकता sārbabhaumiktā

sow *v.* रोप्नु ropnu

soy *n.* सोया soyā

soybean *n.* भटमास bhatmās

space *n.* ठाउँ thaun, अन्तरिक्ष antāriks

spare part *n.* अतिरिक्त पूर्जा atirikta purzā

spark *n.* झिल्को jhilko

sparrow *n.* भँगेरो bhangero

spatial *adj.* अवकाशिक avakāsik

speak *v.t.* बोल्नु bolnu

speaker *n.* वक्ता vakta

special *adj.* विशेष vises

specialist *n.* विशेषज्ञ visesagy

specialize *v.i.* कुनै विषयमा विशेष ज्ञान kunai bisayama bises gyan

specify *v.t.* स्पष्ट उल्लेख गर्नु spast ullekh garnu

specimen *n.* नमूना namunā

spectacle *n.* तमाशा tamāsa, चश्मा casmā

spectator *n.* दर्शक darsak

speech *n.* भाषण bhāsan, बोली boli; चाल cāl; *v.i.* छिटो गर्नु chito garnu

speed limit *n.* गति सीमा gati simā

spell *v.t.* हिज्जे गर्नु hijje garnu

spend *v.t.* खर्च गर्नु kharc garnu

spendthrift *n.* फजुल खर्ची phajul kharci

spice *n.* मसला masālā

spicy *adj.* मसालेदार masāledar

spider *n.* माकुरो mākuro

spiderweb *n.* माकुराको जाल makura ko jāl

spill *v.t.* पोख्नु pokhnu

spin *v.i.* घुम्नु ghumnu

spinach *n.* पालुङ्गोको साग pālungo ko sāg

spine *n.* मेरुदण्ड merudanda

spinster *n.* बूढीकन्या budhi kanyā

spirit *n.* आत्मा ātmā

spiritual *adj.* आत्मिक ātmik

spit *v.t.* थुक्नु thuknu

spite *n.* द्वेष dves

splendid *adj.* शानदार sandār

split *v.* छुट्टिनु chuttinu

splurge *n.* फजुल खर्च phajul kharca

spoil *v.t.* बरबाद गराउनु barbād garāunu

spokesman *n.* प्रवक्ता prabaktā

sponge *n.* स्पंज spanj

spontaneous *adj.* स्वतःस्फूर्त svata sphurta

spoon *n.* चमचा camcā

sport *n.* खेल khel

sportsman *n.* खेलाडि khillāri

spouse *n.* पति पत्नी pati patni

spout *n.* धारा dhārā

spread *n.* फैलाव phailāv; *v.t.* फैलाउनु phailāunu

spring *(season) n.* वसंत vasant; *v.i.* उफ्रिनु uphrinu

sprinkle *v.t.* छर्कनु charkinu

sprout *n.* अंकुर ankur; *v.i.* अंकुरित हुनु ankurit hunu

spy *n.* जासुस jasus, गुप्तचर guptachar; *v.i.* गुप्तचरी guptacari, जासुसी गर्नु jāsusi garnu

square *n.* वर्ग varg

squeeze *v.* थिचनु thichnu

squint *v.i.* तिरछा देख्नु tirchā dekhaunu

squirrel *n.* लोखर्के lokhareke

stab *v.* चक्कु हान्नु churā hānnu

stability *n.* स्थिरता sthiratā

stable *adj.* स्थिर sthir; *n.* तवेला tabela

stadium *n.* रङ्गशाला rangsāla

staff *n.* कर्मचारी karamcāri

stage *(theater) n.* मंच manc, अवस्था avasthā

stain *n.* धब्बा dhabbā; *v.t.* दाग लगाउनु dāg lagaunu

stainless *n.* बेदाग bedāg

stainless steel *n.* खिया नलाग्ने इस्पात khiyā nalāgne ispāt

stair *n.* भरेङ bhareng

stakeholder *n.* सरोकारवाला sarokārwālā

stale *adj.* बासी bāsi

stall *n.* थान thān; *v.t.* टालनु tālnu

stamina *n.* सहने शक्ति sahane sakti

stammer *n.* भकभकाउने bhākbhāune; *v.i.* भकभकाउनु hāklāunu

stamp *n.* डाक टिकट dāk tikat

stampede *n.* भाग दौड bhāg daud

stand *v.i.* उठनु uthnu

standard *adj.* स्तर star; *n.* मानक mānak

standard of living *n.* जीवनस्तर jivanstar

standing *adj.* स्थायी sthāyi

staple *adj.* मुख्य mukhya; *n.* स्टेपल setpal; *v.t.* स्टेपलले बाध्नु stepal bāmdhnu

star *n.* तारा tārā

starch *n.* स्टार्च stārch; *v.t.* कलफ लगाउनु kalaf lagāunu

stare *v.i.* आँखा फादेर हेर्नु aakha faderā hernu

starfish *n.* तारमीन tārmin

stark naked *adv.* पूरा नाङ्गो purā nāngo

start *n.* आरंभ ārambh; *v.t.* शुरु गर्नु suru garnu

starvation *n.* भोकमरी bhokmāri

starve *v.* भोकै मर्नु bhokai marnu

state *n.* प्रदेश prades; हालत halat; *v.i.* बताउनु batāunu

stately *adj.* राजकीय rājkiya

statement *n.* भनाई bhanai

statesman *n.* राजनेता rājnetā

static *adj.* निश्चल nischal

station *n.* स्टेशन stesan; *v.t.* तैनात गर्नु taināt garnu

stationery *n.* लेखन सामग्री lekhan sāmagri

statistical *adj.* सांख्यिकीय sānkhyikiy

statistics *n.* तथ्याङ्क tathyanka, तथ्याङ्क शास्त्र tathyānka sāstra

statue *n.* मूर्ति murti

status *n.* स्थिति sthiti

status quo *n.* यथावत स्थिति yathavat sthiti

statutory *adj.* कानून सबन्धी kanoon sambandhi

staunch *adj.* भर पदो bharpardo

stay *n.* बस्नु basnu

steadfast *adj.* इमान्दार imāndār, निरन्तर nirantar

steady *adj.* स्थिर sthir

steak *n.* गाइको माँसुको टुक्रा gaiko māsuko tukra

steal *v.t.* चोरी गर्नु cori garnu

steam *n.* वाफ bāph

steamer *n.* स्टीमर stimār

steamship *n.* स्टीमर stimar

steel *n.* इस्पात ispāt

steer *v.t.* चलाउनु calāunu

steering wheel *n.* चलाउने चक्का calāune cakkā

stench *n.* दुर्गन्ध durgandha

stenographer *n* स्टेनो ग्राफर stenographer

step *n.* कदम kadam

stepbrother *n.* सौतेनी भाई sauteni bhai

stepdaughter *n.* सौतेनी छोरी sauteni chori

stepfather *n.* सौतेनी बाबु sauteni babu

stepmother *n.* सौतेनी आमा sauteni amma

stepsister *n.* सौतेनी बहिनी sauteni bahini

stepson *n.* सौतेनी छोरा sauteni chora

stereotype *n.* परंपराबाद paramparrbād

sterile *adj.* बाँझ bāmnjh, नपुंसक napunsak

sterilize *v.t.* जीवाणुहीन बनाउनु jivānuhin banaunu

stern *adj.* कडा karā

stethoscope *n.* स्टेथस्कोप stethāskop

stew *n.* उमालेको मासु umāleko māsu

stewardess *n.* परिचारिका paricārika

stick *n.* डण्डा dandā; *v.t.* टाँस्नु tāsnu

stiff *adj.* कडा karā

stiffen *v.i.* कडा हुनु karā hunu; *v.t.* कडा बनाउनु karā banaunu

stigma *n.* अपमानको चिनो apmān ko cino

still *adj.* निश्चल niscal; *adv.* अझै ajhai

stillborn *adj.* जन्मंदै मरेको janmadai mareko

stilletto *n.* खंजर khanjar

stimulant *n.* उत्तेजक uttejak

stimulate *v.t.* प्रेरित prerit

sting *v.* टोक्नु toknu

stink *v.* गनाउनु ganāunu

stinking *adj.* गनाउने ganāune

stipend *n.* भत्ता bhāttā

stir *v.t.* चलाउनु calāunu

stitch *n.* टाँका tāmkā; *v.* सिउनु siunu

stock *n.* (fin.) शेयर seyar; *v.t.* सामान राख्नु saman rakhnu

stock market *n.* धितो बजार dhito bajār

stockbroker *n.* शेयर दलाल seyar dalāl

stocking *n.* लामो मोजा lamo moja

stomach *n.* पेट pet

stomachache *n.* पेट को दुखाई pet ko dukhai

stone *n.* पत्थर patthar

stony *adj.* ढुंगा जस्तो dhungā jasto

stooge *n.* उसको निम्ति प्रयग गरीने aruko nimiti prayog garne

stool *n.* स्टूल stul

stop *n.* रोक rok; *v.t./v.i.* रोक्नु roknu

storage *n.* संग्रहण sangrahan

store *n.* पसल pasal; *v.t.* संग्रह गर्नु sangrah garnu

storehouse n. भंडार bhandār

storeroom n. भंडार गृह bhandār grh

storm n. तूफान tufān

stormy adj. तूफानी tufāni

story n. कहानी kahāni

stout n. तगडा tagrā

stove n. चूल्हो culho

straight adj. सोझो sidhā

straighten v. सोझो बनाउनु sojho banāunu

straightforward adj. इमानदार imāndār

strain v.t. कसेर तान्नु kasera tānnu

strange adj. अचंमको achambhako

strangely adv. अचंम संग achamba sanga

stranger n. अजनबी ajnabi

strangle v.t. गला घोट्नु gala ghotnu

strategy n. रणनीति rananiti

straw n. पराल parāl

strawberry n. स्ट्रवेरी strawberry

stray v. हराउनु harāunu

stream n. धारा dhārā

street n. सडक sarak

strength n. बल bal

strengthen v.t. ताकत takat

stress n. दबाव dabāv; v.t. बल दिनु bal dinu

stressful n. तनाव पुर्ण tanāv purna

stretch v.t. तान्नु tānnu

stretcher n. स्ट्रेचर strecar

strict adj. कडा kadam

strike n. हडताल hartāl; v. हिर्काउनु hirkāunu

striking adj. हडताली hartāli

string n. धागो dhāgo

strip n. पट्टी patti

stripe n. धारी dhāri

stroke (heatstroke) n. लू लाग्नु lu lāgnu

stroke v.t. मस्तिष्क घात mastiska ghat

stroll v. टहल्नु tahalnu

strong adj. बलीयो baliyo

stronghold n. किल्ला killā

structure n. संरचना sanracanā

struggle n. संघर्ष sanghars

struggling adj. संघर्षशील sangharshasil

stubborn adj. हठीलो hathilo

stucco n. भित्तामा सिमेन्टको प्लास्टर bhittāmā siment ko plastar

student n. विद्यार्थी vidyārthi

studio n. कलाकारको काम गर्ने कोठा kalākārko kām garne khotā

studious adj. अध्यनशील adhyansil

study n. पढाई parhāi; v.t. पढनु parhnu

stuff n. सामाग्री sāmagri

stumble v.i. ठक्कर खानु thakkar khanu

stumbling block n. वाधा vādhā

stupid adj. मूर्ख murkh

stupidity n. मूर्खता murkhatā

stutter v. भकभकाउनु bhakbhakāunu

style n. शैली saili

stylish adj. फैशनेबल faisanebal

subcommittee n. उपसमिति upa-samiti

subconscious adj. अचेतन मन acetan man

subcontinent n. उपमहाद्विप upamahādwip

subcontract n. अन्यपक्षलाई ठेक्का दिनु anyapaksa lai theka dinu

subdivide n. सानो सानो टुक्रा गर्नु sāno sāno tukrā garnu

subdue v.t. वश मा ल्याउनु bas ma lyaunu

subject n. विषय visay

subjective adj. आत्मगत ātmagat

subjugate *v.* जित्नु jitnu

sublet *v.* भाडामा लिनेले फेरी भाडामा दिनु bhādāmā line le pheri bhādāma dinu

sublime *adj.* असरदायक asardāyak

submarine *n.* पनडुब्बी pandubbi

submit *v.t.* को अधीनता स्वीकार गर्नु ko adhinata swikar garnu

subordinate *n.* आफू तलको कर्मचारी āaphu talako karmacari

subpoena *n.* अदालतमा हाजिर हुने बाध्यता adālatma hājirhune vādhyatā

subscribe *v.i.* हस्ताक्षर गर्नु hastāksar garnu

subscription *n.* चंदा candā

subsequent *adj.* त्यसपछि tyas pachi

subside *v.* तल खस्नु tala khāsnu

subsidy *n.* आर्थिक सहायता ārthik sahāyatā

substance *n.* तत्व tatva

substandard *adj.* स्तरीय नभएको stariya na bhaeko

substantial *adj.* महत्वपूर्ण mahatvapurna

substantiate *v.* प्रमाण सहित समर्थन गर्नु pramān sahit samarthan garnu

substantive *adj.* निकै धेरै nikai dherai, निकै मात्रामा nikai mātrāmā

substitute *adj.* एक को सट्टामा अर्को ek ko satta ma arko; *n.* एवज evaz; *v.t.* प्रतिस्थापित गर्नु pratisthāpit garnu

substitution *n.* प्रतिस्थापन pratisthāpan

subterranean *adj.* भूमिगत bhumigat

subtitle *n.* उपशीर्षक upsirsak

subtle *adj.* सूक्ष्म suksma

subtract *v.t.* घटाउनु ghatāunu

suburb *n.* उपनगर upnagar

suburbia *n.* समष्टि रुपमा उपनगर samasti rupmā upanagar

subvert *v.* नाश गर्नु nās garnu

subway *n.* सुरंगपथ surangpath

succeed *v.i.* सफल हुनु saphal hunu

success *n.* सफलता saphaltā

successive *adj.* एक पछि अर्को ek pachi arko

successor *n.* उत्तराधिकारी uttarādhikari

such *adj.* यस्तो yasto

such as *pron.* उदाहरणको लागी udāharan ko lāgi

suck *v.t.* चुस्नु cusnu

Sudan *n.* सुडान sudān

sudden *adj.* एकाएक ekāek

suddenly *adv.* अचानक acānak

sue *v.* नालिस गर्नु nālis garnu

suffer *v.i.* सहनु sahanu

suffering *n.* दुख dukha

sufficient *v.i.* पर्याप्त paryāpta

suffrage *n.* मताधिकार matādhikār

sugar *n.* चीनी cini

sugarcane *n.* उखु ukhu

suggest *v.t.* सुझाव दिनु sujhiu dinu

suggestion *n.* सुझाव sujhiu

suicide *n.* आत्महत्या ātamhatyā; **(commit ~)** *v.t.* आत्महत्या गर्नु ātamhatya garnu

suit *n.* सूट sut; *v.t.* अनुकूल हुनु anunku hunu

suitable *adj.* उपयुक्त upyukt

suitcase *n.* सूटकेस sutkes

sulfur *n.* गन्धक gandhak

sulfuric acid *n.* गन्धकको तेजाब gandhak ko tejāb

sullen *adj.* रुखा rukhā

sum *n.* जोड jor; *v.t.* जोड्नु jornu

summarize v. संक्षेपमा भन्नु sanksepmā bhannu

summary n. संक्षेप sanksep

summer n. गरमी garmi

summit n. शिखर shikhar

summon n. समन saman

sun n. सूर्य surya

sunbathe v.i. घाम ताप्नु ghām tāpnu

sunburn n. घामले डढेको gham le dadheko

sundae n. सन्डी sande

Sunday n. आइतबार aitabar

sunflower n. सूरजमूखी surajmukhi

sunglasses n. pl. घाम को चश्मा ghām ko casmā

sunny adj. घाम लागेको ghām lāgeko

sunrise n. सूर्योदय suryodaya

sunset n. सूर्यास्त suryāsta

sunshine n. घाम ghām

sunspot n. सुर्यमा देखिने दाग suryamā dakhine dāg

sunstroke n. लू लाग्ने रोग lu lagne rog

suntan n. घामले डढेको ghamle dadheko

superb adj. उच्चकोटीको uccakotiko

superficial adj. सतही sathi

superintendent n. निरीक्षक niriksak

superior adj. सर्वोच्च sarbacca

superlative adj. सर्वोच्च तहको sarbac tahako

superman n. महामानव mahāmānav

supermarket n. सुपरबजार suparbāzār

supersede v. अर्काको ठाउँ लिनु arkāko thāun linu

superstition n. अन्धविश्वास andhavisvās

superstitious adj. अंधविश्वासी andhavisvāsi

supervise v.t. पर्यवेक्षण गर्नु paryaveksan garnu

supervisor n. पर्यवेक्षक paryaveksak

supper n. बेलुका को खाना beluka ko khana

supplement n. परिशिष्ट parisist; v.t. पूरा गर्नु purā garnu

supply n. सप्लाई saplāi; v.t. सप्लाई गर्नु saplāi garnu

support n. सहारा sahāra; v.t. सहारा दिनु sahāra dinu

supporter n. समर्थक samarthak

suppose v.i. मान लिनु mān linu

suppress v. दबाउनु dawāunu; v.i. दमन गर्नु daman garnu

supreme adj. सर्वोच्च sarvocca

supreme court n. सर्वोच्च अदालत sarvocca adālat

surcharge n. अधिमूल्य adhimuly

sure adj. निश्चित niscit

surely adv. निश्चित साथ niscit sāth

surety n. जमानत jamānat

surf n. समुद्र लहर samudri lahar

surface n. सतह satah

surge v. धेरै बढनु dherai badhnu

surgeon n. शल्य चिकित्सक salya chikitsak

surgery n. शल्यचिकिसा salyacikitsā

surly adj. रुखो rukho

surmount v. वाधालाई जितु bādhā lāi jitnu

surname n. परिवार को नाम parivār ko nām

surpass v.t. बढीकर हुनु badhikar hunu

surplus n. अतिरिक्त atirikt

surprise n. आश्चर्य āscarya; v.t. आश्चर्य गर्नु āscarya garnu

surrealism *n.* अचेतनमन कलामा acetan man kalāmā

surrender *v.t.* आत्ममर्पण गर्नु ātm-samarpan garnu

surrogate *n.* एककाे ठाउँमा अर्काे राख्नु ek ko thāunmā arko rākhnu

surround *v.t.* घेर्नु ghernu

surrounding *adj.* आस-पास काे ās-pās ko

surroundings *n. pl.* पास-पडाेस pās-paros

surveillance *n.* शंकास्पदकाे अवलाेकन sankāspadko avalokan

survey *v.* सर्भेक्षण गर्नु sarveksan garnu

survive *v.i.* जीवीत रहनु jivit rahanu, वाच्नु bānchnu

survivor *n.* वाँचे banche

suspect *v.* शंका गर्नु sankāgarnuu; *n.* शंका गरिएकाे sankā garieko

suspend *v.t.* निलम्बन गर्नु nilambane garnu

suspenders *n. pl.* हाेटिस hotis

suspense *n.* अनिश्चय aniscay

suspension *n.* निलम्बन nilamban

suspicion *n.* संदेह sandeh

suspicious *adj.* संदेहजनक sandehjanak

sustain *v.t.* थामी राख्नु thāmi rakhnu

sustainable *adj.* दिगाे हुन सक्ने digo huna sakne

suttee *(custom of burning widows)* *n.* सती sati

swallow *n.* निल्नु nilnu

swamp *n.* दलदल daldal

swan *n.* राजहंस rājhans

swap *v.* साँटासाँट गर्नु sāntāt garnu

swarm *n.* झुण्ड jhund

swear *v.i.* किरिया खानु kiriya khanu; *v.t.* गाली गर्नु gali garnu

swearing *n.* सपथ ग्रहण sapath graham

sweat *n.* पसीना pasinā; *v.i.* पसीना बहाउनु pasinā bahāunu

sweater *n.* स्वेटर svetar

Sweden *n.* स्वीडन sviden

sweep *v.t.* बढार्नु badharnu

sweet *adj.* मीठाे mitho; *n.* मिठाई mithāi

sweeten *v.t.* मीठाे बढाउनु mitho banāunu

sweetheart *n.* प्रिय priya

swell *v.i.* बढनु barhnu

swelling *n.* सुन्निनु sunninu

swift *adj.* छिटाे chito

swim *v.i.* पाैडी खेल्नु paudi khelnu

swimmer *n.* पाैडी खेल्ने paudi khelne

swimming *n.* पाैडी खेलाई paudi khelai

swindle *v.t.* धाेका दिनु dhoka dinu

swindler *n.* धाेखेवाज dhokebāj

swing *n.* झूला jhulā; *v.i.* डाेल्नु dolnu; *v.t.* झुल्नु jhulnu

Swiss *adj.* स्विजरल्याण्ड निवासी swijarlyand nivāsi

switch *n.* स्विच svic; *v.t.* स्विच खाेल्नु svic kholnu

switchboard *n.* स्विच वाेर्ड swic bord

Switzerland *n.* स्विटजरलैंड swigarlyand

sword *n.* तरवार tarvār

sycophant *n.* झूटाे प्रशंसक jhuto prasansak

syllable *n.* अक्षर aksar

syllabus *n.* पाठ्यक्रम pathyakram

symbol *n.* प्रतीक pratik

symbolic *adj.* प्रतीकार्थ pratikārth

sympathetic *adj.* सहानुभूति राखि sahānubhuti rakhi

sympathize *v.i.* सहानुभूति जताउनु
sahānubhuti jataunu

sympathy *n.* सहानुभूति sahānubhuti

symposium *n.* गोष्ठी gosthi

symptom *n.* लक्षण laksan

synagogue *n.* यहूदिको मन्दिर
yahudi ko mandir

syncretism *n.* विभिन्न धर्म र विचार
समन्वय bivinna dharma ra vicār
samnwan

syndicate *n.* सिन्डीकेट sindiket

synonym *n.* पर्याय paryāy

synopsis *n.* संक्षिप्त sanksipta

syntax *n.* वाक्यविन्यास
vāktavinyās

synthesis *n.* समायोजन samāyojan

synthetic *adj.* नक्कली nakkali

Syria *n.* सिरिया siria

syringe *n.* पिचकारी pickāri

syrup *n.* सिरप sirap

system *n.* प्रणाली pranāli

systematic *adj.* व्यवस्थित
vyavasthit

table 256 tattoo

T

table *n.* टेवल teble

table tennis *n.* टेवल टेनिस tebltenis

tablecloth *n.* टेवल पोश teble posh

tablespoon *n.* चिया चम्चा ciya camcā

tablet *n.* टिकिया tikiyā

tabloid *n.* रोमांचकारी खबरको पत्रिका romānckān khabarko patrikā

taboo *n.* समाजवाट निषेधित samāj bāta nisedhit

tacit *adj.* नवोलेर दिएको स्वीकृति nabolera dieko swikriti

tact *n.* व्यवहार कुशलता vyavahār kusaltā

tactful *adj.* व्यवहारकुशल vyavahārkusal

tactics *n.* रणनीति ranniti

tail *n.* पुच्छर puchhar

tailor *n.* दर्जी darzi

tailor *v.t.* सिलाई गर्नु silāi garnu

tailoring *n.* सिलाई silāi

tailormade *adj.* सिलाइ गर्न लगाएको जस्तो salāi garna laeko jasto

Taiwan *n.* ताईवान Taiwān

take *v.t.* लिएर जानु liyera janu

take off *v.* उड्नु (वायुयान) udnu (vayuyan)

talc *n.* टैल्क tailk

tale *n.* कथा kathā

talent *n.* योग्यता yogyatā

talented *adj.* प्रतिभाशाली pratibhāsāli

talk *n.* बातचीत bātcit; *v.i.* बातचीत गर्नु bātcit garnu

talkative *adj.* गफी gaphi

tall *adj.* अग्लो aglo

tame *adj.* पालतू pātlu; *v.t.* पालतू बनाउनु pātlu banāunu

Tamil *n.* तामिल tamil

tamper *v.t.* गडबड गर्नु garbār garnu

tan *v.t.* ताम्रवर्ण बनाउनु tamrvarn banāunu

tangerine *n.* सुन्तला suntalā

tangible *adj.* वास्तविक vāstavik

tangle *v.t.* उलझाउनु uljhāunu

tank *n.* टंकी tanki

tanker *n.* टंकी जहाज tanki jahāz

tantrum *n.* धेरै रिसाएको dherai risāeko

Tanzania *n.* टान्जालिया tanjānia

tap *n.* धारा dhāra; *v.t.* धारा लगाउनु dhāra lagāunu

tape *n.* फीता phitāa; *v.t.* फीताले बाँध्नु phitāle bādhnu

tape recorder *n.* टेपरेकार्डर teprekārdar

tapestry *n.* चित्रपट citrapat

tardy *adj.* अवेर aber

target *n.* लक्ष्य laksy

tariff *n.* सीमा शुल्क sima shulka

tarnish *v.* विगार्नु bigārnu

task *n.* काम kām

taste *n.* स्वाद svād; *v.t.* स्वाद लिनु svād linu

tasteful *adj.* स्वादिष्ट swādista

tasteless *adj.* नमीठो स्वाद namitho swād

tasty *adj.* स्वादिष्ट svādist

tattoo *n.* जिउमा चिन्ह लगाउने jiumā cinh lagāune

taunt v. व्याङ्ग गर्नु vyanga garnu

tavern n. मदिरा गृह madirā grah

tax n. कर kar

taxable adj. करयोग्य karyogya

taxi n. टैक्सी taiksi

taxing adj. भारी bhāri

tea n. चिया ciyā

teach v.t. पढाउनु padhāunu, सिकाउनु sikāunu

teacher n. अद्यापक adhyāpak

teaching n. पढाउने काम padhāune kām

teakettle n. चियादानी ciādāni

teammate n. एउटै टीममा काम गर्ने eutai timmā kām garne

teapot n. चियादानी ciyāydāni

tear n. (in eye) आँसू āmsu; v.t. च्यात्नु chyatnu

tear gas n. अश्रु ग्यास asru gyās

teardrop n. आँसुको थोपा ānsuko thopā

tease v.t. जिस्काउनु jiskāunu

teaspoon n. चिया चम्चा chiya camcā

technical adj. प्राविधिक prābidhik

technician n. प्राविधिज्ञ prābidhigya

technique n. प्रविधि prabighi

technology n. प्रविधि prabidhi

tedious adj. बोर हुनु bor hunu

teenager n. किशोर kisor

telecommunication n. दूरसंचार duur sancār

telegram n. तार tār

telephone n. भारतको भाषा bhārat ko bhāsa

telescope n. दूरबीन durbin

television n. टी. वी. ti.vi.

tell v.t. वताउनु batiunu

temper n. स्वभाव swabhib

temperament n. व्यवहार vyavahār

temperate adj. संयमी sanyami

temperature adj. ज्वर jwar, तापक्रम tapkram

temple n. मंदिर mandir

temporary adj. अस्थायी asthāyi

tempt v.t. लोभ्याउनु lobhāunu

temptation n. प्रलोभन pralobhan

ten num. दस das

tenable adj. हुन सक्ने huna sakne

tenacious adj. दृढ drrh

tenancy n. मोहियानी हक mohiyani hak

tenant n. मोही mohi

tend v.i. चल्नु calnu

tendency n. झुकाव jhukāv

tender adj. दयालु dayālu

tenderhearted adj. करुणामय karunāmaya

tennis n. टेनिस tenis

tenor n. पुरुषस्वर purussvar

tense adj. कसेको kaseko; n. कडा kadā

tension n. तनाव tanāv

tent n. पाल pāl

tentacle n. स्पर्शक sparsak

tentative adj. प्रयोगात्मक prayogātmak

tenth adj. दसौँ dasaun

tenuous adj. दुब्लो dubalo

tenure n. समयावधि samayābadhi

tepid adj. कुनकुना kunkunā

term n. अवधि avadhi

terminal adj. अन्तिम antim

terminate v.t. समास गर्नु samāpt garnu

terminus n. आखिर ākhir

termite n. धमिरो dhamiro

terrace n. छज्जा chajjā

terrain n. भूमिको किसिम bhumi ko kisim

terrestrial adj. पार्थिव pārthiv

terrible *adj.* भयंकर bhayankar

terribly *adv.* भयंकर रुपले bhayankar rup le

terrific *adj.* भयानक bhayāankar; शानदार sāndar, डर लाग्ने dar lāgne

terrify *v.* डर लाग्ने गराउनु dar lāgne banāunu

territorial *adj.* क्षेत्रीय ksetriya

territory *n.* क्षेत्र ksetra

terror *n.* आतङ्क atanka

terrorism *n.* आतङ्कवाद ātankavād

terrorist *n.* आतङ्कवादी ātankavādi

terrorize *v.* आतङ्कित बनाउनु ātankit banāunu

test *n.* परीक्षा pāriksā; *v.t.* परीक्षा दिने pāriksā dine

testify *v.i.* साक्षी बस्नु sakchhi basnu

testimony *n.* गवाही gabahi

text *n.* पाठ pāth

textbook *n.* पाठ्यपुस्तक pāthyapustak

textile *n.* कपडा kaprā

Thailand *n.* थाइल्याण्ड thailand

than *conj.* ...भन्दा bhanda

thank *v.t.* धन्यवाद दिनु dhankyavād dinu

thank you *interj.* धन्यवाद dhanyavād

thankful *adj.* आभारी ābhāri

thankfulness *n.* आभार ābhār

thankless *adj.* जस नपाउने काम jas napāune kām

that *adj./pron.* त्यो tyo

thaw *v.i.* गल्नु gālnu; *v.t.* गलाउनु galāunu

the *art.* त्यो tyo

theater *n.* थियटर thietar

theft *n.* चोरी chori

their *pron.* उनीहरूको uniharuko

theism *n.* इश्वरमा विश्वास iswarmā biswās

them *pron.* उनलाई unlai

theme *n.* विषय visay

themselves *pron.* आफैले āphaile

then *adv.* तब tab

theology *n.* धर्मशास्त्र dharmāsastrā

theoretical *adj.* सिद्धांतसंबंधी siddhāntsambandhi

theorize *v.* सिद्धान्त बनाउनु siddhānta banānu

theory *n.* सिद्धांत siddhānta

therapeutic *adj.* चिकित्सीय cikitsiya

therapist *n.* चिकित्सक cikitsak

therapy *n.* चिकित्सा cikitsā; रोगको औषधी rogko ausadhi

there *adv.* त्यहाँ tyahan

thereafter *adv.* त्यसपछि tyaspachi

therefore *adv.* यसकारण yskāran

therefrom *adv.* त्याहाँ वाट tyahān bāta

therein *adv.* यही सिलसिलामा yahi silsilāmā

thermal *adj.* ताप संबन्धी tāp sambandhi

thermometer *n.* तापमापी tāpmāpi

thermos *n.* थर्मस tharmas

thermostat *n.* तापस्थायी tāpsthāyi

these *pron.* यी yi

thesis *n.* शोध-प्रबन्ध sodh-prabandh

they *pron.* तिनीहरू tiniharu

thick *adj.* बाक्लो baklo

thicken *v.t.* बाक्लो बनाउनु gārha bānāunu

thickness *n.* मोटाई motāi

thief *n.* चोर chor

thigh *n.* तिघ्रा tigrā

thin *adj.* पातलो patlo

thing *n.* चीज ciz

think *v.i.* सोच्नु socnu

thinkable *adj.* सोच्न सकिने socna sakine

third *adj.* तेस्रो tesro

third world *n.* तेस्रो विश्व teso viswa

thirst *n.* प्यास pyās, तिर्खा tirkhā

thirsty *adj.* प्यासो pyāro

thirteen *num.* तेरह terah

thirteenth *adj.* तेरहौँ terahau

thirtieth *adj.* तीसौँ tisaun

thirty *num.* तीस tis

this *adj./pron.* यो yo

thorn *n.* काँडा kādā

thorough *adj.* पूरा purā

thoroughfare *n.* आम वाटो ām bāto

those *pron.* जो jo

though *conj.* हुन त hunat

thought *n.* विचार vicār

thoughtful *adj.* ख्याल गर्ने khyāl garne

thoughtless *adj.* लापरवाही lāparbahi

thousand *num.* हजार hajar

thousandth *adj.* हजारौँ hajaraun

thread *n.* धागो dhāgo

threat *n.* धमकी dhāmki

threaten *v.t.* धमकी दिनु dhāmki dinu

three *num.* तीन tin

threefold *n.* तीनगुना tinguna

threshold *n.* देहली dehali

thrice *adj.* तीन पटक tin patak

thrift *n.* मितव्यय mitvyay

thrifty *adj.* मितव्ययी mitvyayi

thrive *v.i.* फलनु-फूलनु phalnā-phulnā

throat *n.* घाँटी ghati

throb *v.i.* काम्नु kāmnu

throne *n.* सिंहासन sinhāsan

throttle *n.* गला घोट्नु galā ghotnu

through *adv.* पार pār

throughout *adv.* पूरा purā

throw *v.t.* फ्याँक्नु phyaknu

thrust *v.* धक्का दिनु dhakkā dinu

thug *n.* गुण्डा gundā

thumb *n.* बुढी औँला budhi amnla

thumbnail *n.* बुढि औलाको नङ budhi aunlā ko nang

thunder *n.* गर्जन garajn

thunderbolt *n.* बिजुली गर्जन bijuli garjan

thundershower *n.* गर्जन garjan, बिजुली र वर्षा bijuli ra varsā

thunderstorm *n.* गर्जन संगै वतास garjan sangai batās

Thursday *n.* विहिवार bihibār

thus *adv.* यसरी yasari

Tibet *n.* तिव्वत tibbat

Tibetan *adj.* तिव्वती tibbati

Tibeto-Burmese *n.* तिव्वत वर्मेली tibbati barmeli

ticket *n.* टिकट tikat

tickle *v.i.* झुनझुनी हुनु jhunjhuni hunu

tickle *v.t.* गुदगुदाउनु काउकुति kaukuti lagāunu

tidal *adj.* ज्वार भाटा संवन्धि jwār bhata samband

tide *n.* ज्वार-भाटा jvār-bhātā

tidy *adj.* ठीक-ठीक thik-thik

tie *n.* टाई tai; *v.* बाध्नु bandhnu

tiger *n.* बाघ bagh

tighten *v.t.* कस्नु kasnu

tile *n.* टायल tāyal

till *prep.* सम्म samma; *v.* जोत्नु jotnu

tiller *n.* जोत्ने jotne

tilt *v.* ढल्कनु dhalkanu; *v.i.* झुक्नु jhuknu

timber *n.* काठ kāth

time *n.* समय samay

timely *adj.* सामयिक sāmayik

timetable *n.* समय तालिका samay tālikā

timid *adj.* लाज मान्ने lāj mānne

tin *n.* टिन tin, डिब्बा dibbā

tingle *v.i.* झुनझुनी चढ्नु jhunjhuni carhnu

tint *n.* रगत ragat; *v.t.* रगत दिनु rangat dinu

tiny *adj.* सानो sano

tip *n.* वकस vakas

tiptoe *n.* पंजा panjā; *v.i.* पंजा को बलमा चल्नु panjā ko balma cālnu

tire *n.* टायर tāyar

tired *adj.* थाकेको thakeko

tiredness *n.* थकावट thakāvat

tireless *adj.* अथक athak, नथाक्ने nathakne

tiresome *adj.* थकाउने thakāune

titan *n.* शक्तिशाली व्यक्ति saktisāli vyakti

title *n.* पुस्तक pustak, शीर्षक sirsak

titular *adj.* नाममात्रको nām mātrako

to *prep.* सम्म sāmmā

toad *n.* भ्यागुतो जस्तो जनावर bhyāguto jasto janāwar

tobacco *n.* तमाखु tamāku

today *adv.* आज āja

toddler *n.* बामे सर्ने बालक bāme sarne bālak

toe *n.* खुट्टाको औंला khutta ko aunla

together *adv.* साथ साथ sāth sāth, संग संगै sang sangai

toil *n.* मेहनत mehanat; *v.t.* मेहनत गर्नु mehanat garnu

toilet *n.* सौचालय sauchalaya

token *n.* प्रतीक pratik

tolerable *adj.* सहनीय sahaniya

tolerance *n.* सहनशीलता sahansiltā

tolerant *adj.* सहनशील sahansiltā

tolerate *v.t.* सहनु sahani

toll *n.* सडक कर sadak kar

tomato *n.* गोलभेडा golbheda

tomb *n.* कब्र kabr, चिहान chihān

tombstone *n.* चिहानको ढुंगा cihānko dhungā

tomorrow *adv.* भोली bholi

tone *n.* स्वर svar

tongs *n. pl.* चिमटा cimtā

tongue *n.* जिब्रो jibro

tonic *n.* टनिक tanik

tonight *adv.* आज राती aja rati

tonnage *n.* टनेज tanthār

tonsils *n. pl.* टान्सिल tensil

tonsure *n.* कपाल खौरने kapāl khaurane

too *adv.* पनि pani

tool *n.* औजार aujār

tooth *n.* दाँत dānt

toothache *n.* दाँत दुख्ने dānt dukhne

toothbrush *n.* दाँत को ब्रुश dānt ko brush

toothpaste *n.* टूथपेस्ट tuthpest, मंजन manjan

toothpick *n.* दांत कोट्याउने dānt kotyāune

top *adj.* माथि mathi

top secret *adj.* अति गोप्य ati gopya

topcoat *n.* लामो कोट lāmo kot

topic *n.* विषय visay

topical *adj.* प्रासंगिक prāsangik, सामयिक sāmayik

topmost *adj.* सबभन्दा माथि sabvanda māthi

torch *n.* टार्च tārc

torment *n.* पीडा pirā; *v.t.* यातना दिनु yātnā dinu

tornado *n.* आँधी āndhi

torrent *n.* प्रचण्ड धारा pracand dhārā

tort *n.* करार भंग karār bhang

tortilla *n.* मेक्सिकोमा बनाइनेरोटी mexico mā banāine roti

tortoise *n.* कछुवा kachuwā

torture *n.* उत्पीडन utpiran; *v.t.* उत्पीडन गर्नु utpiran garnu

toss *v.t.* उछाल्नु uchālnu

total *adj.* पूरा purā; *n.* जोड jor

totaling *n.* जम्मा गर्नु jammā garnu

totalitarian *adj.* तानाशाह tanāsah

totality *n.* संपूर्णता sampurnatā

totally *adv.* बिलकुल bilkul

touch *n.* स्पर्श spars; *v.t.* छुनु chunu

touching *adj.* मर्मस्पर्शी maramsparsi

touchy *adj.* चिडचिडा circirā

tough *adj.* कडा karā

tough-minded *adj.* भावुक नभएको bhabuk nabhaeko

toughen *v.t.* कडा गर्नु karā garnu

tour *n.* घुम्नु ghumnu

tourism *n.* पर्यटन paryatan

tourist *n.* पर्यटक paryatak

tournament *n.* प्रतियोगिता pratiyogitā

towards *adv.* को तर्फ ko tarph

towel *n.* तौलिया tauliyā

tower *n.* मीनार minār

towering *adj.* उत्तम uttam

town *n.* नगर nagar

townsman *n.* नगर निवासी nagarniwasi

toxic *adj.* विखालु bikhālu

toy *n.* खेलौना khelāunā

trace *n.* चिन्ह cihn; *v.t.* खाका उतार्नु khākā utārnu

trachea *n.* श्वासनली scāsnali

track *n.* मार्ग mārg, गोरेटो goreto; *v.t.* पत्ता लगाउनु pattā lagāunu

trackable *n.* हिंडन सक्ने hindna sakne

tractor *n.* ट्रैक्टर traiktar

trade *n.* व्यापार vyāpār; *v.t.* व्यापार गर्नु vyāpār garnu

trademark *n.* व्यापारको चिनो vyāpārko cino

trader *n.* व्यापारी vyāpār

tradesman *n.* पसले pasale

tradition *n.* परम्परा paramparā

traditional *adj.* पारम्परिक pāramparik

traffic *n.* यातायात yātāyat

tragedy *n.* दुखान्त dukhānta

tragic *adj.* कारुणिक kārunik

trail *n.* गोरेटो goreto

trailer *n.* ट्रेलर trelar

train *n.* रेलगाडी relgāri; *v.t.* प्रशिक्षित गर्नु prasiksit garnu

trainee *n* प्रशिक्षार्थी prasikshgoretorthi

trainer *n.* प्रशिक्षक prasiksak

training *n.* प्रशिक्षण prasiksan

trait *n.* विशेषता visestā

traitor *n.* देशद्रोही deshdrohi

tram *n.* ट्राम trām

tramp *n.* गुन्डा gundā

trance *n.* भाव-समाधि bhav-samāndhi

tranquil *adj.* शान्त sānta

tranquilizer *n.* औषधी ausadhi

transaction *n.* कारोबार kārobār

transcript *n.* आधिकारिक दस्तावेज dastabej

transfer *n.* एक ठाँउ बाट अर्को ठाँउमा सार्नु ek thau bata arko thauma sarnu

transform *v.* वदल्नु badalnu

transformation *n.* परिवर्तन parivartan

transistor *n.* सानो रेडियो sāno redio

transit *n.* परिवहन parivahan

translate *v.t.* अनुवाद गर्नु anuvād garnu

translation *n.* अनुवाद anuvād
translator *n.* अनुवादक anuvādak
transmission *n.* प्रसारण prasāran
transmit *v.t.* पठाउनु pathaunu
transparence *n.* पारदर्शीता pāradarsitā
transparent *adj.* पारदर्शी parādarsi
transport *n.* परिवहन parivahan
transport *v.t.* वहन गर्नु vahan garnu
transporter *n.* वाहक vahak
trap *n.* फंदा phandā; *v.t.* फसाउनु phasaunu
trash *n.* कचरा kacarā
trauma *n.* घाउ ghāu
travel *n.* यात्रा yātrā; *v.i.* यात्रा गर्नु yātrā garnu
traveler *n.* यात्री yātri
travelogue *n.* यात्रा संस्मरण yātrā samsmaran
tray *n.* किश्ती kisti
treacherous *adj.* विश्वासघाती viswāsghāti
treachery *n.* विश्वास घात biswāsghāt
tread *v.t.* कुल्चनु kulchanu
treason *n.* देशद्रोह desdroh
treasure *n.* कोश kosh, खजाना khajanā
treasurer *n.* कोषाध्यक्ष kosadhyaksha
treasury *n.* ढुकुटी dhukuti, कोश kosh
treat *v.t.* व्यवहार गर्नु vyavyahār garnu
treatise *n.* प्रबन्ध prabhandh
treatment *n.* व्यवहार vyavyahār, उपचार upacār
treaty *n.* संधि sandhi, सम्झौता sanjhautā
tree *n.* रुख rukh
trek *v.* पदयात्रा गर्नु padyātrā garnu
trekker *n.* पदयात्री padyatri

trekking permit *n.* पदयात्री अनुमति पत्र padyatri anumati patra
trekking trail *n.* पदयात्री पथ padyatri path
tremble *v.i.* काप्नु kaapnu
trend *n.* झुकाव jhukāv
trespass *v.i.* अनाधिकार प्रवेश गर्नु anādhikār praves
trial *n.* परीक्षण pariksan; मुद्दा muddā
triangle *n.* त्रिकोण trikon
triangular *adj.* त्रिकोणात्मक trikonātmāk
tribal *n.* जनजाति संबन्धि janjāti sambandhi
tribe *n.* जनजाति janjāti
tribunal *n.* आयोग āyog
tributary *n.* नदीको शाखा nadiko sāpha
tribute *n.* श्रद्धांजलि sraddhānjali
trick *n.* जाल jāl; *v.t.* धोका दिनु dhokā dinu
trickle *n.* थोपा थोपा गरि खस्नु thopā thopā gari khasu; *v.t.* थोपा थोपा thopā thopā
tricolor *n.* तिरंगा tirangā
tricycle *n.* तीन पाङ्गरे tin pangre
trident *n.* त्रिशुल trisul
triennial *adj.* तीन वर्षमा एक पटक teen varsamā ek patak
trifle *n.* तुच्छ वस्तु tucch vastu
trigonometry *n.* त्रिकोणमिति trikonmiti
trillion *n.* एक सय अरब ek saya arab
trim *v.* छाँटकाट गर्नु chātkāt garnu
trimester *n.* त्रिमास trimās
trinity *n.* तीनवटा एक teen bātā ek
trio *n.* तीनजनाको समूह tin janāko samuh

trip *n.* यात्रा yātrā

tripartite *adj.* त्रिपक्षीय tripaksiya

triple *adj.* तीनगुना tingunā

triplet *n.* तिम्लाहा tamlyāhā

triplicate *adj.* तीन प्रति tin prati

tripod *n.* तीन खुट्टे tinkhutte

trisect *v.* तीन टुक्रा पार्नु tin tukrā parnu

triumph *n.* विजय vijay; *v.i.* जीतनु jitnā

trivia *n.* तुच्छ कुरा tucch kura

trivial *adj.* तुच्छ tucch, मामूली māmuli, सानोतिनो कुरा sānotino kurā

trolley bus *n.* ट्रलीवस tralibas

trooper *n.* घुडसवार ghudsawār

troops *n.* सेना senā

trophy *n.* पुरस्कार puraskār, विजयको पुरस्कार vijayako puraskār

tropical *adj.* उष्णकटिबन्धी usnakatibandhi

tropics *n. pl.* उष्णकटिबन्ध usnakatibandh

trouble *n./adj.* गडबड garbar

troubleshooter *n.* गडबड समाधान गर्ने gadbad samādhān garne

troublesome *adj.* गडबड गर्ने garbar garne

trousers *n. pl.* पतलून patloon

trout *n.* असला माछा asalā machā

trowel *n.* करनी karni, पाटा pātā

truce *n.* युद्धविराम yuddhabirām

truck *n.* ट्रक trak

truckload *n.* ट्रकले लैजाने भार trak le laijane bhār

true *adj.* ठीक theek, साँचो sancho

truffle *n.* कवक kavak

truly *adv.* सांचिचकै sachikai

trump *n.* तुरुप turup; *v.t.* तुरुप चल्नु turup calnu

trunk *n.* तना tanā

trust *n.* विश्वास visvās, गुठी guthi; *v.t.* विश्वास गर्नु visvās garnu

trustee *n.* सम्पत्ति व्यवस्थापन sampatti vyavasthāpan

trustworthy *adj.* विश्वसनीय visvasniy

truth *n.* सच्चाई saccāi

truthful *adj.* सत्यवादी satyavādi

try *n.* कोशिश kosis garnu; *v.t.* कोशिश गर्नु kosis

tsunami *n.* समुद्री छाल samudri chāl

tube *n.* नली nali

tuberculosis *n.* क्षयरोग kshaya rog

Tuesday *n.* मंगलबार mangalvār

tuition *n.* शिक्षा शुल्क shikshā shulka

tumor *n.* ट्यूमर tinmar

tuna *n.* टुना माछा tunā māchā, ट्युना tunā

tune *n.* सुर sur; *v.t.* सुर मिलाउनु sur milāunu

Tunisia *n.* टुनिसिया tunisia

tunnel *n.* सुरुङ्ग surung

turban *n.* पगडी pagadi

turbulent *adj.* आन्दोलित āndolit

turkey *n.* तुर्की चरा turki charā

Turkey *n.* तुर्की turki

Turkish *n./adj.* तुर्की को turki ko

Turkmenistan *n.* तुर्कमेनिस्तान turkmenistān

turmoil *n.* खलबली khalbali, गडवडी gadbadi

turn *n.* घुमाव ghumāv, पालो pālo; *v.t.* घुम्नु ghumnu

turtle *n.* कछुआ kachuā

tusk *n.* हात्तीको दाँत hāttiko dānt

tussle *n.* झगडा jhagadā, भिडन्त bhidanta

tutor *n.* प्रशिक्षक prasiksak

TV *n.* टी भी tibhi

twain *n.* दुई dui

twelfth *adj.* वारहौँ bārahaun

twelve *num.* बारह bārah

twentieth *adj.* बीसौँ bisaun

twenty *num.* बीस bis

twice *adv.* दुई पल्ट dui palta

twilight *n.* झिसमिसे jhis mise

twin *n.* जुम्ल्याहा jumlaha

twinkle *v.i.* टल्कनु talkanu

twist *n.* मोड mod; *v.t.* मोडनु modnu

two *num.* दुई dui

two-faced *adj.* दुईमुखे dui mukhe

two-way *adj.* दोहरो dohoro

twofold *adj.* दुई गुना dui guna

tycoon *n.* धनी व्यापारी dhani vyāpari

type *n.* प्रकार prakār; *v.t.* टाइप गर्नु tāip garnu

typewriter *n.* टाइप मशीन tāip masin

typhoid *n.* टाइफड taifad

typhoon *n.* समुद्री आँधी samudri āndhi

typical *adj.* आम ām

typist *n.* टाइपिस्ट tāipist

tyrannical *adj.* अत्याचारी atyācari

tyranny *n.* अत्याचार atyācār

tyrant *n.* अत्याचारी atyācari

U

U.A.E. (United Arab Emirates) *n.* संयुक्त अरव अमीरात samyukta arab emirat

U.S.A. (United States of America) *n.* अमेरिका amerikā

ugly *adj.* नराम्रो narāmro

Ukraine *n.* युक्रेन yukren

ulcer *n.* अल्सर alsar

ultimate *adj.* आखिरी ākhiri

ultimatum *n.* अन्तिमेत्थम antimetham

ultra *n.* अतिवादि ativādi

ultramodern *adj.* अत्याधुनिक atyādhunik

ultrasound *n.* अल्ट्रासाउन्ड ultrāsāund

umbrella *n.* छाता chātā

unable *adj.* असमर्थ asamartha

unabridged *adj.* सानो नबनाएको sāno nabanaeko

unacceptable *adj.* अस्वीकार्य asvikārya

unaccompanied *adj.* साथमा नगएको sāth mā nagayeko

unaccountable *adj.* अनुत्तरदायी anuttardāyi

unaccustomed *adj.* वानी नपरेको bāni napareko

unadulterated *adj.* मिलावट नभएको milāwat na bhaeko

unaffected *adj.* असर नपरेको asar na pareko

unanimous *adj.* एकमत ekmat

unarmed *adj.* निरस्त्र nirastra

unauthorized *adj.* अनधिकृत anadhikrit

unavoidable *adj.* अवश्यंभावी avsambhāvi

unaware *adj.* अनजान anjān

unbearable *adj.* असह्नीय asahaniy

unbecoming *adj.* हुन लायक नभएको huna layak nabhaeko

unbelievable *adj.* अविश्वसनीय aviswasniya

unborn *adj.* नजन्मेको najanmeko

unbroken *adj.* अटूट atut

uncertain *adj.* अनिश्चित aniscit

uncertainty *n.* अनिश्चितता aniscitatā

uncivilized *adj.* असभ्य asabhya

uncle *n.* *(father's sister's husband)* फूफाज्यू phuphāju; *(father's younger brother)* सानोबुबा sanobuva; *(paternal)* काका kakā, मामा māmā

unclean *adj.* फोहर phohar

unclear *adj.* अस्पष्ट aspasta

uncomfortable *adj.* असुविधाजनक asubhidajanak

uncommon *adj.* असाधारण asādhāran

uncommunicative *adj.* संपर्क गर्न नसक्ने samparka garna na sakne

unconditional *adj.* विना शर्त bināsarta, विनाशर्तको binā sartako

unconscious *adj.* बेहोस behos

unconstitutional *adj.* असंवैधानिक asambaidhanik

uncontrollable *adj.* नियन्त्रण गर्न नसक्ने niyantran garna nasakine

uncover *v.t.* नाङ्गो गर्नु nango garnu

undamaged *adj.* नोक्सान नभएको noksān nabhaeko

undecided *adj.* अनिर्णीत anirnit

under *prep.* तल tala, मुन्तिर muntira

underage *adj.* नावालक nabālik

underdeveloped *adj.* अविकसित abikasit

underdog *n.* हार्न सक्ने hārna sakne

underestimate *v.t.* वास्तव भन्दा कम bāstav bhandā kam

undergo *v.i.* अंतर्गत antargat

undergraduate *n.* स्नातक नभएको snātak nabhaeko

underground *adj.* भूमिगत bhumigat

underline *v.t.* रेखांकित गर्नु rekhānkit garnu

undermine *v.* कमजोर पार्नु kamjor parne

underneath *prep.* को तल ko tala

underpants *n. pl.* भित्री कपडा bhitri kapda

underprivileged *adj.* आर्थिक सामाजिक पिछडिएको ārthik sāmajik pichadieko

undersecretary *n.* उपसचिव upasaciv

undersign *v.t.* हस्ताक्षर गर्नु hastāksar garnu

undersigned *n.* तल हस्ताक्षर गर्ने tala hastaksar garne

understand *v.t.* बुझ्नु bujnu

understanding *n.* बुझ्ने शक्ति bujne sakti

understood *adj.* बुझिएको bujhieko

undertake *v.t.* वचन दिनु vacan dinu

undertaker *n.* अन्तिम संस्कार गराउने antim samskar garāune

underwater *adj.* पानी मुनि pāni muni

underwear *n.* तल लगाउने कपडा tala lagaune kapda

underweight *adj.* कम वजन भएको kam wajan bhaeko

underworld *n.* अपराधी गतिविधि गर्ने sparādhi gatibidhi garne

undesirable *adj.* अवांछनीय abanchaniya

undo *v.i.* अन्यथा गर्नु anyathā garnu

undoubted *adj.* विना प्रश्न bina prasna

undress *v.t.* लुगा फुकाल्नु lugā phukālnu

undue *adj.* अनावश्यक anābasyak, अनुचित anusit

unearned *adj.* नकमाएको nakamāeko

unearth *v.* खन्नु khannu

uneasiness *n.* बेचैनी becaini

uneasy *adj.* बेचेन becain

uneducated *adj.* अनपढ anparh

unemployed *adj.* बेरोजगार berojgār

unemployment *n.* बेरोजगारी berojgāri

unending *adj.* अनन्त anant

unequal *adj.* असमान asmān

unequivocal *adj.* विना कुनै शंका binā kunai sankā

unexpected *adj.* सोचदै नसोचेको sochdai nasocheko

unfair *adj.* अनुचित anucit

unfaithful *adj.* वेइमान beimān

unfamiliar *adj.* अनजान anjān, नचिनेको nachineko

unfasten *v.t.* खोल्नु kholnu

unfit *adj.* अयोग्य ayogya

unforgettable *adj.* विर्सन नसक्ने birsana nasakne

unfortunate *adj.* दुर्भाग्य durbhāgya

unfortunately *adv.* दुर्भाग्यवश durbhāgyavas

unfounded *adj.* आधारहीन ādhārhin

unfriendly *adj.* अस्नेही asnehi

unfurnished *adj.* फर्निचर नभएको famicar nabhaeko

ungovernable *adj.* शासन गर्ने नसकिने sasan garna na sakne

ungrateful *adj.* कृतघ्न kritaghna

unhappy *adj.* दुखी dukhi

unhealthy *adj.* अस्वास्थयकर asvisthyakar

unheard of *adj.* कहिले नसुनेको kahile na suneko

unholy *adj.* अपवित्र apavitra

unicameral *adj.* एक सदनात्मक ek sadanātmak

unification *n.* एकीकरण ekikaran

uniform *adj.* एक समान ek smān

unify *v.* एकीकरण गर्नु ekikaran garnu

unilateral *adj.* एक तर्फी ek tarfi

unimpeachable *adj.* विना शंका bina sanka

unimportant *adj.* महत्वहीन mahatvahin

unintelligent *adj.* मूर्ख murkha

unintentional *adj.* जानीजानी नगरेको jāni jāni nagareko

uninterested *adj.* चाख नलिने cakh naline

union *n.* संघ sangha

unique *adj.* बेजोड bejor

unisex *adj.* एकलिंगी ek lingi

unit *n.* इकाई ikāi

unite *v.t.* जोड्नु jornu

united *adj.* एकीकृत ekikrit

United Kingdom *n.* संयुक्त अधिराज्य sanyukta adhirājya

United Nations *n.* संयुक्त राष्ट्र sanyukt rāstra

United States *n.* संयुक्त राज्य sanyukt rājya

unity *n.* एकता ektā

universal *adj.* विश्वव्यापी viswa vyāpi

universe *n.* विश्व visva

university *n.* विश्वविद्यालय visvavidyālay

unjust *adj.* अनुचित anucit

unknowing *adj.* नथहापाएको nathāhāpāeko

unknown *adj.* अंजान anjān

unlawful *adj.* गैर कानूनी gair kānuni

unless *conj.* जबसम्म न...नत्र jabasamma na...natra

unlike *adj.* असमान asamān

unlikely *adj.* असंभाव्य asambhāvya

unlimited *adj.* असीमित asimit

unload *v.t.* माल उतारनु māl utārnu

unlucky *adj.* अभागी abhāgi

unmarried *adj.* अविवाहित avibahit

unnatural *adj.* अप्राकृतिक aprākritik

unnecessary *adj.* अनावश्यक anāvsyak

unoccupied *adj.* खाली khāli

unofficial *adj.* अनौपचारिक anaupacharik

unorthodox *adj.* कट्टर नभएको kattar nabhaeko

unpack *v.t.* सामान निकालनु sāmān nikālnu

unpaid *adj.* अवैतनिक avaitanik

unpleasant *adj.* नरमाइलो naramailo

unpopular *adj.* अलोकप्रिय alokpriyā

unpredictable *adj.* अनुमान गर्न नसकिने anumān garna nasakine

unprepared *adj.* तैयार नभएको tayār nabhaeko

unprintable *adj.* छाप्न लायक नभएको capna lāyak nabhaeko

unproductive *adj.* अनुत्पादक anutpādak

unprofitable *adj.* लाभदायी नभएको lābhdayika bhaeko

unqualified *adj.* अयोग्य ayogya

unreadable *adj.* पढ्न नसकिने padhna nasakine

unreliable *adj.* अविश्वसनीय aviswasaniya, भरपर्दो नभएको bharpardo nabhaeko

unrest *n.* गडबड garbar

unripe *adj.* कांचो kānco

unsafe *adj.* असुरक्षित asuraksit

unsatisfactory *adj.* असन्तोषजनक asantosjanak

unscientific *adj.* अवैज्ञानिक abaigyānik

unscientific *adj.* अवैज्ञानिक avaijyānik

unseen *adj.* अदृश्य adrisya; नदेखिएको nadekhiyeko

unselfish *adj.* स्वार्थी नभएको swārthi nabhaeko

unskilled *adj.* अकुशल akusal

unsociable *adj.* अमिलनसार amilansār

unstable *adj.* अर asthir, अस्थिर asthir

unsuccessful *adj.* असफल asaphal

unthinkable *adj.* असोचनीय asocaniya

untidy *adj.* सफा नभएको saphā nabhaeko

untie *v.t.* खोल्नु kholnu

until *prep.* जब सम्म jab samma

untimely *adj.* असामायिक asāmayik

untiring *adj.* नथाकेको nathākeko

untouchable *adj.* अछुत achut

untrue *adj.* झूठो jhutho

unused *adj.* उपयोग नभएको upayog nabhaeko

unusual *adj.* असामान्य asāmānya

unwell *adj.* अस्वस्थ asvasth

unwilling *adj.* अनिच्छुक anikshuk

unworthy *adj.* अयोग्य ayogya

unwrap *v.t.* खोल्नु kholnu

unwritten *adj.* अलिखित alikhit

up *adj./adv./prep.* माथि māthi

up-to-date *adj.* अहिले सम्म ahile samma

upbringing *n.* पालनपोषण pālan posan

update *v.* समयानुकुल samayānukul

upkeep *n.* देखभाल dekhbhāl

uplift *v.* उठाउनु uthāunu

upon *prep.* माथि māthi

upper *adj.* माथिल्लो māthillo

upper-class *adj.* माथिल्लो वर्ग māthillo varga

uppermost *adj.* सर्वोच्च सबभन्दा माथिको sabbhanda mathiko

uproar *n.* हो-हल्ला ho-hallā

upset *n.* गडबड garbar, चिन्तित cintit; *v.t.* गडबड गर्नु garbar garnu

upsetting *adj.* गडबड गराउने garbar garaunu

upside down *adv./adj.* उलटा पुल्टा ultā pultā

upstairs *adj.* माथि māthi

upward *adv.* माथि तिर māthi tira

uranium *n.* यूरेनियम ureniam

urban *adj.* नगरीय nagriya

urge *n.* इच्छा ichā

urgency *n.* अत्यावश्यकता
  atyāvasyaktā
urgent *adj.* धेरै जरुरी dherai jaruri
urinary *adj.* मूत्रीय mutriy
urinate *v.t.* पिशाब गर्नु pisab garnu
urine *n.* पिशाब pisab
urn *n.* कलश kalas
urologist *n.* मूत्र विशेषक्ष mutr
  visesagya
Uruguay *n.* ऊरुगए urugue
us *pron.* हामीलाई hamilai
usage *n.* प्रयोग prayog
use *n.* प्रयोग prayog; *v.t.* प्रयोग गर्नु
  prayog garnu
used *adj.* उपयोग भई सकेको
  upayog bhai sakeko
useful *adj.* उपयोगी upyogi
useless *adj.* बेकार bekār
user *n.* उपयोगकर्ता upyogkartā
usual *adj.* साधारण sādhāran
usually *adv.* अकसर aksar
utensil *n.* भाडा bhāndā
utility *n.* उपयोगिता upyogita
utilize *v.t.* प्रयोगमा ल्याउनु
  prayogmā lyāunu
utmost *adj.* बढी भन्दा बढी badhi
  bhanda badhi
utter *adj.* बिलकुल bilkul; *v.t.* भन्नु
  bhannu
Uzbekistan *n.* उजवेकिस्तान
  Ujbekistān

V

vacancy *n.* रिक्तता riktatā, रिक्त स्थान rakta sthān

vacant *adj.* खाली khāli

vacate *v.* खाली गर्नु khāli garnu

vacation *n.* छुट्टी chutti

vaccinate *v.* खोप लगाउनु khop lagāunu

vaccination *n.* खोप लगाउनु khop lagaunu

vaccine *n.* खोप khop

vacuum *n.* शुन्य स्थान sunya sthan

vagabond *n.* घुमन्ते ghumante

vagina *n.* योनि yoni

vague *adj.* अस्पष्ट aspast

vain *adj.* बेकार bekār, सित्तैमा sittaimā

valet *n.* टहलुआ tahluā

valiant *adj.* शूरवीर survir

valid *adj.* मान्य mānya

validate *v.* मान्यता दिलाउनु mānyatā dilāunu

validity *n.* मान्यता mānyatā

valley *n.* उपत्यका upatyakā

valuable *n./adj.* मूल्यवान mulyavān

value *n.* मूल्य muly; *v.* महत्त्व दिनु mahatwa dinu

vanguard *n.* रक्षक raksak

vanilla *n.* वैनिला vaililā

vanish *v.i.* हराउनु harāunu

vanity *n.* घमण्ड ghamanda

vapor *n.* वाफ bāph

variable *adj.* परिवर्ती parivarti

variance *n.* विभिन्नता bibhinnata

variation *n.* विभिन्न रुप vibhinn rup

varied *adj.* विविधता पूर्ण vibidhatā purna

variety *n.* विविधता vividhtā

various *adj.* विभिन्न किसिमको bibhinna kisim ko

vary *v.i.* बदलिनु badlinu; *v.t.* बदल्नु badlanu

vase *n.* पात्र pātra

vast *adj.* विशाल visāl

vault *n.* शव-कक्ष sav-kaks

veal *n.* वाच्छाको मासु bācha ko māsu

Veda *n.* वेद ved

Vedanta *n.* वेदान्त vedanta

vegetable *n.* तरकारी tarkari

vegetarian *n./adj.* शाकाहारी sākāhāri

vegetation *n.* हरियाली hariyāli

vehement *adj.* प्रचंड pracand

vehicle *n.* गाडी gāri

veil *n.* परदा pardā

vein *n.* नसा nasā

velvet *n.* मखमल makhmal

vendor *n.* बेच्ने मान्छे bechne mānche

venerable *adj.* आदरणीय ādaraniya

venerate *v.t.* को आदर गर्नु ko ādar garnu

venereal disease *n.* यौन रोग yaun rog

Venezuela *n.* वेनेज्वेला benejuela

vengeance *n.* बदला badlā

vengeful *adj.* वदला लिने badalā line

venom *n.* विष bis

vent *n.* निकास nikās

ventilate *v.t.* हावादार बनाउनु havādār banāunu

ventilation *n.* हावादारी havādāri

venture *n.* साहस sahas

venue *n.* स्थान sthān

verandah *n.* वरण्डा varandā

verb *n.* क्रिया kriyā

verbal *adj.* शाब्दिक sābdik

verdant *adj.* हरियो hariyo

verdict *n.* फैसला faisalā

verge *n.* किनारा kinārā

verification *n.* प्रमाणित गरेको pramānit gareko

verify *v.t.* प्रमाणित गर्नु pramānit garnu

versatile *adj.* धेरै कुरा जानेको dherai kura janeko

verse *n.* श्लोक slok

version *n.* अनुवाद anuvād

versus *prep.* विद्रोह bidroh

vertebra *n.* ढाडको हड्डी dhadko haddi

vertical *adj.* खडा kharā

very *adv./adj.* धेरै dherai

vessel *n.* जहाज jahāz

vest *n.* बनियान baniyān, गञ्जि ganji

veteran *adj.* अनुभवी anubhavi; पूर्व सिपाही purva sipāhi; *n.* अनुभवी व्यक्ति anubhavi vyakti

veterinarian *n.* पशुचिकित्सक pasucikitsak

veterinary *adj.* पशुचिकित्सा pasucikitsa

veto *n.* विशेषाधिकार bisesādhikār

via *prep.* को बाटो बाट ko bāto bata

viable *adj.* व्यवहारिक byābahārik

vial *n.* शीशी sisi

vibrate *v.i.* कम्पायमान हुनु kampāymān hunu

vibration *n.* कंपन kampan

vice *n.* दुर्गुण durgun

vice president *n.* उपराष्ट्रपति uparāstrapati

viceroy *n.* भाइसराय vaisray

vicinity *n.* छिमेक chimek

vicious *adj.* खराब kharāb

victim *n.* पीडित pidit

victimize *v.* पीडित बनाउनु pidit banāunu

victor *adj.* विजयी vijayi

victorious *adj.* विजयी गर्ने vijay garne

victory *n.* जीत jit

video *n.* विडियो vidiyo

Vietnam *n.* वियतनाम viyatnām

view *n.* दृश्य drsya; *v.t.* जाँच्नु jāncnu

vigilante *n.* अवैधानिक समूह abaidhanik samuh

vigor *n.* बल bal

villa *n.* बंगला bangalā

village *n.* गाँउ gaun

villager *n.* गाँउले gāunle

villain *n.* खलनायक khalanāyak

villify *v.* वदनाम गर्नु badnām garnu

vindictive *adj.* बदला लिने badalā line

vine *n.* अंगुरको रुख angur ko rukh

vinegar *n.* सिरका sirka

vineyard *n.* अंगुरको बगैंचा angur ko bagaincha

vintage *n.* अंगुरी anguri

violate *v.t.* भंग गर्नु bhang garnu

violation *n.* भंग bhang

violence *n.* हिंसा himsā

violent *adj.* हिंसापूर्ण himsāpurn

violet *n.* बैंजनी baigani

violin *n.* वायलिन vāyalin

violinist *n.* वायालिन वादक vaylin vādak

viral *adj.* विषाणु visānu

virgin *n.* कुमारी kumāri

virile *adj.* पुरुषत्व purusatwa

virtual *adj.* यथार्थ yathārth, वस्तु vastu

virtue *n.* गुण gun

virus *n.* वाइरस vāiras

visa *n.* वीसा vizā

visibility *n.* देखिनु dekhinu

visible *adj.* देखिने dekhine

vision *n.* दृष्टि dristi

visit *n.* भेंट bhent; *v.t.* संग भेटन जानु sanga bhetna janu

visitor *n.* अतिथि atithi, आगन्तुक āgantuk

visor *n.* अग्र भाग agra bhāg

vista *n.* दृश्य drisya

visual *adj.* आँखा को āmkha ko

vital *adj.* महत्वपूर्ण mahatvapurn

vitality *n.* तेज tej

vitamin *n.* विटामिन vitāmin

vivid *adj.* विशद visad

vocabulary *n.* शब्दावली sabdāvali

vocal *adj.* स्वर को svar ko

vodka *n.* रक्सी raksi

vogue *n.* प्रचलित फेशन pracalit fesan

voice *n.* आवाज āvāz, स्वर swar; *v.t.* आवाज गर्नु āvāz garnu

voiceless *adj.* आवाज विहीन āwaj bihin

void *adj.* शून्य sunya

volatile *adj.* अस्थिर asthir

volcanic *adj.* ज्वालामुखी वाट बनेको jvālamukhi bāta baneko

volcano *n.* ज्वालामुखी jvālāmukhi

volleyball *n.* भोलीबल volibal

volt *n.* वोल्ट volt

voltage *n.* वोल्टता volttā

volume *n.* आयतन āyatan

voluminous *adj.* धेरै थेली भएको dherai theli bhaeko

voluntary *adj.* ऐच्छिक aicchik

volunteer *n.* स्वंय सेवक svayam sevak

vomit *v.i.* वान्ता गर्नु bantā garnu

voodoo *n.* वोक्सीविद्या boksi bidyā

vote *n.* भोट bhot; *v.i.* भोट हाल्नु bhot hālnu

voter *n.* मतदाता matdātā

voucher *n.* वाउचर vāucar

vow *n.* प्रतिज्ञा prātigya; *v.t.* व्रत लिनु vrat linu

vowel *n.* स्वर svar

voyage *n.* यात्रा yātrā; *v.t.* यात्रा गर्नु yātrā garnu

vulerable *adj.* असुरक्षित āsuraksit

vulgar *adj.* अश्लील ashlil

vulture *n.* गिद्ध giddhā

W

wag *v.i.* हल्लनु hallanu

wage *n.* तलब talab

wagon *n.* माल गाडी māl gadi

wail *v.i.* रुनु runu

waist *n.* कमर kamar

wait *v.i.* पर्खनु parkhanu

waiter *n.* बैरा bairā

waiting room *n.* प्रतीक्षालय pratiksilay

waitress *n.* परिचारिका parichārika

waiver *n.* छुट chut

wake *n.* जागरण jāgaran; *v.i.* निद्राबाट जाग्नु nindrā bata jāgaunu; *v.t.* जगाउनु jagāunu

wakeful *adj.* सजग sājag

walk *v.t.* पैदल जानु paidal janu

walker *n.* पैदल हिंडने paidal hidne

wall *n.* पर्खाल parkhāl

wallet *n.* बटुआ batuā

wallpaper *n.* भित्तामा टाँस्ने कागज bhittā mā tasne kagaj, वाल पेपर wal pepar

walnut *n.* ओखर okhar

waltz *n.* एक किसिमको नाच ek kisimko nāc

wand *n.* छडी chari

wander *v.i.* घुम्नु ghumnu

wanderlust *n.* घुम्ने इच्छा ghumne icchā

wane *v.* विस्तारै घट्नु bistari ghatnu

want *n.* इच्छा icchā; *v.t.* चाहनु cāhnu

war *n.* युद्ध yuddh; लडाई ईच्छुक ladāi icchuk

ward *n.* वडा wadā

warden *n.* वार्डेन warden

wardrobe *n.* अलमारी almāri

ware *n.* माल māl

warehouse *n.* गोदाम godām

warfare *n.* द्वन्द dwanda

warm *adj.* न्यानो nyāno

warmth *n.* गरमी garmi

warn *v.t.* चेतावनी दिनु cetāvani dinu

warning *n.* चेतावनी cetāvani

warrant *n.* वारंट vārant

warranty *n.* आक्षासन āksāsan

warrior *n.* लडाकु lādāku

wary *adj.* चौक्न्नु cauknnu

wash *v.t.* धुनु dhunu; **wash dishes** *v.* भाँडा माइन्नु bhānda mājnu; **wash hands** *v.* हात धुनु hāt dhunu

wash-and-wear *adj.* इस्त्री लाउन नपर्ने istri lāuna naparne

washable *adj.* धुनु सक्ने dhuna sakine

washerman *n.* धोबी dhobi

washerwoman *n.* धोविनी dhobini

washing machine *n.* धुलाई को मशीन dhulai ko macine

washroom *n.* चर्पी carpi

wastage *n.* नोक्सानी noksāni

waste *n.* कूडा kurā; *v.t.* वरवाद गर्नु barbād garnu

wasteful *adj.* अपव्ययी apvyayi

wastepaper basket *n.* कूडादान kurādān

watch *n.* घडी ghari; *v.* हेर्नु hernu

watchdog *n.* प्रहरी कुकुर prahari kukur

watchful *adj.* सतर्क satark

watchman *n.* चौकीदार caukidār

watchout *v.* ध्यान दिनु dhyān dinu

water *n.* पानी pāni; *v.t.* पानी दिनु pāni dinu

water buffalo *n.* भैंसी bhainsi

watercolor *adj.* जलरंग को jalrang ko; *n.* जलरंग jalrang

waterfall *n.* झरना jharnā

watermelon *n.* खरबुजा kharbuzā

waterpower *n.* जलविद्युत jal vidyut

waterproof *adj.* पानी नपस्ने pāni napasne

waterproof shoes *n.* पानी नपस्ने जुत्ता pāni napāsne juttā

watershed *n.* जलाधार jalādhār

waterspout *n.* ढुंगेधारा dhunge dhārā

watertight *adj.* पानी नपस्ने pāni napasne

waterway *n.* जलमार्ग jal mārg

watery *adj.* जलीय jaliy

watt *n.* वाट vāt

wattage *n.* वाट-संख्या vāt-sankhyā

wave *n.* लहर lahār; *v.t.* लहराउनु lahāraunu

wax *n.* मैन main

way *n.* बाटो bāto

wayward *adj.* जिद्दी jiddi

we *pron.* हामी hāmi

weak *adj.* कमजोर kamzor

weaken *v.* कमजोर बनाउनु kamjor banāunu

weakness *n.* कमजोरी kamjori

wealth *n.* धन dhan

wealthy *adj.* धनी dhani

weapon *n.* शस्त्र sāstra

wear *v.t./v.i.* लगाउनु lagāunu

weary *adj.* थाकेको thakeko

weather *n.* मौसम mausam

weather forecasting *n.* मौसम पूर्वानुमान mausam purbanuman

weatherman *n.* मौसमविद् mausambid

weave *v.t.* बुन्नु bannu

weaver *n.* जुलाहा julāhā

web *n.* जाला jālā

website *n.* वेबसाईट vebsāit

wedding *n.* विवाह vivāh

wedding anniversary *n.* विवाह वार्षिक उत्सव vivāh varsik utsav

wedding ring *n.* विवाहको औठी vivāhko aunthi

wedge *n.* पच्चर paccar

Wednesday *n.* बुधवार budhvār

weed *n.* खर-पतवार khar-patvār; *v.t.* खर-पतवार सफा गर्नु khar-patvār safa garnu

week *n.* हप्ता hafta, सप्ताह saptāh

weekday *n.* काम को दिन kām ko din

weekend *n.* सप्ताहांत saptāhānt

weekly *adv.* प्रतिहप्ता pratihapta

weep *v.i.* रुनु runu

weeping *adj.* रोइरहेको roiraheko

weigh *v.t.* तौलनु tāulanu

weight *n.* वचन vazan

weightlifting *v.t.* भार उठाउनु bhār uthaunu

weird *adj.* अचम्को achambako

welcome *n.* स्वागतम svāgatam; *v.t.* स्वागत गर्नु svāgat garnu

weld *v.t.* टाँका लगाउनु tāmkā lāgāunu

welfare *n.* भलाई bhalāi

well *adj.* ठीक thik; *interj.* राम्रो सँग rāmro sanga

well-to-do *adj.* संपन्न sampanna

wellwisher *n.* हितैषी hitaisi

werewolf *n.* ब्वासोमा रुपान्तरण गर्न सक्ने bwasomā rupāntar garna sakne

west *adv.* पश्चिमी pascimi; *n.* पश्चिम pascim

western *adj.* पश्चिमी pascimi

Westernization *n.* पश्चिमीकरण paschimikaran

westward *adj.* पश्चिमतिर pascim tira

wet *adj./v.t.* गीलो gilo; *adj.* भिजेको bhijeko; *v.* भिज्न bhijnu

wet-nurse *n.* बुबुधाई bubu dhāi

whale *n.* ह्वेल hvel

whaling *n.* ह्वेलमाछा मार्नु suwl mācha mārnu

wharf *n.* जहाज-घाट jahāz-ghāt

what *adj.* के ke; *pron* जो jo; **what is that?** त्यो के हो? tyo ke ho?; **what time is it?** कति बज्यो kati bajyo?

whatever *adv./pron.* जे सुकै je sukai

wheat *n.* गहूँ gehum

wheel *n.* पाङ्ग्रा pāngrā

wheelbarrow *n.* ठेला thelā

wheeze *n.* घरघराहट ghergharāhat; *v.i.* घरघर गरेर सास फेर्नु gharghargarera phernu

when *adv.* कहिले kahile

whenever *adv.* जुनसुकै बेलामा jun sukai bela ma

where *conj.* जहाँ jahān; **where were you born?** तपाईको जन्म कहाँ भएको हो tapai ko janma kaha bhayeko ho

wherever *adv.* जहाँ सुकै भए पनि jahām sukāi vaye pāni

whether *conj.* या yā

which *adj.* कुन kun

whichever *pron./adj.* जो कोई jo koi

while *conj.* जब सम्म jaba samma; *n.* समय samay; **while you wait** *conj.* तपाई पर्खदा tapāi parkhada

whimsical *adj.* असामान्य asāmānya

whip *n.* कोर्रा korāa

whirl *v.i.* तेजी सँग घुम्नु tezi sanga ghumnu

whirlpool *n.* भँवर bhanvar

whisker *n.* जुँगा jungā

whisky *n.* ह्विस्की hviski

whisper *n.* काने खुसी kane khusi; *v.i.* कानेखुसी गर्नु kāne-khusi garnu

whistle *n.* सीटी siti; *v.i.* सीटी बजाउनु siti bajaunu

white *adj.* सेतो seto

white collar *adj.* कार्यालयमा काम गर्ने karyalaya mā kām garne

white elephant *n.* नचाहिएको कुरा na cāheko kurā

white flag *n.* सेतो झन्डा (हारको प्रतीक) seto jhandā (hār ko pratik)

white wine *n.* सेतो रक्सी seto raksi

whiten *v.t.* सेतो गर्नु seto garnu

whither *adj.* कुन ठाउँमा kun thauma

who *pron.* को ko

whoever *pron./adj.* जो कोई jo koi

whole *adj.* पूरा purā

wholesale *adj.* थोक thok

wholesome *adj.* हितकर hitkar

whom *pron.* जसलाई jaslai

whooping cough *n.* लहरे खोकि lahare khoki

whore *n.* रन्डी randi

whorehouse *n.* रन्डी घर randi ghar

whose *pron.* जसको jasko

why *adv./conj.* किन kina

wick *n.* बत्ती batti

wicked *adj.* दुष्ट dust

wide *adj.* चौडा caurā

wide-awake *adj.* सजग sajag

widen *v.t.* चौडा गर्नु caurā garnu

widespread *adj.* व्यापक vyāpak
widow *n.* विधवा vidhvā
widower *n.* विधुर vidhur
width *n.* चौडाई caurāi
wield *v.t.* चलाउनु calāunu
wife *n.* पत्नी patni, स्वास्नी swāsni, श्रीमति srimāti
wig *n.* नक्कली कपाल nakkali kapāl
wild *adj.* जंगली jangali
wild animal *n.* जंगली जनावर jangali jānvar
wilderness *n.* उजाड ujār
wildlife *n.* जंगली जनावर jangali jānvar
will *n.* इच्छापत्र icchāpatr; *v.* गर्नु garnu
willful *adj.* स्वेच्छाले swecchāle
willing *adj.* इच्छुक icchuk
willingness *n.* इच्छा icchā
willow *n.* भिसा bhisā
win *n.* विजय vijay; *v.t.* जीतनु jitnu
wind *n.* हावा havā; *v.* घुमाउनु ghumāunu
windfall *n.* आशानै नगरी आएको पैसा āsā nai nagari āeko paisa
windmill *n.* हावाको मिल hāwā ko mill
window *n.* झ्याल jhyāl
windstorm *n.* आँधी āndhi
windup *n.* सिद्धाउनु siddhāunu
windy *adj.* हावादार havādār
wine *n.* रक्सी raksi
wing *n.* *(of a plane)* पखेटा pakheta; प्वाँख pwānkh
wink *n.* झ्पकी jhapki; *v.i.* आँखा झ्पकाउनु āṅkhā jhapkāunu
winner *n.* विजेता vijétā
winning *adj.* सफल saphal
winter *n.* जाडो jādo
wipe *v.t.* पुछ्नु puchnu
wire *n.* तार tār

wireless *adj.* बेतार betār
wiretap *n.* टेलिफोनमा जासूसी telephonmā jasusi
wisdom *n.* बुद्धि buddhi
wisdom teeth *n.* बुद्धि वंगारो buddhi bangāro
wise *adj.* बुद्धिमान buddhimān
wish *n.* इच्छा icchā; *v.i.* इच्छा हुनु icchā hunu
wit *n.* होश hos
witch *n.* वोक्सी boksi
witch doctor *n.* झाँकी jhankri
witchcraft *n.* वोक्सी विद्या boksi vidyā
with *prep.* को साथ ko sāth
withdraw *v.t.* हटाउनु hatāunu
withdraw money *v.* पैसा झिक्नु paisā jhiknu
withdrawal *n.* निकासी nikāsi
withhold *v.t.* रोक्नु roknu
within *adv.* को भित्र ko bhitrā; भित्र bhitra
without *adv./prep.* को बिना ko binā
withstand *v.t.* सामना गर्नु sāmnā garnu
witness *n.* साक्षी sakshi
witty *adj.* विनोदी vinodhi
wizard *n.* जादूगर jādugar
wolf *n.* ब्वाँसो bwanso
woman *n.* आईमाई aimai
womankind *n.* महिला mahilā
womb *n.* गर्भाशय garbhāsya
wonder *v.i.* आश्चर्यचकित हुनु āscaryacakit hunu
wonderful *adj.* आश्चर्यजनक āscaryajanak
wood *n.* काठ kāth
woodcarving *n.* काष्ठकला kāsthakalā
woodland *n.* रुखले ढाकेको जग्गा rukhle dhakeko jaggā

woods *n.* जंगल jangal

woody *adj.* काठ भएको kāth bhaeko

wool *n.* ऊन un

woolen *adj.* ऊनी uni

wooly *adj.* उनले ढाकको unledhākeko

word *n.* शब्द sabd

work *n.* काम kām

workday *n.* काम गरेको दिन kam gāreko din

worker *n.* मजदूर mazdur

working *adj.* काम गरेको kām gareko

workman *n.* काम गर्ने kām garne

workshop *n.* कारखाना kārkhānā

world *n.* संसार sansār

worldly *adj.* धर्म निरपेक्ष dharma nirapeksa

worldwide *adj.* विश्वव्यापी visvavyāpi

worm *n.* कीरा kirā

worn-out *adj.* थाकेको thākeko

worried *adj.* चिन्तित cintit

worrisome *adj.* चिन्ताजनक cintajanak

worry *n.* चिन्ता cintā; *v.i.* चिन्ता गर्नु cintā garnu

worse *adj.* अरु खराब aru kharab

worsen *v.* अरु खराब हुनु aru kharāb hunu

worship *n.* पूजा bhakt; *v.* पूजा गर्नु pujā garnu

worst *adj.* खराब kharāb

worthless *adj.* काम नलाग्ने kām nalagne

worthwhile *adj.* उचित ucit

worthy *adj.* योग्य yogya

wound *n.* घाउ ghāu; *v.t.* घायल गर्नु ghāyal garnu

wrap *n.* लपेटनु lapernu, बेर्नु bernu; *v.t.* लपेटनु lapernu

wrath *n.* रोष ros

wreck *n.* सत्यानाश satyānās; *v.t.* नष्ट गर्नु nast garnu

wrench *n.* रिन्च rinc

wrestle *v.t.* कुश्ती लड्नु kusti ladnu

wrestler *n.* कुशतीबाज kustibāz

wrestling *n.* कुश्ती kusti

wrinkle *n.* चाउरी cauri; *v.* चाउरी पर्नु cauri parnu

wrist *n.* नारी nādi

wristwatch *n.* घडी ghari

write *v.t.* लेख्नु lekhnu

write-up *n.* प्रकाशित विवरण prakashit vivaran

writer *n.* लेखक lekhak

writing *n.* लेखन lekhan

wrong *adj.* बेठीक bethik

wrongdoer *n.* गलती गर्नु galti garne

X

X-mas *(abbreviation of Christmas) n.* क्रिसमस krismas

X-ray *n.* एक्स- रे eks-kiran

X-ray *v.t.* एक्स-रे गर्नु eks-kiran garnu

xenophobia *n.* विदेशी प्रति डर vedesi prati dar

Y

yacht *n.* याट yãt
yak *n.* चौंरी गाई chaunro gãi
yam *n.* तरुल tarul
yankee *n.* अमेरिकन amrikan
yard *n.* गज gaj
yarn *n.* सूत sut
yawn *n.* हाई hãi; *v.i.* हाई गर्नु hãi garnu
year *n.* बर्ष varsa
yearly *adj.* वार्षिक varsik
yearn *v.i.* ईच्छा गर्नु icchã garnu
yearning *n.* आकंक्षा ãkãnkchã
yell *v.t.* कराउनु karãunu
yellow *adj.* पहेंलो pahelo
yes *adv.* हो ho
yesterday *n.* हिजो hijo; **day before yesterday** *n.* अस्ति asti
yet *adv.* अहिले सम्म ahile samma
Yeti *n.* हिम मानव him mãnav
yield *n.* उपज upaj; *v.t.* उत्पन्न गर्नु utpann garnu
yoga *n.* योग yog
yogurt *n.* दही dahi
yolk *n.* जर्दी zardi
yonder *adv.* वहाँ vahãm
you *pron.* तिमी timi; *(honorific)* तपाई tapãi
young *adj.* युवक yubak
youngster *n./adj.* जवान javãn
your *pron.* तिम्रो timro; *(honorific)* तपाईको tapaiko;
yourself *pron.* तपाई स्वयम् tapai swayam
youth *n.* युवा javãni

youth hostel *n.* युवालय yuwalaya
youthful *adj.* जवान javãn

Z

Zambia *n.* जाम्बिया jāmbia
zeal *n.* उत्साह utsāh
zealous *adj.* उत्साही utsāhi
zebra *n.* जेबरा zebrā
zen *n.* जापानी बुद्धधर्म japani buddhadharam
zenith *n.* शिरोबिन्दु sirobindu
zero *num.* शून्य sunya
zest *n.* मजा majā
zigzag *n.* घुमाउरो ghumāuro; *v.t.* घुमाउरो वाट हिड्नु bata hidnu
Zimbabwe *n.* जिम्माबी jimbawi
zinc *n.* जस्ता jastā
Zionism *n.* यहूदीको आन्दोलन yahudiko āndolan
zip *v.t.* जिप बंद गर्नु zip band garnu
zip code *n.* जिप कोड zip kode
zipper *n.* जिप zip
zodiac *n.* राशी चक्र rāsi cakr
zonal *adj.* क्षेत्रीय ksetriya
zone *n.* क्षेत्र ksetra, अंचल ancal
zoo *n.* चिडियाघर ciriyāghar
zoological *adj.* प्राणी-विज्ञान संबंधी prāni-vigyān sambandhi
zoology *n.* प्राणी-विज्ञान prāni-vigyān

Nepali-interest titles from Hippocrene Books . . .

NEPALI-ENGLISH/ENGLISH-NEPALI DICTIONARY & PHRASEBOOK *(Romanized)*
Prakash Raj

This two-way dictionary and phrasebook is designed for those who wish to communicate in Nepali and learn its basic vocabulary and grammatical structure. The Nepali is provided in Romanized form, but the Devanagari alphabet is included at the beginning of the book for quick reference. A grammar section, pronunciation guide, and practical cultural information provide further insight into the language and society.

1,500 entries · 978-0-7818-0957-3 · $13.95pb

TASTE OF NEPAL
Jyoti Pandey Pathak

Gourmand World Cookbook Award Winner 2007— Best Foreign Cuisine Cookbook!

One of the very few Nepali cookbooks on the market, *Taste of Nepal* is a thorough and comprehensive guide to this cuisine, featuring more than 350 authentic recipes, a section on well-known Nepali herbs and spices, menu planning, Nepalese kitchen equipment, and delightful illustrations. Instructions are clearly detailed with illustrations, and most ingredients are readily available stateside. There is something for everyone in this book—for the most timid cook Fried Rice (*Baasi-Bhaat Bhutuwa*) or Stir-Fried Chicken (*Kukhura Taareko*) are easily achievable, but the adventurous will be tempted to try Goat Curry (*Khasi-Boka ko Maasu*) and Sun-Dried Fish with Tomato Chutney (*Golbheda ra Sidra Maacha*).

978-0-7818-1309-9 · $19.95pb

Other South Asian Interest Titles from Hippocrene Books...

LANGUAGE GUIDES

Bengali (Bangla)-English/English-Bengali (Bangla)
Dictionary & Phrasebook
978-0-7818-1218-4 · $14.95pb

Gujarati-English/English-Gujarati
Dictionary & Phrasebook
6,800 entries · 0-7818-1051-5 · $13.95pb

Hindi-English/English-Hindi Dictionary & Phrasebook
3,400 entries · 0-7818-0983-5 · $12.95pb

Hindi-English/English-Hindi Children's Picture
Dictionary
625 entries · 0-7818-1129-5 · $14.95pb

Hindi-English/English-Hindi Concise Dictionary
11,000 entries · 0-7818-1167-5 · $14.95pb

Marathi-English/English-Marathi
Dictionary & Phrasebook
978-0-7818-1142-2 · $14.95pb

Teach Yourself Marathi
0-87052-620-0 · $9.95pb

Punjabi-English/English-Punjabi Dictionary
25,000 entries · 0-7818-0940-1 · $24.95pb

Punjabi-English/English-Punjabi
Dictionary & Phrasebook
4,000 entries · 978-0-7818-1300-6 · $13.95pb

Concise Sanskrit-English Dictionary
18,000 entries · 0-7818-0203-2 · $14.95pb

Tamil-English/English-Tamil Dictionary & Phrasebook
(Romanized)
6,000 entries · 0-7818-1016-7 · $14.95pb

Urdu-English/English-Urdu Dictionary & Phrasebook
(Romanized)
3,000 entries · 0-7818-0970-3 · $14.95pb